Sexual Harassment in Education and Work Settings

Sexual Harassment in Education and Work Settings

Current Research and Best Practices for Prevention

**Michele A. Paludi,
Jennifer L. Martin, James E. Gruber, and
Susan Fineran, Editors**

Foreword by Mo Therese Hannah

Women's Psychology
Michele A. Paludi, Series Editor

 PRAEGER™

An Imprint of ABC-CLIO, LLC
Santa Barbara, California • Denver, Colorado

Library of Congress Cataloging-in-Publication Data

Sexual harassment in education and work settings : current research and best
practices for prevention / Michele A. Paludi, Jennifer L. Martin, James E. Gruber,
and Susan Fineran, editors.
    pages cm.—(Women's psychology)
    Includes index.
    ISBN 978-1-4408-3293-2 (alk. paper)—ISBN 978-1-4408-3294-9 (ebook)
1. Sexual harassment in education—United States.   2. Sexual harassment–United
States.   I. Paludi, Michele Antoinette.
    LC212.82.S4985   2015
    371.7'8—dc23   2015008694

ISBN: 978-1-4408-3293-2
EISBN: 978-1-4408-3294-9

19 18 17 16 15   1 2 3 4 5

This book is also available on the World Wide Web as an eBook.
Visit www.abc-clio.com for details.

Praeger
An Imprint of ABC-CLIO, LLC

ABC-CLIO, LLC
130 Cremona Drive, P.O. Box 1911
Santa Barbara, California 93116-1911

This book is printed on acid-free paper ∞
Manufactured in the United States of America

"I decided it's better to scream. . . . Silence is the real crime against humanity."

—Nadezhda Mandelstam

Thank you to my parents for encouraging me to speak out
against silence.
—Michele A. Paludi

This book is dedicated to the activists who work tirelessly to make our
schools, streets, and communities free of harassment.
—Jennifer L. Martin

To all the people who have participated in the International Coalition
Against Sexual Harassment conferences over the past two decades.
—James E. Gruber

For my cadre of colleagues in ICASH, who write, incite, and inspire
all of us to keep the sexual harassment issue central and
consequential in our work and in our lives.
—Susan Fineran

Contents

PART II: HERITAGE OF TITLE IX AND TITLE VII

PART III: SEXUAL HARASSMENT: INCIDENCE AND PSYCHOLOGICAL DIMENSIONS

Series Foreword

Michele A. Paludi

Because women's work is never done and is underpaid or unpaid or boring or repetitious and we're the first to get fired and what we look like is more important than what we do and if we get raped it's our fault and if we get beaten we must have provoked it and if we raise our voices we're nagging bitches and if we enjoy sex we're nymphos and if we don't we're frigid and if we love women it's because we can't get a "real" man and if we ask our doctor too many questions we're neurotic and pushy and if we expect childcare we're selfish and if we stand up for our rights we're aggressive and "unfeminine" and if we don't we're typical weak females and if we want to get married we're out to trap a man and if we don't we're unnatural and because we still can't get an adequate safe contraceptive[s] but men can walk on the moon and if we can't cope or don't want a pregnancy we're made to feel guilty about abortion and . . . for lots of other reasons we are part of the women's liberation movement.

(Author unknown, quoted in *The Torch*, September 14, 1987)

This sentiment underlies the major goals of Praeger's book series, "Women's Psychology."

1. Valuing women. The books in this series value women by valuing children and working for affordable child care; valuing women by respecting all physiques, not just placing value on slender women;

valuing women by acknowledging older women's wisdom, beauty, aging; valuing women who have been sexually victimized and viewing them as survivors; valuing women who work inside and outside of the home; and valuing women by respecting their choices of careers, of whom they mentor, of their reproductive rights, their spirituality, and their sexuality.

2. Treating women as the norm. Thus the books in this series make up for women's issues typically being omitted, trivialized, or dismissed from other books on psychology.

3. Taking a non-Eurocentric view of women's experiences. The books in this series integrate the scholarship on race and ethnicity into women's psychology, thus providing a psychology of all women. Women typically have been described collectively; but we are diverse.

4. Facilitating connections between readers' experiences and psychological theories and empirical research. The books in this series offer readers opportunities to challenge their views about women, feminism, sexual victimization, gender role socialization, education, and equal rights. These texts thus encourage women readers to value themselves and others. The accounts of women's experiences as reflected through research and personal stories in the texts in this series have been included for readers to derive strength from the efforts of others who have worked for social change on the interpersonal, organizational, and societal levels.

A student in one of my courses on the psychology of women once stated:

I learned so much about women. Women face many issues: discrimination, sexism, prejudices . . . by society. Women need to work together to change how society views us. I learned so much and talked about much of the issues brought up in class to my friends and family. My attitudes have changed toward a lot of things. I got to look at myself, my life, and what I see for the future. (Paludi 2002, p. 378)

It is my hope that readers of the books in this series also reflect on the topics and look at themselves, their own lives, and what they see for the future.

I am honored to have *Sexual Harassment in Education and Work Settings: Current Research and Best Practices for Prevention* included in this series on Women's Psychology. This volume offers suggestions for all of us who want to know more about prevention of and responses to sexual harassment in K–12 classrooms, in colleges, and in businesses. All of the contributors to this volume are deeply committed to ensuring educational and employment equity for women and men and the eradication of vio-lence against students and employees. I am honored to have had the opportunity to work with them on this volume.

REFERENCE

Paludi, M. (2002). *The psychology of women.* 2nd ed. Upper Saddle River, NJ: Prentice Hall.

Foreword

Mo Therese Hannah

This volume gives witness to the recent and growing laser-like focus in the United States on the massive societal and personal destruction wreaked by all forms of interpersonal violence. Despite the fact that sexual harassment, domestic violence, and other manifestations of power-and-control dynamics technically are outlawed or at least are not sanctioned in the United States, all of these continue to run rampant in our homes, schools, and workplaces. Those forced to endure harmful behaviors inflicted on them by their coworkers, bosses, peers, or partners have done nothing to deserve such treatment, and they only ask to be able to work, study, recreate, and live in peace and safety. Despite all we know, and even when their pleas reach the ears of designated authorities, whether due to the ignorance or the negligence of those authorities, most victims continue to suffer in silence. That in this day and age—well into the 21st century—a book like this is still so relevant and necessary speaks volumes about the current state of the human condition.

The view, as they say, is not pretty. With all of the progress made over the past several decades as far as detecting, understanding, sanctioning, and preventing interpersonal violence, with all the legal cases, educational campaigns, and White House pronouncements—all aimed to drive a stake into the monster of abusive dynamics—what does it say about our society that, at this late a date, the volume you are reading is still so necessary and relevant? It brings to mind the line from scripture that has proven itself, over and over again, to be a perennial piece of wisdom: *"The spirit is willing but the flesh is weak."*

Yet relevant and necessary this book very much is. Co-editors Michele Paludi, Jennifer Martin, James Gruber, and Susan Fineran, along with the authors, have made a significant contribution to helping us navigate our culture away from sexual harassment and other psychologically toxic behavior patterns that are partly responsible for the array of physical and mental ills that remain at epidemic levels in our culture. Interpersonal violence—unlike physical assaults—leaves few if any visible wounds. But it leaves behind the imprints of often-severe emotional trauma that survivors almost unanimously describe as worse than any physical injury.

As trauma-informed practitioners are well aware, no matter the form the abuse might take, the impacts are the same; whether occurring in the relationship between a manager and her staff, a clergy person and his congregation, or a husband and wife. These sequelae—impaired mental health; reduced work productivity, absenteeism, and job loss; decreased self-esteem; stress-related illnesses; and even suicide and early death—impose unnecessary costs on our society and its inhabitants. These costs are unsustainable and intolerable; they must not and cannot any longer be endured.

This book describes a way out of our morass. It is the desperate measure needed during desperate times. I thank and congratulate those who produced this volume, and I commend its readers for their humane concern for these vital topics.

Acknowledgments

Michele A. Paludi

I thank Praeger senior acquisitions editor Debbie Carvalko for encouraging me to edit this volume and others that deal with gender violence in the workplace and in educational institutions.

I also thank my sisters, Rosalie and Lucille, for their support.

Friends deserve my appreciation for their listening: Steven Earle, Tony LoFrumento, Brad Fowler, Dan Bilodeau, Johanna Duncan-Poitier, and Philip Poitier.

I thank my colleagues at Siena College for their impact on my research, advocacy, and thinking about sexual misconduct.

I also thank the individuals whose complaints I have investigated and on whose behalf I have testified as an expert witness since the late 1980s for sharing their lives with me and giving me opportunities to help them. You have all made me a better person. I want to especially acknowledge Mary Ellen Rosetti who left a legacy with respect to sexual harassment about which her family can be proud.

And to Antoinette and Michael Paludi, my parents. I miss you more as each day passes. Thank you for grounding me in respect, civility, and a home full of love. I continue to carry on your tradition with everyone I know. You were right: It's not easy but worth it.

Jennifer L. Martin

I wish to thank Dr. Michele Paludi, Dr. Julia Smith, Dr. Nancy Brown, and Dr. Michelle Collins-Sibley, for providing me with endless guidance and support throughout the years. I thank my institution, the University of Mount Union, for supporting this work. I thank my students, past and present, for challenging me to do a better job every single day. I thank my friends and my family for their unwavering support of me.

James E. Gruber

I'd like to acknowledge my frequent co-authors, Susan Fineran and Phoebe Morgan, for their creativity, persistence, and good humor.

Susan Fineran

I would like to thank Michele Paludi for organizing our wonderful international conferences on sexual harassment and for spearheading this book. I am very honored to have been asked to be both an editor and contributor in this important endeavor. I also thank my students, who have generously shared their experiences of sexual harassment and discrimination with their classmates and with me, and who have been so enthusiastic about the value of a class on sexual harassment to them. And finally, I thank my husband, Craig, who lives every day as a feminist man in a sexist world and never gives up hope for change.

Introduction

Michele A. Paludi

Freedom from sexual assault is a basic human right . . . a nation's decency is in large part measured by how it responds to violence against women . . . our daughters, our sisters, our wives, our mothers, our grandmothers have every single right to expect to be free from violence and sexual abuse.

> Vice President Joe Biden, January 2014, International Coalition
> Against Sexual Harassment

This edited volume was born of the 2013 Conference of the International Coalition Against Sexual Harassment. In August 2013, scholars, attorneys, advocates, and human resource professionals from the United States, Israel, and Switzerland met to discuss innovative ways to train students, faculty, administrators, and employees on sexual harassment and other forms of sexual misconduct. We discussed new legislation and guidance throughout the world. In the United States, for example, the Campus Sexual Violence Elimination Act (Campus SaVE), and ways that SaVE, and the Office of Civil Rights of the U.S. Department of Education recommend prevention and resolution of complaints of sexual misconduct, discrimination, and harassment on the basis of sex, race, age, disability, religion, pregnancy, and other federally protected categories.

The International Coalition Against Sexual Harassment was formed in 1991, shortly after the Senate Judiciary Confirmation Hearings of Judge

Clarence Thomas. The topic of sexual harassment was relatively new then; at least the label was. The behavior had long been experienced by women in the workplace as well as in undergraduate and graduate programs considerably earlier (Baker 2007). Baker commented:

> In March 1975, a group of feminist activists in Ithaca, New York coined the term "sexual harassment" to name something they had all experienced but rarely discussed—unwanted sexual demands, comments, looks, or sexual touching in the workplace. The experience they wanted to spotlight was one that women in this country had faced since colonial times. Seventeenth-century indentured servants, eighteenth-century black slaves, nineteenth-century factory workers, and twentieth-century office workers all shared the experience of having fended off the sexual demands of those wielding economic power over their lives—masters, overseers, foremen and supervisors. (Baker 2007, 1)

The initial meeting of the International Coalition Against Sexual Harassment was sponsored by the Society for the Study of Social Problems; the group formed to address sexual harassment was identified as Sociologists Against Sexual Harassment. This first meeting was in response to Professor Anita Hill's 1991 testimony before the Senate Judiciary Committee during the confirmation hearings of Supreme Court Justice Clarence Thomas. The organization was renamed the International Coalition Against Sexual Harassment (ICASH), and it holds conferences and provides a Listserv.

NOT ALONE

During the writing of this text, sexual misconduct—including sexual harassment—received national attention as it had in 1991 during Professor Anita Hill's testimony at the U.S. Senate Confirmation Hearings of Judge Clarence Thomas and with the Tailhook Scandal. In January 2014, President Barak Obama initiated a Task Force to Protect Students from Sexual Assault. He noted the national statistics—one in five women experiences sexual violence while at college—and requested guidance from the Task Force on ways for colleges and universities to better prevent sexual assault, as well as respond to survivors of assaults.

On April 29, 2014, the White House Task Force to Protect Students from Sexual Assault released *Not Alone*, a report containing a set of actions and recommendations based on national conversations regarding sexual violence on college campuses. This is the initial report from the Task Force that will directly impact every campus in the United States. *Not Alone* identified two main goals, which are to

- Inform and Demonstrate to Survivors of Sexual Assault That They Are Not Alone, and
- Assist Colleges and Universities in Meeting Their Obligation to Protect Students from Sexual Violence.

Not Alone made several recommendations for preventing and responding to sexual misconduct.

- Conducting campus climate surveys to identify incidence rates as well as individuals' perceptions of the investigative process at the campus.
- Engaging men in education, prevention, and responding to sexual misconduct.
- Responding to sexual misconduct in a manner that is sensitive to all parties and includes
  - Enabling confidential reporting,
  - Developing a comprehensive sexual misconduct policy,
  - Facilitating trauma-informed training for campus officials,
  - Ensuring safe disciplinary systems, and
  - Developing partnerships with the community (e.g., advocates, law enforcement).

Thus, the major focus of the Task Force to date has been to

- Identify the scope of the problem of sexual misconduct on college campuses,
- Help prevent campus sexual misconduct,
- Assist campuses in responding effectively when a student has experienced sexual misconduct, and
- Improve and make transparent the federal government's enforcement efforts.

U.S. senator Claire McCaskill released a report in July 2014 (McCaskill 2014) that indicated colleges and universities are violating federal law by failing to investigate campus sexual assaults. The report included responses from 300 colleges and universities that suggested that more than 20% of campuses permit their athletic departments to supervise cases of sexual assault involving student athletes. Additionally, McCaskill noted that more than 40% of campuses had not investigated a single case of sexual violence in the past five years. Furthermore, public safety officials at 30% of the campuses studied indicated that they have not received training in how to handle reports of sexual misconduct. Another finding drawn from the survey was that 10% of campuses do not have a Title IX coordinator, despite it being required by law.

THE CAMPUS SEXUAL VIOLENCE ELIMINATION ACT

In addition to following the recommendations from the White House Task Force to Protect Students from Sexual Assault, campuses had to comply with new legislation, the Campus Sexual Violence Elimination Act (Campus SaVE), by March 7, 2014. The Campus Sexual Violence Elimination Act was passed in March 2013 as part of the Violence Against Women Reauthorization Act. This Act applies to institutions of higher education; it is directed toward campuses that participate in financial aid programs under Title IV of the Higher Education Act of 1965.

Campus SaVE amends the Clery Act, which requires higher education institutions to report crime statistics and disclose security-related information. Specifically, Campus SaVE

- Includes offenses involving intimate partner violence, dating violence, and stalking with the crimes that institutions must both report to authorities and include in the annual security reports;
- Expands the categories of reportable hate crimes to include crimes based on bias against gender identity or national origin; and
- Campuses' policy statements must now include detailed descriptions of the campus' internal procedures in cases of intimate partner violence, dating violence, and stalking and must include descriptions of the campus education and prevention programs.

Campus SaVE provided definitions of types of misconduct that must be used in the campus policy statement. These definitions are provided below.

Domestic Violence Defined

Felony or misdemeanor crimes of violence are those committed by a current or former spouse of the victim, by a person with whom the victim shares a child in common, by a person who is cohabitating with or has cohabitated with the victim as a spouse of the victim under the domestic or family violence laws of the jurisdiction or by any other person against an adult or youth victim who is protected from the person's acts under the domestic violence laws of the jurisdiction.

Dating Violence Defined

Violence committed by a person—

- Who is or has been in a social relationship of a romantic or intimate nature with the victim; and
- Where the existence of such a relationship shall be determined based on a consideration of the following factors:
  - The length of the relationship,
  - The type of relationship, and
  - The frequency of interaction between the persons involved in the relationship.

Stalking Defined

Engaging in a course of conduct directed at a specific person that would cause a reasonable person to:

- Fear for his or her safety or the safety of others, or
- Suffer substantial emotional distress.

The definition of sexual harassment for campuses to use in its policies is one that has been recommended by the Office for Civil Rights (OCR) and the Equal Employment Opportunity Commission.

Sexual harassment is legally defined as "unwelcome sexual advances, requests for sexual favors, and other verbal or physical conduct of a sexual nature" when any one of the following criteria is met:

- Submission to such conduct is made either explicitly or implicitly a term or condition of the individual's employment or academic standing.
- Submission to or rejection of such conduct by an individual is used as the basis for employment or academic decisions affecting the individual.
- Such conduct has the purpose or effect of unreasonably interfering with an individual's work or learning performance or creating an intimidating, hostile or offensive work or learning environment (Equal Employment Opportunity Commission 1990).

CRITIQUE OF CAMPUS SAVE

According to OCR, resolutions of sexual misconduct must be determined within 60 days. Campus SaVE, on the other hand, indicates that final decisions can be delayed until the eve of the victim's graduation. Murphy (in this volume) has pointed out that this resolution recommended by SaVE violates students' equal access to education; there is simply no equity if the remedy is not in place until graduation. Waiting also puts others on campus at risk for assault.

Additionally, according to OCR, campuses are mandated to act even without a report when the campus authority "knows or should know" about misconduct. SaVE, however, states that no response from the campus is necessary unless the campus receives an "actual report." The concern raised by Murphy and others is that this provision would lead to increased misconduct as well as to students becoming fearful of reporting their experiences.

At the time this volume went into publication, a landmark federal lawsuit had been filed against the Department of Education on behalf of all women students in the United States. This lawsuit was filed to ensure women students' safety and full equality in higher education.

BEHAVIORAL EXAMPLES AND INCIDENCE RATES

Both *Not Alone* and Campus SaVE have relied on national incidence data indicating that women on college campuses are at greater risk of violence than are women in other groups; most incidents of sexual misconduct go unreported; most students are not aware of their campus' reporting options; and most campuses have no staff members trained in the psychology of the victimization process, consequently staffers ask questions of survivors that engender victim blaming. Additionally, research has identified that most individuals do not accurately label rape or other forms of sexual misconduct (Paludi & Kravitz 2011).

Women who have experienced sexual violence in high school are more likely to be sexually assaulted in college (Hall-Smith, White & Holland 2003). The term "the red zone" refers to the high incidence of sexual violence against women on college campuses—for incoming college students, the red zone is the first six weeks of the first semester.

Domestic Violence

Behavioral examples of domestic violence include—but are not limited to—attempting to cause or causing bodily injury by hitting, slapping, punching, hair pulling, kicking, and other forms of unwanted physical contact that cause harm; knowingly restricting the movements of another person; isolating or confining a person for a period; controlling or monitoring behavior; being verbally or emotionally abusive; or exhibiting extreme possessiveness or jealousy.

Estimates of domestic violence range from 960,000 incidents to upward of 4 million incidents annually. Eighty-five percent of survivors of domestic violence are women; 15% are men. Women between the ages of 16 and 24 are at the greatest risk for experiencing nonfatal domestic violence. The likelihood of being killed by an intimate partner also is greater for women than for men. During the six months following a battering episode, one-third of battered women are revictimized (Lundberg-Love & Marmion 2006).

Dating Violence

Dating violence is a pattern of coercive behaviors that serves to exercise control and power in an intimate relationship. The coercive and abusive behaviors can be physical, sexual, psychological, verbal or emotional. Relationship abuse can occur between current or former intimate partners who have dated, lived together, currently reside together on or off campus, or who otherwise are connected through a past or existing relationship. Hall-Smith, White, and Holland (2003) examined dating violence in college women longitudinally for four years. They found that 74.8% of white women and 81.5% of African American women reported being sexually victimized, 76.6% of white women and 81.1% of African American women had been physically assaulted.

Dating violence can occur in opposite-sex and same-sex relationships as well as in transgender relationships. Dating violence includes, but is not limited to, attempting to cause or causing bodily injury by hitting, slapping, punching, hair pulling, kicking, and other forms of unwanted physical contact that causes harm; knowingly restricting the movements of another person; isolating or confining a person for a period; controlling or monitoring behavior; being verbally or emotionally abusive; or exhibiting extreme possessiveness or jealousy.

Stalking

Stalking behaviors include incessant phone calls/e-mails/texts; continually sending gifts or letters professing love; following the target; stealing the target's mail; spying on the target; and killing or threatening to kill the target. Research indicates that 13% of college women have been stalked; 80.3% of those stalked knew or had seen their stalker prior to the misconduct beginning. Thirty percent of women report being injured emotionally from being stalked. Similar to other forms of sexual misconduct on campuses, 83% of stalking incidents go unreported.

Cyberstalking is an extension of the physical form of stalking and is unacceptable at any level. Cyberstalking includes using electronic media such as the Internet, social networking sites, cell phones, or similar devices or mediums to pursue, track, harass, monitor, or make unwanted contact with another person (Chisholm 2006).

Martin (2008) has framed the research on stalking within the context of relationship persistence, which is rewarded in Western culture. According to Martin, "The media portrays images of men pursuing and eventually breaking down the resistance of women in film. . . . These films portray stalking behaviors as necessary to reach the eventual reward: the desired woman. Many men follow these patterns of mild violence in their own relationships" (Martin 2008, 12).

This standard of persistence is an element of the double standard of sexuality, which is part of the reason why gendered violence occurs. As Spitzberg and Rhea (1999) reported, this double standard rewards men for sexual persistence and women for resistance. The standard also penalizes women for being overt in their sexuality. As Martin concluded, "This essentializing system results in a web of mixed messages where silence can become consent, and where no does not necessarily mean no" (Martin 2008, 12). Spitzberg and Rhea's (1999) research on sexual coercion supports Martin's theory: "undue· reliance on nonverbal communication in sexual pursuit can lead to a lack of communicative resources for negotiating appropriate conduct" (Spitzberg & Rhea 1999, 5).

Sexual Harassment

There are two types of sexual harassment situations that are described by the legal definition—quid pro quo sexual harassment and hostile environment sexual harassment. Quid pro quo sexual harassment involves an individual with organizational power who either expressly or implicitly ties an employment or academic decision to the response of an employee or student to unwelcome sexual advances. Hostile environment sexual harassment involves a situation where an atmosphere or climate is created in the workplace, classroom, library, lab, or other work or learning area on campus that makes it difficult—if not impossible—for an employee to work or for a student to study and learn, because the atmosphere is perceived by the individual to be intimidating, offensive, and hostile.

The incidence of sexual harassment among undergraduate students by their peers ranges between 20% and 80% each year. Sexual harassment of college students by professors ranges from 30% to 50% annually, ranging from sexual come-ons to coercing students into a sexual relationship by threatening to lower their grades or threatening to not write a letter of recommendation for a job or graduate school, and including requests for sexual activity in exchange for a higher grade, an internship, or a scholarship (Hill & Silva 2005).

Rape

One in four women is a survivor of rape. In their first six weeks in college, numerous women are likely to be raped, with 80% to 90% of those women assaulted knowing their attacker (McCauley, Ruggiero, Resnick & Kilpatrick 2010). Women who are members of sororities are 74% more likely to experience rape than are other college women; the women who live in a sorority house are more than three times as likely to be raped (Minow & Einolf 2009). Sexual assault is an offense classified as forcible or nonforcible sex offenses under the uniform crime reporting system of the Federal Bureau of Investigation.

NonconsensualSexual Contact Defined

Nonconsensual sexual contact includes the touching of an unwilling or nonconsensual person's intimate parts (such as genitalia, groin, breast, buttocks, mouth, or the clothing covering these areas); touching an unwilling person with one's own intimate parts; or forcing an unwilling person to touch another person's intimate parts.

Nonconsensual Sexual Penetration Defined

Nonconsensual sexual penetration includes any sexual penetration (anal, oral, or vaginal), however slight, with any body part or object that is perpetrated by an individual upon another individual without effective consent.

Sexual Exploitation Defined

Occurs when a person takes nonconsensual or abusive sexual advantage of another person to benefit or advantage anyone other than the individual being exploited, and that behavior does not otherwise constitute another form of sexual misconduct. Examples of sexual exploitation include, but are not limited to, prostitution, nonconsensual video or audio recording of sexual or other private activity, exceeding the boundaries of consent (e.g., permitting others to hide in a closet and observe consensual sexual activity, video recording a person who is using a bathroom), engaging in voyeurism, or engaging in consensual sexual activity with another person when knowingly infected with human immunodeficiency virus (HIV) or other sexually transmitted disease (STD) and without informing the uninfected person of such infection.

IMPACT OF SEXUAL MISCONDUCT ON INDIVIDUALS AND CAMPUSES

Not Alone and Campus SaVE provided empirical evidence of the high costs of sexual misconduct to students, faculty, administrators, and staff.

Sexual misconduct impacts several areas of functioning—including but not limited to—the following:

- Emotional
  - Anxiety
  - Depression
  - Fear
  - Shame
  - Shock
  - Suicidal Thoughts
  - Confusion
- Physical
  - Headaches
  - Substance Abuse
  - Sleep Disturbances
  - Gastrointestinal Disorders
  - Eating Disorders
  - Self-Harm
- Career/Work
  - Change in Career Goals
  - Reduced Productivity
  - Absenteeism
  - Lower Grades/Poor Academic Performance

All of these responses become more pronounced the longer the survivor endures the violence. The costs of discrimination and harassment to campuses include absenteeism, fear, decreased morale, and lack of trust (Paludi 2014; Waits & Lundberg-Love 2008).

TITLE IX

Not Alone and Campus SaVE are the latest guidance and legislation that began with Title IX of the 1972 Education Amendments. According to Title IX, "No person in the United States shall, on the basis of sex, be excluded from participation in, be denied the benefits of, or be subjected to discrimination under any education program or activity receiving Federal financial assistance."

Title IX was enacted as a consequence of several instances of discriminatory treatment and harassment of women, including, for example,

- Failure to admit women to undergraduate programs,
- More difficult or different admission criteria for women,
- Failure of colleges to admit married women,
- Less financial aid provided for women,
- Discouraging women from pursuing traditionally male vocations,
- Sexual harassment of women students,
- Fewer athletic opportunities and resources provided for women, and
- Fewer women allowed to coach or to hold positions in high school or college athletic departments.

Title IX applies to

- Admissions,
- Recruitment,
- Financial Aid,
- Academics,
- Counseling,
- Grading,
- Athletics,
- Housing,
- Classroom Assignments,
- Discipline,
- Vocational Education, and
- Students on Terms Abroad.

The principles of Title IX include

- Thorough, reliable, and impartial investigations of discrimination and harassment;
- Prompt, effective, and equitable resolutions of harassment and discrimination; and
- Remedies to end discrimination, prevent its recurrence, and remedy the impact upon the survivor and community.

Title IX is governed by the Office of Civil Rights (OCR) of the U.S. Department of Education. In April 2011, OCR issued its "Dear Colleague Letter" which identified for campuses their responsibilities in preventing and responding to sexual harassment, sexual misconduct, and discrimination. The OCR "Dear Colleague Letter" discusses, in part, the issues listed below.

- As soon as a campus knows—or reasonably should know—of possible sexual violence, it must take immediate and appropriate investigative action.
- The campus must complete an investigation in less than 60 calendar days.
- If sexual violence has occurred, then prompt and immediate steps must be taken to end the sexual violence, prevent its recurrence, and address its effects.
- Grievance procedures must use the preponderance of evidence standard to resolve complaints, that it is more likely than not that the misconduct occurred.
- The campus must notify both the complainant and the respondent of their appeal rights.
- Campuses must appoint a Title IX coordinator, who oversees investigations, training, and reports of sexual misconduct as well as handling discrimination and harassment issues for the campus.

CULTURAL ISSUES

Not Alone, Campus SaVE, and the "Dear Colleague Letter" all include recommendations for addressing cultural perceptions and reporting sexual harassment experienced by students and employees (Paludi 2014). In North America, Australia, and Germany, for example, sexual harassment is defined as "[u]nwanted verbal or physical overtures." In Brazil the term means "[t]o seduce someone, to be more intimate, to procure a romance." The definition of sexual harassment in South Africa is "[u]nwelcome touching or fondling" (DeSouza & Solberg 2003). Additionally, individuals in Brazil have questioned whether to classify sexual harassment as a crime that incurs punishment, so as to end this form of violence in educational institutions and workplaces (DeSouza & Solberg 2003).

Denga and Denga (2004) identified the distinction in definitions of sexual harassment between the Western view and Nigerian view.

DeSouza and Solberg (2003) reviewed incidence rates of sexual harassment of college students in several countries—Australia, Brazil, China, Italy, Israel, Pakistan, Puerto Rico, Sweden, and Turkey. They reported that incidence rates of sexual harassment are relatively high in all countries surveyed. Mecca and Rubin (1999) reported that African American women college students indicated that they frequently experienced sexual

Table 1. Western and Nigerian Definitions of Sexual Harassment

Western View	Nigerian View
Subtle pressure for sexual activity	Too mild to constitute sexual harassment
Leering or ogling of a woman's body	Regarded as foolishness
Constant brushing against a woman's body	"Superfluous affection"
Sexual harassment	Stalking a woman

touching. For certain students the incidence of campus violence is greater, including for

- People of color;
- Transgender individuals;
- Lesbian, gay, and bisexual individuals; and
- Individuals with physical and emotional disabilities.

Hofstede's (2001) cultural dimensions theory is a framework that can be applied to cultural perceptions of academic and workplace sexual harassment and other forms of campus violence. The dimensions are listed below.

- Power Distance: Extent to which less powerful members of a culture accept that power is distributed unequally.
- Individualism versus Collectivism: In individualistic cultures, emphasis is placed on personal achievements and individual rights.
- Individuals in collectivistic cultures act as members of a cohesive group.
- Masculinity versus Femininity: Refers to the distribution of emotional roles between women and men. Masculine cultures' values include competitiveness, ambition, power, and assertiveness. Feminine cultures emphasize caring, relationships, and the quality of life.
- Uncertainty Avoidance: Extent to which individuals attempt to cope with anxiety by minimizing uncertainty.
- Long-Term Orientation Versus Short-Term Orientation: Extent to which cultures attach importance to the future (Hofstede 2001).

With respect to sexual harassment, individualistic societies emphasize individual identities. There is a greater rate of labeling sexual harassment, and reporting sexual harassment as fighting for one's rights is paramount in an individualistic society. In collectivist cultures, to maintain group harmony individuals are more likely to go along with group definitions and perceptions. In Latino collectivist cultures, for example, individuals are more likely to be offended at unwanted sex-related behavior in the classroom or workplace. The cultural norms of "respeto" and "dignidad" dictate that interpersonal relationships be respected.

In masculine cultures great value is placed on power, competition, and success; thus, sexual harassment is more likely to be condoned. Additionally, in masculine cultures sexual language typically is more prevalent and is not labeled as sexual harassment.

Individuals in high power distance cultures take cues from superiors on behaviors that constitute sexual harassment. People in low power distance cultures label behaviors as sexual harassment by their own morals. Individuals in high uncertainty avoidance will not label or report sexual harassment if their academic grade or their job is jeopardized. Hofstede's dimensions prove essential for modifying training programs on sexual harassment and other forms of campus violence.

Paludi (2014) has recommended novel intervention strategies that are accessible across cultural groups. Additionally, campus officials who are dealing with preventing and responding to complaints of campus violence must be trained to understand and appreciate the differences and how best to protect and deal with the differences in perception, labeling, and reporting. Furthermore, counselors who deal with survivors of campus violence must be appropriately trained to deal with a diverse population of clients.

REASONABLE CARE AS PREVENTION

Policies and Procedures

Legally defensible policies for preventing discrimination, harassment, and other forms of workplace and campus violence require more than a general organizational statement against the behavior (Hedge & Pulakos 2002; Levy & Paludi 2002; Smith & Mazin 2004). Such policies require the efforts and support of administrators, employees, faculty, and students at all levels, and the continual training of all members of the organization (discussed elsewhere in this chapter), as well as the implementing of investigatory procedures that encourage individuals to come forward with complaints (EEOC 1999). This aspect of reasonable care will put campuses and workplaces on stronger footing in a legal action. Additionally, all members of an organization—educational and business—would benefit from a climate of respect and cooperation.

Components of Policies and Procedures

Recommendations identified by OCR, *Not Alone*, and the EEOC have been translated by attorneys, human resource management specialists, and social scientists (e.g., Association of the Bar of the City of New York 1993; Connell 1991; Gutek 1997; Reese & Lindenberg 1999; Smith & Mazin 2004; Trotter & Zacur 2004). The literature on sexual harassment and other forms of campus and workplace violence has identified components of effective policy statements, which are listed below (see Paludi & Paludi 2003).

- Statement of Purpose
- Legal Definitions
- Behavioral Examples
- Definition of Consent
- Definition of Incapacitated
- Statement Concerning Impact of Violence on Individuals and the Organization
- Statement of Individual's Responsibility in Filing Complaint
- Statement of Organization's Responsibility in Investigating Complaint
- Statement Concerning Confidentiality of Complaint Procedures
- Statement Concerning Sanctions Available
- Statement Regarding Retaliation
- Statement of Sanctions for Retaliation
- Statement Concerning False Complaints
- Identification and Background of Individual(s) Responsible for Hearing Complaints

The literature also has identified components for effective complaint procedures for organizations and campuses. Empirical research indicated that individuals feel more encouraged to file a complaint of harassment, discrimination, or sexual misconduct when they understand what the process entails (Levy & Paludi 2002). Thus, all parties to the complaint must be given accurate and adequate information about the complaint procedure, written in understandable language and terms. Failure to provide such information makes the policy statement inhibitive (Trotter & Zacur 2004).

According to Riger's (1991) research with sexual harassment of employees, when policy statements are not clearly written and communicated, women are reluctant to label their experiences as sexual harassment and thus do not report their discrimination incidents. Further, O'Connell and Korabik (2000) reported that there is a reduction in severe sexual harassment incidents when businesses adhere to and enforce their anti-sexual harassment policies.

Thus, simply having a policy does not isolate an organization or campus. The policy must be disseminated to all members of the organization; individuals must be trained on its content (*Frederick v. Sprint/ United Management Company* 2001). Paludi (2014) also recommends the following:

- The policy should contain an alternative procedure for complaints if the investigator is the person alleged to have engaged in discrimination or harassment.
- The policy statement should be made available in languages in addition to English for individuals and their support systems whose native language is not English.
- The policy statement must be made available in Braille and also in large print and also must be made available as an audio recording.

Components of effective procedures include all of the following, at a minimum.

- Informing individuals that the workplace/campus will not ignore any complaint of discrimination, harassment, or sexual violence.
- Informing individuals that the investigator of complaints will not make determinations about the complaint based on the reputations or organizational status of the individuals involved.
- Informing individuals that the investigation of complaints will be completed promptly.
- Informing individuals that the witnesses to incidents or to changes in the parties' behavior will be interviewed.
- Informing individuals that all documents presented by the complainant, respondent, and witnesses will be reviewed.
- Informing individuals that the complainant and the respondent will be subject to an in-depth interview.

SANCTIONS AND DISCIPLINE

A vital part of the policy statement informs individuals what sanctions will be imposed if the policy is violated. Discipline should be designed to end the misconduct and prevent the misconduct from reoccurring. Specific examples of progressive discipline should be provided in the policy statement and procedures, including verbal warning, written reprimand in the individual's personnel file, pay increase denials, pay reduction, transfer of the harasser, demotion, expulsion, or dismissal (Dessler 2009; Smith & Mazin 2004). The policy statement and procedures also should emphasize that the policy provides for stricter penalties for continued misbehavior.

CORRECTIVE ACTION

In addition to disciplining individuals who have violated the policy statement on sexual misconduct, discrimination, and harassment, providing corrective action also is recommended. Discipline does not correct the behavior or performance in question. Depending on the particular situation, other measures might be effective and appropriate, such as individualized training programs on rape, stalking, domestic violence, and dating violence (Salisbury & Jaffe 1996) and counseling through an Employees Assistance Program, counseling center, or community-based therapist (Dessler 2009; Paludi & Paludi 2003).

TRAINING PROGRAMS

There is ample empirical research to indicate that training about discrimination, harassment, and sexual misconduct changes attitudes and behaviors (see, e.g., Anand & Winters 2008; Antecol & Cobb-Clark 2003; Blakely, Blakely & Moorman 1998; Dwairy 2004; Kluge 2008; Pendry Driscoll & Field 2007; Perry, Kulik & Schmidtke 2006; Rynes & Rosen 1995; York, Barclay & Zajack 1997). Research indicates, for example, that training increases knowledge acquisition and reduces the inappropriate behavior of men who had a high propensity to harass. Research also indicates that sexual harassment training is associated with an increased probability—especially for men—of considering unwanted sexual gestures, remarks, touching, and pressure for dates to be a form of sexual harassment (Antecol & Cobb-Clark 2003; Beauvais 1985). Further, men who receive such training have greater knowledge of sexual harassment and have less tolerant attitudes toward sexual harassment than do men who are not trained (Frisbie 2002; Moyer & Nath 2006).

Thus, an important feature of an effective policy statement and investigatory procedure on violence is a training program designed to enforce the policy (Levy & Paludi 2002; Paludi & Paludi 2003; Smith & Mazin 2004). The impact of the absence of effective or enforced policies through training programs includes individuals not fully comprehending what behaviors do, in fact, constitute discrimination, harassment, or sexual misconduct and retaliation, and how the organization will deal with complaints and sanctions for violating the policy (EEOC 1999; Wentling & Palma-Rivas 2002). Training also should encourage individuals who have complaints to promptly report their complaints to the individual charged with investigating them (OCR 2011; EEOC 1990, 1999; Tsai & Kleiner 2001).

Training programs include three major components: (1) needs assessment, (2) facilitating the training programs, and (3) post-training evaluations (DeCenzo & Robbins 2007; Goldstein & Ford 2002). Poorly conceptualized and poorly facilitated training programs on sexual misconduct, discrimination, and harassment cause more harm than good (Chavez & Weisinger 2008; De Meuse, Hostager, Claire & O'Neill 2007; Society for Human Resource Management 2009; Stockdale & Crosby 2004). Stockdale and Crosby (2004) and Sacco and Schmitt (2005) reported that, despite the fact that employees liked participating in training on workplace discrimination, the impact of such training might not translate into sustained, positive organizational results.

Needs Assessment

There are several topics to be discussed in any training program on sexual misconduct, harassment, and discrimination (e.g., legal definitions, behavioral examples, policy and investigatory procedures). In keeping with the literature in human resource management (e.g., Barbazette 2006; Brown 2002; Jones 2000) conducting a needs assessment to identify additional issues participants expect to be covered in a training session is recommended.

Examples of additional topics include: the role of hidden biases and stereotypes (Babcock 2006); the impact of sexual misconduct on individuals' emotional and physical health; self-concept and interpersonal relationships; the role the counseling center, clergy, and health services play in assisting individuals; and the interface of homophobia and violence and race and violence. The topics typically are suggested to the trainer based on prior complaints faced by the campus or organization.

Brown (2002) identified four reasons that needs assessments should be conducted prior to facilitating training programs. These are to (1) identify problem areas, (2) obtain management support, (3) develop data for measuring the effectiveness of the training program, and (4) determine the costs and benefits of the training program. Needs assessments can be conducted through anonymous surveys and focus groups (Lucier 2008; Roberson, Kulik & Pepper 2003; Tyler 2002). Levy and Paludi (2002) recommended the following process.

- Ask individuals to provide answers to question regarding sexual misconduct, harassment, and discrimination via an anonymous mail survey.
- Facilitate two-hour focus groups with randomly selected individuals (no more than 15 to 20 per session) to elicit in-depth responses. Structured interview questions for individuals who participate in the focus groups center around their goals for training, including their needs with regard to better understanding issues such as consent, incapacitation, reporting options.

- Analyze responses from the previous steps using qualitative and quantitative analyses.
- Prepare a written report that summarizes the needs assessment, including suggestions for the following:
  - How to increase awareness.
  - Ways to examine attitudes.
  - Alternatives to stereotyping.
  - Methods of supportive action.
- Make recommendations for post-training evaluations (to be discussed subsequently in this chapter).

The main goal of the needs assessment therefore is to obtain information concerning the manner in which discrimination, sexual misconduct, and harassment are addressed in the organizational climate of the campus. The desired information includes topics such as empowerment, the establishment of mutual trust and respect, methods of inclusion or exclusion, and verbal and nonverbal communication indicative of harassment and discrimination. The process of the assessment is to be consistent with the goal of the training programs in which the individuals subsequently will participate (Tyler 2002). An example of a needs assessment for training content on sexual harassment can be found in Levy and Paludi (2002).

Facilitating Training Programs

Training must be geared toward the accomplishment of campus or organizational mission and organizational goals and must be based on key performance indicators. The training strategy, for example, perhaps is connected to the campus' compliance and ethics goal. Failure to demonstrate that the training is tied to the organization's mission, values, and strategic plan (goals), denies the importance of the role of training in the prevention and intervention of unlawful campus misconduct that diminishes productivity and morale, increases absenteeism and turnover, ruins reputations, and thereby negatively affects the bottom line.

Training Goals

Goals for training programs that have been identified in the scholarly and training literatures include (Bell & Kravitz 2008) the following:

- To provide all members of the campus or organization with a clear understanding of their rights and responsibilities with respect to discrimination, harassment, and sexual misconduct.

- To enable individuals to distinguish between behavior that is and behavior that is not discrimination, harassment, or sexual misconduct.
- To provide individuals with information concerning statements and procedures set up by the campus or organization.
- To discuss the emotional and physical reactions common among survivors.
- To encourage individuals to examine their personal feelings and those of others with respect to discrimination, harassment, and sexual misconduct.
- To dispel myths about sexual misconduct, discrimination, and harassment.
- To empower individuals to take control of their behavior.
- To discuss the concept of unwelcomeness and how this is communicated verbally and nonverbally.
- To create an environment that is free of discrimination, sexual misconduct, and harassment and free of the fear of retaliation for speaking out about these issues.

After the goals have been established, policies and procedures must be revised, taking into account new case law and research from the social sciences and management literatures. The policy statements and procedures are part of the training session content, therefore they must be completed prior to the training.

Training Components

The campus' president or Title IX coordinator should introduce each training session, and provide the strategic rationale regarding why the training is occurring. The trainer should emphasize the campus' or organization's commitment to a respectful, discriminatory, harassment-free and retaliation-free work environment.

Ideally, training sessions should include no more than 20 to 25 participants to facilitate discussion and small-group exercises, and to minimize risk for those participants who are reluctant to speak up and ask questions. Key discussion topic areas for a comprehensive training program include the following:

- Explanation of how the training supports the mission and values and why the training is occurring.
- Legal definitions of all types of discrimination and harassment, including quid pro quo and hostile environment, and examples of

each—must be inclusive of all legally protected classes based on federal and state laws such as sex, race, color, religion, national origin, age, disability, and sexual orientation.

- Definition of welcomeness, severe and pervasive, reasonable person/victim/woman, gender or sexual in nature (e.g., race, disability, religion).
- Organization's policies related to discrimination, sexual misconduct, and harassment including electronic communication, workplace violence, respectful conduct, affirmative action, and, of course, the policy—with an emphasis on intolerance of the misconduct.
- Organization's grievance procedure.
- Who the policy applies to including outside vendors, visitors, and clients.
- Retaliation against anyone involved in a complaint is against the law and against the campus' or organization's policy; include examples of behavior that constitutes retaliation.
- Consequences/impact of the behavior on the target, the work unit, the organization, and the perpetrator.
- Confidentiality.
- The role and responsibility of the bystander/witness.
- Assertive communication.
- Overview of the investigation process and why it occurs.

In addition to these topics, administrators require additional information, including the following:

- That administrators' behavior will be held to a stricter standard than nonsupervisory employees; behavior executed by an employee might not be considered unlawful, but the same behavior committed by a supervisor could be considered unlawful.
- Their role and responsibility in preventing discrimination, sexual misconduct, and harassment.
- Consensual relationships with one of their direct reports.
- Their responsibility to report any discrimination, sexual misconduct, and harassment of which they are aware.
- The issue of knew or should have known.
- Importance of monitoring the campus or workplace environment for any signs or symptoms of potential sexual misconduct, discrimination, or harassment.

Further, discrimination, sexual misconduct, and harassment are emotionally charged topics that are threatening and confusing to many people. Stereotypes about members of protected classes often remain unchallenged unless individuals participate in effective trainer-guided intervention programs, such as a training program in sexual misconduct, discrimination, and harassment awareness (Bell & Kravitz 2008; Paludi & Paludi 2003).

Training programs involve more than a recitation of individuals' rights and responsibilities and what the law and campus or organization policy requires. Training also requires dealing with individuals' assumptions and misconceptions about protected classes and power issues, as well as the anxieties about the training itself. Thus, training sessions must devote ample time to dealing with the participants' feelings, misconceptions, and questions (Levy & Paludi 2002). Trainees frequently want to discuss topics following the training program with the trainer without hearing any comments from other participants. Because these topics are intimate for individuals, they are unlikely to ask questions in public. Thus, the trainer should be available after the formal training program concludes to answer attendees' questions privately.

Ecological Approach to Training

Paludi and Paludi (2003) offered an "ecological approach" for conducting training programs in organizations. It stresses that harassment, sexual misconduct, and discrimination training should be provided in a sequence that ensures optimum assistance for all parties in a complaint resolution (see ordered list below). This sequence for businesses is as follows:

1. Investigators of Complaints
2. Counselors in Employees Assistance Program/Counseling Center
3. Trainers
4. President and Vice Presidents
5. Managers and Supervisors, Deans
6. Department Chairs
7. Employees
8. Students

Levy and Paludi (2002) recommend establishing training programs for employees and faculty within certain departments because they each have unique responsibilities. Training programs should not separate employees by sex, race, disability, national origin, or other protected categories. Conducting separate sessions for women and men on rape or sexual harassment, for example, could perpetuate stereotypes that all women are survivors and all men are perpetrators, which certainly is not supported by research. This type of training also can be divisive. All individuals have the same rights and responsibilities and must be provided with identical information concerning their rights and responsibilities.

Temporary and seasonal workers, board members, transfer students, volunteers, and long-term contract employees should be included in training.

Qualifications of Trainers

The importance to be placed on qualifications of trainers is well known. Courts have stated (for example in *Cadena v. Pacesetter Corp.*) that organizations must ensure that trainers

- Completely understand the complex body of harassment and discrimination laws, and
- Keep up to date with new cases that change the interpretations of these laws.

Educational qualifications of trainers for sexual harassment programs have been identified in the campus violence literature (Holladay & Quinones, 2008).

- Education/training in the psychological issues involved in campus violence.
- Education/training in the legal issues involved in campus violence.
- Publications/presentations on campus violence.
- Ability to work well with constituencies.
- Education/training in psychological issues involved in facilitating a training program.

One of the findings from empirical research on discrimination, sexual misconduct, and harassment concerns the resistance of individuals to talking about these issues. Experiences are difficult to discuss. Additionally, an individual who currently is being trained on the organization's policy could be experiencing a form of the violence being discussed. It thus is important to give legitimacy to the anxieties, confusion, and fears raised by trainees. Some individuals might want to make jokes about the topic because of the sensitivity of the issue. It is important to establish a respectful atmosphere in the training session and to talk up front about the attitudes some individuals have brought with them to the training.

It is advisable to have therapeutic support staff (e.g., counseling center, Employees Assistance Program personnel) attend training programs to assist with flashbacks that can occur (Contrada, Ashmore, Gary, Coups,

Egeth, Sewell, Ewell, Goyal & Chase 2000; Hamilton, Alagna, King & Lloyd 1987; Lundberg-Love & Marmion 2006; Paludi & Paludi 2003).

Pedagogical Concerns

Training must be facilitated in a formal training or meeting room where there is enough space so participants are not crowded together. Ideally, the room should allow learners to be able to see each other so that communication flows among all participants in the training. This facilitates the pedagogy of the training.

Several training methods exist for instructing individuals about harassment, sexual misconduct, and discrimination, including lectures, videos and films, simulation exercises, behavioral rehearsal, and Web-based training (DeCenzo & Robbins 2007; Dessler 2009; Smith & Mazin 2004; Walker 2000). The discipline of educational psychology has offered principles of the psychology of learning to all of these types of training programs (e.g., Slavin 2005).

- Gain the trainees' attention
- Maintain the trainees' attention
- Present material in an interesting way
  - Use trainees' experiences as the basis for examples and applications
  - Provide behavioral examples
  - Make the content immediately applicable
- Structure the learning experience
- Allow opportunities for practicing information from the training program
- Provide feedback
- Provide visual images
- Emphasize importance of concepts
- Use realistic examples, not jargon
- Encourage trainees to learn from each other
- Model desired behavior

Human resource management research has identified benefits and weaknesses of pedagogical methods for training programs on discrimination, sexual violence, and harassment (Callahan, Kiker & Cross 2003; Goldstein & Ford 2002; Stockdale & Crosby 2004; Wentling & Palma-Rivas 2002). Lecture formats, for example, are ideal for disseminating information about legal issues, the organization's policy and procedures, and behavioral examples; however, trainees could become bored or impatient and consequently might not pay attention. This is a serious issue because individuals must understand their rights and responsibilities under Title VII, Title IX, and the organization's or the campus' policy.

Case studies and scenarios encourage trainees to learn through guided discovery and teach individuals to think critically about campus violence (Carter 2002). They do not however, provide direct practice with issues. Trainers also might not provide one right or wrong answer to the cases and consequently individuals might not receive the best guidance in learning how to resolve cases of violence, discrimination, or harassment.

Although behavioral rehearsal or role-playing techniques are a good method for teaching communication and interaction skills, they present opportunities for embarrassment and loss of self-confidence among trainees. Furthermore, role-playing sexual harassment could elicit laughter, which can be perceived negatively by individuals who have experienced this form of violence.

The use of videos in training program is beneficial for trainers because the presenter can repeat part of the video or skip material already presented (Blanchard & Thacker 2003; Dessler 2009). There is a lack of personal contact when using video training, which creates an opportunity for individuals to become bored and not acquire knowledge about the policy and procedures.

Web-based training programs generate high levels of individuals' acquisition and retention of the material presented (Frisbie 2002), and offer fast-paced learning. This pedagogical technique, however, can create frustration in individuals who are not computer literate or who would prefer learning from an individual, not from a computer (Oddsson 2001).

Inevitably, administrators must consider whether to use purchased training programs. Purchased programs are easy-to-use tools because no development time is required, programs often are inexpensive as compared to utilizing an outside consultant/trainer, and all the training materials are provided in a nice neat package. These programs, however, often are not customized (or only minimally customized) for organizations, do not include the organization's pertinent policies, already are outdated upon purchase due to changes in case law, and are designed for anyone to use—including a novice who is not a subject-matter expert. In all likelihood, these programs might not carry much protective weight with the courts.

The complexity of sexual misconduct, discrimination, and harassment makes it unsuitable for asynchronous e-learning. It does not offer the same opportunities to engage in discussion; pose multifaceted and complex questions and receive (immediate) answers, particularly with questions about the more subtle, nuanced types of behaviors; share the social contact of interaction with peers and an instructor; or to partake in meaningful feedback. E-learning sometimes has been described as too simplistic, weak, dull, and monotonous. Learners are free to go through e-learning training at their own pace, which means they frequently could be interrupted by phone calls and by coworkers, coffee and lunch breaks, and meetings; or they might engage in multitasking while progressing through the online program. All of these interruptions interfere with the learning environment.

A study conducted by Bingham and Scherer (2001) showed that participants who attended a short sexual harassment training knew more about sexual harassment and viewed the workplace misconduct as more improper than did a similar group of nonparticipants. Unfortunately, male participants had an unfavorable response to the training, tended to blame the victim, were less tenable in perceiving coercive sexual harassment, and indicated that they were less apt to report sexual harassment. Additionally, men were more likely to perceive social sexual behavior at work as more amiable than were women. These gender differences were not apparent in the group of nonparticipants. Although the authors identified potential theories to help explain the men's reactions, the most likely cause was the inadequacy of the training.

The training program lacked a strategic approach and lasted only 30 minutes (Bingham & Scherer 2001). The authors did not discuss the objectives or teaching methodology of the program, or the expertise of the presenter(s), all of which could influence the effectiveness of the training session. The results of this study should raise a red flag among human resources professionals when designing and implementing harassment and discrimination training programs. According to the authors, attempts at cost reduction by minimizing the quality and quantity (length) of the training can create "inherent dangers . . . when developing sexual harassment programs" (Bingham & Scherer 2001, 145). Organizations that believe the myth that "something is better than nothing" actually could be amplifying potential trouble by implementing an inadequate program.

Research by York, Barclay, and Zajack (1997) demonstrated that combining two training methods—a videotape of five different vignettes and a case study analysis of each vignette—increased participant understanding of sexual harassment. Gender differences in perception and analysis were apparent in that women were more likely to identify sexual harassment in specific videos demonstrating more subtle misconduct; there was no difference in gender perception for the blatant misconduct.

Effective training methods must take into account the learning styles of adults (Knowles, Holton & Swanson 2005) and should empower individuals, help students and employees to think strategically, and help employees communicate effectively. Interactive pedagogy encompasses adult learning principles. Research has identified that adults prefer learning situations which

- Are practical and problem-centered,
- Promote positive self-esteem,
- Integrate new ideas with existing knowledge,
- Show respect for the individual learner,
- Capitalize on their experience, and
- Allow choice and self-direction (Knowles, Holton & Swanson 2005; McNamara 2008).

Thus, training programs must

- Provide overviews, summaries, case studies, and behavioral rehearsals to link research to practice;
- Use collaborative, authentic problem-solving activities;
- Assist individuals in becoming more effective and confident through guided practice and establishing routines;
- Ask individuals what they would like to know about the training topic;
- Provide a quality, well-organized, differentiated experience that uses time effectively and efficiently;
- Validate and respect participants' existing knowledge;
- Create activities that use individuals' experience and knowledge; and
- Be engaging and not repetitive.

The major objective of the training modules and pedagogical techniques is to facilitate transference to the campus or workplace. Transference can be accomplished by the following:

- Association: Having participants associate the new information with something with which they are already knowledgeable.
- Similarity: Presenting information that is similar to material that participants already know (i.e., it revisits a logical framework or pattern).
- Degree of original learning: The degree of original learning for the participants was high.
- Critical attribute element: The information learned by the participants contains elements that are extremely beneficial or critical on the job.

Acknowledgment of Participation in Training

Following the completion of the training program, all individuals must sign an acknowledgment receipt indicating that they participated in the training program. A copy of this acknowledgment should be given to the participants and a copy should be placed in the human resources/personnel office or Title IX coordinator's office (Smith & Mazin 2004).

Post-Training Evaluations

Measuring the effectiveness of training programs is an important aspect of the training program. Evaluations help the organization to determine whether the training delivered or failed to deliver the expected benefits (Hoyle 2006; Morgan & Casper 2000; Tyler 2002). The measures of success for the training programs are those identified in the needs assessment phase. Issues in the measurement phase can be discussed two ways, one is the types of information to measure and another is methods for measuring whether the training effort achieved its goals. It is not enough to merely assume that any training that an organization offers is effective, even if it is legally mandated (Tyler 2002). The transfer of knowledge from the training room to the campus or workplace is the most important measure of success.

Information to Measure

The most well-known model for determining the effectiveness of training programs is the Kirkpatrick Model (Kirkpatrick, 1959; 1998), which comprises four levels—reaction, learning, behavior, and results. The results level concerns the benefits resulted from training. The behavior level taps into what extent trainees change their behavior in the workplace as a result of the training. The learning level asks to what extent trainees improved their knowledge and skills and changed their attitudes as a result of the training programs. The reaction level determines trainees' opinions about components including the structure of the training program, location of the program, and trainer effectiveness.

The most commonly used level of the Kirkpatrick Model is the reactions level; however this is the least valid evaluation technique (Tan, Hall & Boyce 2003). Individuals' opinions are strongly influenced by factors that could have little to do with the training effectiveness. By measuring reactions, organizations do not obtain information regarding individuals' learning; how well participants are integrating the new knowledge and skills; whether training has reduced the incidence of sexual misconduct, harassment, or discrimination; or whether there has been increased reporting post training (Stockdale & Crosby 2004).

Measurement Techniques

Common performance-based evaluations that incorporate any of the Kirkpatrick Model levels are post-training, pre-post-training, pre-post-training performance with control group, and the Solomon Four Group Design.

Post-Training

Individuals' performance, that is, knowledge of the organization's policy, incidence of discrimination, Title VII provisions, and Title IX provisions is measured after the participants have attended the training program to determine whether they have increased their knowledge of this information. Some trainees might have known this information prior to participating in the training program, however. Thus, simply providing a post-training survey or test could overstate the benefits of the training program.

Pre-Post-Training Evaluations

Pre-post-training evaluations can assist with this concern (Sadri & Snyder 1995). The trainer administers a test or quiz prior to the beginning of the training program. The quiz might ask questions regarding the definition, incidence, and explanatory models of various forms of discrimination, harassment, or sexual misconduct, or about the organization's policy statement. Following the training program, the trainer re-administers the quiz and then determines whether scores on the post-test quiz are better than those from the pre-test version. This method can provide more reliable information about whether the training program contributed to increased scores on the post-test quizzes—which is expected, if the training program was effective.

Pre-Post-Training with Control Group

To further answer the question regarding training effectiveness, a pre-post-training with control group can be used. In this method, two groups of individuals are established and evaluated on factors such as their knowledge, attitudes, and behavior. The control group, however, receives no training and the other group does receive training. Both groups take a post-test. This method corrects for factors other than training that could influence employees' performance. The group that received training should have higher post-test scores than those of the control group.

CURRENT VOLUME

The contributors to this volume share the belief that we need to bring together—from a variety of disciplines, including the social sciences, law, and management—concepts, theories, and research such as those dis-cussed in this Introduction, that can be useful to people in making deci-sions about preventing and responding to sexual harassment in educational and workplace settings. Contributors to each of these volumes focus on educational and management strategies that are grounded in case law and empirical research in the social sciences, education, and human resource management. They all recognize that dealing with sexual harassment de-pends on effectively listening to students and employees.

The goal of all chapters in this volume is on working strategically, col-lectively, ethically, respectfully, and effectively with people. Another goal is to motivate our readers to take action against sexual harassment. We edited this volume to provide information to assist individuals, campuses, and employers in intervening when they recognize a threat of sexual ha-rassment—to a friend, classmate, dorm mate, employee, student, or other individual.

REFERENCES

Anand, R., and Winters, M. (2008). A retrospective view of corporate diversity training from 1964 to the present. *Academy of Management Learning and Education 7*, 356–372.

Antecol, H., and Cobb-Clark, D. (2003). Does sexual harassment training change attitudes? A view from the federal level. *Social Science Quarterly 84*, 826–842.

Association of the Bar of the City of New York. 1993. *Law firm policies on workplace sexual harassment. Report from the Committee on Labor and Employment Law, the Association of the Bar of the City of New York.*

Babcock, P. (2006). Watch out for the minefield of hidden bias. In *HR Magazine: Guide to managing people*, edited by Society for Human Resource Management, 44–47. Alexandria, VA: Society for Human Resource Management.

Baker, C. (2007). The women's movement against sexual harassment. New York: Cambridge Press.

Barbazette, J. (2006). *Training needs assessment: Methods, tools and techniques.* New York: John Wiley & Sons.

Beauvais, K. (1985). Workshops to combat sexual harassment: A case study of changing attitudes. *Signs 12*, 130–145.

Bell, M., and Kravitz, D. (2008). What do we know and need to learn about diver-sity education and training? *Academy of Management Learning and Education 7*, 301–308.

Bingham, S., and Scherer, L. (2001). The unexpected effects of a sexual harassment educational program. *The Journal of Applied Behavioral Science 37*, 125–153.

Blakely, G., Blakely, E., and Moorman, R. (1998). The effects of training on percep-tions of sexual harassment allegations. *Journal of Applied Social Psychology 28*, 71–83.

Blanchard, N., Thacker, J., and Blanchard, P. (2003). *Effective training: Systems strategies and practices*. Upper Saddle River, NJ: Prentice Hall.

Brown, J. (2002). Training needs assessment: A must for developing an effective training program. *Public Personnel Management* 31, 569–578.

Cadena v. Pacesetter Corp., 224 F.3d 1203, 1215 (10th Cir. 2000).

Callahan, J., Kiker, D., and Cross, T. (2003). Does method matter? A meta-analysis of the effects of training method on older learner training performance. *Journal of Management* 29, 663–680.

Carter, S. (2002). Matching training methods and factors of cognitive ability: A means to improve training outcomes. *Human Resource Development Quarterly* 13, 71–87.

Chavez, C., and Weisinger, J. (2008). Beyond diversity training: A social infusion for cultural inclusion. *Human Resource Management* 47, 331–350.

Chisholm, J. (2006). Cyberspace violence against girls and adolescent females. *Annuals, New York Academy of Sciences* 1087, 74–89.

Connell, D. (1991). Effective sexual harassment policies: Unexpected lessons from Jacksonville Shipyards. *Employee Relations* 17, 191–206.

Contrada, R., Ashmore, R., Gary, M., Coups, E., Egeth, J., Sewell, A., Ewell, K., Goyal, T., and Chasse, V. (2000). Ethnicity-related sources of stress and their effects on well-being. *Current Directions in Psychological Science* 9, 136–139.

De Meuse, K. P., Hostager, T. J., Claire, E., and O'Neill, K. S. (2007). Longitudinal evaluation of senior managers' perceptions and attitudes of a workplace diversity training programme. *Human Resource Planning* 30 (2), 38–46.

DeCenzo, D., and Robbins, S. (2007). *Fundamentals of human resource management*. New York: Wiley.

Denga, D., and Denga, H. (2004). Sexual harassment: A student's view from a Nigerian University. *The African Symposium* 4 (March).

DeSouza, E., and Solberg, J. (2003). Incidence and dimensions of sexual harassment across cultures. In *Academic and workplace sexual harassment: A handbook of cultural, social science, management, and legal perspectives*, edited by M. Paludi and C. A. Paludi Jr. Westport, CT: Praeger, 3–30.

Dessler, G. (2009). *Fundamentals of human resource management*. Upper Saddle River, NJ: Prentice Hall.

Dwairy, M. (2004). Culturally sensitive education: Adapting self-oriented assertiveness training to collective minorities. *Journal of Social Issues* 60, 423–436.

Equal Employment Opportunity Commission (EEOC) (1999). *Enforcement guidance: Vicarious employer liability for unlawful harassment by supervisors*.

Equal Employment Opportunity Commission (EEOC) (1990). *Policy guidance on sexual harassment*. http://www.eeoc.gov/policy/docs/currentissues.html. Accessed May 11, 2015.

Frederick v. Sprint/United Management Company, 246 F. 3d 1305 (11th Cir. 2001).

Frisbie, S. (2002). Sexual harassment: A comparison of on-line versus traditional training methods. Unpublished doctoral dissertation, Texas Tech University, Lubbock, TX.

Goldstein, I., and Ford, J. (2002). *Training in organizations: Needs assessment, development and evaluation.* 4th ed. Belmont, CA: Wadsworth.

Gutek, B. (1997). Sexual harassment policy initiatives. In *Sexual harassment: Theory, research, and practice,* edited by W. O'Donohue. Boston: Allyn & Bacon.

Hall-Smith, P., White, J., and Holland, L. (2003). A longitudinal perspective on dating violence among adolescent and college-age women. *American Journal of Public Health* 93, 1104–1109.

Hamilton, J., Alagna, S., King, L., and Lloyd, C. (1987). The emotional consequences of gender-based abuse in the workplace: New counseling programs for sex discrimination. *Women and Therapy* 6, 155–182.

Hedge, J., and Pulakos, E. (2002). *Implementing organizational interventions: Steps, processes and best practices.* San Francisco, CA: Jossey-Bass.

Hill, C., and Silva, E. (2005). *Drawing the line: Sexual harassment on campus.* Washington, DC: American Association of University Women Educational Foundation.

Hofstede, G. (2001). *Culture's consequences: Comparing values, behaviors, institutions, and organizations across nations.* 2nd ed. Thousand Oaks, CA: Sage.

Holladay, C., and Quinones, M. (2008). The influence of training focus and trainer characteristics on diversity training effectiveness. *Academy of Management Learning and Education* 7, 343–35.

Jones, C. (2000). Levels of racism: A theoretical framework and a gardener's tale. *American Journal of Public Health* 90, 1212–1215.

Kirkpatrick, D. (1998). *Evaluating training programs: The four levels.* San Francisco, CA: Berrett-Koehler.

Kirkpatrick, D. (1959). Techniques for evaluating training programs. *Journal of the American Society for Training Development* 13, 3–9.

Kluge, A. (2008). What you train is what you get? Task requirements and training methods in complex problem-solving. *Computers in Human Behavior* 24, 284–308.

Knowles, M., Holton, E., and Swanson, R. (2005). *The adult learner.* Oxford: Butterworth-Heinemann.

Levy, A., and Paludi, M. (2002). *Workplace sexual harassment.* 2nd ed. Englewood Cliffs, NJ: Prentice Hall.

Lucier, K. (2008). A consultative training program: Collateral effect of a needs assessment. *Communication Education* 57, 482–489.

Lundberg-Love, P., and Marmion, S. (2006). *Intimate violence against women.* Westport, CT: Praeger.

Martin, J. (2008). Shifting the load: Personality factors and women in the workplace. In *The psychology of women at work: Challenges and solutions for our female workforce,* edited by M. Paludi, 153–200. Westport, CT: Praeger.

McCaskill, C. (2014). *Sexual violence on campus: How too many institutions of higher education are failing to protect students.* Washington, DC: U.S. Senate Subcommittee on Financial and Contracting Oversight.

McCauley, J., Ruggiero, K., Resnick, H., and Kilpatrick, D. (2010). Incapacitated, forcible, and drug/alcohol-facilitated rape in relation to binge drinking, marijuana use, and illicit drug use: A national survey. *Journal of Traumatic Stress* 23 (1), 132–140.

Mecca, S., and Rubin, L. (1999). Definitional research on African American students and sexual harassment. *Psychology of Women Quarterly* 23, 813–817.

Minow, J., and Einolf, C. J. (2009). Sorority participation and sexual assault risk. *Violence against Women* 15 (7), 835–851.

Morgan, R., and Casper, W. (2000). Examining the factor structure of participant reactions to training: A multidimensional approach. *Human Resource Development Quarterly* 11, 301–317.

Moyer, R., and Nath, A. (2006). Some effects of brief training interventions on perceptions of sexual harassment. *Journal of Applied Social Psychology* 28, 333–356.

O'Connell, C. E., and Korabik, K. (2000). Sexual harassment: The relationship of personal vulnerability, work context, perpetrator status, and type of harassment to outcomes. *Journal of Vocational Behavior* 56, 299–329.

Oddsson, F. (2001). Computerized training methods: Effects on retention and rate of responding. *Dissertation Abstracts International* 61, 5546.

Paludi, M. (2014, August). Faculty development workshops for teaching about sexual harassment in undergraduate and graduate training programs. Presentation for the International Coalition Against Sexual Harassment, New York, NY.

Paludi, M., and Kravitz, A. (2011). Sexual harassment of adolescent girls by peers, teachers, employers, and internet providers. In *The psychology of teen violence and victimization*, Vol. 1, edited by M. Paludi, 155–189. Santa Barbara, CA: Praeger.

Paludi, M., and Paludi, C., eds. (2003). *Academic and workplace sexual harassment*. Westport, CT: Praeger.

Pendry, L., Driscoll, D., and Field, S. (2007). Diversity training: Putting theory into practice. *Journal of Occupational and Organizational Psychology* 80, 27–50.

Perry, E., Kulik, C., and Schmidtke, J. (2006). Individual differences in the effectiveness of sexual harassment awareness training. *Journal of Applied Social Psychology* 28, 698–723.

Reese, L., and Lindenberg, K. (1999). *Implementing sexual harassment policy: Challenges for the public sector workplace*. Thousand Oaks, CA: Sage.

Riger, S. (1991). Gender dilemmas in sexual harassment policies and procedures. *American Psychologist* 46, 497–505.

Roberson, L., Kulik, C., and Pepper, M. (2003). Using needs assessment to resolve controversies in diversity training design. *Group and Organization Management* 28, 148–174.

Rynes, S., and Rosen, B. (1995). A field survey of factors affecting the adoption and perceived success of diversity training. *Personnel Psychology* 48, 247–270.

Sacco, J., and Schmitt, N. (2005). A dynamic multilevel model of demographic diversity and misfit effects. *Journal of Applied Psychology* 90, 203–231.

Sadri, G., and Snyder, P. (1995). Methodological issues in assessing training effectiveness. *Journal of Managerial Psychology* 10, 30–32.

Salisbury, J., and Jaffee, F. (1996). Individual training of sexual harassers. In *Sexual harassment on college campuses: Abusing the ivory power*, edited by M. Paludi, 141–152. Albany, NY: SUNY Press.

Slavin, R. (2008). *Educational psychology: Theory and practice.* 9th ed. Boston: Allyn & Bacon.

Smith, S., and Mazin, R. (2004). *The HR answer book.* New York: AMACOM.

Society for Human Resource Management. (2009). www.shrm.org. Accessed March 20, 2015.

Spitzberg, B. H., and Rhea, J. (1999). Obsessive relational intrusion and sexual coercion victimization. *Journal of Interpersonal Violence* 14, 1.

Stockdale, M., and Sagrestano, L. (2011). Resources for targets of sexual harassment. In *Praeger handbook on understanding and preventing workplace discrimination*, edited by M. Paludi, Volume 2. Westport, CT: Praeger.

Stockdale, M. S., and Crosby, F. J., eds. (2004). *The psychology and management of workplace diversity.* Boston: Blackwell Publishing.

Tan, J. A., Hall, R. J., and Boyce, C. (2003). The role of employee reactions in predicting training effectiveness. *Human Resource Development Quarterly* 14, 397–411.

Trotter, R., and Zacur, S. (2004). Corporate sexual harassment policies: Effective strategic human resource management. *Journal of Business and Economics Research* 2, 63–70.

Tsai, P., and Kleiner, B. (2001). Reasonable care of small business to prevent employee discrimination. *Equal Opportunities International* 20, 24–26.

Tyler, K. (2002). Evaluating evaluations. *HR Magazine* 47.

Waits, B., and Lundberg-Love, P. (2008). The impact of campus violence on college students. In *Understanding and preventing campus violence*, edited by M. Paludi, 51–70. Westport, CT: Praeger.

Walker, T. (2000). Effectiveness of multicultural training: Examination of experiential and didactic teaching styles on multicultural awareness training outcomes. *Dissertation Abstracts International* 06, 5324.

U.S. Department of Education, Office of Civil Rights (OCR) (April 2011). "Dear Colleague Letter."

Wentling, R., and Palma-Rivas, N. (2002). Components of effective diversity training programs. *International Journal of Training and Development* 3, 215–226.

York, K., Barclay, L., and Zajack, A. (1997). Preventing sexual harassment: The effect of multiple training methods. *Employee Responsibilities and Rights Journal* 10, 277–289.

Part I

Preventing and Responding to Sexual Harassment in Education and Workplace Settings: Civility, Respect, and Valuing the Dignity of All Individuals

Chapter 1

"Respecting" Our Mission, Core Values, and Strategic Commitments: A Hiring Consideration at St. Bonaventure University

F. Edward Coughlin, OFM

In his best-selling book titled *Good to Great*, Jim Collins (2001) articulated the core concepts and principles that he believed led a company—and by extension any organization or institution—to "make the leap from good to great." Collins argued persuasively that, among other things, an organization must "understand what it could be the best at" to help it to find and retain the "right people" and preserve its "core values and purpose," but also must continually adopt its operating practices to endlessly enable the organization to adapt to a changing world (Collins 2001, 193–195).

Benefitting from the insights of Collins and others, businesses, organizations, and educational institutions—both for-profit and nonprofit—in recent years have learned to attend more carefully and creatively (1) to their stated mission—understanding who they are and what they do best; (2) to creating an institutional culture that supports its stated mission; (3) to hiring competent and skilled individuals who are aware of, have respect for, and are open to assuming an appropriate measure of responsibility for the institution's mission, core values, and strategic commitments;

(4) to providing a variety of ongoing opportunities for all individuals within the institution to grow in their understanding of "their responsibility to promote, or at least to respect" every individual within the community, academic freedom, and the institution's stated mission, core values, and strategic commitments; and (5) to being committed to reviewing as well as revising, as necessary, its priorities and strategic commitments.

This chapter attempts to do two things: (1) provide a working definition of respect as it might apply to individuals, academic freedom, and an educational institution's stated mission, core values, and strategic commitments; and (2) consider how "respect" for individuals, academic freedom, and the institution's mission, values, and commitments ought to be a hiring consideration. Collins' work guided the work of the St. Bonaventure University Ad Hoc Hedgehog Task Force in Fall 2005. After an extensive campuswide conversation to review the Task Force's statement, the University adopted what is now referred to as the "Statement of Distinction" in Spring 2006.

THE MEANING OF "RESPECT"

"Respect," from the Latin *respicio*, means to look back at something or someone "with care," to look with solicitude, to be mindful of the "other as other." In a similar way, the Latin word *capere*, meaning to take hold of or grasp what is seen, implies that the individual "looking/seeing" grasps the objective truth and goodness of what is seen—that is, the value, the dignity of a person as a good in itself, without reference to one's own self or personal interest or preferences. To speak of respect for individuals, academic freedom, an institution's mission, core values, or strategic commitments then is to name essential goods that are considered normative standards. They are non-negotiables. They are standards, therefore, which require ongoing attention and careful assessment. Respect as a core value then challenges both the institution and each individual to attend to an essential quality at the heart of its life in that it provides a foundation for ensuring fidelity to its publically stated commitments. It is presumed here that "respect" for academic freedom, with all of its attendant rights and responsibilities, is one of the University's core values.

Different types of respect have been identified and discussed in the philosophical literature (e.g., Farley 1993). For example, respect for persons, "the dignity of the individual," and the intrinsic worth attributed to every human being have been given the most extensive attention. Other types of respect identified in the literature include evaluative (earned and deserved) respect, directive (required) respect, and a cultural expectation of respect (Dillon 2003).

Robin Dillon (1992; 2003) has also written about "care respect." Dillon describes it as a "felt benevolent concern for" core values including academic freedom and strategic commitments. As such, Dillon understands "care respect" to include the recognition and understanding of an institution's core values and commitments, as well as a sense of "personal" openness to valuing or caring about them (*reverentia*). Care respect demands, therefore, a sense of personal readiness to assume an increasing measure of personal ownership and responsibility for measuring one's attitudes and actions against the standard of, among other things, the institution's overall mission, core values, and strategic commitments. The current formulation of the University's mission, vision as an institution in the Catholic-Franciscan tradition, and core values (discovery, community, and the dignity of all persons) is found for the first time in the University's 2002 catalogue.

In the context of an educational institution, "care respect" might best be understood as a fundamental openness to understanding the practical implications of the institution's commitments, as a recognition of the fact that those commitments lay claims upon "me," independent of "my" personal interests and commitments, and assuming that genuine "care respect" is expressed in "my" conduct while "I" am part of "this" organization (Dillon 2003).

Care respect for the institution's commitments would presume, therefore, that faculty, students, administrators, and employees understand and stand ready to commit themselves, as "they are best able to do" in both their attitudes and actions, to demonstrate care respect for every person, academic freedom, and the University's heritage, mission, values, and strategic commitments (John Paul II 1990).[1]

Practically speaking, the threefold challenge of cultivating a "good and adequate measure" of respect for individuals, academic freedom, and the institution's core commitments as it ought to be expressed in one's attitude and actions is a critical concern in both the hiring process and in the ongoing development of faculty, staff, and administrators in particular. As a normative ideal, it admits to degrees of difference in the measure and manner in which respect might be expressed. At the same time, it attempts to recognize the fact that it challenges individuals to "avoid the extremes" of, for example, either detached indifference or hostility toward individuals, academic freedom, or the institution's mission, core values, and strategic commitments (Coughlin 2006; Karris 2008).

CARE RESPECT: A HIRING CONSIDERATION

Law professor Richardson R. Lynn, in an article titled, "MISSION POSSIBLE: Hiring for Mission in a Vague World" (Lynn 2001) argues that "faculty hiring is the key element in protecting the institution's mission from dilution and irrelevance." In addition to focusing on the role of search committees in mission-driven hiring, Lynn believes that one of the chief academic officer's "primary jobs is always to maintain and strengthen mission." In a law school like his own, Lynn stated his belief that "[f]aculty hiring at a mission-oriented school may be eroded by overemphasizing landing more Supreme Court clerks, Ph.D.'s, or acknowledged narrow specialists." Lynn therefore argues that any educational institution that wants to protect its character and distinctiveness must be committed to faculty hiring that "focuses largely on mission." Similar arguments are made by others, including Larry Braskamp in his guidebook titled *Hiring for Mission*.

In the hiring process, prospective hires must be informed of the institution's mission, core values, and strategic commitments. Candidates also must be asked about their openness and readiness over time and with appropriate opportunities to learn about the meaning and implications of those commitments, to do their part to at least respect, if not promote, as best they are able in their attitudes and actions, the value of every individual, academic freedom, and the institution's mission, core values, and strategic commitments.

CONCLUSION

St. Bonaventure University is a university in the Catholic-Franciscan tradition. As such, it is an independent, coeducational institution governed by an autonomous Board of Trustees. It values the founding vision and partnership model adopted by Nicholas and Mary Devereux, Bishop John Timon, and Friar Pamphilo da Magliano and his friar companions as a paradigm for how it intends to embrace its future. It also continues to value its association with the Franciscan tradition and the Friars of the Holy Name Province (New York, NY) in particular. At the same time, the University also continues to value its historical relationship with the Roman Catholic Church and the contribution it seeks to make to Catholic higher education (John Paul II 1990). These are some of the elements that contribute to St. Bonaventure University's uniqueness.

St. Bonaventure has defined its mission, articulated its core values, and identified its strategic priorities and commitments. The University community is also conscious of the ongoing challenge to both understand the meaning of those commitments and to act in accordance with them. At the same time, the University community understands its responsibility to refashion its strategic commitments, in particular in light of changing situations, new questions, and changing circumstances (Hehir 1995). All members of the campus community thus are challenged continually to be faithful to its essential nature and creatively fulfill its mission, embody its values, and meet the demands of its strategic commitments. These values should be clearly made known to individuals seeking employment. Candidates should be asked to state their openness and readiness to promoting and minimally respecting those commitments, and those hired should be periodically evaluated with respect to their attitudes and behavior with regard to the institution's values, traditions, and core commitments.

NOTES

1. Ex corde ecclesiae, n. 21, envisions an academic community "animated by a spirit of freedom and charity; it is characterized by mutual respect, sincere dialogue, and the protection of the rights of individuals." See also, Part II, Art. 2.4, which states that the "freedom of conscience of each person is to be respected."

2. Ex corde ecclesiae, n. 12, states that every Catholic University "possesses that institutional autonomy necessary to perform its functions effectively and guarantees its members academic freedom, so long as the rights of individual persons and the community are preserved within the confines of the truth and the common good." See also Ex corde ecclesiae, note 15, which includes references to earlier documents in which the Church previously articulated its respect for academic freedom.

3. Ex corde ecclesiae, n. 27, states that "Non-Catholic members are required to respect the Catholic character of the University, while the University in turn respects their religious liberty." Part II, Art. 4, 2, states that "All teachers and all administrators, at the time of their appointment, are to be informed about the Catholic identity of the institution and its implications, and about their responsibility to promote, or at least to respect, that identity." Art. 4.4, states that "Those university teachers and administrators who belong to other Churches, ecclesial communions, or religions, as well as those who profess no religious belief, and also all students, are to recognize and respect the distinctive Catholic identity of the University."

REFERENCES

Collins, J. (2001). *Good to great: Why some companies make the leap . . . and others don't.* New York: Harper Collins.

Coughlin, E., ed. (2006). *Works of St. Bonaventure X: Writings on the spiritual life.* St. Bonaventure, NY: Franciscan Institute Publications.

Dillon, R. (2003). Respect. *Stanford encyclopedia of philosophy.* www.plato.stanford .edu/entries/respect. Accessed October 13, 2014.

Dillon, R. (1992). Respect and care: Toward moral integration. *Canadian Journal of Philosophy* 22, 102–105.

Farley, M. (1993). A feminist version of respect for persons. *Journal of Feminist Studies in Religion* 9, 183–198.

Hehir, J. (1995, Nov.-Dec.). Identity and institutions. *Health Progress* 76–78.

John Paul II (1990). *Ex corde ecclesiae.* www.vatican.va/holy_father/john_paul _ii/apost_constitutions/documents/hf_jp-ii_apc_15081990_ex-corde -ecclesiae_en.html. Accessed October 31, 2014.

Karris, R., ed. (2008). *Works of St. Bonaventure XIII.* St. Bonaventure, NY: Franciscan Institute Publications.

Lynn, R. (2001). Mission possible: Hiring for mission in a vague world. *The University of Toledo Law Review* 33, 107.

Chapter 2

Where Mission Meets Practice: Sexual Violence Prevention, Bystander Intervention Education, and Catholic School Teaching at U.S. Catholic Colleges and Universities

Joy Galarneau and Shannon O'Neill

INTRODUCTION

> I have come to see the role that every person has in changing the way the world is today.
> Everyone has the power to speak up against sexual violence. People just need to be educated on how to do so.
>
> —Student Participants in MVP at Siena College

It is estimated that 20% to 25% of women and 6% of men in the United States experience an attempted or completed sexual assault while attending college (Fisher, Cullen & Turner 2000; Krebs, Lindquist, Warner, Fisher & Martin 2007). Across the nation, institutions of higher learning are beginning to acknowledge sexual violence as an issue of significant concern requiring institutional resources and commitment on campuses. This in large part is due to high-profile federal guidance and legislation such as the "Dear Colleague Letter" issued by the U.S. Department of Education, Office of Civil Rights in April 2011 and the 2014 Campus Sexual Violence Elimination (SaVE) Act, as well as investigations of campuses alleged to be in noncompliance with federal mandates. At present, more than 100 colleges and universities are under federal investigation for possible violations of Title IX specifically related to their handling of sexual violence or sexual harassment cases. In its 2014 report, *Rape and Sexual Assault: A Renewed Call to Action,* the White House described the Campus SaVE Act (Pub. L. No. 113-4 2013) as "a major effort to make our colleges and universities safer—by issuing guidance to help schools understand their obligations to prevent and respond to campus sexual assault, and by stepping up federal compliance and enforcement actions" (White House Council on Women and Girls 2014, 3).

Many campus communities are experimenting with comprehensive, community-based approaches to addressing sexual violence that take their lead from public health models. Their efforts include proactive approaches aimed at preventing incidents of violence from occurring at all, in addition to responsive efforts to address incidents that have occurred. Current prevention approaches have shifted and expanded in focus from programming that was based almost entirely on a risk-reduction model targeting potential victims or perpetrators, to a bystander intervention model that enlists a community-wide pool of potential allies who work together to advance their campuses' antiviolence agendas. This latter model attempts to overcome the limitations of exclusively using the former (such as victim blaming) and to leverage previously untapped populations to create communities in which violence is neither normative nor tolerated.

This chapter presents bystander intervention as an evidence-based best-practice approach to sexual violence prevention in college settings. Using our own institution—Siena College—as a case study, we propose that mission-specific resources can strengthen this pedagogical approach and advance the prevention agenda. In turn, we contend that bystander intervention education can deepen community engagement in promoting the collegiate mission.

The chapter begins with a statistical sketch of sexual violence on college campuses. Building upon this quantitative foundation, it then provides a "bigger picture" of sexual violence. Recognition of the myriad, complex root causes of sexual violence has inspired comprehensive preventive approaches to addressing sexual violence (American College Health Association [ACHA] 2008; Centers for Disease Control and Prevention [CDC] 2004; Curtis & Love 2009; Tabachnick 2008; Virginia Sexual and Domestic Violence Action Alliance 2009; Wilson 2014).

This insight leads into the theoretical examination of bystander intervention education through the practical lens of its implementation at Siena College. Next is a discussion of how Siena's Franciscan Catholic mission is serving as a resource for strengthening our community's prevention efforts (and vice versa) focusing in particular on the Catholic social teaching tradition. We contend that Catholic colleges and universities have a unique opportunity to bring bystander intervention education and Catholic social teaching into constructive conversation that ultimately can both strengthen pedagogical models and build a community free of sexual violence and the structures that support it. At the same time, we see great potential for broadening this "mission meets practice" conversation beyond Catholic institutions of higher learning. The chapter concludes with practical recommendations for leveraging organizational mission in the advancement of sexual violence prevention.

SEXUAL VIOLENCE ON COLLEGE CAMPUSES: A STATISTICAL SKETCH

> I learned some really alarming statistics.
> More than I expected are sexually violated.
> —Student Participants in MVP at Siena College

We begin with a definition of sexual violence. This is the definition that we utilize in our Human Rights Policy at Siena College: Physical acts of a sexual nature, perpetrated against a person's will or when a person is incapable of giving consent (a person who is mentally incapacitated, asleep, physically helpless due to drug or alcohol consumption or unconscious is considered unable to consent). In this policy, sexual violence is a broad umbrella term, and includes sexual coercion, sexual assault, and rape (Siena College Human Rights Policy, http://www2.siena.edu/pages/5685.asp).

In much of the literature cited in this chapter, the term "sexual assault" is used interchangeably with the term "sexual violence," with the definition of sexual assault mirroring the broader definition of sexual violence cited above. In the 1970s, the term "sexual assault" began to be used, first surfacing as a replacement for the term "rape" in state laws. This was advocated by writers such as Susan Brownmiller (1975)—who argued that rape is about power, not sex—as a way of emphasizing the inherently violent nature of the crime.

The following statistics serve as a helpful starting point in framing the issue of sexual violence on U.S. college and university campuses.

Women Are More Likely Than Men to Be Victims of Sexual Violence, But Men Also Are Victims

Young women are especially vulnerable to victimization. In fact, for women, simply attending college is a risk factor for sexual assault victimization. It is estimated that one out of five undergraduate women and about 6% of men will experience an attempted or completed sexual assault while in college (Fisher, Cullen & Turner 2000; Krebs et al. 2007).

First-year and sophomore students are at greater risk for victimization than are juniors and seniors (Krebs et al. 2007).

Most Acts of Sexual Violence on College Campuses Are Facilitated By Alcohol

The majority of sexual assaults in college occur when women are incapacitated. Often, this state of incapacitation is due to alcohol consumption. Alcohol is the number one date rape drug. Less than 1% of rapes are committed using a drug other than alcohol (i.e., "roofies") (Krebs et al. 2007; Krebs, Lindquist, Warner, Fisher & Martin 2009; Mohler-Kuo, Dowdall, Koss & Wechsler 2004).

Most Victims of Sexual Violence Know Their Attackers

The majority of victims of sexual assault are victimized by people they know and trust, rather than strangers: 77% of victims of physically forced assault knew their attacker; and 88% of victims of incapacitated assault knew their attacker. Sometimes this is referred to as "date rape" but in the current context of "hook-up culture" so pervasive on college campuses, in which dating is virtually nonexistent and in which students often do not self-identify their romantic relationships as dating relationships, the term "acquaintance rape" probably is more accurate (Fisher, Cullen & Turner 2000; Krebs et al. 2007). We hesitate to use either term, because both terms too often are interpreted as signaling that perpetrators of non-stranger rape are less responsible for their actions and their actions are less egregious than perpetrators who sexually assault strangers (Lisak 2011).

Men Are More Likely Than Women to Be Perpetrators of Sexual Assault, But Most Men Are Not Perpetrators

More than 90% of perpetrators are male (Krebs et al. 2007). At the same time, research suggests that most males do not commit sexual assault, and that relatively few men (approximately 5% to 15%) are multiple offenders who perpetrate the majority of assaults (Carr & VanDeusen 2004; Lisak 2011; Lisak & Miller 2002).

Most Acts of Sexual Violence Are Not Reported

Based on the statistics given above, sexual violence on college campuses could be considered an epidemic. Yet the consistently low rates of reporting prevent many institutions from acknowledging it as such. About 5% of completed and attempted rapes are reported. Why don't victims report? In their own words:

- They didn't want anyone to know about it;
- They had no proof;
- They thought that nothing could be done about it; and
- Those who reported that they were incapacitated also reported that they didn't think that anything that serious happened, saying things such as, "[S]ince I was passed out, I couldn't say 'no,' so I am not sure if it is really rape" (Krebs et al. 2007).

The U.S. Department of Justice suggests a connection between acquaintance rape and underreporting.

Half of all student victims do not label the incident "rape." This is particularly true when no weapon was used, no sign of physical injury is evident, and alcohol was involved—factors commonly associated with campus acquaintance rape. Given the extent of non-stranger rape on campus, it is no surprise that the majority of victimized women do not define their experience as a rape. These reasons help explain why campus sexual assault is not well reported. (U.S. Department of Justice 2005, 6)

When it comes to sexual violence, the situation on U.S. college and university campuses mirrors the broader national context: The majority of victims are women. Almost 1 in 5 women (18.3%) and 1 in 71 men (1.4%) in the United States have been raped at some point in their lives. Young women are most vulnerable to victimization. Most female victims of completed rape (79.6%) experienced their first rape before the age of 25. The majority of perpetrators are male: 98.1% of female victims of rape reported that the perpetrator was male; 92.5% of female victims of sexual violence other than rape reported that the perpetrator was male. Male rape victims also reported predominantly male perpetrators. The majority of female and male rape victims know their perpetrators. More than half (51.1%) of female victims of rape reported being raped by an intimate partner and 40.8% by an acquaintance; for male victims, more than half (52.4%) reported being raped by an acquaintance and 15.1% by a stranger (Black, Basile, Breiding, Smith, Walters, Merrick, Chen & Stevens 2011).

BEYOND THE STATISTICS: PAINTING A BIGGER PICTURE OF SEXUAL VIOLENCE ON COLLEGE CAMPUSES

The broad umbrella of violence was what I was previously unaware of.
I am a lot more sensitive to the things that I see and hear on campus, things that could contribute to a violence culture.

—Student Participants in MVP at Siena College

As the data provided above indicate, the widespread notion that acts of sexual violence are committed predominantly by social deviants simply is not supported by research. The often-cited depiction of the typical campus rapist as a knife-wielding masked man hiding in the bushes waiting to brutally physically and sexually attack a woman walking alone at night is not the most commonly encountered campus scenario. In the collegiate setting, a woman is much more likely to be sexually assaulted in her residence hall room or at a party by a fellow classmate who uses alcohol to render her more vulnerable or to fully incapacitate her. Research indicates that perpetrators of sexual violence on college campuses comprise a heterogeneous group, although they tend to share some common characteristics. For example, the majority is composed of men who have access to consensual sex (Handeyside, Wickliffe & Adams 2007). The prevalence of rape myths—such as the stranger in the bushes rape scenario—makes it easier to think of offenders as completely different from "us," despite the fact that most sexual assaults are committed by a person that the victim knows and trusts. It is difficult to accept the reality that the majority of perpetrators of sexual violence are fellow community members living in residence, taking classes, and developing friendships with potential victims (Center for Sex Offender Management 2006).

Just as it is easier for us to believe that acts of sexual violence are committed predominantly by mentally ill or psychopathic strangers who are not part of the "normal population," it is more palatable to envision these assaults as isolated random or occasional acts. Unfortunately, this is not the case. The data indicate that sexual violence occurs at alarmingly high rates on college campuses and in our nation at large, and that these acts are perpetrated largely by a relatively small population of serial offenders. What's more, sexually violent crimes such as rape are part of a larger spectrum of sexually harassing and violent behaviors that go well beyond physical acts of sexual violation and also occur with alarming frequency. This continuum includes sexist remarks, rape jokes, tracking sexual conquests with peer approval, touching intimate body parts without the consent or knowledge of the individual, unwelcome "grinding," unauthorized surveillance of sexually intimate acts or of a person's intimate body parts, sexual coercion, rape, and sexual battery. Research indicates that nearly two-thirds of college students report experiences of sexual harassment occurring while in school (Hill & Silva 2005).

Why? Why are sexual violence and sexual harassment so prevalent on our college campuses and in our nation at large? Why are these acts committed so casually, repeatedly, and often by respected members of our communities? Public health experts use the term "risk factors" when naming the various circumstances that influence a person's likelihood to perpetrate acts of sexual violence. The Centers for Disease Control and Prevention (CDC) employs an ecological model to identify these risk factors (CDC 2004). This four-tiered model identifies interrelated risk factors at individual, interpersonal relationship, community, and societal levels, such as attitudes and beliefs that support sexual violence (individual), association with sexually aggressive peers (interpersonal), weak sanctions for perpetrators (community), and structural inequalities based on gender (societal). Cross-cultural studies specific to the collegiate context have identified risk factors including sex-role socialization, rape myths, lack of sanctions for abuse, male peer-group support, pornography, adversarial sexual beliefs, lack of empathy, and all-male membership groups such as fraternities and sports teams (Carr & Van Deusen 2004.)

In this big-picture view, sexual violence—and its frequent perpetration by social nondeviants—is a foreseeable consequence of many interrelated root causes (risk factors). This complex cultural portrait sometimes is referred to as "rape culture." "The basic premise of this concept is that rape does not happen just because one individual chooses to rape another. Rape happens because there are attitudes and norms that allow it to happen" (Guy 2008, 10).

There are many examples of the ways in which rape-supportive attitudes and norms have pervaded campus communities and U.S. society at large. What follows is just a sampling.

- Phrases like "I raped that test" or "That professor raped me on that test" have found their way into the vernacular of students. One of the authors of this chapter once actually heard a star student employee of Women's Center use it in the Center.

- The *Online Slang Dictionary* offers nearly 200 words referring to sexual intercourse. Many of the terms and phrases connote violence, such as: "bang," "beat," "chopped up," "cut," "hit," "hit raw," "hit that," "kick it," "nail," "pound," "ram," "slap and tickle," "slay," "smack," "smash," and "spank" (http://onlineslangdictionary .com/thesaurus/words+meaning+sex+sexual+intercourse.html).

- The English language contains more than 200 words for a sexually promiscuous woman and only about 20 for a sexually promiscuous man. Popular slang words for sexually promiscuous women include: "slut," "ho-bag," and "whore." For men, "player," "stud," or, at worst, "*male* slut" (Benedict 2005; Valenti 2008).

- In April 2013, Dartmouth College cancelled classes after students on its campus received rape and death threats following their participation in a public protest against institutional attitudes toward sexual assault, racism, and homophobia. One anonymous online comment reads: "It's women like these who deserve to get raped" (http:// thinkprogress.org/health/2013/04/24/1911741/dartmouth -protest-cancels-classes/#.UXp916E5NVI.email).

- In October 2013, a string of news stories brought to light an e-mail with the subject line "luring your rapebait"; apparently written by a member of Georgia Tech's Phi Kappa Tau fraternity to teach his fraternity brothers "the 7 E's of HOOKING UP!" at parties (http://www.huffingtonpost.com/2013/10/08/georgia-tech-frat-email-rapebait_n_4063101.html).

- In August 2012, in Steubenville, Ohio, two popular high school football players were convicted of sexually assaulting a teenager who was incapacitated by alcohol, while fellow athletes videotaped or photographed the event. Some of the bystanders sent the photos to friends or posted them on social media, but none of them contacted the police. In November 2013, several adults—including the superintendent of Steubenville schools—were charged with felonies such as obstructing justice and tampering with evidence as a result of an investigation into a possible cover-up of the case (http://www.ny-times.com/2013/11/27/sports/in-steubenville-rape-case-a-lesson-for-adults.html?pagewanted=2&_r=0).

Individually these examples might be easy to dismiss, but when taken together along with current statistics about sexual violence in our campus communities, they depict a culture characterized in real and complicated ways by the normative presence of a continuum of violence that is fueled by certain attitudes, behaviors, and structures. This complex, messy nexus of belief and behavior helps to explain why acts of sexual violence are committed not only by strangers, mentally ill persons, or psychopaths but also—and more often—by the boy next door, the star athlete, the student leader, or the straight-A student. It also helps to explain why survivors of sexual violence are so reluctant to report these crimes. We live in a culture that minimizes, tolerates, and even encourages sexual violence—particularly against women—through a combination of cultural cues that signal to us that a man is entitled to do whatever he likes with a woman's body and that she is at least partially responsible for his assaultive actions upon her body if, for example, she is drunk, wearing revealing clothing, or is not a virgin. We live in a culture that tells us that sexual violence against women is inevitable and socially acceptable. We habitually justify this collective perception with tactics that demean women; downplay the egregious nature of sexual violence; conflate sex and violence; discourage reporting of sex offenses; cover up incidents of sexual violence; protect perpetrators from being held accountable; and blame, shame, and further victimize survivors of sexual assault. This is a powerful cultural matrix of attitudes, behaviors, and norms with which we must reckon when addressing sexual violence.

A caveat before we move on: The recognition of this formidable tide of cultural signals that minimize, tolerate, or even promote sexual violence does not discount individual human agency. At the end of the day, each of us is responsible for his or her own actions, regardless of whether we are bombarded with cultural cues that legitimize violence. As noted above, research shows that although sexual violence against women is rampant and largely facilitated by men, not all or even the majority of men are per-petrating these acts. In fact, research tells us that men are more likely to commit sexual violence in communities where sexual violence goes un-punished. Lack of accountability for perpetrators is a community-level risk factor for sexual violence. Bystander intervention programs are most successful when supported by institutional policies that hold perpetrators accountable for their actions (CDC 2004; Tabachnick 2008).

TRANSFORMING VALUES INTO ACTION: USING BYSTANDER INTERVENTION TO PREVENT SEXUAL VIOLENCE ON COLLEGE CAMPUSES

> I was always willing to be an active bystander in extreme situ-ations, but now I know HOW to be an active bystander for all kinds of troubling situations.
>
> —2012–2013 P.E.E.P.s Founding Member

> My beliefs have been reaffirmed. I now know actions to take that go along with my beliefs.
>
> —2012 Student Participant in "Mentors in Violence Prevention" at Siena College

Given the complexity of rape culture both in terms of its causes and effects, it follows that efforts to eradicate sexual violence must be multifac-eted and broad ranging in scope. Indeed, the same public health experts cited above are encouraging the implementation of comprehensive pre-ventive approaches to address risk factors at all levels of the ecological model that influence individuals' decisions to perpetrate acts of sexual violence and support a culture of violence. The ultimate goal of these community-oriented approaches is the creation of violence-free communi-ties. Their success is dependent upon collective action; thus, responsibility for enacting lasting change resides with the entire community rather than only those directly affected by sexual violence (ACHA 2008; CDC 2004; Curtis and Love 2009; Virginia Sexual and Domestic Violence Action Alliance 2009; Wilson 2014).

Public-health approaches to preventing sexual violence endorse the use of three forms of prevention: primary, secondary, and tertiary. Primary pre-vention takes place before violence has occurred, and the latter two forms of prevention focus on immediate and long-term responses, respectively, to acts of violence that already have occurred. The authors of "Sexual Violence Prevention: Beginning the Dialogue" note, "While the major purpose of interventions that take place after violence has occurred is to reduce or ameliorate the negative effects of the violence, some of these approaches may have the advantageous effect of preventing a recurrence of violence" (CDC 2004, 4). Examples of interventions that take place after violence has occurred are community-wide awareness-raising and victim-support events such as "Take Back the Night," strong sanctions for perpetrators, and training programs for first responders and investigators.

According to Lee, Guy, and Perry, the best primary prevention approaches to sexual violence "combine the socio-political analysis of the feminist anti-rape movement and the systematic approach to promoting healthy behaviors central to public health theory" (Lee, Guy & Perry 2008, 7). These efforts do not disparage the necessary direct services to survivors of sexual violence and risk-reduction education for potential victims and perpetrators. Rather, they recognize both the value and limitations of preventive approaches aimed at selected audiences, and seek to augment them with strategies aimed at inspiring whole communities to work together to enact the broader social change that will prevent sexual violence before it happens—change that will eradicate sexual violence completely.

College and university educators across the nation are beginning to turn to bystander intervention programs as a primary prevention educational tool for combating the epidemic of sexual violence in their campus communities. This marks a shift away from only providing risk-reduction programs that target potential victims—such as self-defense courses, "Watch your drink," and "Don't walk alone" campaigns—or programs geared toward potential perpetrators. The risk-reduction approach has been criticized for limitations such as participant resistance to seeing themselves in the role of victim or perpetrator, which undercut the prevention message. Programs that focus exclusively on teaching women how to avoid being victimized have been further criticized for perpetuating injustice against women by signaling that women are solely responsible for preventing violence (Banyard, Plante & Moynihan 2004; Cissner 2009).

Bystander intervention programs attempt to prevent or de-escalate potentially harmful acts by enlisting the active support of persons—bystanders—who bear witness to these acts as they are unfolding. In the case of sexual violence, sometimes this involves intervening at the moment a bystander realizes that another person is in imminent danger of being sexually assaulted. At other times, it means intervening *either* to prevent acts along the continuum of violence described above *or* to name and challenge the attitudes, behaviors, and structures that support these acts. Collegiate bystander intervention programs are built on the premise that most members of the campus communities are potential allies in prevention who can be mobilized to action if equipped with the appropriate blend of awareness of the problem, motivation to assume responsibility and commit to action, and necessary practical skills to appropriately and safely intervene (Berkowitz 2009; Carr 2008; Curtis & Love 2009). Bystander intervention programs, according to Berkowitz, are "designed to help individuals express their personal and organizational values in action when encountering problems" (Berkowitz 2009, 6). The American College Health Association's (ACHA) 2007 "Position Statement on Preventing Sexual Violence on College and University Campuses" describes bystander intervention.

> Bystander techniques are skills that allow students, faculty, and staff to recognize the continuum of violence and empower them to intervene, prevent, or stop inappropriate comments and actions. The goal is to create a culture shift from bystander apathy to bystander intervention, thus creating a culture in which violence cannot occur. (ACHA 2007, 2)

As the ACHA makes clear, the ultimate goal of bystander intervention is culture change. In other words, the method of teaching individual intervention skills is intended as a means to a more ambitious end—the creation of violence-free communities. This outcome depends upon community endorsement of active bystander behavior in two ways: (1) a critical mass of community members proficient in bystander intervention skills practices active bystander behavior, and (2) institutional conditions that support active bystander behavior. These are addressed in turn.

A variety of programs—such as Mentors in Violence Prevention (MVP) and Green Dot—have been developed and shown to be effective in training college and university students in bystander intervention (Cissner 2009; Coker, Cook-Craig, Williams, Fisher, Clear, Garcia & Hegge 2011). These bystander intervention programs share several characteristics. They appeal to all members of the community as being able to play a role in violence prevention and having a stake in doing so; include well-trained professionals in program coordination and facilitation; enlist the support of male and female peer role models; address barriers to intervention; obtain commitment to intervene; teach many options for safely intervening that accommodate different personalities and the particulars of the situation; include a lot of time for practice; and provide booster sessions (ACHA 2007; Berkowitz 2009; Carr 2008).

Curtis and Love (2009) advocate the implementation of a multilevel approach to bystander intervention that utilizes bystander intervention to addresses the root causes of sexual violence at all levels of the ecological model: individual, interpersonal relationship, community, and societal. Curtis and Love also encourage the development of bystander intervention programs that address risk factors for sexual violence at all of the levels of the ecological model (e.g., sexism, homophobia, and male privilege and entitlement) rather than only teaching individuals to intervene when acts of sexual violence are imminent.

At Siena College, the evolution and current structure of our bystander intervention campaign reflects the ongoing efforts to incorporate these best-practice elements into our programs, and (as is discussed in this chapter) our understanding of how Siena's mission supports active bystander behavior and culture. We employ a combination of nationally recognized and homegrown programs, including the following examples.

"Who Are You?" Orientation Program

Students come to this program already having completed a mandatory online course (MyStudentBody, https://www.mystudentbody.com/) that introduces them to the issues of sexual violence, dating violence, and stalking; including general information, Siena-specific resources, and active bystander messaging. The "Who Are You?" orientation program is mandatory for all incoming students and has been in place for several years (it formerly was called "Speak Out and Stand Up"). Over the years, the program has evolved based upon anecdotal feedback and formal assessment data from student participants. In its current format, "Who Are You?" is preceded in the orientation schedule by a mandatory large-group session—"Who are We?"—facilitated by the dean of students and vice president for student affairs. This mixed-gender session begins with discussion of personal values and institutional mission, which leads into a presentation designed to educate and empower students to recognize and report incidents of sexual violence, dating violence, and stalking. The students are then transitioned into same-gender small-group sessions facilitated by a faculty member, administrator, or staff member. The facilitator leads the participants through an interactive discussion about becoming an active bystander, with a special focus on preventing sexual violence. We anchor the discussion in a video titled "Who Are You?" (http://www.whoareyou.co.nz/), which takes students through a potential sexual violence scenario that is then broken down to show the multiple bystander intervention opportunities and strategies that could be employed by a variety of people to prevent the sexual assault from being perpetrated. The session is designed to empower students with knowledge, commitment, and practical skills to become active bystanders who confront the continuum of violence and who apply their skills to address a broad range of behaviors and attitudes that violate personal and community values.

We use social norms techniques to support our message and affirm that Siena is a community where active bystander behavior is normative and supported. For example: we show short student-produced video clips of

Siena students talking about their successful active bystander experiences. We also share statistics from various campuswide surveys such as these drawn from the 2013 Health Survey: 98% of Siena students say they would intervene to stop sexual assault, 94% of Siena students say they have a responsibility to contribute to the well-being of other students, four out of five Siena students say their campus encourages them to be an active bystander.

Program assessment data show that we are meeting our desired outcomes: 97% of 2013 program attendees reported that they left with both useful bystander and reporting techniques and with a feeling of responsibility for the safety and well-being of their peers.

Mentors in Violence Prevention (MVP)

This intensive multisession evidence-based program (Katz n.d.) is offered each semester to students who are recommended by faculty, staff, student leaders, and program alums. MVP has been shown to reduce sexist attitudes and increase participant self-efficacy around active bystander behavior (Cissner 2009). We specifically target student leaders for this program including members of the Residence Hall Association (RHA), Student Senate, Student Events Board (SEB), and athletes. We collaborate with our community partners (two local sexual violence agencies) as MVP facilitators. This program has grown—and more men take part—each semester. We attribute program success largely to peer recommendations.

In our program assessment data, a large majority of participants report that they plan to utilize the information and skills gained from this training in their leadership roles on campus and beyond, and many provide specific examples such as creating a hall program, applying to be a peer educator, informally educating their friends, getting involved with the Women's Center, supporting survivors, and addressing offensive language. "If I see a situation on campus I will be more likely to help and have a better understanding of what should be done." Many also reported changes that already had occurred in their beliefs and actions as a result of the training, such as increase in victim empathy; reduction in victim blaming, sexist attitudes, and buy-in of gendered stereotypes; recognition of and decrease in tolerance for attitudes and behaviors that support rape culture; understanding that sexual violence can occur in the context of romantic relationships; and more recognition of potential intervention opportunities and increased comfort in intervening in these situations.

Peer Education & Empowerment Program at Siena

The Peer Education & Empowerment Program at Siena (P.E.E.P.s) group was founded by participants in the first cohort of MVP and the

Women Studies service-learning course "Sexual Assault: Peer Advocacy." These students were seeking more ways to educate their peers who would not normally self-select for MVP or the Women's Studies course. The P.E.E.P.s collaborate with faculty who teach in our first-year seminar program, bringing semester-long interactive peer education sessions on recognizing, reporting, and preventing sexual violence into these classrooms. The non-self-selected aspect of the "P.E.E.P.s in the Classroom Program" is important in that it reaches a largely male audience in many of the classrooms. The P.E.E.P.s have expanded their focus, which now includes discussion and activities related to healthy relationships and dating violence. The P.E.E.P.s also partners with other student groups in residence hall programming, and P.E.E.P.s members participate as leaders in large-scale community awareness-raising activities such as Take Back the Night and One Billion Rising. Current P.E.E.P.s members actively recruit, select, and train incoming P.E.E.P.s members. On our feedback forms for first-year students who participated in the "P.E.E.P.s in the Classroom Program," one first-year student reported that "you can't unlearn this stuff." One student reported that the most rewarding aspect of being a member of the P.E.E.P.s was "having students come up to you and asking how they can become involved on campus in regards to preventing sexual violence."

Mission Possible Active Bystander Training Program

This program was developed and is facilitated by the three deans in the Office of the Dean of Students after they received student requests for more active bystander training that is intensely practical, skill-based, and covers a broad range of bystander intervention opportunities in addition to potential acts of sexual violence. "Mission Possible" aims to teach students to learn and apply bystander intervention skills to address a variety of behaviors and attitudes that violate their personal and our community values, including bullying, hazing, homophobia, racism, sexism, sexual violence, and dating violence. The workshop is highly interactive and includes a variety of teaching methods, such as storytelling, brief self-reflective writing exercises, small-group work, large-group conversations/report-outs, role playing, and using popular media clips. The teaching style is intentionally personal, inductive, and very practical, with the goal that student participants will leave feeling increased empathy, ownership, and empowerment vis-à-vis their role and ability as active bystanders.

In the summer of 2013, resident assistants (RAs), orientation leaders (SAINTS), and Affinity student group leaders all participated in this training. In all sessions, 100% of the participants could identify intervention opportunities they might encounter on campus; 98% of RAs and Affinity group leaders could identify strategies for intervening in problematic situations (SAINTS were not asked this question on their evaluation); 100% of

RAs reported that the workshop provided them with realistic scenarios that they might encounter as an RA; 99% reported that they felt more prepared to be an active bystander in a variety of everyday situations. One participant reported: "This is one of the most beneficial training sessions of SAINTS training because it gets you ready for real life situations and gives you the knowledge that you can pass down to your freshmen to show them that this is the way that we deal with things at Siena."

All of our bystander intervention training programs are anchored in a four-stage learning process designed to help participants understand the culture of sexual violence and recognize intervention opportunities; engender victim empathy and commitment to act; and empower participants with confidence and intervention skills. These stages also are designed to help bystanders overcome the factors that inhibit action, such as fear of embarrassment or retaliation, misperceptions regarding how others present feel about or will respond to the situation, and lack of skills. The four stages are: (1) notice the event, (2) interpret it as a problem, (3) feel responsible for dealing with it, and (4) choose to act (Berkowitz 2009).

To illustrate how we might work through these four stages during a bystander intervention training workshop, let's return to the comment "That professor raped me with that exam."

Stages One and Two: Notice the Event. Interpret It As a Problem

To get students to intervene when they hear a fellow classmate use this phrase, we have to first get them to actually "hear" and then interpret comments such as this one as problematic. To achieve this outcome, we might engage students in conversations in which we situate this behavior on the continuum of sexual violence by discussing why sexual violence has infiltrated our language and how it contributes to a culture that minimizes, tolerates, or even encourages sexual violence. For example, it desensitizes us to the violence that rape is, and it minimizes the suffering of rape victims. We find these educational conversations work best when they are actual conversations (rather than mini-lectures) that incorporate inductive methods that invite students to deeply and thoughtfully engage these issues with skilled facilitators. One of the authors of this chapter often opens up this dialogue by asking, "Have you ever heard someone say, 'That professor lynched me with that exam?' (The answer is always "no.") "Why not?" "Why do you think some people view 'raped' as an acceptable term to use in casual conversation but not 'lynched'?"

Stage Three: Feel Responsible for Dealing with It

It is imperative that we facilitate our conversations with students in a way that motivates students to feel responsible for acting. Some of the talking points from our "stage one" conversations help us move students through stage two, such as a discussion about the potentially negative consequences of using these kinds of flip phrases about rape. Another way to do this is to personalize the situation enough to get workshop participants to feel responsible for dealing with it: What if you heard this phrase used in front of someone you care about who has survived an act of rape? How do you think they would feel? Other talking points might address some of the reasons that keep people from intervening: If you are uncomfortable with this comment, it is likely that others are as well, even if they don't speak up. (Addresses misperceptions about other bystanders' nonintervention.) Don't assume someone else will address the behavior (addresses diffusion of responsibility). Finally, as discussed in more depth in the next section, at Siena we appeal to students' personal values and our institutional mission when attempting to motivate students to feel responsible for acting.

Stage Four: Choose to Act

Getting students to a place where they feel empowered to act involves two steps. First we have to get them to buy into the notion that they have power as bystanders. The sharing of personal active bystander success stories by fellow students has been an effective tool in our Siena community, and often helps students to overcome their fears of losing social status as a result of intervening. Examples include P.E.E.P.s sharing their personal intervention stories during their classroom visits and student active bystander video clips shown at "Who Are You?" orientation sessions. During the "Who Are You?" active bystander workshop at new student orientation we use an additional method to empower students: We facilitate a conversation around the question "Do bystanders have power?" Of course our answer is "Yes." To "prove our point" we begin by inviting students to "do the numbers." That is, we share the research that indicates that only a small number of people in our community are actually hurting people with sexual violence, and we show a visual to back this up—one side of the PowerPoint slide is loaded with potential active bystanders and the other side has a few perpetrators on it. We then engage students in a discussion of how bystanders have power whether they act or don't act—by their passivity (normalizing or condoning behavior) or by acting to prevent violence. We tell session participants that we are focusing on them precisely because of how much power they have. As mentioned, we conclude with social norms techniques.

The second step of stage four is very practical and context specific: To appropriately empower students to become active bystanders, we have to suggest and practice multiple safe ways to intervene, such as these three strategies offered by Berkowitz (2009).

- Strategy 1: Direct confrontation: "I think that's a poor choice of words. Getting raped is a lot worse than having to take an unfair exam."
- Strategy 2: Shifting the focus: "I have an exam that I'm really worried about that I have to take tomorrow."
- Strategy 3: Shifting the Person: "Oh, you mean it was an unfair exam?" (*"You're not kidding."*) "That means the professor raped you?" (*"Yeah, he raped me."*) "And you'll be traumatized for a long time to come?" (*"You're getting carried away."*) "Well, I'm wondering how a survivor of rape would interpret that remark, or if it might minimize a rapist's behavior?" (*"I guess so."*) "But I'm sorry the exam was so unfair. Are you worried about how you did?" (*"You bet."*) "Well, I understand your frustration" (Berkowitz 2009, 55).

Berkowitz contends that the third strategy has the most educational potential and also potentially is most effective at gaining allies in addition to stopping the behavior. It also takes the most preparation. Conversely, the more blunt first strategy might be more daunting for students who are more reserved. At Siena we are realistic about students' abilities and willingness to employ different strategies. Our active bystander training sessions often promote the following three intervention strategies: Direct (direct confrontation), delegate (enlisting the help of others, such as friends, fellow bystanders, college officials), or distract (somewhat akin to strategy two above—shifting the focus—this strategy diffuses the situation by shifting attention away from it). During our training workshops we invite students to do some discernment about the strategies they will, might, or will never use, depending upon factors such as their particular personalities, comfort levels, and skills. We jump-start this conversation by sharing the strategies that are most comfortable and most uncomfortable for us (facilitators). In determining which intervention method to use, it also is important to consider who will be the target of the intervention (the person doing the behavior or the person[s] affected by the behavior), when it is most appropriate to intervene (in the moment or after the fact), and if it is safe to intervene. Practice is key to successfully empowering students to become active bystanders. Our "Mission Possible" Active Bystander workshop and "P.E.E.P.s in the Classroom" visits incorporate a lot of role-playing to help students practice intervention strategies in a safe space. We believe that this has resulted in creating and reinforcing a community norm of active bystanders. In our 2013 campus Health Survey, four out of five students reported that Siena encourages them to be an active bystander and half of these students were able to provide an example of how they have been an active bystander at Siena. Following are some examples of what students shared when asked how they have been an active bystander at Siena.

- I haven't had to be one yet but someone has for me and I greatly appreciate that.
- I have intervened in the use of racial slurs at a basketball game.
- A boyfriend and girlfriend were fighting upstairs and I told her RA it was getting serious.
- I have seen a female friend and a female stranger being pursued uncomfortably by a male and told that male to stop and stayed by the females' sides for the remainder of the time.
- When I heard a group of male students talking inappropriately about females I asked them to stop.
- Told my friend to stop pursuing a girl that was drunk.
- At a party I took a drunk girl away from a guy that was trying to bring her to a bedroom in one of the townhouses because I knew she would regret it in the morning and was too intoxicated to make her own decisions.

Bystander intervention programs are most successful when they are supported by a variety of institutional conditions. At Siena we support our bystander intervention training programs within an intentionally comprehensive, holistic approach to addressing sexual violence that includes the following:

- *The Siena College Anti-Violence Task Force*: A collaborative group of faculty, staff, and students whose mission is to provide programs and resources to assist our community in recognizing, reporting, and preventing sexual violence, relationship violence, and stalking.
- *The Siena College "Recognize, Report, Prevent" Campaign*: A comprehensive passive programming campaign that includes resource pamphlets, poster series, bulletin board kits, and a website—all designed around a standard, recognizable, visual brand.
- *Social Norms Campaign*: This campaign supports pro-social behavior through the use of campus climate data. Materials are designed using the "recognize, report, prevent" brand.
- *Student-produced videos*: Show students sharing successful active bystander stories, athletes speaking out against violence, and community members holding up signs explaining why they are participating in events such as One Billion Rising.
- *Weekly emails to the Siena community*: E-mail messages that celebrate active bystanders in our community, reinforce the active bystander message ("remember the three D's!"), and share resources (such as Public Safety's anonymous tip line, resources for survivors, and consent checklist).

- *Mandatory active bystander training programming*: Required for all incoming students at orientation, as well as for resident assistants, orientation leaders, and various student leadership groups. Self-selected training programs complement mandatory training and recruit peer leaders.

- *Inclusion of active bystander messaging into related mandatory Title IX training programs*: Such as those for student athletes, Resident Assistants, and campus employees.

- *Siena College Human Rights Policy*: Includes our policies regarding investigating and adjudicating reports of sexual violence. The policy is annually disseminated to all members of the community electronically and in print to students, and is readily accessible online.

- *Siena College Welfare of the Community Policy*: Akin to an amnesty policy, this policy makes it easier for students to intervene who at the time might be involved in behaviors that violate college policy (such as drinking) without fear of getting in trouble for these other violations.

- *Residence Hall Programs*: RA programs that incorporate active bystander messaging, as well as programs that focus on promoting other pro-social behaviors such as healthy relationships.

- *Sr. Thea Bowman Center for Women:* The Center's student-led peace and nonviolence committee provides opportunities for advocacy on issues related to violence against women.

- *Community-wide awareness raising and survivor support events*: like "One Billion Rising," "Operation Red Zone," "Red Flag Campaign," "Clothesline Project," "Take Back the Night," and "White Ribbon Campaign."

WHERE MISSION MEETS PRACTICE: HOW CATHOLIC SOCIAL TEACHING CAN STRENGTHEN BYSTANDER INTERVENTION EDUCATION AT CATHOLIC COLLEGES AND UNIVERSITIES

Focusing on Siena's mission and values infused this year's RA training with a greater sense of purpose and helped me see a deeper inspiration and meaning to my day-to-day activities. Tying the mission into Siena's antiviolence efforts made the mission more real; it's not just words about affirming the dignity and worth of each person, and creating a more just and peaceable world, it's what we do and why we do it. It helped me place my role as an active bystander into the framework of my faith and personal values, which energized and inspired me! I recognize, report, and prevent any type of violence because I recognize the dignity and beauty of each individual I encounter. That's what I do and why I do it.

—Student Participant in Resident Assistant Training

As a Franciscan community, Siena strives to embody the vision and values of St. Francis of Assisi: faith in a personal and provident God, reverence for all creation, affirmation of the unique worth of each person, delight in diversity, appreciation for beauty, service with the poor and marginalized, a community where members work together in friendship and respect, and commitment to building a world that is more just, peaceable, and humane. . . . As a Catholic College, Siena affirms the dignity of the individual while pursuing the common good.

—Excerpt from Siena College Mission Statement

The previous sections of this chapter presented sexual violence as a complex epidemic whose eradication from our campuses is a daunting yet feasible goal requiring institutional resources and active commitment of our entire communities. We submitted bystander intervention education programs—supported by holistic primary prevention campaigns—as best-practice means for achieving our the goal of violence-free communities. Using Siena College as a case study, we provided a snapshot of what this approach might look like in practice.

The remaining sections of this chapter propose that this approach can be strengthened by leveraging an institution's mission resources. To support and explicate this proposal we turn again to Siena College, focusing on resources rooted in our community's Franciscan Catholic heritage. Our attention is primarily directed to the Catholic social teaching tradition that inspires our institutional mission. Before we can delve into the specifics of how we at Siena are leveraging our mission resources to advance our anti-violence agenda, we first need to introduce the Catholic social teaching tradition and its potential as a resource for eradicating sexual violence, strengthening bystander intervention pedagogy, and in the words of the Siena College mission statement, for "building a more just, peaceable and humane world."

Catholic social teaching (CST) is a difficult concept to unpack. Sometimes the phrase is used as a broad umbrella term referring to a vast tradition of reflection and action on social issues spanning the entirety of Catholic history. More commonly, CST is defined as a collection of teaching documents that have been generated over the last 100 years or so in response to current political, economic, and social issues. These documents are written by various leaders within the global organizational structure of the Catholic Church, such as popes, global meetings of church leaders such as the Second Vatican Council (1962–1965), and governing bodies such as the United States Conference of Catholic Bishops (U.S.C.C.B.). Although no official list exists, a number of resources endeavor to provide a comprehensive—if not exhaustive—bundle of primary sources. Pope Leo XIII's 1891 encyclical letter, *Rerum Novarum,* is widely used as a benchmark for the beginning of this formal tradition (e.g., O'Brien & Shannon 2009).

Catholic social teaching represents an ever growing, living tradition of reflection and action. Documents are created and circulated as church leaders deem necessary in response to current issues such as war, the economy, the environment, and family life. As discussed elsewhere in this chapter, the internal coherency of this eclectic, evolving collection rests on key principles that are woven throughout, such as human dignity realized in community, the common good and our participation in it, solidarity, and preferential option for the poor. These principles are rooted in reflections on the Hebrew and Christian scriptures (the Bible) and more broadly on Christian tradition (encompassing 2,000 years of theological and philosophical inquiry and reflection on lived experiences of Christian faith.) The U.S. Bishops unpack CST and situate it within Catholicism in the following manner.

> Catholic social teaching is a central and essential element of our faith. Its roots are in the Hebrew prophets who announced God's special love for the poor and called God's people to a covenant of love and justice. It is a teaching founded on the life and words of Jesus Christ, who came "to bring glad tidings to the poor . . . liberty to captives . . . recovery of sight to the blind" (Lk 4:18–19), and who identified himself with "the least of these," the hungry and the stranger (cf. Mt 25:45). . . . The Church's social teaching is a rich treasure of wisdom about building a just society and living lives of holiness amidst the challenges of modern society. (U.S.C.C.B. 1995, para. 1 ff)

As the Bishops make clear, the Catholic social teaching tradition has as its ultimate goal active participation in the creation of peaceful and just communities. In other words, this teaching tradition is intended to inspire and mobilize Christians and all people of goodwill to action. Like bystander intervention education, it is intended to transform values into action. Byron (1998) contends that "principles, once internalized, lead to something. They prompt activity, impel motion, direct choices. A principled person always has a place to stand, knows where he or she is coming from and likely to end up. Principles always lead the person who possesses them somewhere, for some purpose, to do something, or choose not to" (Byron 1998, para. 1).

We contend that the key principles of CST compel action against sexual violence and its root causes. At the same time, we acknowledge that there are tensions in CST's treatment of sexual violence and in the way it addresses the issue of justice for women. The *Catechism of the Catholic Church* strongly condemns rape as "the forcible violation of the sexual intimacy of another person," which "does injury to justice and charity," and which "deeply wounds the respect, freedom, and physical and moral integrity to which every person has a right" (Catholic Church 1992, para. 2356). Yet there is no systematic treatment of sexual violence in CST documents. For example, a review of 23 documents written by popes and global councils of church leaders yields two mentions of rape (see Appendix). This list includes all of the papal and conciliar documents usually found in bound print collections plus a few extra documents. In his 1995 "Letter to Women," Pope John Paul II asserts that "the time has come to condemn vigorously the types of *sexual violence* which frequently have women as their object and to pass laws which effectively defend them from such violence" (John Paul II 1995, para. 5). The Pope's condemnation of sexual violence quickly gives way to his profession of gratitude for women who keep their babies conceived as a result of rape. Pope Francis (2013) similarly mentions rape in the context of a discussion about abortion, although his nuanced remarks are couched within the following assertion of shortcomings in terms of the Church's support for suffering women.

> It is not "progressive" to try to resolve problems by eliminating a human life. On the other hand, it is also true that we have done little to adequately accompany women in very difficult situations, where abortion appears as a quick solution to their profound anguish, especially when the life developing within them is the result of rape or a situation of extreme poverty. Who can remain unmoved before such painful situations? (Pope Francis 2013, para. 214)

In the more localized U.S. context of CST, a review of the vast collection of documents issued by the U.S.C.C.B. turns up several miscellaneous references to rape, often in the context of broader discussions of violence (e.g., U.S.C.C.B. 1995, U.S.C.C.B. 2000). Several documents focus on child sexual abuse, and one exemplary document—"When I Call For Help"—addresses sexual violence in the context of domestic violence (U.S.C.C.B. 2002).

In the 23 papal and conciliar documents where rape is mentioned twice, abortion is mentioned almost 100 times (Appendix). Pope Francis speaks to the implications of emphasizing certain issues while neglecting others.

> [I]n preaching the Gospel a fitting sense of proportion must be maintained. . . . For example, if in the course of the liturgical year a parish priest speaks about temperance ten times but only mentions charity

or justice two or three times, an imbalance results, and precisely those virtues which ought to be most present in preaching and catechesis are overlooked. (Pope Francis 2013, para. 38)

Adams is more pointed in an assessment of the consequences of the Church's lack of attention to the epidemic of sexual violence against women, "As long as violence is both invisible and unnamed, it is tacitly, although perhaps unintentionally, condoned." (Adams 2005, 80).

When it comes to CST's treatment of the broader, related issue of justice for women, results also are mixed. From its inception, CST documents defended the dignity of women, but often nuanced this by claiming that a woman's nature made her more or less suited to certain roles than men (Pope Leo XIII 1891, para. 42). As Himes (2001) points out, one can see a clear evolution in CST's affirmation of women as equal to men in both dignity and rights, which is evidenced by contemporary CST's strong condemnation of discriminatory practices in cultural life, at work, and in government. But there persists in CST a tendency toward a theology of complementarity that favors certain roles for women on the basis of natural law or the perceived will of God (such as motherhood) and denies them access to other roles (such as priesthood) (Pope John XXIII 1963, para. 19, 41; Vatican Council II 1965, para. 29, 60; Pope Paul VI 1971, para. 13; Pope John Paul II 1995a, para. 99; Pope John Paul II 1995b; Pope Francis 2013, para. 103). It is important to note that the ministerial roles denied to women carry with them institutional authority in the public sphere. This has led to criticism of the Catholic Church for promoting sexism through its institutional power structure. Heyer (2007) challenges CST for the way in which it so often presents "women's issues" as limited to reproductive issues such as abortion.

In contrast to the church's public voice on issues like abortion and same sex marriage, too seldom do we find the magisterium emphasizing physical or sexual violence against women or the dehumanizing conditions limiting women in many parts of the world. Given these realities, a Catholic witness that remains blind to [the] full experience of women not only risks inattentiveness to the anawim, but also risks complicity. (Heyer 2007, 2)

Heyer balances this critique of CST with an acknowledgment of its potential as a source of support and empowerment for justice for women.

Whereas many inside and outside the church cast feminism and Catholicism as incompatible ideologies, both approaches affirm equal human dignity, seek justice for the vulnerable, and liberation for the oppressed. A feminist concern for women's experience precisely as disadvantaged and for their equal social power both reflects and challenges Catholic social thought. (Heyer 2007, 2)

Similarly, we assert that CST's key principles support and strengthen bystander intervention education and broad-based efforts to eradicate sexual violence in the following ways.

CST Supports the Underlying Premise of Bystander Intervention Education: Sexual Violence Is Not Inevitable; It Can Be Eradicated

In "Confronting a Culture of Violence," the U.S. bishops contend that "Our social fabric is being torn apart by a culture of violence that leaves children dead on our streets and families afraid in our homes. . . . It doesn't have to be this way. It wasn't always this way. We can turn away from violence; we can build communities of greater peace" (U.S.C.C.B. 1995, para. 1). This claim is not the result of naive optimism. Rather, it is a faith-filled affirmation—with very practical implications—that acknowledges both the magnitude and complexity of recognizing and addressing this culture of violence. Like bystander intervention education, CST affirms the notion that all members of a community have a role to play in eradicating violence (U.S.C.C.B. 2002).

Catholic Social Teaching's Approach to Combatting Violence Aligns with Public Health Models That Address the Root Causes of Sexual Violence in Their Prevention Efforts

The U.S. Bishops' quote given above acknowledges and condemns the existence of a culture of violence in our country. In the same text the bishops name many of the attitudes, behaviors, and norms that encourage and sustain it.

> The celebration of violence in much of our media, music and even video games is poisoning our children. Beyond the violence in our streets is the violence in our hearts. Hostility, hatred, despair and indifference are at the heart of a growing culture of violence. Verbal violence in our families, communications and talk shows contribute to this culture of violence. Pornography assaults the dignity of women and contributes to violence against them. (U.S.C.C.B. 1995, para.1)

Documents including "Confronting a Culture of Violence" and "When I Call for Help" begin with this broader analysis and then offer a framework for action that translates CST principles into specific acts that challenge the culture of violence and promote the building of just, peaceable, violence-free communities (U.S.C.C.B.1995; U.S.C.C.B. 2002). In "When I Call for Help," the bishops include the added steps of acknowledging the ways in which interpretations of scripture and Church teachings have contributed to women's suffering and then model how to draw upon scriptural passages and theological concepts to condemn the abuse of women, support and empower survivors, and hold perpetrators accountable (U.S.C.C.B. 2002).

Catholic Social Teaching's Foundational Principles—Human Dignity Realized in Community and Participation in Building the Common Good—Clearly Align with Bystander Intervention Education's Shifting of Responsibility for Eradicating Sexual Violence to the Whole Community

Human dignity realized in community is the twofold foundational claim of CST. Mining the creation stories in the Hebrew Bible, CST teaches that all people possess equal human dignity because they are created in the image of God. Because human dignity is a gift from God, it cannot be surrendered or taken away. Catholic social teaching concretizes the concept of human dignity by championing and enumerating inalienable human rights rooted in human dignity (Pope John XXIII 1963; Vatican Council II 1965). What's more, CST asserts that, because human beings are created in the Trinitarian image of God, we are created for one another and only reach our full human potential in community. This notion is the underlying premise for the interrelated concepts of the common good and participation in it. Thompson explains, "The idea of the common good is that the good of each person is bound up with the good of the community; all are responsible for it" (Thompson 2010, 59). In "Economic Justice for All," the U.S. Bishops are more blunt, "Human dignity can be realized and protected only in community" (U.S.C.C.B. 1986, para. 28). If individuals are truly bound up with and responsible for the good of the community, then each of us has an obligation to speak out and stand up *against* sexual violence and *for* a just, peaceable and humane community (Pope John XIII 1961; U.S.C.C.B. 1986; Vatican Council II 1965). Documents such as "When I Call for Help" propose multiple practical strategies for action to several different audiences, in much the same way that active bystander training provides students with many developmentally, contextually appropriate strategies for intervention (U.S.C.C.B. 2002).

Catholic Social Teaching's Principles of Solidarity and Preferential Option for the Poor Support and Strengthen Bystander Intervention Education by Deepening and Concretizing the Potential Active Bystander's Commitment to Engaging in the Community's Sexual Violence Prevention Efforts

"(Solidarity) is not a feeling of vague compassion or shallow distress at the misfortunes of so many people, both near and far. On the contrary, it is a firm and persevering determination to commit oneself to the common good" (Pope John Paul II 1987, para. 38). Applied to bystander intervention training, the principle of solidarity can help increase victim empathy by reminding us that we are all deeply affected and hurt when any one member of our community is harmed or hurts another. As mentioned above, to assist students in working through stage three of the four stages of bystander intervention (assume responsibility) we often use techniques that personalize the situation for students: What if the person being harassed was your sister? Because we have begun drawing explicitly upon CST in our training, we now add, "Our community values call us to treat everyone as our sister or brother." The virtue of solidarity also helps us articulate bystander intervention as a way of life, rather than an occasional isolated act.

When CST uses the phrase "preferential option for the poor," it refers to an expansive understanding of what it means to be poor, which includes not only those who are economically disadvantaged, but also persons who are oppressed and marginalized by unjust behaviors and structures (Vatican Council II 1965). This concept is rooted in biblical stories of God's special care for the most vulnerable persons among us. On the basis of these stories, CST asserts that the way people draw closer to God is by getting closer to the poor: "As Christians, we are called to respond to the needs of all our brothers and sisters, but those with the greatest needs require the greatest response" (U.S.C.C.B. 1986, para. 16). In collegiate and broader contexts, in which sexual violence is pandemic and women are particularly vulnerable to victimization, the preferential option for the poor elevates action that challenges this culture of violence to a privileged place at the top of our personal and community agendas.

Catholic Social Teaching's Dual Emphasis on Works of Charity and Justice Supports Bystander Intervention Education That Focuses on Interventions across the Levels of the Ecological Model

More broadly, CST holds the potential to aid colleges and universities in their quest to strike an appropriate balance between various proactive and responsive approaches to addressing sexual violence; including bystander intervention training, risk-reduction programs, and direct services to survivors. Himes clarifies CST's dual concern for charity and justice.

A common distinction made between charity and justice is to see the former as addressing immediate need through direct aid while the latter looks at longer-term solutions through social analysis and change. Another way of putting it is to see charity as a response to the *effects* of personal and social ills while justice aims at remedying the *causes* of such ills. . . . Both charity and justice are important responses to the challenge of the gospel, and both are praised in CST, and both are needed if we are to build a world where human beings live with dignity. (Himes 2001, 45–46)

In CST, participation in the common good necessitates that we address *both* individual acts of misbehavior *and* broader structural injustices that threaten the common good. "We see in the world a set of injustices which constitute the nucleus of today's problems and whose solution requires the undertaking of tasks and functions in every sector of society . . . if justice is really to be put into practice" (Synod of Catholic Bishops 1971, para. 20). Like bystander intervention education, CTS is a model that allows us to be practical visionaries—to do the work of creating the "what could be" (what Christians call "building the kingdom of God") while acknowledging and managing the "what is." When it comes to addressing sexual violence, this means that we share resources between programs that focus on remedying the effects of violence and those that aim at preventing it. It also supports the provision of some risk-reduction programming, but in a way that is intentionally designed to avoid any victim-blaming messages.

Catholic Social Teaching Provides a Theological Mandate for Active Bystander Programs

CST provides language to name sexual violence as sin—which the bishops explicitly direct pastors to do in "When I Call for Help"—and to understand it as sinful on a personal and structural level.

Education [for justice] demands a renewal of heart, a renewal based on the recognition of sin in its individual and social manifestations. It will also inculcate a truly and entirely human way of life in justice, love and simplicity. It will likewise awaken a critical sense, which will lead us to reflect on the society in which we live and on its values; it will make people ready to renounce these values when they cease to promote justice for all people. . . . This education is deservedly called a continuing education, for it concerns every person and every age. . . . It is also a practical education: it comes through action, participation and vital contact with the reality of injustice. (Synod of Bishops 1971, para. 51–53)

Thompson contends that CST encourages "new methods of education for justice that yield not only information but the transformation of persons, who then work to change society" (Thompson 2010, 296). We propose that a mission-driven model of bystander intervention education can serve as one such method of education for justice. As one of our students beautifully and succinctly put it, "I joined the P.E.E.P.s because it is my social justice mission to end sexual violence at Siena College." At Siena, we are leveraging CST as a key mission resource to strengthen our active bystander programs and advance our antiviolence agenda. The progressive evolution of our efforts to leverage mission in support of prevention efforts includes the following.

Mission Literacy Training for Siena Faculty, Staff, and Administrators

At Siena, we have learned that mission literacy is essential to achieving endorsement and collaboration in the implementation of a community-wide, mission-driven approach to sexual violence prevention on our campus. Mission literacy refers to both general education about Siena's Franciscan Catholic heritage and more focused conversations on the connections between institutional mission and violence-prevention efforts. Division of Student Affairs retreats always include a session devoted to general mission education. In January 2014, the authors were invited to facilitate a presentation and conversation about the ways in which CST can support and strengthen bystander intervention education. The antiviolence task force has approached this more focused conversation through inductive exercises such as reviewing Siena's mission and looking for elements that support our task force mission. These educational opportunities have led to brainstorming sessions on how to engage students in similar conversations, which in turn have generated the programs highlighted below.

The Inclusion of Mission-Specific Language in Electronic and Print Resources

On the landing page of our violence-prevention website (www.Siena .edu/SexualViolencePrevention) we explicitly state that Siena's violence-prevention efforts are rooted in its Franciscan and Catholic tradition, which affirms the unique worth of each person and shares a commitment to building a world that is more just, peaceable, and humane. These elements of our mission are rooted directly in the foundational principles of CST. We go on to assert that violence of any type—including sexual violence—is antithetical to our values and to our vision of what it means to live and learn in a safe, respectful, and inclusive community. A "mission tagline" is included on all antiviolence task force communications and weekly e-mails to the college community; it reads, "building a more just, peaceable and humane world." Lastly, in community newsletters the antiviolence task force has featured student active bystander stories titled "Partners in Mission" and has included an excerpt from the college's mission statement.

The Formal Inclusion of Values Conversations and Education about CST in Active Bystander Training Workshops for Students

The Mission Possible workshop is the school's first comprehensive effort to design a mission-driven active bystander training curriculum. The program begins with an interactive, inductive conversation about values. Participants are asked to write down three of their personal values. The facilitators then invite students to share these values out loud with the group. During this exercise, one of the facilitators takes notes on a large whiteboard. The facilitators then project Siena's mission statement on a screen and invite the participants to identify Siena values that also were mentioned as personal values of group members. Invariably there is much overlap. The facilitators draw attention to this, then transition into how values such as respect for everyone's dignity and worth, equality, courage, practicing what you preach, and responsibility align with active bystander behavior.

Next the facilitators ask the students where they learned their values. Once again, the students share out loud with the large group, naming the people in their lives who have educated them, such as Mom, Dad, Grandpa, Grandma, my sister, Coach Smith, Pastor Rob, Professor Jones, and my youth minister. The facilitators then explain that Siena's values also "come from somewhere," that is, they are rooted in a particular tradition: Siena's Franciscan Catholic heritage. They are careful to note that this does not mean that Catholicism has a monopoly on these values or that only Catholics can support Siena's mission. This leads into a discussion of CST much like the one provided above, which introduces students to CST and ties it into bystander intervention. The discussion is geared toward the student audience with stories of St. Francis, Jesus, and biblical figures to make the principles less abstract and more accessible. Throughout the rest of the workshop, facilitators refer back to these introductory exercises and conversations about values and mission. Of the RAs who attended, 100% reported that, as a result of attending 2013 RA training, they are able to articulate how Siena's antiviolence efforts are informed by our Franciscan and Catholic values. At orientation and P.E.E.P.s training we also employ this method of introducing students to Siena's mission and its connection to the sexual violence prevention and bystander intervention.

As a result of our campaign to increase mission literacy among our colleagues, we are beginning to see the implementation of our mission-driven model of bystander intervention education in other areas of the Division of Student Affairs, such as LGBT Ally Training.

We contend that just as CST can strengthen and support bystander intervention education, the reverse is true. With a critical mass of buy-in, the mission-driven model of bystander intervention can empower our communities to constructively inform the living tradition of CST. We believe that mission-driven active bystander programs have the potential to spark a "call to action" to the institutional Catholic Church—including Catholic institutions of higher learning—to speak out and stand up *against* sexual violence and *for* justice for women. This call to action challenges the Catholic Church to practice what it preaches and to examine ways in which its institutional practices might support rape culture. As the bishops prophetically state in *Justitia in Mundo* ("Justice in the World"), the Church itself must be just (1971). If the Church were to answer this call, the results could be truly transforming. The Church is a significant moral voice on many issues, such as immigration. Imagine what could happen if this massive global organization used its moral voice to speak out against sexual violence and to challenge the structures that perpetuate it.

CONCLUSION: RECOMMENDATIONS FOR IMPLEMENTING THE MISSION-DRIVEN MODEL OF BYSTANDER INTERVENTION EDUCATION

Using Siena College as our case study, we have endeavored to support our contention that Catholic colleges and universities have a unique opportunity to bring bystander intervention education and Catholic social teaching into constructive and mutually beneficial conversation in the service of sexual violence–prevention efforts. We also see great potential for broadening this "mission meets practice" conversation beyond Catholic institutions of higher learning. Based on our particular experiences at Siena College, we conclude with the following practical recommendations for implementing the mission-driven model of bystander intervention education in the advancement of sexual violence prevention.

1. Implement a comprehensive, customized approach that includes a combination of homegrown and national evidence-based anchor programs that train students to be active bystanders, and ensure that these programs are supported by a wide range of institutional initiatives (e.g., standardized brand for messaging; social norms; sexual violence policy).

2. Secure widespread buy-in of faculty, staff, and students vis-à-vis program development, facilitation, participation, and endorsement. The development of an antiviolence task force—which is tasked and empowered to create programs—is one way to bring together and mobilize members of these key constituencies. Student participation is essential, especially that of recognized student leaders. Participation by senior administrators—such as the Dean of Students and the Title IX Coordinator—also is key. If your school has a person or office specifically tasked with mission promotion, then it is important to invite that person or office to the table.

3. Enlist the support and expertise of partners in community agencies already doing this work.
4. Whenever possible, utilize peer educators in program development and delivery. Make sure peer education programs are guided by skilled and committed advisers.
5. Ensure that potential collaborators are mission literate. Enlist the support of skilled facilitators who are mission literate and able to translate and share mission resources in accessible and inviting ways. Employ inductive conversations to build literacy in a safe space. Be honest and open about potential areas of tension between institutional mission and antiviolence efforts. Also ensure that potential partners receive adequate training in bystander intervention and around the issue of sexual violence.
6. Weave mission intentionally, explicitly, and carefully into programs and supporting materials—and in the case of religiously affiliated institutions, especially keep in mind community members who do not self-identify with their institution's religious affiliation.
7. Employ an ongoing feedback loop—using formal and informal assessment channels—to improve programs and services. Program assessment data also can help to secure institutional resources.
8. Develop a model that is both efficacious in supporting a sexual violence–prevention agenda and is a broad-based curriculum with wide-scale applicability to other campus issues (e.g., bullying, dating violence, LGBT ally training, alcohol abuse).

APPENDIX: PAPAL AND CONCILIAR CATHOLIC SOCIAL TEACHING DOCUMENTS

Rerum Novarum, Pope Leo XIII, 1891
Quadragesimo Anno, Pope Pius XI, 1931
Mater et Magistra, Pope John XXIII, 1961
Pacem in Terris, Pope John XXIII, 1963
Gaudium et Spes, Vatican Council II, 1965
Dignitatis Humanae, Vatican Council II, 1965
Populorum Progressio, Pope Paul VI, 1967
Octogesima Adveniens, Pope Paul VI, 1971
Justitia in Mundo, Synod of Bishops, 1971
Evangelii Nuntiandi, Pope Paul VI, 1975
Laborem Exercens, Pope John Paul II, 1981
Solicitudo Rei Socialis, Pope John Paul II, 1987
Mulieris Dignitatem, Pope John Paul II, August 15, 1988
Centesimus Annus, Pope John Paul II, 1991
Evangelium Vitae, Pope John Paul II, 1995
Letter to Women, Pope John Paul II, 1995

Letter of His Holiness John Paul II to Mrs. Gertrude Mongella Secretary General of the Fourth World Conference on Women of the United Nations, Pope John Paul II, 1995

Fides et Ratio, Pope John Paul II, 1998

Compendium of the Social Doctrine of the Church, Pontifical Council for Justice and Peace, 2004

Deus Caritas Est, Pope Benedict XVI, 2005

Sacramentum Caritatis, Pope Benedict XVI, 2007

Caritas in Veritate, Pope Benedict XVI, 2009

Evangelii Gaudium, Pope Francis, 2013

REFERENCES

Adams, C. (2005). "I just raped my wife! What are you going to do about it, pastor?" The church and sexual violence. In *Transforming a rape culture,* edited by E. Buchwalk, P. Fletcher, and M. Roth. Minneapolis, MN: Milkweed Editions.

American College Health Association (ACHA) (2008). *Shifting the paradigm: Primary prevention of sexual violence.* Linthicum, MD: American College Health Association. http://www.acha.org/sexualviolence/docs/acha_psv_toolkit.pdf. Accessed April 6, 2015.

American College Health Association (ACHA) (2007). Position statement on preventing sexual violence on college and university campuses.

Banyard, V., Plante, E., and Moynihan, M. (2004). Bystander education: Bringing a broader community perspective to sexual violence prevention. *Journal of Community Psychology* 32, 61–79.

Benedict, H. (2005). The language of rape. In *Transforming a rape culture,* edited by E. Buchwalk, P. Fletcher, and M. Roth. Minneapolis, MN: Milkweed Editions.

Berkowitz, A. (2009). *Response ability: A complete guide to bystander intervention.* Chicago, IL: Beck and Company.

Black, M. C., Basile, K. C., Breiding, M. J., Smith, S. G., Walters, M. L., Merrick, M. T., Chen, J., and Stevens, M. R. (2011). *The national intimate partner and sexual violence survey (NISVS): 2010 summary report.* Atlanta, GA: National Center for Injury Prevention and Control, Centers for Disease Control and Prevention.

Brownmiller, S. (1975). *Against our will: Men, women and rape.* New York: Simon and Schuster.

Byron, W. J. (1998, October 31). Ten building blocks of Catholic social teaching. *America: The National Review.* http://americamagazine.org/issue/100/ten-building-blocks-catholic-social-teaching. Accessed April 7, 2015.

Campus Sexual Violence Elimination Act ("Campus SaVE Act"), Pub. L. No. 113-4, § 304, 127 Stat. 89 (2013) https://www.govtrack.us/congress/bills/113/s128/text. Accessed April 7, 2015.

Carr, J. L. (2008). Preventing sexual violence through empowering campus bystanders. In *Shifting the paradigm: Primary prevention of sexual violence,* edited by American College Health Association, 16–18. Hanover, MD.

Carr, J. L., and VanDeusen, K. M. (2004). Risk factors for male sexual aggression on college campuses. *Journal of Family Violence* 19, 279–289.

Catholic Church (1992). *Catechism of the Catholic Church.* Vatican: Libreria Editrice Vaticana.

Center for Sex Offender Management (2006). *Understanding sex offenders: An introductory curriculum.* U.S. Dept. of Justice. http://www.csom.org/train/etiology/3/3_1.htm. Accessed April 7, 2015.

Centers for Disease Control and Prevention [CDC] (2004). *Sexual violence prevention: Beginning the dialogue.* Atlanta, GA: Centers for Disease Control and Prevention.

Cissner, A. (2009). *Evaluating the mentors in violence prevention program: Preventing gender violence on a college campus.* Center for Court Intervention. http://www.courtinnovation.org/sites/default/files/MVP_evaluation.pdf. Accessed April 7, 2015.

Coker, A. L., Cook-Craig, P. G., Williams, C. M., Fisher, B. S., Clear, E. R., Gracia, L. S., and Hegge, L. M. (2011). Evaluation of Green Dot: An active bystander intervention to reduce sexual violence on college campuses. *Violence against Women* 17, 777–796.

Curtis, M., and Love, T. (2009). *Tools for change: An introduction to the primary prevention of sexual assault.* Austin: Texas Association Against Sexual Assault.

Fisher, B. S., Cullen, F. T., and Turner, M. G. (2000). *The sexual victimization of college women.* Washington, DC: National Institute of Justice, Bureau of Justice Statistics.

Handeyside, A. K., Wickliffe, S. L., and Adams, J. (2007). *Striving for justice: A toolkit for judicial resolution officers on college campus. Responding to sexual assault and dating and domestic violence.* University of Michigan. http://sapac.umich.edu/files/sapac/StrivingForJustice.pdf. Accessed April 6, 2015.

Heyer, K. (2007, November 9). *A feminist appraisal of Catholic social thought.* University of San Francisco Lane Center for Catholic Studies and Catholic Social Thought. Fall Lecture Series. https://www.usfca.edu/uploaded-Files/Destinations/Institutes_and_Centers/Lane/Publications/. Accessed April 6, 2015.

Hill, C., and Silva, E. (2005). *Drawing the line: Sexual harassment on campus.* Washington, DC: American Association of University Women Educational Foundation.

Himes, K. (2001). *Responses to 101 questions on Catholic social teaching.* Mahwah, NJ: Paulist Press.

Katz, J. (n.d.). *Mentors in Violence Prevention (MVP): Gender violence prevention education and training.* http://www.jacksonkatz.com/mvp.html. Accessed April 5, 2015.

Krebs, C. P., Lindquist, C. H., Warner, T. D., Fisher, B. S., and Martin, S. L (2009). College women's experiences with physically forced, alcohol- or other drug-enabled, and drug-facilitated sexual assault before and since entering college. *Journal of American College Health* 57 (6), 639–647.

Krebs, C. P., Lindquist, C. H., Warner, T. D., Fisher, B. S., and Martin, S. L. (2007). *The campus sexual assault (CSA) study.* https://www.ncjrs.gov/pdffiles1/nij/grants/221153.pdf. Accessed April 6, 2015.

Lee, D. S., Guy, L., and Perry, B. (2008). Sexual violence prevention. In American College Health Association, *Shifting the paradigm: Primary prevention of sexual violence,* 7–9. Hanover, MD.

Lisak, D. (2011). Understanding the predatory nature of sexual violence. Sexual Assault Report. *Civic Research Institute* 14 (1), 49–57. http://www.davidlisak.com/wp-content/uploads/pdf/SARUnderstandingPredatoryNatureSexualViolence.pdf. Accessed April 7, 2015.

Lisak, D., and Miller, P. M. (2002). Repeat rape and multiple offending among undetected rapists. *Violence and Victims* 17 (1), 73–84.

Mohler-Kuo, M., Dowdall, G., Koss, M., and Wechsler, H. (2004). Correlates of rape while intoxicated in a national sample of college women. *Journal of Studies on Alcohol* 65, 37–45.

O'Brien, D. J., and Shannon T. A. (2009). *Catholic social thought: The documentary heritage.* Maryknoll, NY: Orbis Books.

Pope Francis (2013). *Evangelii Gaudium.* Vatican: Libreria Editrice Vaticana.

Pope John XXIII (1963). *Pacem in terris.* Vatican: Libreria Editrice Vaticana.

Pope John Paul II (1995a). *Evangelium vitae.* Vatican: Libreria Editrice Vaticana.

Pope John Paul II (1995b). *Letter to women.* Vatican: Libreria Editrice Vaticana.

Pope John Paul II (1987). *Solicitudo rei socialis.* Vatican: Libreria Editrice Vaticana.

Pope Leo XIII (1891). *Rerum novarum.* Vatican: Libreria Editrice Vaticana.

Pope Paul VI (1971). *Octogesima adveniens.* Vatican: Libreria Editrice Vaticana.

Tabachnick, J. (2009). *Engaging bystanders in sexual violence prevention.* National Sexual Violence Resource Center. http://www.nsvrc.org/. Accessed April 7, 2015.

Thompson, J. M. (2010). *Introducing Catholic social thought.* Maryknoll, NY: Orbis Books.

U.S. Conference of Catholic Bishops (U.S.C.C.B.) (2002). *When I call for help: A pastoral response to domestic violence against women.* http://www.usccb.org. Accessed April 7, 2015.

U.S. Conference of Catholic Bishops (U.S.C.C.B.) (2000). *Responsibility, rehabilitation, and restoration: A Catholic perspective on crime and criminal justice.* http://www.usccb.org. Accessed April 6, 2015.

U.S. Conference of Catholic Bishops (U.S.C.C.B.) (1995). *Confronting a culture of violence: A Catholic framework for action.* http://www.usccb.org/

U.S. Conference of Catholic Bishops (U.S.C.C.B.) (1986). *Economic justice for all.* http://www.usccb.org/upload/economic_justice_for_all.pdf

U.S. Department of Education, Office for Civil Rights (2011, April 4). *"Dear Colleague" letter guidance, supplementing the OCR's revised sexual harassment guidance.* http://www2.ed.gov/about/offices/list/ocr/letters/colleague-201104.pdf. Accessed April 3, 2014.

U.S. Department of Justice, Office of Justice Programs, National Institute of Justice (2005). *Sexual assault on campus: What colleges and universities are doing about it.* https://www.ncjrs.gov/pdffiles1/nij/205521.pdf. Accessed April 4, 2015.

Valenti, J. (2008). *He's a stud, she's a slut, and 49 other double standards every woman should know.* Berkeley, CA: Seal Press.

Vatican Council II (1965). *Gaudium et spes.* Vatican: Libreria Editrice Vaticana.

Virginia Sexual and Domestic Violence Action Alliance (2009). *Guidelines for the primary prevention of sexual violence and intimate partner violence.* Richmond: Virginia Sexual and Domestic Violence Action Alliance. http://www.communitysolutionsva.org/index.php/resources. Accessed April 2, 2015.

White House Council on Women and Girls (2014). *Rape and sexual assault: A renewed call to action.* Washington, DC: The White House. http://www.white house.gov/sites/default/files/docs/sexual_assault_report_1-21-14.pdf. Accessed April 6, 2015.

Wilson, R. (2014, June 6). Why colleges are on the hook for sexual assault. *The Chronicle of Higher Education.* http://chronicle.com/article/Why-Colleges -Are-on-theHook/146943/. Accessed April 7, 2015.

World Synod of Catholic Bishops (1971). *Justitia in mundo.* Vatican: Libreria Editrice Vaticana.

Part II

Heritage of Title IX and Title VII

Chapter 3

From Explicit Equity to Sports to Sexual Assault to Explicit Subjugation: The True Story Behind Title IX and Women's Ongoing Struggle for Equality in Education

Wendy Murphy

Much of the public narrative related to Title IX and the problem of campus sexual assault put forth during the period from 2000 to 2014 was mysteriously misleading. Splashy news stories in major publications suggested that positive reforms—especially from 2010 to 2014—grew out of an organic groundswell of student activism, and that in response to this activism Congress was enacting laws to make things better. President Obama held numerous press events and talked about a new task force and other initiatives that would help stop sexual assault from occurring on college campuses. What *actually* was going on during this period was that Congress was pushing through a new federal law known as the "Campus Sex Violence Elimination Act" (SaVE) also known as the 2013 Clery Amendments to the Violence Against Women Act (VAWA). The legislation weakens women's rights on campus, limits the ability of regulatory agencies to hold schools accountable for the mistreatment of victimized women, and expressly allows schools to subject women to second-class treatment in the redress of gender-based violence on campus.

Many advocates and students *supported* Congress in that effort and were celebrated in the media for doing so. As supporters awkwardly cheered for a new law that would hurt women, a few relentless individuals working behind the scenes fought hard to stop SaVE and to preserve women's constitutional and fundamental civil right to full equality in higher education.

I was one of those people.

Our fight to protect women's educational equality involved political strategies aimed at shaming Congress, alongside use of aggressive litigation tactics in federal oversight agencies and in the courts when going up against some of the most powerful schools in the country. The media never reported the truth about what Congress was doing, so the public had no way of knowing that a bill had been proposed that would give schools authority to mistreat women on campus. Nor did the media report on what we were doing behind the scenes to try and stop SaVE, and how our strategies would eventually lay the groundwork for a future body of law in which SaVE will have no effect on any college campus, and women, once and for all, will enjoy *full* equality in education.

This chapter is an overview of the history of Title IX with an emphasis on what actually worked to move women forward toward full equality, alongside disturbing tactics—often used by women's rights groups themselves—that made progress more difficult to achieve.

THE EARLY YEARS

Equality in education—like equality in larger society—depends on a strong legal baseline in fundamental rights and constitutional principles. Such laws comprise the core values from which other legal doctrines evolve. The stronger the baseline, the more weight a court must assign the rights at stake in legal controversies.

Very strong roots of legal protection for the concept of educational equality were established in 1964 when Congress passed landmark civil rights legislation. One section, Title IV of the Civil Rights Act of 1964, prohibited segregation and discrimination in *public* places—including colleges and universities—on the basis of "race, color or national origin." Another section, Title VI of the same Act prohibited discrimination in all federally funded programs and activities, including public *and* private schools. Discrimination on the basis of sex initially was not covered under Title IV or Title VI, but it was included in Title VII, which prohibited discrimination in employment on the basis of "race, color, religion, sex or national origin." Title VII, however, exempted educational institutions with regard to "educational activities" such that faculty and most administrators were not protected.

In 1965, President Lyndon Johnson issued an executive order forbidding employment discrimination in federal contracts on the basis of "race, color, religion and national origin." He amended the order in 1968 to also forbid employment discrimination in federal contracts on the basis of sex.

In 1969, Dr. Bernice Sandler suffered sex discrimination and was denied a job in higher education for which she was qualified. She was surprised to learn that, although Title VII forbade sex discrimination in employment, colleges and universities were exempted from the law. Sandler soon discovered the amended 1968 executive order and realized that, although universities could discriminate on the basis of sex in employment regarding "educational activities," they were forbidden to do so under the executive order if they were parties to federal contracts. Sandler researched the law and learned that the executive order could be enforced through the filing of a complaint with the U.S. Department of Labor. An employee there, Vincent Macaluso, secretly helped Sandler gather data, which enabled Sandler to file a complaint requesting that the department investigate an "industry-wide" pattern of discrimination against women in higher education with regard to hiring practices, promotions, and salary differentials. That data—which showed widespread sex discrimination in higher education—then were presented to Congress during hearings before a special education subcommittee headed by Representative Edith Green (D–Ore.), who later became known as the "Mother of Title IX." Sandler earned the title "Godmother of Title IX." (Dr. Sandler recently dubbed me the "Goddaughter of Title IX.") Those hearings became the foundation for what eventually would become Title IX.

Congress continued to hold hearings, while Sandler spread the word to advocates around the country about the importance of filing complaints with federal oversight agencies on matters related to gender discrimination in higher education with regard to both employment and admissions. Many people followed Sandler's lead, and Sandler herself filed approximately 250 complaints on behalf of other women. One noteworthy complaint was filed in 1970 with the Department of Health, Education, and Welfare on behalf of women at Harvard. Later that same year, the Department of Labor issued "Sex Discrimination Guidelines" for federal contractors.

Aware that Congress was planning to enact a new federal law to prevent sex discrimination in all aspects of higher education that would affect both *public and private* universities, Harvard, Princeton, Yale, and Dartmouth lobbied unsuccessfully for an exemption that would allow them to limit their admissions of women. Such an exemption initially was allowed for service academies, but it was removed through subsequent legislation.

A bill guaranteeing women protection in *public* education was enacted in 1972 when Title IV was amended to add "sex" to the list of protected-class categories. A similar proposal to ensure women's full equality in private education by simply amending Title VI to add "sex" was rejected, purportedly on the grounds that civil rights activists feared it might open Title VI to other amendments that could hurt the interests of the black community in achieving racial equality in private schools. In truth, it was not likely antiracism activists who objected to adding "sex" to Title VI. Considering that a small group of Ivy League universities previously had lobbied openly and unsuccessfully for an exemption that would have allowed them to discriminate against women in admissions, it is more likely that, having failed to win an exemption, those same elite schools changed their strategy and lobbied Congress behind the scenes to prevent *any* amendment to Title VI that would add "sex" to the list of protected-class categories. The antiracism argument was likely only a smokescreen, but because women's rights activists were reluctant to be seen as causing harm to the fight for racial equality, the apparent opposition of antiracism activists silenced women's groups on their demand that "sex" be added to Title VI.

As a result, the plan to amend Title VI was abandoned, and in 1972 Congress instead enacted Title IX as a separate, stand-alone law that promised equality and prohibited discrimination "on the basis of sex" in schools that accepted federal funds. Because Title IX covered *all* schools that accepted federal funds, it applied with equal force to public and private schools alike. Also, although Title IX was codified as an Education Amendment it nonetheless was a civil rights law that guaranteed women the same rights and protections as those guaranteed under Title VI to other protected-class categories, such as race and national origin. This was made clear by Congress' use of the exact same language in Title IX as had been enacted in Title VI. In fact, after its enactment Title IX *was* interpreted and enforced as requiring exactly the same substantive standards of legal protection as are required under Title VI. The U.S. Supreme Court affirmed this basic principle a few years later in *Cannon v. University of Chicago*, yet widespread understanding of Title IX *as a civil rights law* for women would not develop for decades, largely because Title IX quickly became propagandized in society as a sports-equity rule.

The misframing of Title IX as a sports-equity rule began in 1975, when the Title IX regulation was enacted requiring schools to provide, among other things, "prompt and equitable" redress of sex discrimination on campus. That same year, Texas congress member John Tower proposed a new federal law to exempt athletics programs from compliance with Title IX. This was met with strong opposition from women's rights advocates who successfully fought to maintain a federal mandate that would ensure Title IX's applicability to athletics as well as to other educational programs and activities.

Between 1975 and 1980, the Department of Health, Education and Welfare released several policy statements regarding the scope and purpose of Title IX. In 1980, the Office for Civil Rights (OCR) at the Department of Education (DOE) was established and was given primary oversight responsibility for

Title IX's enforcement. From 1975 to 1990, the OCR developed various Title IX publications in which sports equity for women was not emphasized, yet media attention and Title IX litigation focused nearly exclusively on the relationship between Title IX and sports.

In 1992, the U.S. Supreme Court decided *Franklin v. Gwinnett County Public Schools*. In this case the court explicitly recognized sexual assault as a form of sexual harassment under Title IX. The OCR issued new guidelines in 1997 emphasizing the importance of Title IX's role in preventing student-on-student sexual assault and harassment, but the public narrative continued to frame Title IX as a sports equity rule—even after another landmark Supreme Court case in 1999, *Davis v. Monroe* (526 U.S. 629 (1999), held that Title IX clearly applies to sexual assault and harassment between peers.

Although Title IX was being misunderstood in society as a law related to women and sports, Title IV and Title VI were consistently being framed and understood in society as laws aimed at producing equality and preventing harassment and violence on behalf of students from protected-class categories such as race and national origin.

Widespread public awareness of the relationship between Title IX and gender-based violence and harassment did not begin until 2002, when the faculty of Arts and Sciences at Harvard adopted a controversial rule requiring campus sexual assault victims to produce "sufficient, independent corroboration" for their complaints. In the absence of such proof, Harvard would not provide redress or take action against an offender.

Decades earlier, a similar corroboration rule in the criminal justice system had been abolished as being profoundly sexist, which made Harvard's new policy seem particularly anathematic. The motivation for such an arcane idea soon became apparent, however, when it was revealed that a mandatory corroboration policy would enable Harvard to underreport sexual assault incidents on campus by not counting cases in which the victim could not produce adequate corroboration.

Finding ways to undercount crimes on campus was a big concern for colleges and universities in the early 2000s because of changes made to the federal Clery Act (Clery) in 1998. Originally enacted in 1990, Clery requires that schools must—among other things, such as issue timely warnings of crimes on campus, notify students of rights, conduct prevention programs, and adopt anti-retaliation policies—produce annual "report cards" revealing to the public the number and types of crimes occurring on campus in a given year. As initially enacted, Clery provided no sanctions for noncompliance; thus, many schools simply did not comply. As a result, Congress amended Clery in 1998 to provide that noncompliant schools could be ordered to pay substantial fines.

Because sexual assault was (and still is) among the most prevalent forms of violence on college campuses, schools were particularly reluctant to publicize truthful numbers fearing that parents would not send their daughters to colleges that appeared to be unsafe for women. Whether a school's Clery information is correct was (and still is) difficult to ascertain because the public has no access to reliable comparative data sources. Nonetheless, it is obvious that virtually every school dramatically under-reports the truth. This is evidenced by the fact that multiple studies find students endure very high rates of sexual assault on campus, ranging from one in three (Freyd et al. 2014); to one in four (Humphrey & White 2000); to one in five (Krebs et al. 2009). On a campus of 1,000 students, this would mean that between 100 and 300 students are sexually assaulted during college—yet no school has ever reported such high numbers. Although many incidents go unreported for reasons that cannot be attrib-uted solely to school officials hiding the truth, these data prove that Clery reports are obviously not reflective of reality.

After Clery was amended in 1998 to allow for sanctions, pressure mounted on schools to reveal accurate numbers. Not telling the truth could be expensive, but releasing true data also could have economic re-percussions by affecting a school's reputation as an unsafe place for women. Many schools correctly complained that high numbers of sexual assaults did not necessarily indicate an unsafe campus and that, in fact, a school with high numbers *could be* especially safe for women because it was an indication that problems were not being swept under the rug and that women were being encouraged to file reports.

Some schools began to devise strategies that would enable them to avoid fines without revealing accurate (high) numbers. Harvard's manda-tory corroboration requirement, as an example, would generate artificially low numbers because only cases with "sufficient" and "independent" proof would be counted. Moreover, reporting rates would decline because students would know that their word alone was insufficient to establish a violation. In other words, requiring corroboration would deter victims from reporting *and* would allow Harvard to undercount incidents, thus technically complying with Clery but without telling the truth.

I was a Visiting Scholar at Harvard Law School when the corroboration rule was adopted by Harvard College. Students were angry, and they sought advice from advisers and professors, but no one had any understanding of Title IX with regard to its relationship to sexual assault, or had even a basic understanding of the fact that students could file complaints with federal oversight agencies. Even so-called experts in women's rights at Harvard Law School had little understanding of feminist criticisms of rape law and why the corroboration rule had been abolished in the criminal justice system decades earlier. Additionally, no one at Harvard was teaching key theoretical concepts about rape law, such as autonomy theory and bodily integrity.

As a visiting scholar, having just finished a year as an assistant profes-sor of law in the Mary Joe Frug Chair at New England Law–Boston, my work at Harvard focused on the status of women in their capacity as victims in the criminal justice system, and centered around the redesign of rape law at the baseline, with an emphasis on autonomy theory. Autonomy theory recognizes that nonconsent—alone—is enough to prove rape; although in most states the absence of consent is not enough. The use of force also must be proved, and in the absence of force there is no crime. Put another way, women's autonomy is not valued in law because nonforcible sexual intrusions without consent are perfectly legal. I had lectured many times on this topic at Harvard, therefore the students there knew of my work, and they came to me for help when the corroboration rule was announced.

I had been looking for a good Title IX test case at the time, in the hope of increasing public awareness of the relationship between sexual assault and Title IX. As an impact litigator, my practice often involves filing legal actions that provoke systemic reforms. I knew a carefully planned complaint against Harvard, filed with the OCR at the DOE, would greatly enhance the public's understanding of Title IX and maybe even force Harvard to repeal its corroboration policy. I volunteered to represent the Harvard students and I drafted a complaint alleging that Harvard's corroboration rule was inequitable and discriminatory under Title IX because it devalued the word of a woman as inherently inadequate to merit redress of her complaint. I emphasized that such a policy could not pass muster as "equitable" under Title IX where no similar burden was being imposed on other students who alleged civil rights violations under Title VI, on the basis of categories such as race and national origin.

I told the students that I needed a live controversy where the corroboration rule had been applied to an actual case on campus, but the students I talked to understandably feared that having a real student file a complaint against Harvard would lead to retaliation, and could be damaging to their careers. I also was concerned that it could take years for an actual case involving application of the corroboration rule to make its way through the hearing process on campus and reach the stage where we would be ready to file yet still have enough time to obtain a meaningful remedy before the victim graduated. Doing nothing in the meantime, however, could be viewed as a sign that women on campus did not see the corroboration rule as offensive or facially invalid under Title IX.

I decided that the corroboration rule was too dangerous for us to wait for an actual case, and in June 2002 I filed a complaint with the OCR at the DOE on behalf of women as a class at Harvard. I argued that the corroboration rule on its face violated Title IX's regulatory mandate that Harvard respond in a "prompt and equitable" manner to sexual assault on campus.

The complaint was groundbreaking in that no OCR complaint had ever been filed under Title IX on behalf of women as a class and without an actual victim. I argued that the OCR had authority to open an investigation and preemptively prevent application of the corroboration policy, regardless of the fact that no student had yet suffered harm, because the Title IX regulation mandates "equity." I pointed out that with "equity" as its guiding legal principle, the OCR should have authority to issue "equitable" remedies, such as injunctions, much like courts of equity in the real world that routinely issue injunctions on behalf of entire classes of people in civil rights cases. Although I believed in my argument, I expected the OCR to reject the complaint on the grounds that it only decides "live controversies" and not abstract debates about policy.

Weeks later, I received notice that the OCR accepted the complaint on behalf of women as a class and would investigate Harvard under Title IX for the first time in history. This signaled that the OCR agreed with me that the corroboration rule was illegal under Title IX, because federal oversight agencies generally open investigations only when they see a need to expend resources and use their regulatory authority to coerce a change in policy or to remedy a past violation of rights.

Then president of Harvard, Lawrence Summers, when asked how he felt about Harvard being under federal investigation, replied that sexual assault had nothing to do with Title IX. I remember thinking when I heard that comment that it was a little late for Summers to object to the OCR's jurisdiction given that Harvard already was under investigation. Stranger still, if the president of the world's most prestigious university didn't understand the relationship between Title IX and sexual assault, what were the chances *any* university president saw the connection? I made a decision at that moment to ramp up efforts against other schools and to target elite schools in particular—because when schools of influence are forced to change their policies such change trickles down. When lower-tiered colleges get in trouble, change does not "trickle up." A Harvard official said to me years later, "Ms. Murphy, we are quite aware of the OCR ruling against Georgetown. Perhaps you haven't noticed, but this is not Georgetown."

During the six months that Harvard was under investigation, it tried to persuade the OCR that it should be allowed to retain a policy requiring women to produce some corroboration, even if not "sufficient" or "independent." I was shocked because I expected Harvard to be embarrassed and, as Emerson College (MA) did when it came under investigation by the OCR in 2013, apologize publicly and rush to make things right.

Despite its efforts, Harvard was forced to retract the corroboration rule and, as is typical of the OCR after a school fixes its problems, a letter was written at the end of the investigation declaring that Harvard was not in violation of Title IX. That the OCR typically deals with serious problems in such a nonpunitive way is fine, but it's confusing to the public when virtual "love letters" are issued at the conclusion of investigations. It would be more effective in terms of public awareness if the OCR regularly made clear in its decision letters that a school had been in violation, and that problems were remedied during, and because of, a federal investigation.

Word quickly spread in higher education that corroboration policies were unlawful and that students (and others) could file OCR "policy complaints" under Title IX to challenge sexual assault policies without there being an actual victim involved in the complaint process. This was revolutionary and is one of the most significant legal developments in the history of Title IX enforcement, as it greatly enhanced the ability of the OCR to clamp down on noncompliant schools. Indeed, I was able to file complaints against schools across the country, in a matter of minutes and with the push of a button, by using the OCR's online form. I wrote about this exciting new process in articles for the National Sexual Violence Resource Center and *Security on Campus* in 2003, explaining what I did in the Harvard case and describing how students could file similar complaints using Title IX's "prompt and equitable" mandate to force schools to change *any* inequitable policy. In 2006, I turned those early articles into the first-ever law review article describing the legal relationship between sexual assault and Title IX. In the years that followed, public awareness and advocacy groups expanded exponentially, as did the filing of OCR complaints.

The next big wave of public attention to the problem of campus sexual assault began in the fall of 2010 when Harvard again came under investigation. Harvard Law School hired me earlier that year to consult on a Title IX matter, in connection with which I informed them that several of their policies were noncompliant with Title IX. Harvard Law School officials knew from my 2002 corroboration rule case that I would file a complaint with the OCR if necessary, but they ignored my complaints and declined to change the law school's policies. Harvard owed me a lot of money when the day came for me to decide whether to file a complaint. I assumed that I wouldn't get paid if I filed, but I filed anyway. (Eventually Harvard did pay me.) I initially filed on behalf of a particular student after she gave me authority, in writing, to file a complaint for her because of the Title IX violations that had occurred in her specific case, but she was persuaded by women's rights advocates at Harvard Law School (MacKinnon and Rosenfeld) to change her mind on the grounds that it would be "explosive" and that Harvard officials would be furious. I filed anyway, and informed the OCR that the student had been coerced to change her mind. I urged the OCR to open an investigation on behalf of women as a class and irrespective of the student's involvement. If OCR accepted the complaint, then I could advocate for the rights of the student who had been coerced to change her mind and also address the law school's Title IX problems generally, on behalf of all women. In late fall 2010, I learned that the OCR accepted my complaint and agreed to investigate Harvard Law School for myriad Title IX policy violations on behalf of women as a class. This was great news all around because Harvard's policies had many serious problems. Additionally, because the complaint was filed before Harvard officials reached their final decision in the actual student's case then being resolved on campus, that victim prevailed in her matter.

At the same time that I filed against Harvard Law School, I also filed an OCR complaint against Princeton University on behalf of an actual victim *and* as a policy complaint. The Princeton complaint alleged many of the same violations as had been alleged in the complaint against Harvard Law School. The similarity of problems at both schools was not surprising, as I had been told of an "inter-Ivy" consortium of administrators that regularly got together to share strategies regarding the development of sexual-assault policies. I received notice from the OCR in November 2010 that my complaint against Princeton had been accepted for investigation. Among the issues to be addressed by OCR during its investigations of Harvard Law School and Princeton was that both schools were refusing to apply a "preponderance of the evidence" standard in sexual assault matters. Both schools instead imposed a much more demanding burden of proof such that the word of a credible victim was insufficient to establish a violation or justify disciplinary action against her assailant.

Later that fall, I sent both cases to the OCR's headquarters in Washington, DC, along with a letter requesting that the DOE issue some form of "global guidance" that would apply to all schools, because many of the problems at Harvard and Princeton were systemic in higher education. Letters of support for my request were sent from advocacy organizations including Security on Campus and the National Center for Higher Education Risk Management. The OCR agreed and released "global guidance" in the form of a "Dear Colleague Letter" (DCL) on April 4, 2011.

Although my 2010 cases against Harvard Law and Princeton were by far the most significant OCR investigations since the Harvard corroboration rule case almost 10 years earlier, there was almost no media attention given to those cases or, for that matter, to the issue of campus sexual assault generally, until Vice President Joseph Biden went to the University of New Hampshire to announce the DCL on April 4, 2011. The DCL was excellent, agreed with my positions on all the issues I had raised in my complaints against Harvard Law and Princeton, and provided new clarity for all schools regarding their Title IX obligations. Oddly enough, although the DCL had been written in response to my cases against Harvard Law and Princeton, Vice President Biden mentioned neither school in his announcement of the DCL. I chalked it up to politics, the fact that President Obama was a Harvard Law graduate and that the vice president did not want or need to embarrass Harvard. I didn't care. I was grateful, as an activist, that the DCL was such a strongly worded document.

Only days after the DCL was announced, however, the SaVE Act was submitted to Congress, supported by intense lobbying on behalf of higher education. Initially marketed to advocacy groups as a law that would "codify" the DCL, some of SaVE's seemingly favorable provisions were quickly removed and harmful provisions were added in their place, making it clear that the bill was intended not to codify the DCL, but rather to overturn its most helpful provisions. The members of Congress who spearheaded efforts to add harmful provisions to SaVE were mostly Democrats. For example, the person who led the charge to remove the preponderance of evidence standard from an early iteration of SaVE was Senator Patrick Leahy (D-Vt.), a self-proclaimed supporter of women's equality. Republicans were also eager to support SaVE and undermine women's educational equality. Indeed, one congressman was strikingly candid about the reason he wanted the guarantee of "equitable" treatment for women removed from an early version of SaVE.

> The majority bill said that college campuses must provide for "prompt and equitable investigation and resolution" of charges of violence or stalking. . . . But if established on a barely "more probable than not" standard, reputations can be ruined unfairly and very quickly. The substitute [which removed the word "equitable"] eliminates this provision. (Testimony of Senator Charles Grassley (R-Ia.), 158 Cong Rec. S 2761, Congressional Record, Sen., 112th Congress, 2nd Session Senate, April 26, 2012; Violence Against Women Reauthorization Act of 2011, Reference: Vol. 158, No. 61)

I spoke out aggressively against SaVE, and I wrote many columns about the bill's serious problems for Women's eNews and the *Patriot Ledger* newspaper. In several columns, I specifically criticized the lead sponsor of the Senate bill, Robert Casey (D-Pa.); in the immediate aftermath of which I was terminated as an advisory board member from the nonprofit group *Security on Campus*, which is based in Pennsylvania, Casey's congressional district. I suffered many other forms of retaliation. When I publicly criticized Senator Kirsten Gillibrand (D-N.Y.), for her role in supporting SaVE and another law that would diminish women's rights on campus, for instance, my invitation to speak at Buffalo State University was rescinded.

I sent my columns criticizing SaVE to various listservs, and tried to rally the voices of groups that purported to be advocating for women's equality. Every establishment group stayed silent, however, including Legal Momentum and the National Women's Law Center. One brave soul from the National Organization for Women complained about the bill, but then lost her position at NOW. Then even that group fell silent.

When a few grassroots advocates started complaining, the bill's popular title was renamed from the "Campus SaVE Act" to the "Clery

Amendment"—a tactic obviously designed to confuse people about whether there was more than one bill, and whether problems with SaVE had been repaired by the seemingly new "Clery Amendment." When criticisms of the bill began to mount, SaVE was tacked on to the Violence Against Women Reauthorization Act, which is a major funding bill for women's and victims' groups, and everyone clammed up. SaVE's proponents assured advocacy groups that SaVE would not weaken Title IX because it was technically filed as an amendment to Clery, not as an amendment to Title IX itself. That distinction was intellectually dishonest, however, because Congress routinely amends federal laws indirectly by modifying *related* laws. SaVE was *obviously* related to Title IX, and it would undermine women's civil rights because it gave schools explicit permission to treat *all* violence against women under second-class legal standards on campus.

SaVE sailed through Congress, supported by student advocates such as Laura Dunn, Alexandra Brodsky, and Andrea Pino, all of whom were given positions of prominence and opportunities to create "training" programs and websites that touted SaVE as a good thing. None of these women or the groups that they founded—such as "Know your IX"—provide information about the numerous ways in which SaVE subjects victimized women to second-class treatment on campus, affords women lesser legal protection than Title IX, and prevents effective oversight by the OCR.

WHY PARTICULAR PROVISIONS IN SaVE ARE HARMFUL TO WOMEN

By far the most serious overarching problem with SaVE is a provision allowing schools to not provide "equitable" treatment for victimized women. Under Title IX "equitable" treatment is mandatory, but under SaVE, Congress replaced the word "equitable" with "fair," thus allowing schools to treat victimized women under inequitable standards. The word "equitable" is critically important because it means a school's policies must not only be relatively fair, but also must be substantively on par with standards applied in the redress of all other civil rights violence on campus based on categories such as race and national origin. That Congress would remove the word "equitable" is disturbing. That Congress would do so in 2013 with the support of students and women's rights groups is hard to believe, and suggests that advocates were intellectually unable to appreciate the problem, or were being misled about the legal importance of the word "equitable," or were willing to compromise women's equality in exchange for money because of the bill's funding provisions that would pay advocacy groups to conduct training and education programs. At minimum, women's and victims' groups could have and should have insisted that language be included in SaVE declaring that the law "shall not be construed to weaken Title IX," because such language is commonly included in statutes that *might* be interpreted as allowing the diminution of civil rights. This would have enabled advocates to at least argue that "equitable" redress is mandatory irrespective of SaVE, but that language was not included because nobody asked for it.

Other important problems with SaVE include the following:

- Schools can define *civil rights* violence against women using much more onerous *criminal law definitions* when assessing whether a victim suffered a *civil rights* injury. For example, under SaVE, whether a sexual assault occurred is measured by whether the victim did not "consent," and whether "force" was used. Prior to SaVE, a sexual assault under Title IX could be defined *only* by whether the act was "unwelcome" and "offensive." These are much easier standards to prove than "non-consent" and "force." More importantly, women's autonomy is better protected under Title IX because "unwelcome" is entirely a subjective question, which means the victim *alone* gets to decide whether she *wanted* another person's sexual contact. Under criminal law standards such as "non-consent," "force," and even "affirmative consent" and "'yes' means 'yes'" rules, a woman does *not* have exclusive authority to decide who touches her because her subjective experience of nonconsent is offset by her attacker's claimed *perception* of her nonconsent. Simply put, under criminal law definitions, a victim's 100% authority over her body is diminished by the amount of weight a school chooses to accord an offender's claimed mistaken opinion about a victim's actual authority. This diminution of women's autonomy is illegal under Title IX's "unwelcomeness" standard, but is permitted under SaVE's criminal law provisions. Additionally, because SaVE applies *only* to violence against women, SaVE harms *only* women's autonomy on college campuses. This is because "unwelcomeness" remains a mandatory definition in the redress of all other civil rights violence when it occurs on the basis of categories such as race and national origin.

- Schools can impose a burden of proof more onerous than "preponderance of the evidence." "Preponderance" means that if a student victim's report is slightly more credible than her attacker's denial of responsibility, then the school must take effective steps to redress the harm. Before SaVE was enacted, and under the DCL, the "preponderance" standard was mandatory. But SaVE gave schools authority to apply a greater burden of proof such that a victim's report—even if more credible than an offender's denial—would be deemed inherently inadequate to establish that an offense occurred. Regulations enacted in 2014 purport to forbid schools to apply a burden of proof more onerous than preponderance, but regulations cannot trump federal statutes, which means schools that want to apply a more onerous burden of proof will point to the language of SaVE as giving them authority to do so, and note, correctly, that a statute predominates a regulation.

- Schools can "run out the clock" on a victim's complaint such that a final determination is not reached for years, if ever. This means a victim might never learn that her rights were violated and, even if she does, she will have no meaningful recourse. This is because although the OCR technically has jurisdiction to resolve a complaint even after a victim completes her education, a victim has no hope of achieving equitable redress on campus—or educational equality— after graduation.

- The OCR has only limited authority to hold schools accountable for the mistreatment of victims because it has no jurisdiction to address violations of victims' rights when they occur under SaVE or under generic misconduct policies. To prove this point, with the help of my law student Alison Shea, I sent a policy complaint to every regional OCR office in the country right after SaVE took effect in March 2014, asking for an investigation to be opened against schools whose generic sexual misconduct policies—which had been adopted in 2013 pursuant to SaVE—violated Title IX. In every instance I received a letter stating that the OCR has no authority to review violations of rights when they occur under generic misconduct policies or SaVE. This limitation on the OCR's authority arguably is the most dangerous aspect of SaVE because although the OCR is more coercive than punitive, it nevertheless gave students and their families at least some hope that a school *could* be held accountable for treating a victim unfairly. Not surprisingly, after SaVE's enactment schools began relying on "advisors" and "counselors" to persuade victims to choose redress under generic misconduct polices and SaVE, rather than under Title IX. These "advisors" and "counselors" do not tell victims that the consequences of choosing redress under anything other than Title IX. They are not told that the choice results in worse legal standards being applied; that the victim's inherent credibility is devalued; the policies are not "equtable"; the definitions of offenses do not protect the victim's autonomy; *and* the victim then has no recourse with the OCR if her rights are violated. These "advisors" and "counselors" often are paid consultants working for the schools— which raises serious conflict of interest concerns. Even seemingly independent organizations such as the Victims' Rights Law Center often have financial ties to the very schools that send them victims seeking advice and counseling. Even more disturbing, many schools have the victims *file* their complaints under Title IX, but after the victim receives "advice and counseling" those complaints are downgraded to non–Title IX matters and are treated as generic misconduct problems under SaVE. The victim, however, *thinks* that her case is being handled under Title IX every step of the way, because she *filed* it as a Title IX matter with the Title IX coordinator.

- Schools cannot be held responsible for what they "should have" known. Before SaVE and under the DCL, schools were responsible for all incidents—reported or unreported—about which officials had constructive knowledge such that they "knew or should have known." Because SaVE requires actual "reports," the "should have known" rule is no longer applicable. This is particularly dangerous for women because it gives school officials an added incentive to "look the other way" to avoid "actual" knowledge—even in the face of reasonable grounds to believe that actual harm has occurred.

Collectively, problems with SaVE create falsely low incidence rates, and it is very difficult for the public to prove falseness. Although police reports—as public records—might reveal discrepancies, many victims do not file police reports. Regardless, most schools have memoranda of understanding with civilian law-enforcement officials such that police files are treated as confidential school records. A proposed new federal law, known popularly as the Campus Safety and Accountability Act (CASA), will make these memoranda of understanding mandatory.

Reporting rates similarly are difficult to assess for accuracy because of SaVE, but certainly will decline given that SaVE significantly limits the OCR's jurisdiction, makes violence against women more difficult to prove, and does not require "equitable" treatment of women. Reporting rates already were abysmally low before SaVE, primarily because victims did not want to bear the burdens and added traumas associated with seeking redress. SaVE adds even more burdens to the plight of victims, thus it further inhibits reporting.

WHERE DID SaVE COME FROM?

SaVE came from the higher education lobby. Obviously, women would never have supported SaVE if they had known from the beginning that SaVE was designed to undermine women's rights. Between the time that SaVE first was filed with Congress in 2011 and when it took effect three years later, however, SaVE was heavily marketed in the media as a law that would be great for women. Even *Ms. Magazine* trumpeted SaVE as a good law for women in a strange article that lacked meaningful insight or legal analysis (Heldman & Dirks 2014).

Several victims were featured in news stories leading up to SaVE's enactment, and, although they no doubt were sincerely committed to the cause, they had no way of knowing how dangerous SaVE was. Some students even testified before Congress in support of SaVE without understanding why SaVE was such an offensive law and how they were being used to facilitate support for the explicit subjugation and mistreatment of women.

In 2011 problems with SaVE were being ignored, but Yale was taking a lot of heat for being under investigation by the OCR. There was no press whatsoever about the fact that the Yale investigation had been spawned by people at Harvard, however. Women's rights advocates at Harvard Law School contacted students at Yale right after learning that the OCR would investigate Harvard Law School. They offered themselves up to the Yale students (unsolicited) to "help" them with their sexual harassment problem on campus. (Yale had been in the news because a group of men on campus got together and chanted, "No means yes, yes means anal.") The Yale students felt fortunate to have legal help from Harvard Law School—and had no idea that they were being used to provide cover for Harvard. The Harvard women who offered to help did not reveal to the Yale students that Harvard Law School already was under federal investigation. They did, however, tell the Yale students that they wished to remain anonymous while they helped the students secretly prepare an OCR complaint against Yale.

Prior to being contacted by people from Harvard, the Yale students had no plans to file an OCR complaint. The Women's Center at Yale reportedly was shocked upon learning that students had filed an OCR complaint in March 2011 and that it had been instigated by Harvard. That OCR complaint was accepted for investigation only two weeks later—just days before Vice President Biden's long-planned visit to the University of New Hampshire (UNH) on April 4 to announce the DCL. The public learned that Yale would be investigated by the OCR from numerous news stories published only days before the vice president's visit to UNH. It appeared to the public, however, that the DCL had been issued *because of* Yale when, in fact, the DCL was issued *because of* Harvard Law and Princeton. Yale was but a convenient whipping girl.

This is not to say that Yale didn't deserve to be investigated. It did, and I soon became a consultant on a novel lawsuit against Yale on behalf of an employee there who suffered retaliation for years' worth of efforts to force Yale to comply with Title IX. The lawsuit was the first time that an employee—not a student—sued under Title IX for retaliation endured as a result of her efforts to make Yale respond more effectively to sexual assault on campus.

Harvard, Princeton, and Yale all had similar policy problems, including that they applied a burden of proof more onerous than mere preponderance.

The vast majority of universities at the time were correctly applying the preponderance standard in accordance with federal law, but many elite schools stubbornly refused. The complaints I filed against Harvard and Princeton in 2010 eventually forced both schools to adopt the preponderance rule. The University of Virginia (UVA) though not an Ivy League school also had been refusing to apply the preponderance rule, until I filed an OCR complaint against it in 2009. Frustratingly, even after the standard itself was changed at UVA, school officials there failed to *apply* the standard correctly. For example, they would find a victim compelling and credible, but then rule in favor of the perpetrator.

Although the OCR typically resolves complaints within 180 days (U.S. Department of Education, Office for Civil Rights 2005; noting that the OCR resolved 91% of complaints within its benchmark 180-day time limit), Harvard Law and Princeton remained under investigation on their 2010 complaints for four years—longer than any other school. Even after the DCL was issued in 2011 and clearly and directly addressed all the issues then under investigation at both schools, the schools remained under investigation while SaVE was becoming law from 2011 to 2014. During this time, many lower-tier schools made headlines for coming under investigation by the OCR, yet those news stories either ignored SaVE altogether, touted it as a good thing, or were very misleading about the bill's many dangerous provisions.

No newspaper correctly reported on the story, but one of the most misleading stories by far was published in the *New York Times*. In March 2013 it published a front-page story that showcased problems at the University of North Carolina and Occidental College, and specifically noted that students at the University of North Carolina "had taken inspiration, and a few strategic cues, from students who last fall drew attention to the mishandling of sexual assaults at Amherst College in Massachusetts. The Amherst students had, in turn, consulted extensively with women at Yale" (Pérez-Peña 2013). That *New York Times* story failed to note that Yale, which came under investigation in 2011, was *not* the school that started it all, and did not mention that Harvard Law School and Princeton had been under investigation by the OCR for violating Title IX since 2010, *long before Yale and Amherst*. The *New York Times* simply left out any mention of Harvard and Princeton. The paper also failed to note that the Yale investigation was *instigated by Harvard Law School* right after Harvard learned that it would be investigated by the OCR, although many knew that story, too. Most significantly, the *New York Times* said nothing about problems with SaVE— or even noted that SaVE had been signed into law only days earlier, on March 7, 2013 (slated to take effect one year later). It also was not stated that SaVE potentially would benefit Harvard Law School and Princeton in connection with the OCR's then-pending investigations of both schools, because SaVE gave all schools permission to do many of the things that had been illegal before SaVE—the very actions for which Harvard and Princeton were being investigated.

In an interesting development a year later, right after SaVE took effect in March 2014, the *New York Times* wrote another substantial story about campus sexual assault involving Florida State University. That story, like others, nowhere mentioned Harvard Law School, Princeton, or problems with SaVE. Weeks after that misleading story ran, the executive editor at the *New York Times*, Jill Abramson, was fired without explanation. She is an alumna of Harvard Business School.

One of the many obvious problems with such news coverage is that parents are led to believe that their daughters are safer at elite schools, even though the opposite seems to be the case. In my experience, elite schools have some of the highest incidence rates of violence against women, probably because they have the greatest concentrations of the most entitled males, and because these schools take the most aggressive steps to hide the truth because they have the most to lose in terms of money and reputation. The media routinely fail to apprise families of this fact, or of the fact that women are arguably more likely to be sexually assaulted if they go to college than if they do not. Women are even more likely to be sexually assaulted in college than in the hypermasculine environment of the military (Defense Manpower Data Center 2013, 2). These disturbing facts are cruelly ironic given that Title IX was enacted to provide women *better* protection from violence and discrimination in the "special" environment of education as compared to the "real world." This utterly backward result is the product of inadequate external oversight mechanisms that hold schools accountable and ensure effective enforcement of Title IX.

For example, although Title IX lawsuits can be filed against schools that violate women's rights, they are very difficult to win because a victim must prove that school officials had actual knowledge of a problem and were "deliberately indifferent" thereafter. Schools have long understood the need to avoid liability by offering victims support and counseling to ensure that they do not appear "indifferent." Such an onerous liability standard inhibits lawyers from filing suit in most cases.

Oversight agencies such as the OCR offer victims a less burdensome option because complaints can be filed at no cost and without proof of deliberate indifference, and the OCR can bring pressure to bear on noncompliant schools. But the remedies are meager because the OCR is coercive, not punitive. Few cases even make it to the OCR anymore because the OCR only has jurisdiction to deal with Title IX and not with violations of rights under generic misconduct policies and SaVE. Additionally, victims at most schools are being unwittingly coerced to accept redress only under generic misconduct policies and SaVE.

Although other federal agencies such as the Department of Justice (DOJ) can get involved in certain cases and even can impose substantial fines against noncompliant schools, the DOJ—presumably for political reasons—intervenes in matters involving violence against women. No school ever has suffered a financial sanction—not even for the most egregious violations of Title IX.

Without meaningful oversight and accountability, schools have a powerful incentive to favor offenders and mistreat victims, not because schools want rape to occur but because favoring offenders helps schools avoid public scandals and expensive lawsuits. Not surprisingly, new research shows that this unconscionable approach causes substantial harm not only to victims but also to their families. This unique form of suffering is known as "institutional betrayal trauma," which occurs when trust is shattered by the systematic discrediting of victims alongside institutionalized disrespect for their suffering (Smith & Freyd 2013). Other recent data from a survey of students at Boston College arguably corroborate this betrayal theory, as they show that women graduate from Boston College feeling less confident than when they entered. This loss of confidence seems a predictable result at any university where secrecy is prioritized over openness and accountability, and where women are subjected to second-class treatment in response to gender-based violence—the most severe expression of sex discrimination.

My cases against Harvard Law and Princeton were not resolved until late 2014, long after SaVE's March 7, 2014, effective date. The OCR determined in both cases that the schools' policies were noncompliant with Title IX, as I had alleged in my complaints four years earlier. I won the Princeton case in November 2014, although interestingly no reporter who wrote about the case contacted me or mentioned me in a story. Accounts did, however, quote "advocates" who had nothing to do with my case, but who supported the enactment of SaVE and work closely with schools to deter victims from pursuing redress on campus exclusively under Title IX. When I won my case against Harvard Law School a month later, the same thing happened. Even the *Boston Globe* interviewed people who had nothing to do with my case, and the reporters not only barely mentioned me in a throwaway line on the second page of the article, they literally wrote that Murphy "claims" that she filed the complaint that ended with an unprecedented victory against Harvard Law School. This from reporters who *knew* it was my case because the *Globe* had written about it in 2010 when I first filed suit.

The OCR ruled that both Harvard and Princeton would remain under scrutiny by OCR while further modifications were made to their policies because even after a four-year investigation the revised versions still had problematic provisions. Some of those problems must be addressed in future federal lawsuits and through OCR complaints, in which advocates should challenge the constitutional legitimacy of *any* provision in *any* policy that subjects victimized women to disparate policies and legal standards in connection with the redress of gender-based violence.

I raised a host of constitutional objections to SaVE's disparate treatment provisions in a landmark federal lawsuit filed right before SaVE's effective date in March 2014. With help from the "Godmother of Title IX," Dr. Bernice Sandler, I drafted a long and detailed complaint against the DOE and the Department of Health and Human Services (DHHS). I filed suit with help from my local counsel, James Marsh, in the Federal District Court for the District of Columbia. We asked the court to issue an order forbidding the enforcement of SaVE on the grounds that its disparate legal standards violate women's equal protection and due process rights. We also argued that SaVE was unconstitutional because Congress has no authority to regulate violence against women or sexual violence of any kind. Hence, it can hardly claim authority to legislate the legal standards schools must apply in the redress of gender-based violence on college campuses. A major purpose of the lawsuit was to increase pressure on the parties drafting regulations pursuant to SaVE—regulations that were supposed to provide more detailed definitions of certain statutory terms that had been enacted in SaVE.

The lawsuit was filed specifically on behalf of a victim from UVA, but it also implicated Harvard Law School and Princeton. We urged the federal court to approve the suit prior to March 7, 2014, because my UVA client had a case pending at the OCR, and if her case were analyzed under pre-SaVE standards, we would prevail. If the case was analyzed under SaVE's worse standards, however, we would lose. We included Harvard Law School in the lawsuit because that investigation had been opened on behalf of women as a class and we were trying to stop SaVE on behalf of a particular UVA client and for all women. We included references to the Princeton investigation because the OCR in that case refused to say whether it would apply SaVE's standards if that investigation was resolved after March 7.

After refusing to even accept our complaint for docketing for more than a week, the federal court finally approved the suit to proceed at the end of the day on March 6, 2014. Attorney General Eric Holder filed a response on behalf of the DOE and the DHHS on May 20, 2014, in which he avoided the constitutional questions and urged the federal court to dismiss the lawsuit on procedural grounds. The administration's silence on SaVE's constitutional defects to me was a concession of Mr. Holder's awareness that SaVE is unfair to women. Tellingly, President Obama made public comments right after my lawsuit was filed indicating a need for reparative legislation and an executive order. Soon thereafter, Senator Claire McCaskill convened new hearings on the issue of campus sexual assault. McCaskill, Senator Kirsten Gillibrand, and others ultimately proposed new legislation in a bill known as "CASA," which enables schools to further avoid accountability for the mistreatment of victimized women by allowing greater secrecy of victims' reports to school officials and civilian law enforcement officials, and by enabling schools to partner with confidential "advisors" and "counselors" who are not obligated to file formal, counted reports to responsible school officials.

A few weeks after we filed suit to stop SaVE, Dr. Sandler and I were invited to address an alumni group at Harvard. I explained the problems with SaVE in general and the issues with Harvard's sexual assault policy in particular because of its reliance on SaVE. I emphasized the need for Harvard to adopt a singular umbrella policy that would address violence against women under the exact same standards as violence against other protected-class categories, such as race and national origin. About a month later, Harvard announced a revised policy in which several of SaVE's most dangerous provisions were removed. The policy guaranteed "equitable" redress, mandated application of a "preponderance of the evidence" standard, and removed all criminal law definitions of offenses in favor of civil rights definitions. This rejection of criminal terms such as "force" and "non-consent," in favor of "unwelcome" and "offensive" was particularly important as it was an unprecedented embrace of a legal standard that would expressly value women's autonomy by assessing only her subjective experience, without regard for an offender's mistaken opinion of her actual state of mind. This bold move set Harvard apart as being the best of the elite schools on this key issue, which soon led to protests from Harvard professors who complained on behalf of offenders that applying a subjective test would be unfair to perpetrators. I published an op-ed in the *Boston Globe* at the end of 2014 and rebutted that claim and pointed out that, under civil rights laws, an offender who truly believes that he has permission to act is protected by civil rights laws because they require not only proof of "unwelcomeness" but also of "offensiveness." This legal buffer means an unwelcome act will not lead to sanctions unless decision makers on campus find that the act also was objectively "offensive." All schools would be wise to follow Harvard's lead and abandon the use of criminal law terms in favor of "unwelcome and offensive," because the use of criminal terms eventually leads to costly civil rights lawsuits in which victims argue that application of civil rights definitions is mandatory in the redress of all forms of violence against women.

Harvard's new policy is excellent on "unwelcomeness," but remains problematic in other ways, including that it allows victims' complaints to drag on for years before a "final determination" is made. Still, its rejection of SaVE's worse substantive standards was a big step in the right direction.

In early 2015, our federal lawsuit to stop SaVE was dismissed on procedural grounds, which means the court declined to reach the constitutional questions. This is an all too common result of impact litigation aimed at developing strong doctrinal support for women's full constitutional equality. The lawsuit was successful in many ways nonetheless because it had been held up as a "Damocles Sword" for an entire year, which forced schools everywhere to adopt the preponderance of evidence standard. The ruling also was helpful in that it included a determination that SaVE can have "no effect" on Title IX, which in time should trickle down to prevent schools from applying disparate standards in response to any form of sexual violence on campus. Federal courts and agencies over the years consistently have ruled that *all* sexual assaults are civil rights matters, and although a school can have two different policies—one labeled "Title IX" and one labeled "sexual misconduct"—the legal standards must be the same for both and both sets of standards must comply with civil rights laws.

The lawsuit also had an important effect on federal regulations that were being drafted pursuant to SaVE while my lawsuit was pending. When the regulations were released at the end of 2014—right before my suit was dismissed—many of SaVE's constitutional defects identified in the lawsuit were repaired, including most significantly SaVE's use of *mandatory* language that required schools to adopt disparate policies for women. The regulations made clear that there were no mandates, that SaVE was a discretionary bill, and that, despite SaVE's use of terms such as "shall," schools could opt out altogether, reject SaVE in its entirety, and choose to apply *only* Title IX's fully equitable standards to all matters involving violence against women. It remains to be seen how courts will interpret a regulatory attempt to turn a mandatory statutory term into a permissive one, and I am dubious that a substantive provision within a regulation ever can be construed to "redefine" or "trump" a federal statute when the statutory language is clear. Simply put, a school that wants to ignore provisions in the regulations that are good for women lawfully can do so on the grounds that a statute is stronger than a regulation. This controversy surely will lead to future litigation in which the larger constitutional questions about Congress' authority to enact SaVE in the first place, and secondly to *mandate* that schools mistreat women, will need to be addressed.

The lawsuit's effect on Harvard was particularly important because it inspired officials there to do the right thing; when Harvard sets high standards, other schools fall in line. This bodes well for my client from UVA, whose OCR case (as of this writing) is still pending, and involves especially shocking allegations of egregious misconduct. For example, UVA's forensic nurse, Kathryn Laughon, not only changed a medical report to state falsely that there were no vaginal injuries consistent with sexual assault (there were many), she also "lost" or destroyed photographs *that she took* of the victim's vaginal injuries after applying a special dye and inserting a catheter. The nurse's original medical report noted, and of course the victim recalled, that many such photographs were taken, but none were mentioned at the hearing on campus at which the nurse instead informed the board that there were no injuries consistent with sexual assault. The board found in favor of the offender and noted the absence of genital injuries as one of the reasons for its determination.

When the victim's family read the board's decision and saw the conclusion that there were "no injures," they asked the UVA nurse and the UVA hospital where the rape exam was conducted for copies of the photographs depicting the injuries. The hospital balked at the family's request and the family complained to university officials demanding that the photographs be produced. A frustrating series of e-mails went back and forth before a dean (who later resigned) replied that the photographs did not exist.

The victim's family was incredulous. How could the photographs "not exist"? They appealed the school's ruling without the benefit of the photographs, and the university rendered its final decision in favor of the offender in June 2012. I then filed various complaints with several oversight entitles including the nursing licensing board in Virginia and the association that certifies Sexual Assault Nurse Examiners (SANE) because the UVA nurse claimed to be "certified" by the SANE association. I also filed complaints with several federal agencies including the DOJ and the OCR at the DOE under Title IV and Title IX, and filed an unprecedented complaint with the little-known OCR at the DHHS because that agency handles Title IX complaints when violations occur in connection with health care on campus.

Shockingly, the nursing licensing board in Virginia concluded that the nurse—who changed the victim's medical record to state that there were no injuries and who couldn't account for the lost photographs—did nothing wrong. The SANE association also did nothing because it claimed it had no authority to discipline a SANE-trained nurse who violated SANE protocols by failing to preserve photographs or to even create a log to identify the number and type of photographs taken.

I pointed out to the various agencies the many conflicts of interest in the case, including that the nurse who was supposed to be an objective medical professional was employed by UVA and was married to a senior prosecutor in the county attorney's office (which had declined to file criminal charges). It goes without saying that a powerful university should not have close ties with law enforcement and other civilian authorities responsible for making discretionary decisions about whether campus sexual assault cases are investigated and prosecuted. Yet such close ties are exceedingly common and often provide exactly the sort of insulation from accountability that enables schools to violate women's civil rights with impunity.

Lacking the same legacy and political "value" and influence as male offenders, victimized women often are at the mercy of school officials who are highly motivated to rule against them. It is no wonder then that from one in three to one in five women is likely to be sexually assaulted in college (Freyd et al. 2014, one in three; Humphrey and White 2000, one in four; Krebs et al. 2009, one in five). Even using the more conservative one in five statistic, and considering that about six million women currently are enrolled as undergraduates in four-year schools, this means that *more than a million of these women will experience sexual assault during college*. This number is substantially greater than the number of students who suffer any other type of interpersonal violence on campus.

Indeed, although no formal comparative data exist, violence against women clearly is more prevalent than all other forms of civil rights harassment and violence against students from other protected-class categories combined (U.S. Department of Justice 2001; the report did not measure gender-based bias crimes and found an average of only 3.8 hate crimes on campus for all of 1998, for a total of 334 incidents in 411 schools. During the same period, the FBI ascertained that 241 incidents of hate crimes were reported from 222 of 450 schools.) This disturbing fact has been ignored for decades—even though in the early 1970s Congress member Shirley Chisholm remarked during congressional hearings to support the passage of Title IX that during her political career she had endured far more discrimination on the basis of sex than she ever endured on the basis of her status as an African American.

Whether the correct number is one in four or one in five, it bears repeating that this number is arguably greater than the number of women who do not attend college and are sexually assaulted. Women are even more likely to be sexually assaulted in college as compared to women in the hypermasculine environment of the military (Defense Manpower Data Center 2013, 2). One in six women experiences "unwanted sexual contact"; a number that is less than the rate on campus even though the military uses a much broader definition of harm as compared to the definition of "sexual assault" used to measure incidents on campus.

It should come as no surprise then that women are more likely to report sexual assault in larger society: 36% of rapes, 34% of attempted rapes, and 26% of sexual assaults are reported to police (Rennison 2002); and in the military: 46% reporting rate (U.S. Commission on Civil Rights 2013), as compared to colleges which have a 12% reporting rate (Kilpatrick et al. 2007). These data suggest that the military and "real-world" systems, although woefully inadequate at addressing violence against women, are more likely to hold offenders accountable as compared to the colleges and universities systems.

It might be easier (and cheaper) in the short term for schools to sweep violence against women under the rug by claiming that cases are difficult to resolve "he said–she said" situations; this rarely is true. In fact, most cases are more fairly described as "she said–he took the Fifth," or "she said–he hired a lawyer," or "she said–he lied." A disturbing number of cases involve not only careful planning but also the intentional use of rape drugs—which is a convenient strategy for an offender who is hoping to avoid responsibility. A victim who can't remember what happened certainly can't file a report. Drugs that cause amnesia are cheap and easy to get on the Internet, or can be made in a dorm room sink with materials available at Home Depot. By the time a victim recovers a reliable—if fuzzy—memory about what happened, any hope of finding drugs in her blood or urine is long gone because rape drugs dissipate quickly. Schools are well aware that rape drugs are a serious problem, yet most rely on the absence of forensic proof as an excuse to do nothing on the grounds that the absence of memory makes the case unprovable.

Schools that sincerely care about preventing drug-facilitated attacks should adopt clear policies informing all students that an inference of drugging will be drawn from behavioral symptoms alone—irrespective of negative forensic tests—and that victims will be given access to hair-testing technology at no cost, because rape drugs remain detectable in hair for months and studies show that hair testing is an extremely effective method of detection (Kintz 1996). As compared with urinalysis, the rate of detection using hair samples far supersedes that of urine samples for a wide variety of drugs. Simply changing school policy to alert students that there is a drug-testing policy is an effective deterrent to drugging (Martinez 1998), and the very existence of hair-testing procedures, along with inferences from behavioral symptoms alone, will reduce incidence rates on campus by deterring some offenders. Indeed, studies suggest that the more robust the testing policy the greater the deterrent effect (Martinez 1998).

Important new research found that perpetrators of sexual assault on campus are not heterogeneous, and that one in four male college students commits an act of sexual coercion by the end of his fourth year (Swartout et al. 2015). Studies also show that many perpetrators are repeat offenders (Lisak & Miller 2002). These data compel schools to understand the benefits of taking swift and harsh steps in response to first-time offenders as another obvious way to keep incidence rates low.

It might seem preferable to simply side with an offender by imposing some of the blame on victims who become incapacitated, but this approach ignores the findings of numerous studies that show that alcohol isn't a cause of rape so much it is a weapon used by offenders to facilitate the offense by targeting vulnerable victims who have been drinking. Schools that decline to act by allocating responsibility—as if the victim attacked herself—and by exploiting a victim's feelings of self-blame, only motivate predatory offenders to target intoxicated victims and help cause their incapacitation. Schools should work harder to change the harmful narrative that most sexual assaults on campus are nothing more than "bad sex" or "sex with a buzz." If individual autonomy is to be valued, then harm-doers must always bear the burden of restraint and the risk of getting in trouble if they choose to act against a student whose capacity to make decisions is diminished. Policies should make very clear that *diminished capacity is a vulnerability, not a liability,* and that unclear situations regarding whether a person is "too intoxicated" to make a voluntary decision should evoke feelings of reluctance, and not titillation.

In addition to adopting a more civilized approach to situations involving intoxication, schools that properly apply the "preponderance of the evidence" will better deter violence against women by holding many more offenders accountable. Holding schools accountable for correctly applying a burden of proof is not easy, however, and many schools—despite having a "preponderance" standard in place as a matter of policy—will *apply* a more onerous burden of proof on victims. This allows officials to *claim* that they believe the victim, to send her off to counseling but continue to receive tuition payments from her parents, and to claim that they simply didn't believe the victim *enough* to justify punishment of her attacker.

Blaming a victim's inadequate credibility for a school's inability to punish an offender shifts responsibility away from the school, much like "bystander" programs shift responsibility. There's nothing wrong with asking students to help protect each other from harm, but the problem of rampant sexual assault on campus will not get better because school officials tell women not to drink and tell bystanders to watch out for them if they do drink. Sexual assault rates will diminish when women are respected as fully equal citizens at all times—including when they seek redress on campus in the aftermath of sexual assault.

Schools have been getting away with treating women unequally for a very long time, in part by not teaching students to understand Title IX as a civil rights law that applies to sexual assault matters on campus, and by using tactics that deter victims from filing reports and seeking redress. For decades after Title IX was enacted, and to this day, if a victim asks for help, barely able to talk because her body is sore from her mouth to her knees, and she cannot relate what happened because she was drugged or she simply cannot not bring herself to face the horrifying reality of having been violated by a trusted fellow student, it is common for school officials to advise her to "move on" and focus on her studies. Most victims heed this advice because they desperately want to believe that moving on will make everything OK, but the reality is much more grim. Simply moving on fixes nothing and usually makes things worse. In fact, research shows that unresolved trauma has long-term consequences that recur over the lifespan (Chadwick's Child Maltreatment 2014; McCloskey 1997). If the victim accepts the advice to "move on," however, then the problem—at least for the school and for the moment—goes away.

Yet, unjustly refusing to hold offenders accountable, and relying on boondoggle policies adopted under SaVE to legitimize inaction, will be increasingly costly to schools in many ways. For example, victims are more aware of their rights today than ever before, and they are much more willing to file civil lawsuits even if the case will not result in substantial damage award. Moreover, SaVE requires tremendous time and resources, but swift and equitable enforcement of Title IX—and only Title IX—does not. Most importantly, any school that adopts SaVE and authorizes the systematic unfair treatment of an entire class of people will suffer a loss of civility on campus as the university itself becomes weak at its core. To adopt SaVE is to authorize the second-class treatment of women, which causes students to internalize harmful ideas about the value of women in society. After graduation, women and men graduates alike enter the real world scarred with toxic feelings about women, like leaves that in spring-time emerge shriveled from a rotting tree.

A school's values do not exist in Latin words on shiny crests; they live in the actions of its representatives. Some university officials simply do not understand why sexual assaults on campus are so destructive to the fabric of an academic community and so ruinous to the human condition. How can a single act be at once devastating to one person and profoundly pleasurable to another? This question often is at the center of campus disputes and is pondered by decision makers who assess conflicting information through the biased lenses of their own sexual life experiences. Such biases produce unfair results in both directions, with males (usually) identifying with the offender and females (usually) identifying more with the victim.

That two people could feel exceedingly different emotions about the same event makes simple solutions seem elusive. If the frame through which the problem is evaluated is oriented around ideas such as personal autonomy and bodily integrity rather than sex, however, then resolving disputes is simple. Put bluntly, the old adage "my right to swing my fist ends before it hits you in the nose" applies to penises and vaginas, too. Higher-education officials should be focused on guiding the millions of young people in their care toward a deep understanding of why individual autonomy and women's full equality—not sex—are the driving forces behind a school's antiviolence policies.

Although effective solutions won't come from universities alone, leadership that begins in academia has the potential to change behavior far beyond the campus environs—starting with aggressive classroom attention to autonomy theory, alongside consistent application of disciplinary rules that promote the value of each student's exclusive right to decide the circumstances under which another person gains intimate access to his or her body.

Training and education programs are fine, but people cannot be taught not to rape any more than they can be taught not to be racist. Meaningful prevention requires changing the way students think about women and sex, and giving them a compelling reason to think differently—for example, by comparing sexual assault to slavery. No, they aren't exactly the same social harms, but *freedom and authority over the self are compromised in both contexts.* Just as we enlighten young people to reject the argument that some African American slaves "liked" working in the fields even though they were not free to choose otherwise, we need to teach young people to reject claims that there is freedom to be had in a woman's "choice" to be penetrated violently while barely conscious. There isn't.

To be sure, sexual violence emanates not only from a failure of university leadership, but also from a long history of gender inequality in society. Laws related to civil rights in education were not expected to change things overnight, but today—more than 40 years after the enactment of Title IX—women have waited long enough.

For centuries, universities have enjoyed a place of privilege in society, although some believe that it is an undeserved privilege and that higher education is like any other industry except for the benevolent gloss and tax-exempt status. Higher education, however, remains a source of hope for those of us who feel confident that, even as most industries strive only to produce better profits, most colleges and universities sincerely endeavor to produce better people.

Better people do not graduate from universities where sexual assault occurs with impunity. Better people come from schools where equality for women is as important as equality for everyone—including gays, Irish, Muslims, African Americans, and students with disabilities. The very idea that the redress of violence against women should be subjected to worse legal standards as compared to violence against all other students on campus is offensive to the essence of what it means to be a college student in the United States. Women do not need solicitous protection or "special" rights. They want, need, and deserve only meaningful equality in the critically important environment of higher education—where our next generation of leaders, parents, lovers, spouses, friends, and neighbors is living, growing, and learning together about how the world works—and where women fit in. Nobody should leave college having *learned* that violence against women is more acceptable and less serious than targeted violence against any other class of people; yet, under SaVE, that is exactly what Congress has authorized universities to teach their students.

Most schools would be embarrassed to have a reputation as being a place where victimized women are subjected to unequal treatment. This is why all college presidents should proudly speak out against rape the way that the University of Oklahoma president spoke out against racism in 2015—with immediate and public condemnation and the punishment of offenders. Indeed, sexist violence always is a more serious civil rights injury than are racist words. Too many of the most influential university presidents don't care what the public thinks about gender discrimination and sexual violence on campus, however; and they have enough power to get away with not caring.

Let's hope that this is the type of power that parents increasingly find repulsive when they think about where to send their children to college. Schools that treat women as fully equal citizens on campus should be rewarded with lots of tuition dollars and loud public support. Schools that do not should be publicly shamed by those of us who find it abhorrent that girls and women are safer not becoming educated, and that even after half a century of civil rights laws too many schools think this situation is just fine.

REFERENCES

Berry v. Chicago Transit Authority, 618 F.3d 688 (7th Cir. 2010).

Cannon v. University of Chicago, 441 U.S. 677 (1979).

Defense Manpower Data Center (DMDC) (2013). 2012. Workplace and gender relations survey of active duty members. http://www.sapr.mil/public/docs/research/2012_workplace_and_gender_relations_survey_of_active_duty_members-survey_note_and_briefing.pdf. Accessed April 7, 2015.

Franklin v. Gwinnett County Public Schools, 503 U.S. 60 (1991).

Freyd, J., Rosenthal, M., and Smith, C. (2014). *Preliminary results from the University of Oregon sexual violence and institutional behavior campus survey*. http://dynamic.uoregon.edu/jjf/campus/UO-campus-results-30Sept14.pdf. Accessed May 10, 2015.

Heldman, C., and Dirks, D. (2014). One in five women students on college campuses will experience sexual assault. *Ms. Magazine* (Winter/Spring).

Humphrey, J., and White, J. (2000), Women's vulnerability to sexual assault from adolescence to young adulthood. *Journal of Adolescent Health* 27, 419–424.

Kilpatrick, D. G., Resnick, H. S., Ruggiero, K. J., Conoscenti, L. M., and McCauley, J. (2007, February 1). *Drug-facilitated, incapacitated, and forcible rape: A national study*. https://www.ncjrs.gov/pdffiles1/nij/grants/219181.pdf. Accessed April 7, 2015.

Kintz, P. (1996). Drug testing in addicts: A comparison between urine, sweat, and hair. *Therapeutic Drug Monitoring* 18, 450–455.

Krebs, C. P., Lindquist, C. H., Warner, T. D., Fisher, B. S., and Martin, S. L. (2009). College women's experiences with physically forced, alcohol- or other drug-enabled, and drug-facilitated sexual assault before and since entering college. *Journal of American College Health* 57 (6), 639–647.

Lisak, D., and Miller, P. M. (2002). Repeat rape and multiple offending among undetected rapists. *Violence and Victims* 17, 73–84.

Martinez, A. (1998). A statistical analysis of the deterrence effects of the military services' drug testing policies. Master's Thesis. Naval Postgraduate School, Monterey, CA.

McCloskey, L. (1997). The continuum of harm: Girls and women at risk for sexual abuse across the lifespan. In *Developmental perspectives on trauma: Theory, research, and intervention, Rochester Symposium on Developmental Psychopathology,* Book 8, edited by D. Cicchetti and S. Toth, 553–578. University of Rochester Press.

Pérez-Peña, R. (2013, March 20). College groups connect to fight sexual assault. *New York Times.* http://www.nytimes.com/2013/03/20/education/activi sts-at -colleges-network-to-fight-sexual-assault.html?pagewanted=all&_r=0. Accessed April 7, 2015.

Rennison, C. M. (2002). *Rape and sexual assault: reporting to police and medical attention, 1992–2000.* Washington, DC: U.S. Department of Justice, Bureau of Justice Statistics, NCJ 194530.

Smith, C., and Freyd, J. (2013). Dangerous safe havens: Institutional betrayal exacerbates sexual trauma. *Journal of Traumatic Stress* 26, 119–124.

Swartout, K., Swartout, A., Brennan, C., and White, J. 2015. Trajectories of male sexual aggression, from adolescence through college, a latent class growth analysis. *Journal of Aggressive Behavior* 37: 1–11.

U.S. Commission on Civil Rights (2013). *2013 Statutory report on sexual assault in the military.*

U.S. Department of Education, Office for Civil Rights (2005). *Annual report to Congress: Fiscal year 2004,* 4.

U.S. Department of Justice (2001, January 11). *Title IX legal manual.* http://www .justice.gov/crt/about/cor/coord/ixlegal.pdf. Accessed May 10, 2015.

U.S. Department of Justice, Office of Justice Programs, Bureau of Justice Assistance (2001, October). *Hate crimes on campus: The problem and efforts to confront it.* https://www.ncjrs.gov/pdffiles1/bja/187249.pdf. Accessed April 7, 2015.

Chapter 4

A Problem with the U.S. Legal Definition of Sexual Harassment

Sandra Ellenbolt and William E. Schweinle

"Sexual harassment" is a term that is familiar to almost everyone in the working world today. If you have worked for a larger organization, you have more than likely sat through a Human Resources orientation on sexual harassment that describes what is acceptable and unacceptable in the workplace. Yet, sexual harassment continues to be prevalent (c.f. Benagiano, Carrara & Filippi 2010; McDonald 2012). Why do we continue to hear example after example of workplace sexual harassment? Why do existing remedies not work?

A Los Angeles, California, sexual harassment attorney notes that, "While sexual harassment is a term that many of us have frequently heard, its definition is often lost in obscurity." Similar observations have been made by—and about—sexual harassment researchers (Popovich & Warren 2010). This chapter furthers the argument that in the United States we need to better define sexual harassment to better protect citizens.

SEXUAL HARASSMENT LAW

Sex discrimination only has been illegal in the United States since the passage of the 1964 Civil Rights Act. The Act commonly is referred to as "Title VII" and prohibits employment discrimination based on race, color, sex, religion, or national origin and is the basis of our sexual harassment laws today. According to the Equal Employment Opportunity Commission (EEOC) website, in 1980 the EEOC issued guidelines declaring sexual harassment to be a violation of Section 703 of Title VII, establishing criteria for determining when unwelcome conduct of a sexual nature constitutes sexual harassment, defining the circumstances under which an employer may be held liable, and suggesting affirmative steps that an employer should take to prevent sexual harassment. Then, in a 1986 landmark decision, the Supreme Court ruled that sexual harassment can be sex discrimination prohibited by Title VII. In *Meritor Savings Bank v. Vinson*, 477 U.S. 57 (1986), the U.S. Supreme Court held that a claim of "hostile environment" sexual harassment is a form of sex discrimination that is actionable under Title VII.

Courts and employers generally use the definition of sexual harassment contained in the guidelines of the U.S. Equal Employment Opportunity Commission (EEOC). This language has also formed the basis for most state laws prohibiting sexual harassment. The guidelines state the following:

Unwelcome sexual advances, requests for sexual favors, and other verbal or physical conduct of a sexual nature constitute sexual harassment when:

1. Submission to such conduct is made either explicitly or implicitly a term or condition of an individual's employment,
2. Submission to or rejection of such conduct by an individual is used as the basis for employment decisions affecting such individuals, or
3. Such conduct has the purpose or effect of unreasonably interfering with an individual's work performance or creating an intimidating, hostile, or offensive working environment (29 C.F.R. § 1604.11 [1980]).

Under the heading "Sexual Harassment" on the EEOC website it states that it is unlawful to harass a person (an applicant or employee) because of that person's sex. Harassment can include "sexual harassment" or unwelcome sexual advances, requests for sexual favors, and other verbal or physical harassment of a sexual nature.

Further stated, harassment does not have to be of a sexual nature, however, and can include offensive remarks about a person's sex. For example, it is illegal to harass a woman by making offensive comments about women in general. Both victim and the harasser can be either a woman or a man, and the victim and harasser can be the same sex. The harasser can be the victim's supervisor, a supervisor in another area, a coworker, or someone who is not an employee of the employer, such as a client or customer.

Although there are different legal definitions and courses of prosecution in different countries, nowhere do any of the above solutions seem to prevail in its approach. Tsen-Ta describes it best in *Workplace Sexual Harassment in Singapore: The Legal Challenge,* when he asserts that "laws against sexual harassment can only be effective if they can accurately identify the behavior to be proscribed" (Tsen-Ta 1999, 28). Further, Nora contends that "The law itself is in a state of flux and not capable of addressing all of the problems. Clear harassment policies can be effective deterrents" (Nora 1994, S117). To have clearer policies we must first break down our definitions. Definitions should be more precise and concentrate on levels similar to the current legal definition. Then perhaps our laws can begin to advance, giving greater protections to all.

WHAT IS LEGAL (BUT UNCIVIL)

Interestingly, the law does not prohibit simple teasing, offhand comments, or isolated incidents that are not very serious. In these cases, the harassment is illegal when it is so frequent or severe that it creates a hostile or offensive work environment, or when it results in an adverse employment decision (such as the victim being fired or demoted). Similarly, U.S. law does not directly address harassment of a sexual nature beyond the workplace. This suggests that a better definition is warranted, because harassment of a sexual nature is not limited to workplaces.

Sexual harassment research and the law are two dynamic areas that, over time, can impact each other positively. Although some researchers have taken care to define their terms, more often the terms sexual "abuse," "harassment," and "mistreatment" have been used broadly and without the precision that tends to accompany careful policy legislation (Nora 1994, S116).

Sexual harassment does occur outside of workplaces and can come from strangers; in this context it usually evokes more fear and a more negative reaction from victims than sexual harassment by someone the victim knows (Macmillan, Nierobisz & Welsh 2000). There is substantial empirical evidence that sexual harassment—regardless of setting—causes psychological and sometimes physical consequences for the harassed (Benson & Thomson 1982; Charney & Russell 1994; Collinsworth, Fitzgerald & Drasgow 2009; Fitzgerald, Drasgow, Hulin, Gelfand & Magey 1997; Funk & Werhun 2011; Gutek 1985; Rederstorff, Buchanan & Settles 2007; Richman, Flaherty & Rospenda 1996; Richman, Rospenda, Nawyn,

Flaherty, Fendrich, Drum & Johnson 1999; Schneider, Swan & Fitzgerald 1997; Yagil 2008; Yoon, Funk & Kropf 2010). For instance, women who have been sexually harassed, irrespective of setting, often experience fear, anger humiliation, depression, reduced self-esteem, helplessness, anxiety, and nervousness (Gutek & Koss 1993; Van Roosmalen & McDaniel 1998).

Some investigators have found that the psychological abuse which often accompanies physical abuse in a relationship is more detrimental to the victim than the physical injuries (c.f. Folingstad & Dehart 2000; Street & Arias 2001). Perhaps these empirical results about domestic violence can be generalized to sexual harassment, but direct empirical findings have not yet been reported.

Recently, Schweinle (2012) argued on the basis of recent scientific evidence and emerging theory that sexual harassment of women—regardless of the setting or the relationship between harasser and victim—is maliciously (rather than playfully or seductively) motivated. For instance, there is a strong association between engaging in bullying during childhood—which is maliciously intended behavior—and engaging in sexual harassment during adulthood. Further, there is an association between authoritarian personality characteristics—specifically anger and hate—and sexual harassment. Lastly, Schweinle describes his own research demonstrating that sexual harassers have a biased lack of accurate empathy that is identical to the biased perceptions of men who are aggressive toward their wives. Schweinle concludes that sexual harassment appears to be maliciously motivated retaliation against some erroneously perceived slight or rejection by women.

More recent research reported by Gabrovec, Erzen, and Lobnikar (2014) demonstrated significant positive correlations between physical abuse, verbal abuse, and sexual harassment of medical workers in Slovenia. These results further point out and support the conclusion that sexual harassment is a form of aggression that is meant to harm.

If this conclusion is correct, then the present formulation of American sexual harassment statutes is not appropriately addressing the nature of the problem. Other U.S. statutes deal with aggression as the intent to do harm. It seems appropriate that sexual harassment policies follow suit. When investigating allegations of sexual harassment, the EEOC examines the whole record: the circumstances, such as the nature of the sexual advances, and the context in which the alleged incidents occurred. A determination on the allegations is made from the facts on a case-by-case basis.

According to *HR Magazine* (Maatman 2000), although the laws in many countries do not compare to the laws of the United States, most major commercial jurisdictions in the world have adopted workplace harassment laws during the last decade, and many of these are similar to the U.S. system consisting of state and federal employment discrimination statutes. The laws of some nations, however, go even further than U.S. law.

The article further states that employment discrimination and workplace harassment laws exist in most areas of the world. This trend began in Western Europe and has spread to Asia, as well as to South America and Central America. Although workplace harassment laws reflect the employment environments of each particular country, generally there are three regulatory models:

- A statutory prohibition and individual remedies model,
- A criminal law model, and
- A termination indemnity model based on an employee's right to quit his or her employment due to harassment.

Australia, Canada, The Netherlands, Sweden, and the United Kingdom follow the first model. The laws specify prohibited conduct and allow employees to seek individual remedies. In Italy, the Philippines, Taiwan, and Venezuela the second model prevails. Sexual harassment is defined as a criminal offense, and penalties and remedies are provided in statutory penal codes. Germany, Spain, and Thailand fall within the third model.

Nora states, "Labeling such a wide variety of behaviors and activities as sexual harassment in our research may contribute to sloppy speech in daily discussion about these issues. Sexual harassment and harassers are value-laden terms. Real harm can accrue when these label are misapplied" (Nora 1994, S116).

Addressing the issue of the law, the law is too broad and is not capable of addressing all the areas of sexual harassment. Because of this, victims could decide that the harassment that they have experienced does not rise to a level of importance and as a result might be reluctant to complain to the proper authorizes. Many times victims feel humiliated and think they might have done something to invite the behavior. Additionally, many victims sometimes think that filing a complaint is futile; charges of sexual harassment often are ignored or downplayed.

According to Conte (2014) there are many forms of conduct that can make for a hostile environment including sexual comments made in e-mails or Facebook postings, threats to impose a sexual quid pro quo, discussions of sexual activities, telling off-color jokes, inappropriate touching, commenting on physical attributes, the display of sexually suggestive pictures, the use of demeaning or inappropriate "pet names," the use of indecent gestures, undermining the victim's work, engaging in hostile physical conduct, granting job favors to those who participate in consensual sexual activity, and using crude and offensive language.

Microinequities are subtle forms of sexual harassment and gender discrimination that are not always illegal but do negatively impact morale, job performance, and opportunities for promotions and training (Bernstein

& Lenhart 1993, 137). Examples include language that minimizes women (e.g., referring to women as "girls" or "babes"), treatment of women as invisible, negative perceptions of women's ability based on gender, and elimination of women from informal networks. Microinequities are not legally actionable, however, when multiplied they can contribute to a valid hostile environment claim.

The law should address sexual harassment in levels, much as it does homicide. For example, there is first degree, second degree, manslaughter, negligence—and the list goes on. Currently, the definitions of sexual harassment are too broad and should be clarified in a manner enabling the law to address ALL harassment, so as to not minimize a person's trauma.

REFERENCES

Benagiano, G., Carrara, S., and Filippi, V. (2010). Social and ethical determinates of human sexuality: 2. Gender-based violence. *European Journal of Contraception and Reproductive Health Care* 15, 220–231.

Benson, D., and Thomson, G. (1982). Sexual harassment on a university campus: The confluence of authority relations, sexual interest and gender stratification. *Social Problems* 29, 236–251.

Bernstein, A. E., and Lenhart, S. A. (1993). *The psychodynamic treatment of women.* Washington, DC: American Psychiatric Press.

Charney, D., and Russell, R. (1994). An overview of sexual harassment. *The American Journal of Psychiatry* 151, 10–17.

Code of Federal Regulations (C.F.R.) §1604.11, Sexual Harassment. http://www .ecfr.gov/cgi-bin/text-idx?SID=c97c882dc6c18447ec02c516c724cb39&node =29:4.1.4.1.5.0.21.11&rgn=div8. Accessed April 8, 2015.

Collinsworth, L., Fitzgerald, L., and Drasgow, F. (2009). In harm's way: Factors related to psychological distress following sexual harassment. *Psychology of Women Quarterly* 33, 475–490.

Conte, Alba (2014). *Sexual harassment in the workplace—law and practice.* 4th ed. Vol. 1, 1–31.

Equal Employment Opportunity Commission (EEOC) (1990). Policy guidance on current issues of sexual harassment. http://www.eeoc.gov/policy/docs /currentissues.html. Accessed April 8, 2015.

Fitzgerald, L., Drasgow, F., Hulin, C., Gelfand, M., and Magey, V. (1997). Antecedents and consequences of sexual harassment in organizations: A test of an integrated model. *Journal of Applied Psychology* 82, 578–589.

Folingstad, D., and DeHart, D. (2000). Defining psychological abuse of husbands towards wives: Contexts, behaviors and typologies. *Journal of Interpersonal Violence* 15, 891—920.

Funk, L., and Werhun, C. (2011). "You're such a girl!" The psychological drain of the gender-role harassment of men. *Sex Roles* 65, 13–22.

Gabrovec, B., Erzen, I., and Lobnikar, B. (2014). The prevalence and nature of violence directed at the medical staff in psychiatric healthcare in Slovenia. *Health Medicine* 8, 228–234.

Gutek, B. (1985). *Sex and the workplace.* San Francisco, CA: Jossey-Bass.

Gutek, B. A., and Koss, M. P. (1993). Changed women and changed organizations: Consequences of and coping with sexual harassment. *Journal of Vocational Behavior* 42, 28–48.

Maatman, G. L. Jr. (2000). Legal trends—A global view of sexual harassment. *HR Magazine* 45 (7). http://www.shrm.org/Publications/hrmagazine/EditorialContent/0700/Pages/0700legal.aspx. Accessed April 8, 2015.

MacMillan, R., Nierobisz, A., and Welsh, S. (2000). Experiencing the streets: Harassment and perceptions of safety among women. *Journal of Research in Crime and Delinquency* 37, 306–322.

Mann and Elias. (2015). Los Angeles, California, Sexual Harassment Attorneys. http://www.Mannelias.com/sexual-harassment.htm. Accessed April 8, 2015.

McDonald, P. (2012). Workplace sexual harassment 30 years on: A review of the literature. *International Journal of Management Reviews* 14, 1–17.

Meritor Savings Bank v. Vinson, 477 U.S. 57 (1986).

Nora, L. (1994). "Sexual harassment in medical education: A review of the literature with comments from the law." *Academic Medicine* 71, S113–S118.

Popovich, P., and Warren, M. (2010). The role of power in sexual harassment as counterproductive behavior in organizations. *Human Resource Management Review* 20, 45–53.

Rederstorff, J., Buchanan, N., and Settles, I. (2007). The moderating roles of race and gender role attitudes in the relationship between sexual harassment and psychological well-being. *Psychology of Women Quarterly* 31, 50–61.

Richman, J., Flaherty, J., and Rospenda, K. (1996). Perceived workplace harassment experiences and problem drinking among physicians: Broadening the stress/alienation paradigm. *Addiction* 91, 391–403.

Richman, J., Rospenda, K., Nawyn, S., Flaherty, J., Fendrich, M., Drum, M., and Johnson, T. (1999). Sexual harassment and generalized workplace abuse among university employees: Prevalence and mental health correlates. *American Journal of Public Health* 89, 358–363.

Schneider, K., Swan, S., and Fitzgerald, L. (1997). Job-related and psychological effects of sexual harassment in the workplace: Empirical evidence from two organizations. *Journal of Applied Psychology* 82, 401–415.

Schweinle, W. (2012). Sexual harassment is not playful or seductive; it is abuse. In *Violence and abuse in society: Understanding a global crisis,* edited by A. Browne-Miller. Vol. 2. Westport, CT: Praeger.

Street, A., and Arias, I. (2001). Psychological abuse and posttraumatic stress disorder in battered women: Examining the roles of shame and guilt. *Violence and Victims* 16, 65–78.

Tsen-Ta, Jack Lee (1999). Workplace sexual harassment in Singapore: The legal challenge. 11 *S. Ac. L.J.* (28). http://ssrn.com/abstract=648404. Accessed April 8, 2015.

Van Roosmalen, E., and McDaniel, S. (1998). Sexual harassment in academia: A hazard to women's health. *Women and Health* 28, 33–54.

Yagil, D. (2008). When the customer is wrong: A review of research on aggression and sexual harassment in service encounters. *Aggression and Violent Behavior* 13, 141–152.

Yoon, E., Funk, R., and Kropf, N. (2010). Sexual harassment experiences and their psychological correlates among a diverse sample of college women. *Journal of Women and Social Work* 25, 8–18.

Chapter 5

GPS for Title IX, the Clery Act, and the Violence Against Women Reauthorization Act: Navigating the Current Legal Landscape

Jeffrey J. Nolan

INTRODUCTION

The legal landscape surrounding college and university responses to sexual violence has changed dramatically in recent years. Institutions have come under increased scrutiny from the federal government, victims' advocates, and the media; and guidance documents regarding sexual violence issued by the U.S. Department of Education's Office of Civil Rights ("OCR") in 2011 and 2014, issuance of a White House Task Force report on sexual violence in 2014, and unprecedented enforcement activities and social media campaigns have required colleges and universities to focus closely on their sexual violence prevention and response systems.

In 2014, colleges and universities also had to add mastery and implementation of the requirements of the college- and university-specific portions of the Violence Against Women Reauthorization Act of 2013 ("VAWA Amendments") to their "to do" lists. The VAWA Amendments—which went into effect on March 7, 2014—amended the Jeanne Clery Disclosure of Campus Security and Campus Crime Statistics Act, 20 U.S.C. § 1092(f)

("Clery Act") to add several sexual violence–related mandates, and to add new requirements regarding how colleges and universities address domestic violence, dating violence, and stalking. Institutions must now balance the pressure to deal effectively with reported misconduct against the need to deal fairly with all of their students and employees.

This chapter maps out recent developments regarding Title IX, the VAWA Amendments, related administrative enforcement issues, and civil action–related issues. It also highlights briefly how institutions should involve their campus threat-assessment and management teams when they receive reports of domestic violence, dating violence, sexual assault, and stalking. The chapter concludes with the suggestions that education and prevention efforts provide the best hope for progress (as satisfaction with even the best disciplinary and response process is likely to be low, and it is obviously preferable to avoid harm, rather than respond to it), and that by complying with the new legal requirements and guidance—and moving beyond mere compliance and instead innovating in the areas of education and prevention—colleges and universities can make campuses safer from the risks posed by domestic violence, dating violence, sexual assault, and stalking.

APPLICABLE LAW AND GUIDANCE

Title IX

Title IX of the Education Amendments of 1972, 20 U.S.C. §§ 1681 et seq. ("Title IX") prohibits discrimination on the basis of sex in education programs or activities operated by recipients of federal financial assistance. The Office of Civil Rights has issued relatively noncontroversial regulations to implement Title IX (see 34 C.F.R. Part 106). Historically, OCR also offered guidance through a number of "Dear Colleague" Letters, which are issued without following the customary notice and comment rulemaking process. Most OCR guidance documents have not been particularly controversial because they have stayed well within the bounds of generally accepted nondiscrimination and anti-harassment law principles.

April 4, 2011, Dear Colleague Letter

OCR's April 4, 2011, "Dear Colleague Letter" ("2011 DCL") regarding sexual violence involving students (http://www2.ed.gov/about/offices /list/ocr/letters/colleague-201104.pdf), expands substantially the basic nondiscrimination principle stated in Title IX's simple statutory language, which states that "[n]o person in the United States shall, on the basis of sex, be excluded from participation in, be denied the benefits of, or be subjected to discrimination under any education program or activity receiving federal financial assistance." Although the 2011 DCL technically does not have the force of law, the reality of OCR's enforcement process (described below) strongly encourages colleges and universities to follow its many substantive pronouncements regarding how sexual violence–related issues should be handled in the student-on-student context. The 19-page 2011 DCL contains numerous pronouncements regarding OCR's view of what it means for institutions to avoid discrimination on the basis of sex when handling student-on-student sexual assault cases (the 2011 DCL does not address institutional responses to sexual violence against employees, even though Title IX does cover employees as well as students). The letter begins by emphasizing that sexual harassment of students is a form of sex discrimination and that sexual violence (defined to include "rape, sexual assault, sexual battery, and sexual coercion") is a form of sexual harassment. Thus, the letter is framed as supplementing OCR's *Revised Sexual Harassment Guidance* issued in 2001 (see http://www2.ed.gov/about/offices/list/ocr/docs/shguide.pdf) ("2001 Guidance"). It must be acknowledged, however, that in outlining specific procedural and substantive elements that OCR requires or would like institutions to apply in sexual violence cases, the April 2011 DCL goes well beyond the guidance offered in the 2001 Guidance. These new requirements and preferences have had a profound impact on how colleges and universities have responded to sexual violence cases since 2011.

With respect to the identity of the Title IX Coordinator, OCR states in the 2011 DCL that "Title IX coordinators should not have other job responsibilities that may create a conflict of interest. For example, serving as the Title IX coordinator and a disciplinary hearing board member or general counsel may create a conflict of interest." This statement about general counsel is not controversial given a general counsel's ultimate ethical obligation to his or her client (the institution), but the statement about disciplinary hearing board members created substantial concern, because it required institutions to consider whether others with responsibilities in the campus disciplinary process, such as deans of students, would similarly be viewed as having a "conflict of interest." As a result, many institutions appointed Title IX coordinators from outside the traditional student affairs realm (such as, for example, human resources directors). This required non-student-affairs professionals to take on substantial new responsibilities, usually in addition to their existing job duties. It also required those individuals to step outside their traditional areas of practice, become educated, gain experience, and exercise leadership in the unfamiliar and highly sensitive area of student-on-student sexual violence.

The 2011 DCL also stated many new procedural requirements and preferences. For example, although OCR has for some time advised that an alleged victim of sexual harassment should not have to work through the problem directly with the alleged harasser, and that the alleged victim must be notified of the right to end an informal process and proceed with a formal complaint, the 2011 DCL declared that "in cases involving allegations of sexual assault, mediation is not appropriate even on a voluntary basis." This is noncontroversial in cases in which the allegations clearly describe nonconsensual sexual activity, but it has created some concern among student affairs professionals who think that a trauma-informed, structured mediation might be the best option for both parties in highly ambiguous cases.

The 2011 DCL also emphasized that institutions should discontinue the relatively common practice of delaying or suspending internal disciplinary proceedings while a criminal investigation or prosecution is pending. The Office of Civil Rights emphasized in this context that institutions should only delay their internal fact-finding for the short period that it "typically" would take for law enforcement officials to conduct their initial evidence-gathering stage, and stated for example (citing a conversation with one prosecutor) that completing this stage typically takes three to ten calendar days. This position has created some tension between institutions and law enforcement, particularly in cases in which law enforcement does not want an institutional investigation to interfere with the criminal investigation, but the criminal investigation moves at a slower pace than the "three to ten calendar days" time frame suggested in the 2011 DCL.

Also emphasized is that a "preponderance of the evidence" (that is, more likely than not) standard of proof must be used in internal disciplinary proceedings. The OCR rejected the "clear and convincing evidence" standard used by some institutions as being inconsistent with how other civil rights issues are adjudicated in a noncriminal, civil context. Not carving out a higher standard of proof for sexual violence cases makes good sense, yet this position in the 2011 DCL nonetheless has spurred criticism from some advocacy groups, such as the American Association of University Professors. Groups have expressed concerns about the potentially career-ending implications of a professor being found responsible—under a relatively less stringent standard of proof—for sexual violence or sexual harassment.

An even more broad-reaching position taken in the 2011 DCL requires that both parties to a sexual violence case receive equal procedural opportunities to, for example, review all of the evidence, attend all meetings and hearings on an equal basis, have the same rights to have an adviser present, and have an equal right to appeal a disciplinary decision. This position required substantial changes at institutions that had previously viewed a complainant more as a witness than as an equal party to the case.

Lastly, on the procedural front, the 2011 DCL outlined detailed rules regarding the information that complainants should receive regarding the outcome of a disciplinary process. The letter noted that although the Family Education Rights and Privacy Act ("FERPA") restricts an institution's ability to share detailed information from a respondent's education and disciplinary records with a complainant (particularly in sexual harassment cases that do not involve sexual violence), institutions can and should share information about responsibility and sanctions that would directly relate to a complainant. Such information would include, for example, information that a complainant would need to evaluate whether continuing contact with a respondent would be likely to occur postadjudication, such as whether the respondent had been suspended or restricted from certain areas of campus. The letter also noted that for cases that involve sexual violence that rises to the level of a "non-forcible sex offense" under the Clery Act. The letter noted that when a disciplinary proceeding involves alleged Clery Act crimes, FERPA permits an institution to share the final results of the proceeding with the complainant even if the respondent is found not responsible for the crime, and permits the institution to share the final results with anyone if the respondent is found responsible for the crime. The 2011 DCL recommended that notice of outcomes be provided to the parties "concurrently" and in writing.

One noteworthy aspect of the 2011 DCL that was repeated almost verbatim from the 2001 Guidance concerned an institution's obligations when an alleged victim reports sexual violence, but requests that the alleged perpetrator not be notified of the complaint and that no investigation or disciplinary action be initiated. The 2011 DCL emphasized that the institution should respect the alleged victim's confidentiality preferences unless breaking that confidentiality was necessary to move forward in the interest of campus safety, and then outlined factors that the institution could consider in determining how to proceed. The letter included some examples of nonspecific intervention measures (such as general training) that an institution could take if it determined that it was able to respect an alleged victim's request for complete confidentiality. Nonetheless, given the 2011 DCL's simultaneous statements to the effect that when an institution knows or reasonably should know about possible harassment, it "must investigate to determine what occurred and then take appropriate steps to resolve the situation," and given OCR's increased enforcement efforts following the issuance of the 2011 DCL, institutions felt more acutely the tension between respecting a request for complete confidentiality and remedying a reported instance of harassment or sexual violence.

The final five pages of the 2011 DCL are devoted to discussion of OCR's expectations and suggestions regarding institutional education and training programs and remedies that should be considered and implemented when sexual violence has been found to have occurred.

The VAWA Amendments to the Clery Act

As noted, the VAWA Amendments to the Clery Act cover domestic violence, dating violence, and stalking cases in addition to sexual assault cases, and were signed into law on March 7, 2013, and went into effect on March 7, 2014. Like Title IX, the Clery Act applies to institutions that receive federal funds. Among other things, the Clery Act requires institutions to collect and publish campus crime statistics and to publish numerous policy statements in an Annual Security Report ("ASR"). The Clery Act also requires institutions to adopt emergency notification, response, and testing procedures and to provide "timely warnings" to the community regarding listed crimes that are reported to campus security or local law enforcement, in cases where the information received indicates that there could be a continuing threat to employees or students. Guidance on the many detailed requirements of the Clery Act is provided in the Department of Education's February 2011 *Handbook for Campus Safety and Security Reporting* (http://www2.ed.gov/admins/lead/safety/handbook.pdf).

The Clery Act has long required the adoption of sexual assault policies with certain features, but the breadth and detail of these requirements were expanded significantly by the VAWA Amendments. The amendments apply many of the principles and definitions of the Violence Against Women Act of 1994 (42 U.S.C. § 13925 et seq.) to the college and university context (see generally 20 U.S.C. § 1092(f)). The Violence Against Women Act as passed originally in 1994 was designed to improve the response of the criminal justice system to domestic violence, dating violence, sexual assault, and stalking.

Under the VAWA Amendments, each covered institution must develop and distribute in its ASR policies and statements that include

- The institution's programs to prevent domestic violence, dating violence, sexual assault, and stalking;
- The procedures that the institution will follow once an incident of domestic violence, dating violence, sexual assault, or stalking has been reported;
- Notification about existing counseling, health, mental health, victim advocacy, legal assistance, and other services available to victims both on campus and in the community;
- Notification about a victim's right to either choose to notify law enforcement (with institutional support) or to decline to notify law enforcement;
- Notification about the availability of protective orders and institutional sanctions;
- Notification about steps that victims should take to preserve evidence of covered violence or stalking; and
- The provision to victims of information about options for, and available assistance in, changing academic, living, transportation, and

working situations, if such assistance is requested by the victim and if such accommodations are reasonably available (regardless of whether the victim chooses to report to campus police or local law enforcement).

The VAWRA amendments to the Clery Act also codify some—but not all—of the procedural requirements and preferences stated in the 2011 DCL. As codified in the VAWA Amendments, these procedural features are now required as a matter of positive law, as opposed to administrative guidance. The VAWA Amendments, for example, require colleges and universities to publish notice of "prompt, fair and impartial investigation and resolution" procedures, in which parties must be "simultaneously" informed in writing of the outcome of covered disciplinary proceedings that describe any procedures "for the accused and the victim to appeal the results of the institutional disciplinary proceeding," and that provide that "the accuser and the accused are entitled to the same opportunities to have others present during an institutional disciplinary proceeding, including the opportunity to be accompanied to any related meeting or proceeding by an advisor of their choice." The VAWA Amendments also require that institutions specify which standard of evidence will be used in institutional disciplinary proceedings (without specifying what that standard needs to be), but given OCR's continued insistence that any standard higher than a preponderance standard is inappropriate, institutions now likely will continue to specify in their policies that the preponderance standard will apply to their proceedings.

Institutions generally have adapted easily to these requirements, given their move toward compliance with the similar positions expressed in the 2011 DCL, but the "advisor of their choice" language has caused more concern. Traditionally, many institutions have banned attorneys from their disciplinary proceedings, and many have only allowed advisers who are members of the campus community (that is, no parents or other outsiders have been allowed to attend). The unqualified "advisor of their choice" language of the VAWA Amendments appeared on its face to require institutions to literally allow parties to choose any person to serve as their adviser, and despite efforts of colleges and universities in the related negotiated rulemaking process to highlight the potential unintended consequences of allowing attorneys to be present at campus disciplinary meetings and hearings, it was clear that no qualification will be read into this language and that institutions cannot limit the choice of an adviser. The draft regulations do provide, however, that institutions may restrict the extent to which advisers may participate in the proceedings. Thus, unless the draft regulation on this point is changed before finalization in late 2014, institutions may preclude advisers from speaking to an investigator or hearing panel and allow them only to speak privately with the partyadvisee (often called a "potted plant" approach), so long as any such restrictions apply equally to both parties.

Finally, in terms of procedure-related provisions, the VAWA Amendments impose a very substantial training requirement through such a provision. Specifically, the amendments provide that institutional disciplinary proceedings must "be conducted by officials who receive annual training on the issues related to domestic violence, dating violence, sexual assault, and stalking and how to conduct an investigation and hearing process that protects the safety of victims and promotes accountability." Institutions have certainly expanded their sexual assault–related training programs for administrators, staff, and hearing panels following the advice of the 2011 DCL, but the VAWA Amendments' specification of annual training in positive statutory law, and the addition of domestic violence, dating violence, and stalking issues to the apparently required curriculum, is a substantial change that must be addressed by covered institutions.

Institutions also must address the fact that the VAWA Amendments require that both students and employees have the benefit of the listed policies and procedures. This is consistent with other elements of the Clery Act, which require the provision of campus crime statistics and campus safety–related information to employees as well as students. Again, many institutions have worked diligently to conform their student-related policies to the requirements of the 2011 DCL and can adapt easily to the codification of those requirements in the VAWA Amendments, but it is fair to say as of October 2014 that substantial work likely remains to be done to conform employee handbooks, faculty contracts, and collective-bargaining agreements to the procedural requirements imposed by the VAWA Amendments.

In terms of education, prevention, and training requirements, in addition to the annual training for officials practically required by the procedure-related provisions discussed above, the VAWA Amendments require covered institutions to implement extensive training programs for students, faculty, and staff regarding domestic violence, dating violence, sexual assault, and stalking. Specifically, the VAWA Amendments require that each covered institution's ASR must describe "primary prevention and awareness programs for all incoming students and new employees," which must include

- A statement that the institution prohibits the offenses of domestic violence, dating violence, sexual assault, and stalking;
- The definition of domestic violence, dating violence, sexual assault, and stalking in the applicable jurisdiction (or jurisdictions, if an institution operates in more than one jurisdiction);
- The definition of "consent" in reference to sexual activity in the jurisdiction (or jurisdictions);

- Training on "safe and positive options for bystander intervention that may be carried out by an individual to prevent harm or intervene when there is a risk of domestic violence, dating violence, sexual assault or stalking against a person other than such individual"; and

- "[I]nformation on risk reduction to recognize warning signs of abusive behavior and how to avoid potential attacks."

Institutions also must offer "ongoing prevention and awareness campaigns for students and faculty" that address the information outlined above (see 20 U.S.C. § 1092(f)(8)).

These training requirements are daunting. In ensuring that they develop generally offered "primary prevention and awareness programs for all incoming students and new employees" and "ongoing prevention and awareness campaigns for students and faculty" that include all of the VAWA Amendments' required elements, it should be relatively easy for institutions to use their (probably newly developed) state law–specific policy language regarding offense and sexual activity consent definitions in such programs. In recent years, colleges and universities have become relatively more aware of sexual assault–related issues such as sexual assault trauma and reasons why sexual assault reports might be delayed, therefore institutions should be adept at developing or evaluating curricula on those issues as well.

Conversely, institutions will likely have to become more educated themselves, and work with internal or external experts to develop curricula regarding domestic violence, dating violence, and stalking, regarding "safe and positive options for bystander intervention that may be carried out by an individual to prevent harm or intervene when there is a risk of" a covered offense against another person, and regarding "information on risk reduction to recognize warning signs of abusive behavior and how to avoid potential attacks."

QUESTIONS AND ANSWERS ON TITLE IX AND SEXUAL VIOLENCE, APRIL 29, 2014

On April 29, 2014, OCR issued a guidance document titled "Questions and Answers on Title IX and Sexual Violence" (http://www2.ed.gov/about/offices/list/ocr/docs/qa-201404-title-ix.pdf) ("2014 Q&A"). The cover letter to the 2014 Q&A states that it was intended to "further clarify the legal requirements and guidance articulated in the [2011 DCL] and the 2001 Guidance and [to] include examples of proactive efforts schools can take to prevent sexual violence and remedies schools may use to end such conduct, prevent its recurrence, and address its effects."

Several sections of the 2014 Q&A essentially reiterate prior guidance and add more detail. This is true of the guidance's section on institutional obligations to respond to sexual violence and its discussion of students protected by Title IX (which, for example, notes unsurprisingly that sexual violence involving parties of the same sex should of course be handled with the same diligence as cases in which the parties are of different sexes, and discusses some special considerations that apply when complainants are individuals with disabilities or are international students). This also is true of the guidance's section on required procedural elements and the role of the Title IX coordinator, though the guidance does contain new language to the effect that the Title IX coordinator, when properly trained, is "generally in the best position to evaluate a student's request for confidentiality in the context of the school's responsibility to provide a safe and nondiscriminatory environment for all students." This section also elaborates further on—and further exacerbates the tension created by—the 2011 DCL's guidance regarding who should not serve as Title IX coordinator given OCR's view of "conflict of interest" issues. Specifically, in addition to repeating the advice that general counsels should not serve as Title IX coordinators, the 2014 Q&A states that

> [o]ther employees whose job responsibilities may conflict with a Title IX coordinator's responsibilities include Directors of Athletics, Deans of Students, and any employee who serves on the judicial/ hearing board or to whom an appeal might be made. Designating a full-time Title IX coordinator will minimize the risk of a conflict of interest.

Given this language, the increasing workload that Title IX coordinators are being faced with in light of training and expertise expectations, expanded related VAWA requirements, and the increased caseload likely resulting from better outreach and more welcoming disciplinary procedures, many institutions are indeed finding that it is becoming necessary to appoint an individual whose job responsibilities focus in whole or in substantial part on Title IX/VAWA and related compliance issues.

In terms of relatively new guidance, the 2014 Q&A elaborates more than previous guidance on the definition and responsibilities of "responsible employees" (including resident assistants) who must report certain information about sexual violence reports to the Title IX coordinator. The guidance also dovetails with the approach to confidentiality preferred in the White House's *Not Alone Report* (discussed below), in that it emphasizes explicitly that "[b]efore a student reveals information that he or she may wish to keep confidential, a responsible employee should make every effort to ensure that the student understands" the employee's reporting obligations, the student's option to request that the institution maintain confidentiality (which the institution might or might not be able to respect, given countervailing campus safety considerations), and the availability of alternative confidential resources, such as licensed counseling service professionals and—where designated as confidential by the institution—sexual assault–related services. The 2014 Q&A's section on confidentiality issues similarly emphasizes that OCR wants institutions to "take requests for confidentiality seriously" and gives examples of safety-related factors beyond those outlined in the 2001 Guidance and 2011 DCL that Title IX coordinators might consider in deciding whether a confidentiality request can be respected. The 2014 Q&A also discusses in some detail that licensed counselors and pastoral counselors do not, under either Title IX or the Clery Act, have an obligation to disclose reports of sexual violence that are provided to them on a confidential, privileged basis by students. In general, the very explicit discussion of confidentiality in the 2014 Q&A should serve to alleviate some of the concern that institutions had following the 2011 DCL that if they respected a student's request for confidentiality, then they could be criticized by OCR for not being sufficiently proactive in investigating alleged sexual violence, preventing its recurrence, and addressing its effects. Nonetheless, institutions should be vigilant to document their decision-making process surrounding requests for confidentiality, and to take non-identifying remedial action as appropriate (such as general training and monitoring as described in the 2014 Q&A) in cases where they do not move forward with an investigation.

Much of the investigation-related section of the 2014 Q&A is similarly consistent with, but contains some elaboration on, previous guidance. A few items nonetheless are worth mentioning here. In accordance with the discussion of non-hearing-based investigation processes discussed in the White House's "Not Alone Report" (see discussion below), the 2014 Q&A notes that "Title IX does not necessarily require a hearing." Apparently correcting the tension likely created by the 2011 DCL's suggestion that at least one prosecutor believed that initial law enforcement fact-gathering "typically" takes between three and ten days, the 2014 Q&A states that "OCR understands that this example may not be representative and that the law enforcement agency's process often takes more than ten days." In terms of relatively new procedure-related information, the 2014 Q&A notes that

> [q]uestioning about the complainant's sexual history with anyone other than the alleged perpetrator should not be permitted. Further, a school should recognize that the mere fact of a current or previous consensual dating or sexual relationship between the two parties does not itself imply consent or preclude a finding of sexual violence.

This clarification that information about sexual history between the parties could be relevant to provide context, but that it is certainly not dispositive of the question of consent, is helpful. The guidance also emphasizes in the context of investigations and appeals that the effects of trauma on complainants should be recognized and accommodated by, for example, minimizing the number of times a complainant has to repeat a description of the incident to multiple investigators, and training appeals adjudicators or panels on the dynamics of and trauma associated with sexual violence.

The last substantive section of the 2014 Q&A emphasizes that the Clery Act does not affect the Title IX obligations of covered institutions, and that the VAWA Amendments have no effect on institutional responsibilities under Title IX as outlined by OCR. This means, essentially, that institutions must comply with both laws simultaneously.

NOT ALONE: THE FIRST REPORT OF THE WHITE HOUSE TASK FORCE TO PROTECT STUDENTS FROM SEXUAL ASSAULT

On the same day that the 2014 Q&A was issued, April 29, 2014, the White House issued "Not Alone, The First Report of the White House Task Force to Protect Students from Sexual Assault" ("Not Alone Report") (https://www.notalone.gov/assets/report.pdf). This document is not positive law or regulation, and it does not have the "significant guidance document" status or connection to OCR enforcement activities of the 2011 DCL and 2014 Q&A. Nonetheless, given the pressure to follow "best and promising practices" that social media campaigns and media reports can exert on colleges and universities, institutions should at least be conversant with the recommendations in the "Not Alone Report" and be prepared, if necessary, to explain why they chose not to adopt policies and practices consistent with such recommendations.

The "Not Alone Report" encourages colleges and universities to conduct campus climate surveys, advocates the enhancement of prevention programs (particularly those that engage men, which dovetails with the "It's On Us" campaign launched by the White House on September 19, 2014), discusses how the task force thinks institutions can most effectively respond to reports of sexual assault, and discusses steps that the government will take to increase the transparency and effectiveness of enforcement efforts. The report focuses more of its discussion on "responding effectively" than on any other topic, so that topic is addressed primarily here. As noted, the April 29, 2014, OCR Q&A clarifies that OCR is serious about allowing institutions to respect an alleged victim's request for confidentiality as is possible, and the April 29, 2014, "Not Alone Report" provides some likely insight into why that is so. The "Not Alone Report" emphasizes that the problem of a victim's losing control of the extent to which an institution would take nonconfidential investigative and remedial measures once a report is made was "by far, the problem [the Task Force] heard most about" in a series of public listening sessions it conducted. To help solve this problem, the report suggests that institutions should identify trained, confidential victim advocates who can provide emergency and ongoing support, and consider adopting elements of a "sample reporting and confidentiality protocol" that was published with the report. The sample protocol language emphasizes, like the corresponding language of the 2014 Q&A, that institutions should describe clearly in policy the distinct reporting, action, and confidentiality obligations of "responsible employees" versus confidential resources. Again, this coordinated clarification of how the federal government would view requests for confidentiality provides some comfort to institutions that they can make difficult decisions regarding such requests without facing a virtually equal chance of being criticized however the question is resolved. That conundrum was reasonably feared by institutions following issuance of the 2011 DCL but before April 29, 2014, so the clarification is welcome. It bears repeating, however, that institutions still must consider nonidentifying remedial measures where practicable, and document their decision-making process and related communications in this sensitive area.

The "responding effectively" section of the "Not Alone Report" next cites a Checklist for Campus Sexual Misconduct Policies published with the report. Institutions that review the checklist will likely find that their post-2011 DCL policies already are consistent with many of the suggestions in the checklist, but it is useful as an organizational tool, and its suggested definition of "consent" to sexual activity is particularly comprehensive and helpful.

Suggestions regarding training for school officials also are offered in the "responding effectively" section of the "Not Alone Report." Specifically, the report states that the Justice Department's National Center for Campus Public Safety will develop a training program for campus officials involved in investigating and adjudicating domestic violence, dating violence, sexual assault, and stalking cases that is consistent with the VAWA Amendments' requirement that officials receive such training annually. The report emphasizes that this training will be "a trauma-informed program consistent with the new requirements." The report also states that the Department of Justice will launch a comprehensive technical assistance project for campus officials and that the Department of Education will develop trauma-informed training materials for campus health center staff. This section of the report also discusses "new" investigative and adjudicative protocols, such as "single-investigator" models in which parties are not required to attend or state their case in disciplinary hearings. The report observes that "[p]reliminary reports from the field suggest that these innovative models, in which college judicial boards play a much more limited role, encourage reporting and bolster trust in the process, while at the same time safeguarding an alleged perpetrator's right to notice and to be heard." It is fair to say that it appears, anecdotally at least as of October 2014, that many institutions are in fact considering, and some are adopting, single-investigator models. Finally, the "responding effectively" section encourages institutions to partner more effectively with local resources by, for example, entering into memoranda of understanding with local rape crisis centers and local law enforcement that address coordinated responses to sexual violence cases.

WHITE HOUSE TASK FORCE PUBLICATIONS, SEPTEMBER 19, 2014

Consistent with the status of the "Not Alone Report" as a first report and part of an ongoing effort, the White House released additional policy language recommendations on September 19, 2014. This release coincided with the White House's announcement of a bystander education campaign called "It's On Us," (http://itsonus.org). The September 19th policy suggestions outline, for example, how institutions might describe the role and responsibilities of their Title IX coordinator (in terms that summarize, in greater detail, Title IX coordinator responsibilities outlined in previous OCR guidance) (see https://www.notalone.gov/assets/role-of-title-ix-coordinator.pdf), and they contain a comprehensive definition of "sexual exploitation," a form of sexual misconduct that does not necessarily involve physical sexual conduct, but occurs when a person takes sexual advantage of another person for the benefit of anyone other than that person without that person's consent (see https://www.notalone.gov/assets/definitions-of-prohibited-conduct.pdf). The September 19th release also contained suggested policy language regarding interim and supportive measures (see https://www.notalone.gov/assets/interim-and-supportive-measures.pdf).

In sum, the period from April 2011 through October 2014 (when this chapter was finalized for publication) saw an unprecedented level of developments in the statutes, regulations, administrative guidance, and "best practices advice" relevant to sexual assault, domestic violence, dating violence, and stalking. In light of the likely late 2014 release of final VAWA Amendments regulations and the White House's commitment to further publications and agency guidance regarding sexual assault response, it is obvious that institutions should expect, and be attuned to, additional developments in these areas.

ADMINISTRATIVE ENFORCEMENT OF TITLE IX AND THE CLERY ACT

Title IX Enforcement

The 2011 to 2014 period also saw a dramatic increase in OCR enforcement activity and related complaints. To enforce Title IX, OCR investigates individual complaints, conducts agency-initiated compliance reviews, and provides technical assistance to promote voluntary compliance. Theoretically, negative OCR findings can result in the loss of federal funding through Department of Education proceedings, or referral to the Department of Justice for litigation. Although OCR reportedly has threatened to initiate administrative proceedings to cut federal funding during 2013 and 2014, it is still fair to say that resolutions are negotiated with recipients, which take "voluntary remedial actions" to avoid an escalation of the process. Fines are not levied in the OCR enforcement process. Relatively recent OCR enforcement activity is discussed in a "Title IX Enforcement Highlights" document that was published by the Department of Education in June 2012 (see http://www2.ed.gov/documents/press-releases/title-ix-enforcement.pdf).

Whether an OCR investigation is initiated by an individual complaint or an agency compliance review, OCR investigations usually entail a broad-ranging inquiry into the institution's Title IX–related administrative structure (e.g., how the mandatory Title IX coordinator's duties are handled and communicated to the institutional community), its sexual discrimination, harassment, and violence policies and procedures, and its history of handling Title IX–related complaints. In recent years, OCR has issued and publicized detailed Resolution Letters that outline identified deficiencies in institutions' Title IX–related policies and procedures, and Resolution Agreements that describe how institutions will remedy such deficiencies and implement extensive training requirements.

A particularly noteworthy recent investigation at the University of Montana–Missoula involved both OCR and the Department of Justice (DOJ). The DOJ apparently became involved due to allegations that there were systemic defects in how campus police and local off-campus law enforcement responded to sexual assaults. The related Letter of Findings was extensive (see http://www2.ed.gov/documents/press-releases/montana-missoula-letter.pdf), and the related Resolution Agreement outlined a particularly broad array of policy change, training, and ongoing monitoring requirements (see http://www2.ed.gov/documents/press-releases/montana-missoula-resolution-agreement.pdf). The OCR/DOJ press release referred to the agreements reached as "a blueprint for colleges and universities across the country to take effective steps to prevent and address sexual assault and harassment on their campuses." (See http://www.ed.gov/news/press-releases/departments-justice-and-education-reach-settlement-address-and-prevent-sexual-as.) Although, since the press release, OCR officials have stated that the Montana agreement applies only to the University of Montana, all institutions should be cognizant of the prospect that similar enforcement approaches could be employed if deemed justified by federal enforcement authorities.

In sum, it is clear that OCR currently is taking its enforcement role very seriously, and that institutions should be cognizant of OCR's requirements and preferences—as reflected in the guidance discussed above—when developing Title IX–related policies and procedures.

Clery Act Enforcement

The Clery Act is enforced by the U.S. Department of Education's Federal Student Aid office ("FSA"). After years of relative inactivity—for which the department was criticized in the mid-2000s—the department ramped up its enforcement activity significantly. In 2008, Eastern Michigan University paid a record fine of $350,000, and other six-figure fines have been levied since. In 2012, the per-violation fine amount was increased from $27,500 to $35,000, making substantial fines for noncompliance even more likely. The FSA can base investigations on complaints from individuals, or can conduct a compliance audit if it chooses to do so. Letters from the FSA describing fines levied and the bases therefor are available on the department's website. In a noteworthy decision issued in October 2013, the FSA fined Lincoln University $275,000 for various recordkeeping and policy statement violations, which included a $27,500 fine for the university's failure to include a statement about the potential sanctions for sexual assault in its ASR. Institutions should pay particular attention to this area of potential sanctions when revising their ASRs to incorporate all of the new policy-related statements required by the VAWA Amendments.

Alleged underreporting of sexual assaults appears to be a matter of particular interest to the FSA, and alleged victims and victims' groups recently have paired Clery Act administrative complaints with Title IX administrative complaints. Such complaints, particularly when coupled with advocate-driven social media campaigns and the resulting media interest, must be taken seriously.

TITLE IX AND CLERY ACT CIVIL ACTION–RELATED ISSUES

Title IX Civil Action–Related Issues

Under *Gebser v. Lago Vista Indep. Sch. Dist.*, 524 U.S. 274 (1998), the implied private right of action available to parties who would challenge an institution's response to sexual harassment or sexual violence only provides for damages where the institution's response evinces "deliberate indifference." As summarized in 2012 by the Ninth Circuit Court of Appeals, this means that

Damages under Title IX are available only if an official with authority to address the alleged discrimination and institute corrective measures has actual knowledge of the discrimination and fails to adequately respond—i.e., acts with deliberate indifference. See *Gebser v. Lago Vista Indep. Sch. Dist.*, 524 U.S. 274, 290 (1998). The test for deliberate indifference is "whether a reasonable fact-finder could conclude that the [official]'s response was clearly unreasonable in light of the known circumstances." *Oden v. N. Marianas Coll.*, 440 F.3d 1085, 1089 (9th Cir.2006) (internal quotation marks omitted). Summary judgment is properly entered when a school's response to the harassment was not clearly unreasonable as a matter of law. *Davis v. Monroe Cnty. Bd. of Educ.*, 526 U.S. 629, 649. (1999)

Doe v. University of Pacific, 467 Fed. App. 685 (9th Cir. 2012). This high threshold has resulted in the dismissal of many sexual violence–related claims, as occurred in the University of the Pacific case (see *Doe v. University of Pacific*, 467 Fed. App. 685). Courts of Appeals, however, have denied summary judgment (that is, a favorable judgment without a jury trial) where inspired by the facts of certain cases. Potentially substantial civil damages and attorney's fees awards are available in sexual violence cases that survive summary judgment under the stringent *Gebser* standard.

It is noteworthy that courts have accorded substantial deference to OCR's regulations and a nonregulatory policy interpretation document in the context of assessing whether institutions are complying with the athletics equity requirements of Title IX. (See *McCormick v. Sch. Dist. of Mamaroneck*, 370 F.3d 275, 290 [2004]; holding that deference to Department of Education's nonregulatory policy interpretation regarding Title IX's athletics equity requirements was appropriate because it is "both persuasive and not unreasonable.") At least one court has extended the holding of the *McCormick* decision to also accord deference to OCR Dear Colleague letters regarding Title IX athletics equity issues (see *Biediger v. Quinnipiac University*, 728 F. Supp. 2d 62, 92–93 [D. Conn. 2010]).

It is less clear whether such deference would similarly be applied to the 2011 DCL in the event of litigation. First, Title IX athletics equity cases present the relatively straightforward question of whether the institution is discriminating in its athletics programs on the basis of sex; such cases do not involve a higher threshold for liability like that imposed by the "deliberate indifference" standard. Second, the 2011 DCL does not purport to address the question of what constitutes "deliberate indifference" for liability purposes. It obviously is concerned instead with OCR's administrative enforcement positions. Third, an institution pressed to defend itself in litigation might well argue that the 2011 DCL is not entitled to deference under the "persuasive and not unreasonable" standard, or entitled to the deference accorded the Department of Education's other guidance, because so many of its mandates and suggestions clearly are the product of OCR's preferences, with relatively loose connection to the straightforward nondiscrimination requirement imposed by Title IX's statutory language. Only time will tell whether these arguments could prevail in court.

Clery Act/VAWA Civil Action–Related Issues

The Clery Act cannot be enforced through a private right of action. Specifically, the statutory language (20 U.S.C. § 1092(f)(14)(A)) provides that

Nothing in this subsection may be construed to—

(i)   Create a cause of action against any institution of higher education or any employee of such an institution for any civil liability; or
(ii) Establish a standard of care.

The Clery Act also provides further that "Notwithstanding any other provision of law, evidence regarding compliance or noncompliance with [the Act] shall not be admissible as evidence in any proceeding of any court, agency, board, or other entity, except with respect to an action to enforce [the Act]." Despite this clear language, plaintiffs nonetheless have attempted to base claims on Clery Act provisions. These attempts appear to have failed uniformly. The law on this point was referenced recently in the court's decision in *Moore v. Murray State University*, 2013 WL 960320 (W.D. Ky. 2013), which held:

Moore fails to state a claim under the Jeanne Clery Act, 20 U.S.C. § 1092 et seq. because there is no private right of action under that statute. The Clery Act "is a landmark federal law . . . that requires colleges and universities across the United States to disclose information about crime on and around their campuses."

Summary of the Jeanne Clery Act, Clery Center for Security on Campus (http://www.securityoncampus.org/summary-jeanne-clery-act accessed March 8, 2013). "The Act is enforced by the United States Department of Education."
Indeed, the Act itself provides:

[quoting 20 U.S.C. § 1092(f)(14)(A)] Relying on the language of the statute, other courts have concluded that there is no private right of action under the Act. See *Doe v. Univ. of the S.,* 687 F. Supp. 2d 744, 760 (E.D. Tenn. 2009); *King v. San Francisco Cmty. Coll. Dist.,* No. C 10–01979 RS, 2010 WL 3930982, at *4–5 (N.D. Cal. Oct. 6, 2010) ("[T]he Act itself does not provide any private right of action.") [citation omitted].

Because no private right of action exists, Moore's cause of action under the Clery Act fails as a matter of law. *Moore,* 2013 WL 960320, *3.

Obviously, institutions defending sexual violence–related cases will have to be vigilant to ensure that the no "private right of action/no evidence" mandates of 20 U.S.C. § 1092(f)(14)(A) and (B) are respected fully in their cases (Cf. *Kleisch v. Cleveland State University*, 2006 WL 701047 (Ohio App. 10 Dist. 2006) (referencing fact that both the plaintiff's and the university's expert witnesses had offered evidence in bench trial regarding the university's alleged compliance or noncompliance with the Clery Act, and affirming trial court's reliance on the university's expert's opinion to the benefit of the university).)

Related Standard of Care Issues

As noted, institutions involved in sexual violence–related civil actions should be able to keep VAWA Amendment–related compliance issues out of such actions by relying upon 20 U.S.C. § 1092(f)(14)(A) and (B). Further, to the extent that portions of the OCR's 2011 DCL were incorporated into the VAWA Amendments, § 1092(f)(14)(A) and (B) arguably also could effectively preclude the admission of evidence in civil cases regarding noncompliance with those portions of the 2011 DCL.

Institutions should be thoughtful, however, as to whether their noncompliance with other elements of the 2011 DCL might be admitted into evidence by a court to show that the institution failed to follow a standard of care, or to implement appropriate procedures. A detailed analysis of what are known as "negligence per se" principles is beyond the scope of this chapter, but it should suffice to note that institutions defending themselves in sexual violence–related cases should be prepared to respond to arguments to the effect that noncompliance with 2011 DCL requirements constitutes negligence per se. (Cf. *Restatement (Third) of Torts:* Liability for Physical and Emotional Harm, § 14 (stating the principle that violation of a statute, regulation, or ordinance constitutes negligence per se if the statute, regulation, or ordinance was designed to protect against the type of accident that the actor's conduct causes, and if the accident victim is within the class of persons that the law was designed to protect).) Institutions will certainly argue that the 2011 DCL does not have the stature of the types of positive law described in *Restatement* § 14, but institutions should also anticipate that even if they are successful on the negligence per se argument, it is likely that plaintiffs also will argue that violation of 2011 DCL standards is at least evidence of negligence, if not negligence per se. It is fair to anticipate that various inventive approaches will be attempted by plaintiffs who are intent on getting alleged "DCL noncompliance" evidence before a jury.

One approach of potential concern would seek to put 2011 DCL "suggestions" before a jury through the testimony of an expert witness. It is noteworthy by comparison that even nonbinding guidance documents issued by voluntary standards organizations can be admissible as to the standard of care, even though practices that do not conform to the suggestions of such documents are not in violation of any law. For this reason, institutions should be prudent regarding the prospect that even the obviously nonbinding suggestions in the "Not Alone Report" and the various model policies offered on the White House's Not Alone website (some of which are discussed above) could be cited as evidence of "best practices" that an institution allegedly failed to follow in a particular case.

In *Lees v. Carthage College*, 714 F.3d 516 (7th Cir. 2013), the Seventh Circuit Court of Appeals held that a plaintiff's expert in a sexual violence case should be allowed to rely in his testimony on a "door prop alarm" suggestion from a 1996 International Association of Campus Law Enforcement Administrators (IACLEA) manual, even though the manual provided explicitly that it was not intended, given the wide variability in campus environments, to establish particular safety standards. (*Lees v. Carthage College* at 525.) The court's rationale for this holding was that although the IACLEA manual does not establish a binding standard of care, the expert's consultation of the manual's suggestions was a methodologically sound approach to take for purposes of the rules that govern the admissibility of expert testimony (*Lees v. Carthage College* at 525). Of concern is that a jury might focus more on the claim that the "standard" cited by the expert was allegedly violated, and less on whether the standard was or was not a legally binding standard.

By analogy, it would not be surprising if a similar approach were adopted by plaintiffs attempting to put 2011 DCL or "Not Alone Report" "suggestions" before a jury—particularly those suggestions regarding personnel training, student education, and prevention efforts. Institutions defending themselves in sexual violence–related cases of course would resist such attempts, but for prospective planning purposes, it is more prudent to avoid the issue altogether by assuring institutional compliance with all aspects of the 2011 DCL, and considering carefully, at least in general terms, how to align institutional practices with the suggestions found in the "Not Alone Report" and related model policies.

INTERACTION BETWEEN THREAT ASSESSMENT AND DOMESTIC AND DATING VIOLENCE, SEXUAL ASSAULT, AND STALKING

As institutions become more conversant with how to respond effectively to domestic violence, dating violence, sexual assault, and stalking cases, they should not miss the opportunity to recognize that campus threat assessment and management ("TAM") teams can be valuable resources in such cases. Misconduct along these lines might first come to the institution's attention through a student affairs– or employment-related disciplinary process, but in appropriate cases, officials involved in administering such processes should inquire whether the TAM team has been involved. If not, then officials should consider involving the TAM team. Given the potential life-and-death gravity of the issues that can be involved in such cases, institutions should avoid a "silo mentality" that might allow a disciplinary process to progress in a "business-as-usual" manner and remain the sole institutional response, without recognizing that greater safety-related issues could be in play. Because most institutions now use TAM teams to assess and manage risks of targeted violence, institutions should recognize that domestic violence, dating violence, and stalking are likely to fall within the team's area of expertise, and should not hesitate to involve such teams in parallel with other more traditional (and VAWA Amendments–required) campus disciplinary processes.

Institutions also should recognize that the adoption and publication of VAWA Amendments–required policies will likely result in an increase in the reporting of domestic violence, dating violence, and stalking. If planning to involve the TAM team in assisting as necessary, institutions should consider whether their teams are up to speed on the literature and practices regarding the assessment and management of threats in the domestic violence, dating violence, and stalking contexts. Institutions that are seeking to learn more about the interaction between threat assessment and domestic violence, dating violence, sexual assault, and stalking might wish to review several of the chapters in the recently published *International Handbook of Threat Assessment* (Meloy & Hoffmann 2014). Further, institutions should consider whether their TAM teams require some additional training to respond effectively to the threat assessment and management needs that are likely to arise in these areas.

CONCLUSION

The VAWA Amendments' merger of Title IX, VAWA, and Clery Act elements; an increase in administrative enforcement activity; and the White House's "Not Alone" initiative have created new policy, procedural, response, and training requirements and goals for colleges and universities in the areas of domestic violence, dating violence, sexual assault, and stalking. Regulations resulting from the VAWA Amendments–negotiated rulemaking process will detail further the Department of Education's expectations for institutional responses in these areas. Unprecedented social media–driven advocacy campaigns and related media interest also have sharpened the focus on institutional responses to sexual assault. Nonetheless, institutions must balance the pressure to deal effectively with reported misconduct against the need to deal fairly with all of their students and employees.

Education and prevention efforts provide the best hope for progress, as satisfaction with even the best disciplinary and response process is likely to be low, and it is obviously preferable to avoid—rather than respond to—harm. By complying with the new legal requirements and guidance, and moving beyond mere compliance and becoming innovators in the areas of education and prevention, colleges and universities can make their campuses safer from the risks posed by domestic violence, dating violence, sexual assault, and stalking.

NOTES

1. See, e.g., Revised sexual harassment guidance (2001), http://www2.ed.gov /about/offices/list/ocr/docs/shguide.pdf; Dear colleague letter on harassment and bullying (2010), http://www2.ed.gov/about/offices/list/ocr/letters/ colleague-201010.pdf; Dear colleague letter on retaliation (2013), http://www2 .ed.gov/about/offices/list/ocr/letters/colleague-201304.html.

2. See U.S. Department of Justice (http://www.ovw.usdoj.gov), Office on Violence Against Women website http://www.whitehouse.gov/sites/default /files/docs/vawa_factsheet.pdf; "The Violence Against Women Act: Overview, legislation, and federal funding, Congressional Research Service" (May 10, 2012), https://www.fas.org/sgp/crs/misc/R42499.pdf.

3. A summary of the voluminous body of research and advocacy-related information regarding domestic violence, dating violence, and stalking is well beyond the scope of this chapter, but the following websites and the resources available through the sites should be helpful to institutions that are working to understand and evaluate training curricula developed by internal and external subject matter experts: DOJ's Office on Violence Against Women website, http://www.ovw .usdoj.gov/publications.html; Stalking Resource Center website, http://www .victimsofcrime.org/our-programs/stalking-resource-center; Centers for Disease Control and Prevention website, http://www.cdc.gov/violenceprevention /intimatepartnerviolence/teen_dating_violence.html; National Criminal Justice Reference Service website, https://www.ncjrs.gov/teendatingviolence/.

4. Example OCR Resolution Letters and Resolution Agreements are posted in the "Reading Room" section of OCR's website. Noteworthy documents posted as of September 2014 include, for example: University of Notre Dame press release, http://www.ed.gov/news/press-releases/civil-rights-office-announces -settlement-agreement-discrimination-investigation-notre-dame;University of Notre Dame Resolution Letter, http://www2.ed.gov/about/offices/list/ocr/docs /investigations/05072011-a.html; University of Notre Dame Resolution Agreement, http://www2.ed.gov/about/offices/list/ocr/docs/investigations/05072011-b .html; Eastern Michigan University Resolution Letter, http://www2.ed.gov/about /offices/list/ocr/docs/investigations/15096002-a.pdf; EMU Resolution Agreement, http://www2.ed.gov/about/offices/list/ocr/docs/investigations/15096002-b .pdf; Notre Dame College Resolution Letter, http://www2.ed.gov/about/offices /list/ocr/docs/investigations/15096001-a.pdf; Notre Dame College Resolution Agreement, http://www2.ed.gov/about/offices/list/ocr/docs/investigations /15096001-b.pdf; Yale University press release, http://www.ed.gov/news/press

-releases/us-department-education-announces-resolution-yale-university-civil
-rights-invest; Yale Resolution Letter, http://www2.ed.gov/about/offices/list
/ocr/docs/investigations/01112027-a.html; Yale Resolution Agreement, http://
www2.ed.gov/about/offices/list/ocr/docs/investigations/01112027-b.html; State
University of New York Resolution Letter, http://www2.ed.gov/documents
/press-releases/suny-new-york-letter.doc; State University of New York Resolution
Agreement,   http://www2.ed.gov/documents/press-releases/suny-new-york
-agreement.doc.

5. See http://studentaid.ed.gov/about/data-center/school/clery-act.

6. See http://studentaid.ed.gov/sites/default/files/fsawg/datacenter/cleryact
/lincoln/1871_001.pdf.

7. See, e.g., *Simpson v. University of Colorado Boulder,* 500 F.3d 1170 (10th Cir.
2007); *Williams v. Board of Regents of University System of Georgia,* 477 F.3d 1282 (11th
Cir. 2007).

8. See also *Lewen v. Edinboro University of Pennsylvania,* 2011 WL 4527348, *4
(W.D. Pa. 2011) (relying upon 20 U.S.C. § 1092(f)(14)(A)(i) to support dismissal of
attempted Clery-based civil claim); *Doe v. University of the South,* 687 F.Supp.2d
744, 759 (E.D. Tenn. 2009) (dismissing plaintiffs' request for declaratory judgment
to effect that university violated Clery Act sexual assault policy requirements in
part because the no private right of action/no evidence mandate of 20 U.S.C. §
1092(f)(14)(A)(i) rendered the question of Clery Act compliance "completely irrelevant to Plaintiffs['] tort claims").

9. See Dobbs, *The law of torts,* § 164 ("As a sword, the plaintiff can show the defendant's violation of a safety custom as some evidence that defendant failed to act
as a reasonable person under the circumstances. In some cases, evidence of the
custom is presented by an expert, but the rule is no less applicable if the custom is
institutionalized in advisory standards of the relevant industrial association" (citing, e.g., *Hansen v. Abrasive Eng'g & Manufacturing, Inc.,* 317 Or. 378, 856 P.2d 625
(1993) (ANSI advisory standard deemed admissible but not conclusive).

The court in *Getty Petroleum Marketing, Inc. v. Capital Terminal Co.,* 391 F.3d 312
(1st Cir. 2004), provided a fair, balanced summary of the law in this area:

> Many cases involve voluntary industry standards that do not have the force of
> law in the relevant jurisdiction. The overwhelming majority of such cases are
> negligence actions where the industry standard is offered as evidence of the
> appropriate standard of care. See, e.g., Miller v. Yazoo Mfg. Co., 26 F.3d 81, 83
> (8th Cir. 1994) (in personal injury action, American National Standards
> Institute lawnmower safety standards were offered to establish standard of
> care); Matthews v. Ashland Chem., Inc., 770 F.2d 1303, 1310–11 (5th Cir. 1985)
> (in personal injury action, NFPA, National Electric Code, and the American
> National Standard Specifications for Accident Prevention Signs were offered
> to establish standard of care); Boston & Me. R.R. v. Talbert, 360 F.2d 286, 290
> (1st Cir. 1966) ("certain nationally recognized standards concerning the design
> of highway and railroad crossings" were offered to establish standard of care,
> with trial judge's warning that they were "not completely authoritative");
> Dickie v. Shockman, No. A3-98-137, 2000 WL 33339623, *3 (D.N.D. July 17,
> 2000) (in personal injury action, NFPA standards "and other codes applicable
> within the propane industry" were offered to establish standard of care).

These voluntary standards do not irrefutably establish the standard of care in a negligence case. Rather, they constitute "one more piece of evidence upon which the jury could decide whether the defendant acted as a reasonably prudent person in the circumstances of th[e] case." Boston & Me. R.R., 360 F.2d at 290. The defendant is free to argue that the standard is unduly demanding, either in general or in the particular instance, and that it does not reflect industry practice or the standard that a reasonably prudent person would employ. After all, voluntary standards are not law; in essence, they are simply recommendations written by experts who may not themselves be available for cross-examination. In short, the merits of the standard are "for the jury's consideration like any other evidence in the case." Boston & Me. R.R., 360 F.2d at 290.

Consequently, courts have generally treated such standards as factual evidence that the court may admit or exclude based on ordinary evidentiary principles. See, e.g., *Miller*, 26 F.3d at 83–84 (voluntary standard was properly admitted); *Matthews*, 770 F.2d at 1310–11 (voluntary standards were properly excluded); Boston & Me. R.R., 360 F.2d at 290 (voluntary standards were properly admitted); *Dickie*, 2000 WL 33339623, at *3 (admitting expert testimony regarding voluntary standards).

Getty Petroleum, 391 F.3d at 326–27. See also *Kent Village Assocs. Joint Venture v. Smith*, 657 A.2d 330, 337 (Md. Ct. Spec. App. 1995) ("safety standards . . . may be admitted to show an accepted standard of care, the violation of which may be regarded as evidence of negligence"). See also Feld, *Annotation, Admissibility in evidence, on issue of negligence, of codes or standards of safety issued or sponsored by governmental body or by voluntary association,* 58 A.L.R.3d 148 (1974 & 2010 Supp.).

10. Example chapters of interest include, Kropp, P. R., and Cook, A. N., Intimate partner violence, stalking and femicide; Scalora, M. J., Electronic threats and harassment; Dormand, K., Domestic violence threat assessment: Putting knowledge and skills into practice; and Deisinger, E. R., Randazzo, M. R., and Nolan, J. J., *Threat assessment and management in higher education.*

REFERENCES

"Dear Colleague Letter" ("2011 DCL"). http://www2.ed.gov/about/offices/list /ocr/letters/colleague-201104.pdf. Accessed May 12, 2015.

Meloy, J. R., and Hoffmann, J. eds. (2014). *International handbook of threat assessment.* New York: Oxford University Press.

Part III

Sexual Harassment: Incidence and Psychological Dimensions

Chapter 6

Denial, Blame, Betrayal, and the Conspiracy of Silence: Educator Sexual Harassment of K Through 12 Students

Susan Strauss

School should be a fun place where students are on a quest to learn and explore new worlds and relationships in a safe and secure milieu. Sometimes, however, the joy of inquiry is sabotaged by the very people whom students and parents believe they can trust to create and support a positive learning environment—educators, administrators, and other school staff. Probably the most egregious behavior in which these trusted adults can engage to undermine student safety, success, and health is that of sexual harassment of students. The phenomenon is confounded when school officials do not aggressively act to prevent and stop such misconduct (Fossey & DeMitchell 1995; Shakeshaft 2004).

Sexual harassment of students by educators is loathsome and abhorrent—and unfortunately occurs with more frequency than anyone would like to think. According to the U.S. Department of Education, between kindergarten and 12th grade, more than 4.5 million children are targets of sexual harassment by a school employee (Shakeshaft 2004). For the purposes of this chapter, the term "educator" is used to encompass any school employee, including administrators, counselors, janitors, bus drivers, coaches, aides, secretaries, and teachers.

DEFINING SEXUAL HARASSMENT

Confusion is abundant as to what term to use to define sexual misconduct perpetrated upon students by adult educators. "Sexual abuse," "rape," "molestation," "sexual exploitation," and "sexual harassment" are words and phrases frequently used to describe educator sexual misconduct (Shakeshaft & Cohan 1995). "Sexual harassment" is the term primarily used for this discussion. Sexual harassment is broader in scope than the other terms listed; it includes a continuum of behaviors from the more subtle, such as staring, to the egregious misconduct of sexual assault and rape. Sexual harassment can be electronic/digital, physical, verbal, and visual. It is prohibited by the Civil Rights Act Title IX and is defined by the U.S. Department of Education, Office of Civil Rights as

> Unwelcome sexual advances, requests for sexual favors, and other verbal, nonverbal, or physical conduct of a sexual nature by an employee, by another student, or by a third party, which is sufficiently severe, persistent, or pervasive to limit a student's ability to participate in or benefit from an education program or activity, or to create a hostile or abusive educational environment. (U.S. Department of Education 2000, 264)

Additionally, the National Advisory Council on Women's Educational Programs asserted that "Academic sexual harassment is the use of authority to emphasize the sexuality or sexual identity of the student in a manner which prevents or impairs that student's full enjoyment of educational benefits, climate, or opportunities" (Paludi & Barickman 1991, 4).

RESEARCH, PREVALENCE, AND EXAMPLES

Most school educators are trustworthy and committed to teaching their students. Based on the very few studies of sexual harassment and sexual misconduct perpetrated by educators upon students in school, it is a small percentage of educators who engage in this repugnant behavior (Hendrie 1998g; Shakeshaft & Cohan 1995). Colleagues and administrators believe the behavior would be overtly obvious to others within the school. Principals and teachers, although knowing the behavior occurs, just don't believe it is common or that it would occur in *their* school, so they often overlook the signs and symptoms of its presence. Even after a trial in which a colleague has been found guilty of criminal sexual misconduct or sexual harassment, fellow teachers might deny the outcome. It is estimated that

0.04% to 5% of teachers sexually abuse students, and roughly 25% of school districts are challenged with the problem. Unfortunately, the behavior can go unabated for years despite rumors, a gut sense, or even actual formal allegations, as offenders spend decades with students before getting caught—suggesting that "districts are being too lax, too trusting, or too languid about the possibility of employees abusing students" (Graves 1994, 14). By transferring schools, the perpetrators often stay one step ahead of being caught.

Research on school sexual abuse is virtually nonexistent (Sorenson 1991). A four-year analysis of reported cases (from 1987 to 1999) of child sexual abuse in schools reported in the *Education Law Reporter* and found using a Westlaw computer search unveiled a small but steady increase. The increase, however, does not necessarily reflect an actual increase in abuse. It is estimated that a minimum of one-eighth of children are sexually abused by someone other than a family member.

The No Child Left Behind Act of 2001 required a national research study be conducted on sexual abuse in the schools. As a result, Shakeshaft (2004) created a synthesis of existing literature on educator sexual misconduct at the request of the U.S. Department of Education. Shakeshaft found only a few empirical studies and only one study, conducted by the American Association of University Women (AAUW), that was based upon a representative national sample (AAUW 1993; 2001). Although the AAUW's two studies examined the sexual harassment of students with an emphasis on student-on-student harassment, the sexual harassment by educators was also assessed. Shakeshaft (2003) then reexamined the results from the AAUW's studies, concentrating on educator sexual harassment alone.

The 1993 AAUW study surveyed more than 1,600 students in grades 8 through 11 in 79 public schools (AAUW 1993) and found that 25% of females and 10% of males (18% of the total number of students) had been sexually harassed by a school employee. The 2000 study replicated the 1993 study, and surveyed slightly more than 2,000 students (AAUW 2001). Students responded to questions inquiring about their sexual harassment experiences during their entire time in school; they also identified the harasser—such as student, teacher, and other school staff.

The AAUW data were subjected to reanalysis by Shakeshaft (2003) who found that a slightly less than 10% of students reported sexual harassment by educators. Fewer than 9% reported noncontact sexual harassment, approximately 7% indicated they had been subjected to contact or physical sexual harassment, and some students experienced both. Shakeshaft's study estimated that 4.5 million students are sexually harassed by an educator at some point between kindergarten and 12th grade.

Corbett, Gentry, and Pearson (1993) found that 48% of students experienced verbal comments and looks, 23% were subjected to inappropriate touching, and a full 29% experienced affairs or dating relationships with their teachers. Examples of noncontact harassment included insulting comments, looks, and gestures. Contact harassment encompassed unwanted sexual touch and intercourse.

Shakeshaft and Cohan (1995) conducted a four-year study of 225 cases of sexual abuse of students by educators using results of interviews with school administration, teachers, attorneys, and parents. The majority of cases that superintendents disclosed—38%—had occurred in elementary schools; 20% occurred in middle schools, 36% in high schools, and 6% were attributed to other categories. The noncontact harassment, such as educators' exposing themselves to students and showing students pornographic pictures, were not perceived by superintendents as being harmful. If the sexual harassment was verbal in nature, the superintendents were more likely to label it as a "language indiscretion" and as not very serious—even when teachers made such comments as, "What's the matter? Isn't your boyfriend giving you enough? Can't he get it up?" Superintendents did not label such comments as sexual harassment and typically didn't see what harm was caused by these types of comments.

Contact abuse complaints predominantly were lodged against male teachers by female students (Shakeshaft & Cohan 1995). Often the teachers were popular coaches of athletics, drama, art, and music. The male harassers' victims were female in 76% of the cases and male in 24% of the cases. In the cases in which the harasser was female, 86% of the victims were female and 14% were male. A superintendent described the behavior of a male teacher who touched elementary students' breasts and genitals as being "not serious." In another district, a special education student who was emotionally and developmentally disabled was told by the school district to "stay away from the teacher" in response to the teacher performing fellatio on the student in a shopping center parking lot in the middle of the afternoon.

The Texas Civil Rights Project (Cedello 1997) found the greatest percentage of students sexually harassed by educators. In response to the question, "In the most serious incident, who harassed you?" females reported that 42% of those incidents were committed by school administrators, 29% by teachers or counselors, and 58% by other school staff. In contrast, male students reported 8% of the incidents were perpetrated by school administrators, 26% by teachers or counselors, and 15% by school staff. These statistics are particularly alarming when considering that students reported only the "most serious" incidents.

Education Week conducted a six-month study of sex offenses committed upon students by school employees. Researchers used everything available—from newspapers to computer databases—to gather data on 244 cases of abuse (Hendrie 1998g). Perpetrators' ages ranged from 21 to 75, with 28 as the average age. Seven out of 10 were teachers; however, janitors, bus drives, principals, and librarians also were accused. Student victims were in grades kindergarten through 12, and 66% of victims were older the age 14, and 66% were female and 33% were male. Of the accused harassers, 20% were women. Only two cases were determined to have been false. A solid 33% of allegations were against coaches of athletics, music, or drama.

Bithell (1991) found that 1% of adults said that they were sexually abused by teachers in elementary school, and 3% experienced sexual abuse in high school. Bithell estimated that approximately 1 in 20 teachers has sexually harassed students, including everything from sexually noxious comments to sexual intercourse.

Examples of the sexual harassment include sexually offensive verbal comments, such as calling female students "boobies," complimenting a girl on her nice legs, and commenting on the student's sex life (Shakeshaft & Cohan 1995). Corbett, Gentry, and Pearson found comments such as, "nice ass," "great boobs," and "you could make me want to cheat on my wife," and a coach telling female athletes that they "opened their legs wider than that for their boyfriends" (Corbett, Gentry & Pearson 1993, 98). Flattery, consoling, and writing love letters are examples identified by Hendrie (1998c). Shakeshaft and Cohan (1995) included exhibitionism, showing students sexually explicit pictures, and various obscene gestures as examples of noncontact sexual harassment, which they labeled "level I."

Physical examples—referred to as "level II" contact sexual abuse—include touching a female's breasts and legs, requesting hugs, kissing, sexual intercourse (Corbett, Gentry & Pearson 1993; Shakeshaft & Cohan 1995), touching genitals, fondling, tickling (Shakeshaft & Cohan 1995), and pinning the students against walls and lockers (Hendrie 1998c). Male victims' complaints of sexual harassment were taken more seriously by school officials than were female victim's complaints. The female accuser's honesty sometimes was questioned, whereas there were rarely any misgivings about a male student's accusations (Hendrie 1998d). This discounting or minimizing of female students' experiences further victimizes them due to their gender. An emerging trend for educator harassers is the use of text messaging, twitter, e-mail, Facebook, MySpace, and other electronic means to groom and harass their student victim (Maxwell 1997). Text messaging has become the new "digital come-ons" (Maxwell 1997, 1). The electronic tools allow the harasser to extend his or her luring tentacles beyond the school to the point of stalking the student victim. If there is anything positive about the digital come-ons, it is that it leaves evidence of the wrongdoing that school officials can use to support students' allegations.

Sexual abuse committed by teachers and other school employees is challenging to study because students generally do not report it to their parents (AAUW 1993) or to school officials (Shakeshaft & Cohan 1995). When schools are made aware of allegations, they are hesitant to share the data with researchers (Shakeshaft & Cohan 1995). Newspaper articles provide evidence of sexual harassment (and criminal abuse) but are not written in a scholarly mode, and generally no follow-up information is provided.

CHARACTERISTICS OF THE HARASSER

Those educators most likely to sexually harass often are well respected by their colleagues, administrators, students, and parents (Shakeshaft & Cohan 1995). They are more likely to be male (Bagley & King 1990), and actively involved in coaching students enrolled in extracurricular activities such as music, athletics, and debate, for example (Shakeshaft & Cohan 1994). Between 1995 and 2003, Jennings and Tharp (2003) discovered that 25% of Texas educators who sexually harassed students were either music teachers or coaches. According to Shakeshaft (2004), 18% of students are harassed by teachers, 15% by coaches, 13% by substitute teachers, 12% by bus drivers, 6% by principals, and 5% by counselors.

To research the gender of the perpetrator for the Department of Education's national report on sexual misconduct in U.S. schools, Shakeshaft (2004) analyzed the data from the newspaper analysis, states' education disciplinary records, interviews with adults, and surveys of both adults and students. The search for data yielded the following study results. Jennings and Tharp (2003) found that approximately 13% of female teachers and 87% of male teachers were disciplined for sexual misconduct. Hendrie (1998d) concluded that 20% of harassers were female and 80% were male. Shakeshaft and Cohan (1994) discovered that males comprised 96%, and females 4% of sexual offenders. The AAUW (1993) study results showed that slightly more than 57% of harassers were male and about 42% were female. A review of the child abuse literature demonstrated that males are much more likely to be the offender than are females; though the number of female perpetrators could be underreported due to a belief that males should be flattered by a female's sexual "interest" (Shakeshaft 2004).

Female harassers/offenders often are researched separately from male harassers (Hendrie 1998a; Shoop 2004). Years ago, a male making a complaint of being sexually harassed—including sexual assault—was uncommon. If it did occur it most likely was discounted, largely because of the stereotype that any male would enjoy the behavior (Sutton 2004). It is now acknowledged, however, that even consensual sex between an adult and a student younger than age 18 (or even younger, depending on state law) is a crime. According to Sutton (2004), almost 43% of educator sexual offenders are women; however this could be a low percentage.

According to psychological analysis, female harassers typically are considered socially immature rather than sexually perverse (Driedger 2003). Women form a romantic love attachment to the victim, which is in contrast to the profile of male offenders who instead tend to abuse a series of students over time, a behavior rare in women offenders (Hendrie 1998a). Women are reported to rarely use force or threats to keep their victims silent. They are more likely to acknowledge their misconduct and usually engage in the behavior later in life. Women who sexually abuse teens also typically are not particularly disturbed, in contrast to the male offender who generally is more disturbed and difficult to treat. Corbett, Gentry, and Pearson (1993) found that female teachers sexually harass their male students by exposing themselves and infringing on the student's body space. According to one boy, this was accomplished by the teacher having sex every other weekend with a friend of the student.

Considering a female to be a sexual predator is somewhat foreign to the courts, schools, and communities (Hendrie 1998a), and traditionally has led to schools and courts dealing with the issue in alternative ways. Two of the most well-known cases are those of Mark Kay LeTourneau and Julie Anne Fell. LeTourneau, who was married with children, began a sexual relationship with one of her male 6th grade students. LeTourneau became pregnant as a result of their relationship, was caught by the authorities, and spent seven years in prison. LeTourneau and the former student later married and have two children. In the other case, Fell, a 31-year-old married speech coach, English teacher, and mother, had a sexual relationship with one of her 10th grade students (who at the time still played with action figures, which indicates his level of maturity). The Fell case ended differently than the LeTourneau case, with Fell's victim informing the judge that he thinks his former teacher manipulated him for her own sexual pleasure, and that he believes Fell to be a monster. Fell served seven years in prison for her offense.

The study conducted by *Education Week* found 250 cases of educator sexual harassment, of which 43 involved female harassers (Hendrie 1998a). In the cases of the 43 women, 5 of the victims were female and the rest were male. It is suggested that more women might be offending but are not reported due to stereotypes and machismo. If a boy claimed he was having sex with a female teacher, the response of his friends could very well be, "Wow, you are one lucky dude!" according to Shakeshaft (2003).

Same-sex sexual harassment or abuse does not denote homosexual abuse. Shakeshaft and Cohan (1994) discovered that 24% of men who harassed males identified themselves as heterosexuals. Shakeshaft's (2003) reanalysis of the AAUW's 2001 study suggested slightly more than 15% male-to-male harassment, and 13% female-to-female sexual harassment. There appear to be fewer women who target other females, which also was demonstrated in Shakeshaft and Cohan's findings of 3%. The total percentage of same-sex harassment was 27% for Shakeshaft and Cohan's study and 28.3% for Shakeshaft's (2003) AAUW reanalysis.

CHARACTERISTICS OF THE TARGET

Students that are vulnerable or excluded from friendships with other students frequently are the targets of educator harassers because such students often are grateful for any adult attention (Shakeshaft & Cohan 1994). Another study found that the victims shared the attributes of being shy, average or above average students, attractive, had dysfunctional backgrounds, and defined themselves as outcasts. Children who struggle with low self-esteem, who are less likely to have close relationships with their parents, who participate in precarious behavior or whose parents partake in the same behavior, often are the desired prey (Hendrie 1998c; Shakeshaft & Cohan 1994). They are easy marks because they often crave attention and are more likely to not report the harasser. Additionally, these students are less likely to be perceived as scrupulous if they lodge a complaint against a well-liked teacher (Hendrie 1998c; Shakeshaft & Cohan 1994).

Females are the more likely targets of educator sexual harassment (Bagley & King 1990; Hendrie 1998; Shakeshaft 2003; Shakeshaft & Cohan 1994). It could be possible, however, that females are more likely to report their victimization than are males (Shakeshaft 2003). Shakeshaft (2003) concluded that Latino, African American, and American Indian students are more frequent targets of educator sexual harassment than are Caucasian and Asian students.

In Sorenson's study (1991), 22 cases involved male harassers and female victims, 11 were male to male, 2 involved a male harasser and students of both genders, one instance of female harasser and male victim, and one of female-to-female harassment. Twenty of the cases included multiple actual and alleged victims; 30 cases involved accusations of multiple incidents against the same victim. This suggests that many more victims could be involved than the number of cases indicates. Eighteen cases targeted elementary students, 3 involved middle school students, 18 were high school students, 1 was a preschool student, and 3 of the victims were disabled students from various grades. Seventeen of the cases were identified ambiguously as sexual molestation. Five cases included complaints of fondling or exposure, 11 victims were raped or experienced "deviate sexual intercourse" (Sorenson 1991, 464), and 4 victims experienced actual or alleged intercourse. These cases encompassed oral, anal, and other penetration resulting in severe emotional sequelae to the children. Students with disabilities are more likely to experience sexual abuse (Sobsey, Randall & Parrila 1997; Sullivan & Knutson 2000), but there are no data describing the sexual harassment of students with disabilities in schools.

PATTERNS OF EDUCATOR SEXUAL HARASSMENT

The teacher who sexually harasses his or her students behaves like any other sexual predator by using manipulative techniques such as isolation, blame, and lying (Shakeshaft & Cohan 1994). They are experts at taking advantage of a student's immaturity (Hendrie 1998c). Those that target the elementary schoolchild (children younger than seventh grade) are well liked; often are recognized as master teachers; and often are lauded by students, parents, administrators, and other teachers (Shakeshaft 2003). These teachers frequently even are the recipients of the "Teacher of the Year" award or have been recognized for their excellence in teaching (Shakeshaft & Cohan 1994). The harassers' reputation of excellence coupled with their popularity creates a dilemma for the school administrator who receives a complaint of sexual harassment from a marginalized child. In fact, the recognition of excellence is one of the avenues the harasser uses to abuse victims because it adds to the educators' professional credibility when a complaint is made.

The harasser of middle and high school students varies from the harasser of an elementary student (Shakeshaft & Cohan 1994). These educators might or might not be recognized for their excellence and mastery of teaching. According to the authors, when an older child is targeted, it is more likely the result of an opportunity or poor judgment rather than a premeditated event.

"Pedophile" is the label often used to describe an individual who abuses children (age 13 years and younger), but it does not apply in most cases of educator harassment (Hendrie 1998d). Hebephilia refers to those who target adolescents, and sometimes is used to define educators who sexually abuse teens. Educators who harass students, however, typically do not fall into any one category that labels those who commit sexual offenses. Some experts believe that educators who harass might behave this way because of other factors, such as immaturity or stress, or not having a clear sense of professional boundaries. Others might be considered narcissists, concerned only with their own sexual gratification at the expense of the target's pain. Still others could be considered romantic "bad-judgment" abusers who target teens. The labels tend to stem from various fields of study such as psychology or law, but for the purposes of behavior in the schools, it doesn't really matter because the behavior and consequences are the same (Shakeshaft 2003).

"Grooming" is the term (Robins 2000, cited in Shakeshaft 2004; Shoop 2004; Patterson & Austin 2008) often used to describe the process of a planned progression that the harasser instigates to:

1. Begin the selection process of the victim,
2. Assess the student's ability to not tell,

3. Determine the child's compliance,
4. Desensitize the child through increased sexual touch,
5. Proffer experiences the child enjoys and wants to continue, and
6. Manipulate the child into believing that he or she is responsible for the abuse because he or she didn't tell the abuser to stop.

According to Shoop, grooming can run the continuum of questionable boundary crossing to obvious inappropriate behavior.

The process of grooming often begins with the educator giving preferential attention to the target, sometimes inquiring about the student's personal life, boyfriend or girlfriend, and dating relationship while demonstrating sincere interest and understanding, and touching the student (Robins 2000 cited in Shakeshaft 2004; Shoop 2004). Sometimes additional help is given in school subjects, music, or athletics that creates a closer relationship with the child (Shoop 2004). The harassing educator might begin sexual conversations with the student, including discussions about the educator's sex life. The student then might feel special because this teacher—who the student admires and even might feel love for—is treating her or him as an adult. The relationship progresses to sexual intercourse with the teacher indicating a love relationship, and the teacher telling the student that when the student graduates, the teacher will leave his or her spouse and they will be together. Because children believe in these "loving relationships," they often do not define their experience as abuse (Robbins 2000, cited in Shakeshaft 2004).

Some of the sexual harassment occurs in the educator's home, in their car, or some other location outside the school (Shakeshaft 2004). Most sexual harassment occurs in school hallways, offices, and classrooms that sometimes are filled with students. An example is sexual intercourse occurring during class in a storage room attached to the classroom (Shakeshaft 2003; Shakeshaft & Cohan 1994). In another case, the teacher would call specific boys up to his desk allegedly to discuss homework (Shakeshaft & Cohan 1994). As each boy stood at the desk, the teacher caressed and groped the student's penis—and every other child in the classroom was cognizant of what was occurring. For 15 years this teacher abused boys in his classroom until finally one student told a school official.

ALLEGATIONS AND SCHOOL RESPONSE

In Shakeshaft's reanalysis of the AAUW data, 71% of students indicated they would inform a school official if sexually harassed by a school employee (Shakeshaft 2003). The reality appears quite different, however. Of those students who were sexually harassed by a school employee, 11.6% told a teacher, and 10.6% reported the misconduct to another school employee. Students are not likely to report the milder forms of sexual harassment—such as those that are verbal or visual—and are much more likely to report physical forms including hugging, kissing, sexual assault, and rape. According to Shakeshaft and Cohan (1994), approximately 90% of complaints to superintendents consisted of physical sexual harassment. Unfortunately, most of those complaints were not believed or were ignored. Victims as well as other students who know of the harassment soon learn that they cannot trust school officials, teachers, coaches, and other people in positions of trust to protect them. This results in a sense of increased vulnerability, betrayal, and helplessness. Students state they don't tell school officials because of the fear that they won't be believed (Robbins 2000, cited in Shakeshaft 2004). Female victims of teacher Kenneth DeLuca—who sexually abused 13 students who were between the ages of 10 to 18 to more than 21 years old—were not believed and were told to transfer to other schools. Their parents were threatened with lawsuits.

The study by *Education Week* cited numerous failings by school officials including the following (Hendrie 1998b; 1998e):

- Failure to believe students and thereby failure to respond to a complaint.
- Failure to report suspected abuse to agencies such as law enforcement and child protection.
- Failure to conduct—or incompetently conducting—investigations.
- Failure to document incidents, complaints, and investigations.
- Failure to investigate after a student recants her or his complaint, not recognizing that the recant might be in response to threats or manipulation to protect the abuser.
- Failure to fire the harasser despite numerous complaints.
- Failure of the teaching profession to police itself at the state level.
- Failure of school districts to implement quality recruitment and hiring practices by not asking the right questions, seeking references, and fingerprinting.
- Providing positive—even glowing—references for the harasser when he or she moves on to the next school district to teach.
- Failure to revoke educator's licenses for sex crimes.
- Cutting deals with the offender by the district agreeing to remain silent about a student's allegations if the educator quietly resigns.

The child victim often is blamed for her or his own victimization (Hendrie 1998b). For example, when one vice principal caught a teacher kissing a student in his classroom, the vice principal rebuked the student (Hendrie 1998b). Another incident involved a school official bringing the victim and the alleged harasser together, allowing the teacher to manipulate her into recanting her complaint. Another principal, after a nine-year-old third grader cried to her that her teacher had fondled her genitals, told the girl she was wrong, called the teacher to her office, and instructed the student to hug her teacher and "make up." The same principal expressed doubt when the parents of a fifth grade girl exposed their daughter's teacher for touching her breast and running his hands up to her underwear. As a result of the principal's lack of response, the parents went to law enforcement and child protection. Although no criminal charges were filed, social services determined that the teacher should be on the child abuse registry. The teacher continued to teach, however, and school officials claimed that they were unaware that his name was listed on the registry.

Unfortunately, school districts, parents, and students fail to report incidents of educator misconduct to law enforcement agencies or social services (Shakeshaft & Cohan 1994). When the police are notified, it most often is by parents. Because law enforcement is not informed of the physical harassment that could constitute a crime, the abusers are not subjected to criminal sanctions and public knowledge, but rather might receive only school sanctions, which are private and meager.

The school sanctions could very well be nothing more than a reprimand, or the teacher might be allowed to resign quietly, or might be fired and go to another school district and repeat the sexual harassment. This phenomenon sometimes is called "passing the trash," the trash meaning "mobile molesters" (Hendrie 1998e). Sometimes molesters leave when allegations arise but can't be substantiated, or before accusations surface, allowing abusers to stay a step ahead of the law, and to continue their egregious sexual misconduct unabated. When and if a harasser is finally exposed, questions arise as to how this mobile molester's behavior could be stifled and neglected.

The issue of false accusations is a concern of school officials and educators that contributes to the likelihood of students not being believed (Shakeshaft 2004). There are no studies examining the frequency of false accusations, but child sexual abuse research suggested that they are infrequent. The study conducted by Shakeshaft and Cohan (1994) demonstrated that, of the 225 complaints of educator sexual misconduct, all were shown to have occurred. Of these incidents, however, there were several in which the superintendent did not label the behavior as sexual misconduct but rather as touching with no sexual intent. Many school districts are more concerned about being sued by the adult harasser for defamation of character, violation of due process rights, or even being suspended to conduct an investigation than they are about lawsuits brought by victimized students (Hendrie 1998b).

After being informed of potential sexual harassment, school administrators sometimes feel as though they are restricted in the permitted aggressiveness of their actions by union contracts, laws, and privacy rights (Hendrie 1998b). Sexual harassment also often is subtle or imperceptible and therefore difficult to prove. Victims and their families, however, describe jarring testimony demonstrating the failure of school officials to respond to complaints of educator sexual harassment and keep students safe. Throughout the country, courts have responded in kind by awarding victims damages that sometimes are millions of dollars.

One mistake that school administrators make is to think that, because law enforcement is conducting its investigation, the school district can breathe a sigh of relief because it is "off the hook" and does not need to conduct its own investigation (Hendrie 1998f). Conversely, administrators sometimes falsely believe that if they conduct an investigation and determine the validity of the accusation, then they do not need to contact law enforcement. Any time there is a rumor or allegation of sexual misconduct that includes physical contact, law enforcement must be contacted to conduct an investigation. School administrators usually are not trained to conduct any type of investigation much less a criminal investigation, and law enforcement officers state that, when administrators attempt this type of investigation, they do more harm than good and could be accused of obstructing justice. If law enforcement concludes that no crime was committed, the school district must conduct its own investigation to determine whether the student's civil rights were jeopardized in the form of sexual harassment, or if inappropriate behavior did occur but did not rise to the level of sexual harassment. Because of the potential for a conflict of interest, and because the superintendent knows the educator, it is highly recommended that an outside investigator—a trained and competent expert in investigating allegations involving children as victims—be retained. This tactic also helps minimize allegations of a cover-up, because the outside investigator is impartial.

A conspiracy of silence (Corbett, Gentry & Pearson 1993; Winks 1982) is said to exist when administrators, teachers, and students keep silent and thereby cover up student-educator sexual harassment. The conspiracy adds to the detrimental consequences to the victim and the district.

Shakeshaft and Cohan (1995) found that most districts were lacking in reporting procedures as well as policies for dealing with allegations against educators. In most cases, the superintendent was the individual charged with questioning the student victim—sometimes with the parents present, and sometimes without the parents having any knowledge. The questioning usually was incomplete and conducted in such a way that students were fearful. If the superintendent perceived the allegation as serious, then the school's attorney, board president, and teachers' union president were contacted. Questioning the alleged harasser also fell to the superintendent, most often with another person present such as the district's attorney, a union representative, or another administrator. Rarely were the police, district attorney's office, or child protection/social services contacted. Investigations either were nonexistent or inadequate. If the accused teacher stated that the allegation was a lie, it generally ended the "investigation."

Superintendents were discriminatory in their handling of complaints against male teachers compared to complaints made against females (Shakeshaft & Cohan 1995). Allegations against women were viewed through a more critical lens, resulting in women being terminated from employment, whereas the men might receive nothing more than a reprimand. Additionally, male targets' experiences were perceived as more serious in nature than those experiences of the female victim. Female victims were accused of lying, and male victims' honesty was rarely questioned. Same-sex and homosexual allegations were taken more seriously, and believed to have caused more harm than heterosexual or opposite-sex behaviors.

Often superintendents were confused about the dilemma in which they found themselves—protect their educator/abuser or protect the student (Shakeshaft & Cohan 1995)? Superintendents' thoughts were mixed on whom to support—the victim or the teacher. Superintendents empathized with the male abuser, recognizing that what the educator did was wrong but at the same time making statements such as, "Gee, the way these girls dress." That dilemma was confounded when the abuser was this outstanding teacher, sometimes even a friend, and the student victim was a "bad girl" with few friends.

The superintendent's sense of a dilemma was the antithesis of the sentiment of the harasser's peers, who strongly supported their accused colleague to the point of interfering with any attempted investigation and intimidating the victim (McGrath 1994; Shakeshaft & Cohan 1995). Fellow teachers tended to overreact to the accusation, to accuse the superintendent of a witch hunt (McGrath 1994) based on accusations of abhorrent behavior made about a wonderful teacher, and they therefore perceived the superintendent as not supporting the teaching staff. Shakeshaft and Cohan discovered that, as a result, educators switch from discussing the safety and well-being of their students to the safety and well-being of the accused.

Several disciplinary actions are open to the school district (ultimately the school board) in handling complaints of sexual harassment that are found to be true. According to Shakeshaft and Cohan (1995), the consequences to the perpetrator included the following:

- Resigned, left district, retired—38.7%
- Terminated or not rehired—15%

- Suspended then resumed teaching—8.1%
- Verbal or written reprimand—11.3%
- Informal "speaking" to—17.5%
- False allegations—7.5%
- Unresolved allegations—1.9%

Schools continued to minimize the seriousness of the perpetrator's behavior by encouraging the perpetrator to retire or resign—even offering retirement benefits and agreeing not to inform a potential future school employer of the reason that the teacher was leaving the district (Shakeshaft & Cohan 1995). Superintendents legitimized their actions indicating that terminating the perpetrator could end up costing the district in time and money if the terminated educator decided to sue the district. Some perpetrators taught in other districts that were unaware of the allegations against their new staff member, which Hendrie (1998e) called "passing the trash." However, 37% of accused harassers maintained their teaching contracts in the same district, irrespective of the superintendent accepting the teacher as guilty of sexual abuse.

One superintendent shared his frustration of having to return a teacher to his teaching staff after he was found criminally guilty of sexual abuse when a state hearing panel recommended suspension for two years, counseling, and then reinstatement. Another superintendent allowed the perpetrator to remain in the district teaching because the educator hadn't *intended* to sexually abuse the child. A perpetrator was allowed to continue teaching after making an apology to the children's parents (not to the children) for sexual touching and sexual comments. One teacher who abused elementary children was transferred to a high school, and another who abused female special education children, was allowed to work with male students only.

Sixty percent of the school districts offered no remedial help to the student victims (Shakeshaft & Cohan 1995). The other victims were offered counseling, and most superintendents presumed that if the abuse no longer was occurring, then there was no problem. Nothing was done to prevent or intervene in the tremendous backlash and retaliation against the victim by students, school staff, and the community, resulting in many victims leaving the district and sometimes leaving the community (Shakeshaft & Cohan 1995).

Interestingly, some students in the Corbett, Gentry, and Pearson (1993) study did not perceive the sexual harassment between students and educators to be particularly serious. One student stated, "I heard about a teacher being sexually active with a student outside of school, but I thought that it was appropriate" (Corbett, Gentry & Pearson 1993, 100). Another student indicated that coaches slept with students but because the girls wanted to, it wasn't harassment. Yet another student said, "He had sex with her. She was consenting. She was the school slut" (Corbett, Gentry, and Pearson 1993, 100). Roughly 36% of students said that they were aware of students and educators having sex, and 68% perceived that the student and the teacher were equally interested in the relationship.

COMMUNITY BACKLASH

The consensus by student victims and their families is that the schools that are more protective of the adult harasser and the school's reputation than they are of the best interests and safety of their students further victimize students (Hendrie 1998f). As a result, students and their families become disillusioned and angry and feel as though their voices went unheeded by the school district. Many believe that schools are more concerned about the reputation and liability than about the students' well-being. Some school officials become antagonistic and hostile to the families who complain. As a result, families decide to take the matter to court in hopes of catalyzing the school district to hear their pleas and to prevent another child's victimization. As news about the student complaint or potential lawsuit trickles into the community, the community responds by turning on the student and her or his family—sometimes to the point of making the family feel that it must to move out of town.

Even if the perpetrator acknowledges his or her guilt, or if the perpetrator is found guilty of criminal sexual conduct or civil sexual harassment in a court of law, colleagues, students, parents, and the community often continue to support the educator—particularly if he is a favored and successful coach. Examples include letters to the editor in the community paper, community petitions to the school district in support of the teacher's continued employment as a teacher (and coach), and angry crowds of parents and community citizens who were livid because they believed that a teacher was being falsely accused.

Victims lose their friends when a popular teacher is accused, and the victims are labeled as liars by friends, educators, and the community at large (Hendrie 1998g). The retaliation can be severe and have long-lasting emotional ramifications for the student. The student becomes an outcast of the school and the student and the student's family could be ostracized by their church, social networks, and community.

LEGAL ELEMENTS

Numerous state and federal laws outlaw sexual misconduct in the public schools. The sexual misconduct could be covered under criminal laws such as child abuse statues, sexual assault and rape, and other criminal penalties resulting in imprisonment and fines (Shakeshaft & Cohan 1995).

The behavior also is covered under the Civil Rights Act, Title IX (including retaliation), 42 U.S.C § 1983 (Davis 2009), and state, county, and municipal laws replicated after Title IX. Sanctions under Title IX and Section 1983, or comparable state laws, include punitive damages, monetary compensation to the victim, lack of federal funding to the district (Title IX only), and other penalties to the school (Shakeshaft & Cohan 1995). The U.S. Supreme Court in 2009 ruled that students can sue schools simultaneously with Title IX under the U.S. Constitution (42 U.S.C. § 1983) (Davis 2009). Additionally, regulations for licensure of teachers and other state regulations can result in a revoking of the teacher's license—thereby taking away his or her ability to teach (Shakeshaft & Cohan 1995).

Title IX of the Civil Rights Act of 1972 states that for behavior to constitute sexual harassment, it must be unwelcome, sufficiently severe, or pervasive enough to interfere with a student's ability to attain an education, based on the perspective of a reasonable *student,* and the behavior must be sexual or gender based (U.S. Department of Education Office of Civil Rights 2001). There are two broadly accepted elements to sexual harassment—quid pro quo, in which sexual activity is demanded from a student in exchange for some benefit such as a good grade, a recommendation to a college, or conversely, a threat of punishment if the student does not succumb to the demand. A second type of sexual harassment is hostile environment, which generally does not include any threats. This harassment can be more subtle and nuanced and be harder to distinguish than quid pro quo.

Several U. S. Supreme Court cases have defined how Title IX is enforced under the law for teacher sexual harassment. The first case heard by the Court was *Franklin v. Gwinnett County Public Schools* in 1992. The Court ruled that a student may sue the school district for monetary damages under Title IX. Lacking from the Court's opinion, however, was the critical element about the circumstances under which a school district could be held liable. The ambiguity of the Court's decision was addressed in an unpopular 1998 decision.

The 1998 case, *Gebser v. Lago Vista Independent School District,* centered on an eighth-grade student who was sexually *involved* with a teacher for more than a year, and who sued the school district claiming it had violated her rights under Title IX. The Court opined that the student would not receive monetary compensation for damages unless a school official who had the authority to take corrective action had "actual knowledge" of the misconduct and was "deliberately indifferent" to it. Although the court ruled against Gebser, it left the door open for students to sue, but under a very strict standard. This decision raised the questions of what position within the school district constituted "authority," and what behavior, or lack of behavior, constituted deliberate indifference. In *Gebser,* the district was not liable because when the school discovered the teacher's sexual harassment, they fired him, thus avoiding deliberate indifference.

The Supreme Court's *Gebser* decision established new roadblocks for plaintiff students wishing to file suit for educator to student sexual harassment (Beck 2006), thus some plaintiffs might fare better by following state law. According to McGrath (1994), state courts may award monetary damages for administrator's failure to supervise, investigate, train, hire carefully, to warn others, and to report child sexual abuse.

A coalition of 17 civil liberties and women's groups immediately wrote key officials in Congress and the Clinton administration requesting that they counter the effects of the *Gebser* ruling with federal legislation (Hendrie 1998h). The coalition's fear was that the ruling would be a successful catalyst for school officials "to insulate themselves from being informed about sexual harassment to avoid financial liability" (Hendrie 1998h, 18). In essence, *Gebser* rewards a district for ensuring ignorance of sexual harassment, allowing the perpetrator to continue to harass children.

The Supreme Court ruled in 2005 that retaliation claims can be brought under Title IX (Davis 2008). According to Brett Sokolow, president of the National Center for Higher Education Risk Management (NCHERM), "The money behind retaliation cases is bigger than money victims get under Title IX sexual assault cases" (Davis 2008, 6).

Until a 2009 U. S. Supreme Court decision was issued, the circuit courts had long disagreed on whether § 1983 could be brought forward if Title IX also was being used to sue a school district (Davis 2009). *Fitzgerald v. Barnstable School Committee* cleared the way for simultaneous lawsuits with Title IX and § 1983. Section 1983 allows students to seek redress for sexual harassment claims for equal protection violations, which prohibits anyone acting "under color of state law," for example, police, school board, or other government employees or organizations (Katz 2008) from denying an individual her or his constitutional rights. Under § 1983, a student plaintiff does not have to prove deliberate indifference as is required by Title IX, thereby employing a less strict standard. Section 1983 holds that schools have a duty to students to prevent sexual abuse perpetrated by educators (McGrath 1994). In *Doe v. Taylor Independent School District,* the court opined that a principal *personally* could be liable for failing to ensure a student's right to bodily integrity in sexual abuse by an employee.

Under § 1983, the constitutional amendments most likely to be tapped related to sexual harassment include the following (Back to Basics 2008, 10):

1. Fourteenth Amendment (the Equal Protection Clause), guaranteeing citizens freedom from government discrimination on any basis, including race, color, sex, religion, national origin, age, or disability.

2. Eighth Amendment, which forbids cruel or unusual punishment by government officials [school officials].

In *Doe v. Dickenson*, the plaintiff student filed a claim under the Equal Protection Clause of the Fourteenth Amendment, claiming that the customs, practices, and policies of the police department of the City of Phoenix resulted in Dickenson, the school resource officer who allegedly sexually abused a 14-year-old boy, not receiving adequate training and supervision. As a result of the city's negligence, the boy suffered egregious emotional trauma which, in turn, caused his parents to suffer, and continue to suffer emotional anguish, medical costs, and other damages. The plaintiffs won their case under the constitutional right of familial association. As a result of the recent Supreme Court's § 1983 decision, school districts must acclimate themselves to the broad range of constitutional claims that now could be brought forward in sexual harassment liability. Three criteria are required to establish liability under Section 1983.

1. If school officials create and maintain a practice, custom, or policy that condones the abuse of or injury to students,
2. If school officials are liable for injuries to people with whom they have a "special relationship," and
3. If officials face potential liability when they create a danger that causes student injury (Lane 1995, 13).

In 2001, the Eighth Circuit Court of Appeals, for *P.H. v. School District of Kansas City, Missouri,* held that a teacher's sexual harassment of a student would violate § 1983 if the school district failed to receive, investigate, and act upon complaints of sexual abuse; failed to act when provided notice of alleged inadequacy of its employee training procedures required to support a § 1983 claim for failure to train employees to protect students from sexual abuse; and failed to act when provided actual notice of sexual abuse to suffer Title IX liability. In this suit, there had to be proof that the district's failure to train demonstrates deliberate indifference, and that the district had notice that its procedures were inadequate and likely to cause a due process violation of the Fourteenth Amendment. If the need for training is obvious because there is a clear and present pattern of misconduct within the district, then the failure to train demonstrates a violation of § 1983.

There are offenses perpetrated by teachers against students that do not rise to the level of a crime—or even are considered a civil offense or sexual harassment—yet the behavior requires aggressive action by school officials. School officials, in fact, could be sued for not responding to teacher sexual harassment behaviors (Graves 1994). School administrators have been assigned culpability in civil lawsuits, and sometimes criminal complaints, for their failure to act on teacher sexual harassment.

The U.S. Department of Education, Office for Civil Rights (OCR), is the regulatory agency tasked with ensuring that school districts adhere to Title IX or risk losing federal money (Sutton 2004). The OCR published guidelines for schools, which require prompt and equitable resolution of sex discrimination complaints including sexual harassment. The Title IX amendment of 1972 does not directly deal with educator sexual harassment, but has a broader scope including *any* sex discrimination, whether from a student or from school personnel.

A school district might be out of compliance with Title IX if its policies and procedures have been executed but its staff does not understand the policy's complexity and depth (Davis 2008). This emphasizes the importance of conducting yearly training for all school employees ensuring, among other aspects, that they are competent in understanding and using the district's policy.

In *Gebser*, the Court held that a school can be liable for monetary damages to the student-victim when a teacher sexually harasses a student if two criteria are established: (1) The supervisory school official who has authority to institute corrective measures to end the harassment has actual knowledge of the behavior; and (2) if that official demonstrates deliberate indifference in his or her failure to adequately respond to the behavior. This is in contrast to the role of the OCR, which exists to enforce Title IX's mandate of nondiscrimination even if a claim of nondiscrimination does not give rise to monetary damages. In other words, a school district might not be in compliance with the U.S. Department of Education Office of Civil Rights (OCR), for example, because it did not conduct training, publicize the antidiscrimination policy, or identify a Title IX coordinator, and yet not be in violation of Title IX law, because items 1 and 2 (above) were met.

There probably are few people who support educators and students having sex, yet 20 states have no criminal laws against it if students are 16, 17, or 18 years old, depending on the state (Hendrie 1998i). Some people, however, see some gray in the seemingly black-and-white issue—consensual sex between an educator and an older teenager—especially if the particular state's laws state that the age of consent can be as young as 16, 17, or 18 years old. In fact, The National School Board Association (NSBA), the American Federation of Teachers (AFT), and the National Education Association (NEA) do not have a policy absolutely outlawing the behavior.

RECOMMENDATIONS

Sexual harassment of students by educators is a problem that crushes students, parents, teachers, school districts, and the entire community. It is critical that districts acknowledge the problem, educate about it, and implement steps for the prevention and intervention of the misconduct. The following are recommendations for school officials to implement.

- Develop and widely disseminate and publicize an educator sexual harassment/misconduct policy and reporting procedure to students, parents, teachers, and school staff; ensure that the policy is followed.

- Establish a zero-tolerance policy statement regarding retaliation by students, teachers, and staff, as well as prohibiting the use of educator-student electronic communication such as e-mail or Facebook.

- Take all complaints seriously and follow up with an investigation even if the complaint is not formal, is a rumor, or is a gut feeling.

- Provide in the yearly overall sexual harassment training of students and staff-specific training on educator sexual harassment and boundaries, informing all staff members of their responsibility to report questionable behavior to social services, child protection, and administration; failure to report can result in liability.

- Implement effective hiring practices, including conducting background checks and fingerprinting of all potential teachers and school staff.

- Use highly trained individuals or law enforcement to conduct investigations of any allegations and rumors.

- When an allegation or confirmed sexual harassment occurs, denote only one or two spokespersons from the district to deal with the media to ensure accurate information dissemination and to minimize gossip and innuendo.

- Warn other districts in which the alleged harasser is seeking employment—some state laws require this action.

- Report the misconduct to the state licensing agency.

- Monitor the district's environment—listen for rumors, don't ignore the signs, trust your professional instinct about questionable employee conduct, such as prolonged hugging of students, spending time together outside of school, and making sexual comments.

- Document all allegations, investigations, and outcomes—do not expunge findings.

- Contact the parents of the victim prior to interviewing the student.

- Don't make "deals" with the perpetrator—for example by agreeing to expunge his or her records if the educator leaves quietly, or to let them retire with full benefits.

- Only 7% of students report their victimization—make your school district one in which students trust that they will be believed and will not be retaliated against if they come forward to complain.

- Provide a support mechanism for victims.
- Designate one or two Title IX coordinators that are responsible for receiving all sexual harassment and sexual abuse complaints.

Schools have a long way to go in taking the necessary steps to combat sexual harassment by educators (and students). In addition to the suggestions above, state licensing boards and state legislatures should implement stricter rules and laws to effectively prevent and intervene in educator sexual misconduct. Only then can children have more assurance of attending school in an environment that respects them and ensures their safety.

REFERENCES

American Association of University Women Educational Foundation (AAUW) (2001). *Hostile hallways: Bullying, teasing and sexual harassment in school.* Washington, DC: Author.

American Association of University Women Educational Foundation (AAUW) (1993). *Hostile hallways: AAUW survey on sexual harassment in American schools.* Washington, DC: Author.

Back to Basics (2008). Section 1983 and additional avenues for students, employees to pursue claims for sexual harassment. *Educator's Guide to Controlling Sexual Harassment* 16 (1), 9–11.

Bagley, C., and King, K. (1990). *Child sexual abuse: The search for healing.* London: Tavistock/Routledge.

Beck, J. (2006). Entity liability for teacher-on-student sexual harassment: Could state law offer greater protection than federal statutes? *Journal of Law and Education* 35 (1), 141–151. Retrieved from ProQuest database.

Bithell, S. B. (1991). *Educator sexual abuse: A guide for prevention in the schools.* Boise, ID: Tudor House Publishing.

Cedello, S. (1997). *Peer sexual harassment: A Texas-size problem.* Austin: Texas Civil Rights Project.

Corbett, K., Gentry, C., and Pearson, W. Jr. (1993). Sexual harassment in high school. *Youth and Society* 25 (1), 93–103. Retrieved from EBSCO database.

Davis, M. R. (2009). High court broadens school liability, allows pursuit of Title IX, § 1983 claims. *Educator's Guide to Controlling Sexual Harassment* 16 (6), 1–2, 5–6.

Davis, M. R. (2008). Educator misconduct: Schools can face lawsuits in sexual assault cases for damages to the parent-child relationship. *Educator's Guide to Controlling Sexual Harassment* 16 (11), 3, 9.

Doe v. Taylor Independent School District, 15 F.3d 443 (1994).

Driedger, S. (2003). The teacher lesson. *Maclean's* 116 (20), 56. Retrieved from EBSCO database.

Fitzgerald v. Barnstable School Committee, 128 S. Ct. 788.

Fossey, R., and DeMitchell, T. (1995, April). "Let the master respond:" Should schools be strictly liable when employees sexually abuse children? Paper presented at the annual meeting of the American Educational Research Association, San Francisco, CA.

Franklin v. Gwinnett County Public Schools, 503 U.S. 60 (1992).

Gebser v. Lago Vista Independent School District, 524 U.S. 274 (1998).

Graves, B. (1994). When the abuser is an educator. *School Administrator* 51 (9), 8–14, 16–18. Retrieved from EBSCO database.

Hendrie, C. (1998a). Abuse by women raises its own set of problems. *Education Week* 18 (4), 1, 14–15, 17. Retrieved from EBSCO database.

Hendrie, C. (1998b). Cost is high when schools ignore abuse. *Education Week* 18 (15), 1, 14–16. Retrieved from EBSCO database.

Hendrie, C. (1998c). In youth's tender emotions, abusers find easy pickups. *Education Week* 18 (14), 17. Retrieved from EBSCO database.

Hendrie, C. (1998d). Labels like "pedophile" don't explain the many faces of child sexual abuse. *Education Week* 18 (14). 16. Retrieved from EBSCO database.

Hendrie, C. (1998e). "Passing the trash" by school district frees sexual predators to hung again. *Education Week* 18 (15), 16–17. Retrieved from EBSCO database.

Hendrie, C. (1998f). Principals face a delicate balancing act in handling allegations of misconduct. *Education Week* 18 (16), 14. Retrieved from EBSCO database.

Hendrie, C. (1998g). Sex with students: When employees cross the line. *Education Week* 18 (14), 1, 12–14. Retrieved from EBSCO database.

Hendrie, C. (1998h). Shifting legal ground on harassment has made it harder for victims to win. *Education Week* 18 (15), 18. Retrieved from EBSCO database.

Hendrie, C. (1998i). "Zero tolerance" of sex abuse proves elusive. *Education Week* 18 (16), 1, 12–15. Retrieved from EBSCO database.

Jennings, D., and Tharp, R. (2003, May 4, 5, 6). Betrayal of trust. *The Dallas Morning News*. Retrieved from ProQuest Newspapers database.

Katz, A. (2008, December 2). Commentary: Fitzgerald v. Barnstable, annual supreme court review. *Legal Momentum*. www.legalmomentum.org/news-room/press-releases/commentary-fitzgerald-v.html. Accessed April 1, 2014.

Lane, F. (1995). Sexual misconduct of school employees: Supervisory school officials' liability under Section 1983. *School Law Bulletin* 46 (2), 9–16. Retrieved from Minitex database.

Maxwell, L. A. (1997). Digital age adds new dimension to incidents of staff-student sex. *Education Week* 27 (13), 1. Retrieved from Galegroup database.

McGrath, M. J. (1994). The psychodynamics of school sexual abuse investigations. *School Administrator* 51 (9), 28–30, 32–35. Retrieved from EBSCO database.

P. H. v. School District of Kansas City, Missouri, 265 F .3d 653 (8th Cir. 2001).

Paludi, M. A., and Barickman, R. B. (1991). Academic and workplace sexual harassment: A resource manual. Albany, NY: SUNY Press.

Patterson, M. A., and Austin, D. F. (2008, December). Stop the grooming. *American School Board Journal*, 18–20.

Shakeshaft, C. (2004). *Educator sexual misconduct: A synthesis of existing literature.* U.S. Department of Education Office of Under Secretary, DOC 2004-09, Washington DC. http://www.specialeducationmuckraker.com/Shakeshaft _SchoolSexualAbuse.pdf. Accessed April 21, 2015.

Shakeshaft, C. (2003, Spring). Educator sexual abuse. *Hofstra Horizons* 10–13.

Shakeshaft, C., and Cohan, A. (1995). Sexual abuse of students by school personnel. *Phi Delta Kapan* 76 (7). 513–520. Retrieved from EBSCO database.

Shakeshaft, C., and Cohan, A. (1994, January). In loco parentis: Sexual abuse of students in schools: What administrators should know. *Administration and Policy Studies Hofstra University.*

Shoop, R. J. (2004). *Sexual exploitation in schools: How to spot it and stop it.* Thousand Oaks, CA: Corwin Press.

Sobsey, D., Randall, W., and Parrila, R. K. (1997). Gender differences in abused children with and without disabilities. *Child Abuse and Neglect* 21 (8), 707–720. Retrieved from ScienceDirect database.

Sorenson, G. P. (1991). Sexual abuse in schools: Reported court cases from 1987– 1990. *Educational Administration Quarterly* 27 (4), 460–480. Retrieved from Sage database.

Sullivan, P. M., and Knutson, J. F. (2000). The prevalence of disabilities and maltreatment among runaway children. *Child Abuse and Neglect* 24 (10), 1275–1288. Retrieved from ScienceDirect database.

Sutton, L. C. (2004, December). Educator sexual misconduct: New trends and liability. *School Business Affairs,* 6–8

U.S. Department of Education, Office of Civil Rights. (2000). Revised sexual harassment guidance: Harassment of students by school employees, other students, or third parties (Federal Document No. FR Doc. 01-1606). *Federal Register* 66 (13), 5512. http://www.ed.gov/offices/OCR/archieves/pdf /shguide.pdf. April 21, 2015.

Winks, P. (1982). Legal implications of sexual contact between teacher and student. *Journal of Law and Education* 11 (4), 433–477.

Chapter 7

Microaggressions in the Workplace: Recommendations for Best Practices

Lindsey Sank Davis, Chassitty Whitman, and
Kevin L. Nadal

Although there has been a significant increase in federal and state laws that protect women's civil rights, sexism toward women still exists in both overt and subtle forms (Swim, Hyers, Cohen & Ferguson 2001). Such discrimination has been described in multiple ways, including as "overt sexism" (Swim & Cohen 1997), "covert sexism" (Swim & Cohen 1997), and "subtle sexism" (Swim, Mallett & Stagnor 2004). In the field of business, the term "microinequities" has been utilized to identify the pattern of being overlooked, underrespected, and devalued because of one's gender or race (Sue, Capodilupo, Torino, Bucceri, Holder, Nadal & Esquilin 2007). In recent years, several authors have investigated the subtle forms of discrimination in the lives of various marginalized communities—including women; people of color; people with disabilities; and lesbian, gay, bisexual, and transgender (LGBT) people—and have labeled such experiences as "microaggressions" (Nadal 2011, 2013; Sue 2010a, 2010b; Sue et al. 2007).

Microaggressions are defined as "brief and commonplace daily verbal, behavioral, or environmental indignities, whether intentional or unintentional, that communicate hostile, derogatory, or negative slights and insults toward members of oppressed groups" (Nadal 2008, 23). Researchers have found microaggressions have detrimental impacts on targeted groups, such as Black Americans (Pierce, Carew, Pierce-Gonzalez & Willis 1978; Sue et al. 2008); Asian Americans (Sue, Bucceri, Lin, Nadal & Torino 2010); Latina/Latino Americans (Nadal, Mazzula, Rivera & Fuji-Doe 2014); women (Nadal 2010); lesbian, gay, and bisexual people (Nadal, Issa, Leon, Meterko, Wideman & Wong 2011); and transgender people (Nadal, Skolnik & Wong 2012). Empirical research has found microaggressions to negatively influence mental health–related symptoms (Nadal, Griffin, Wong, Hamit & Rasmus 2014), self-esteem, binge drinking (Blume, Lovato, Thyken & Denny 2012), and emotional intensity (Wang, Leu & Shoda 2011).

Microaggression theorists assert that there are three ways that microaggressions can manifest: (1) microassaults, (2) microinsults, and (3) microinvalidations (see Sue 2010a for a review). "Microassaults" often are known as "old-fashioned" forms of discrimination in that perpetrators are conscious of their statements or behaviors, but might or might not be intentional in hurting others. A coworker who makes a joke about people with disabilities or uses homophobic language, for example, might be conscious that the language is discriminatory. If confronted about this behavior, however, the individual could dismiss accusations of prejudice and insist that the language is harmless. "Microinsults" are verbal or nonverbal communications that convey rudeness and insensitivity, often negatively stereotyping a target person, belittling a person's heritage or identity, or both. One example is a person of color who receives substandard service in comparison to white customers at a restaurant; another example is a lesbian couple met with unwelcoming stares or whispers when they hold hands in public. "Microinvalidations" are statements that often are unintentional and exclude, negate, or nullify the realities of individuals of marginalized groups. When a male coworker tells a woman that she complains about sexism or is "too sensitive" about gender issues, for instance, he is communicating that her reality is bogus or wrong and that his perception is correct.

Microaggression theorists also discuss the four psychological dilemmas that arise from experiences with microaggressions: (1) clash of realities, (2) invisibility of unintentional bias, (3) perceived minimal harm of microaggressions, and (d) the catch-22 of responding to microaggressions (Sue 2010b). "Clash of realities" describes how people can perceive or interpret microaggressions differentially, based on their identities, worldviews, and experiences. If a person of color perceives that he or she is being treated poorly as a customer at a store, it could be difficult to "prove" that it is because of race. Because this type of experience can be common in a person of color's everyday life and because he or she can compare the treatment received with how white customers are treated, the interaction could be attributed to racial bias. If he or she were to confront the store clerk in this situation, the clerk might deny the accusation, attribute the behavior to something other than race, or accuse the person of being paranoid or overly sensitive. Because the store clerk could become angry when accused of being a racist, she or he might become defensive and be unable to understand the person of color's point of view or be unwilling take any responsibility for her or his actions.

The second psychological dilemma, "invisibility of unintentional bias," describes the notion that, because discrimination is heavily embedded in American society, people have become socialized to engage in prejudiced behaviors and thus often are not aware of how their biased behavior (Sue 2010a). Because heterosexuals have been socialized to believe that heterosexuality is normative, for instance, they might not even be aware of the privileges that they have as heterosexuals (e.g., many heterosexuals would not think twice about showing public displays of affection). Moreover, heterosexuals might not be aware of how they assume that other people are heterosexual (e.g., when first meeting a female coworker, a heterosexual might ask her if she has "a husband and kids"—unaware that this suggests that being heterosexual and having the legal right to marry is the norm). This type of unintentional and unconscious bias can be found with any privileged identity and often is the root of microaggressive interactions.

The third psychological dilemma, "perceived minimal harm of microaggressions," describes how many people label microaggressions as being harmless, particularly because microaggressions often are brief interactions (Sue 2010b). People of privileged groups (e.g., Caucasians, men, heterosexuals) might tell people of target groups to "get over it," or could claim that microaggressions are no more harmful than the everyday stressors that all people experience. Despite this claim, preliminary research finds that the impact of being victimized by microaggressions can cause emotional or physical discomfort, confusion, and even mental health problems (Balsam, Molina, Beadnell, Simoni & Walters 2011; Nadal 2011; Nadal, Wong, Issa, Meterko, Leon & Wideman 2011; Sue, Bucceri et al. 2010; Sue et al. 2007, 2008). Thus, although people might dismiss microaggressions, it is clear that such experiences do have a negative influence on people's lives.

Finally, the fourth psychological dilemma, the "catch-22 of responding to microaggressions," illustrates the difficulty of responding to microaggressions, primarily because the target individual must weigh the consequences of responding, which could lead to psychological distress (Sue 2010b). If a gay male couple notices that passersby are staring at them in disgust as they show affection in public, for instance, the couple might choose to confront the microaggressors angrily or assertively. In doing so, however, the couple also must consider whether their safety would be compromised or if they would be willing to engage in an argument or heated discussion. At the same time, if they do not say anything, they realize that the perpetrators could continue to engage in such behaviors; that he or she might continue to view LGBT people as abnormal, weak, or inferior—or worse.

Specific to the workplace, Nadal, Griffin, and Wong (2011) describe an instance in which a woman believes that her male coworkers are using sexist language and challenges them on this behavior. As a result, the men become angry with her, which then leads to a hostile working environment and potentially even jeopardizes the woman's position in the company. Given this scenario, it becomes clear that when microaggressions occur there are potential benefits and consequences of addressing them directly. On one hand, the individual could choose to endure the microaggressions because he or she does not foresee any change; however, this results in feelings of distress due to having to deal with this regular discrimination. Conversely, if the person does say something, he or she could face real consequences, such as a tense work environment or even the loss of employment.

Although Title VII of the Civil Rights Act of 1964 protects individuals from egregious employment discrimination, employees generally are not legally protected from microaggressions in the workplace (Lukes & Bangs 2014). Yet research and anecdotal evidence indicate that these experiences are plentiful in workplace settings, even in academic and social-service institutions that seek to promote the ideals of diversity and inclusivity. The purpose of this chapter is to present a review of the research regarding microaggressions and their common manifestations and consequences in the workplace, with a particular emphasis on microaggressions related to race, gender, sexual orientation, and gender identity. Recommendations for employers and future research directions also are discussed.

RACIAL MICROAGGRESSIONS IN THE WORKPLACE

The term "racial microaggression" originally was introduced to describe the "subtle, stunning, often automatic, and non-verbal exchanges which are 'put downs'" (Pierce et al. 1978, 66) experienced by Black Americans. This concept originated from the fact that, despite landmark legal developments in the 1960s, African Americans continued to experience discrimination in less obvious forms. More recently, racial microaggressions have been defined in the literature as "commonplace verbal, behavioral and environmental indignities, whether intentional or unintentional, that communicate hostile, derogatory, or negative racial slights and insults to the target person or group" (Sue et al. 2007, 273).

Sue and colleagues (2007) proposed the first taxonomy to organize the myriad manifestations of microaggressions toward people of color, providing instances of the many types of microaggressions that can occur. For instance, "ascription of intelligence" refers to statements or behaviors that imply that African Americans and Latinos are intellectually inferior, or that Asians are superior at math and science. "Denial of racial reality" refers to statements that negate a person of color's lived experiences with racism and discrimination. The "myth of meritocracy" refers to statements made toward people of color that convey that racism and systemic barriers no longer exist, and that all people can succeed if they try hard enough. By extension, this myth also conveys that people of color who have not achieved academic or professional success have only themselves to blame for their limitations.

Although microaggression research still is a budding area, there are some studies that describe the types of racial microaggressions that people of color endure. Nadal, Wong, and colleagues (2014) found that racial microaggressions predicted reduced self-esteem for college students of color. Alleyne (2004) interviewed 30 black individuals employed by the National Health Service, in education, and in social services, and found that participants reported that colleagues frequently ignored them; failed to provide supportive remarks; refused to make eye contact; excluded them; acted less friendly toward them; and described black people as being aggressive, scary, or angry. Similarly, Constantine, Smith, Redington, and Owens (2008) reported that Black Americans in academic positions commonly have their credentials questioned, an experience unlikely to occur in jobs requiring less education.

These workplace experiences extend to other racial minority groups, both before and after obtaining a position. For example, in an experimental study of discrimination against Latina/Latino job applicants (Bendick, Jackson, Reinoso & Hodges 1991), an applicant for a receptionist position was one of many who received subtly discriminatory treatment. Although the "applicant" identified herself as "Juanita," she was later referred to as "Carmen" by the employer's representative. She was also told that the position for which she applied had already been filled, even though another "applicant" called moments later and received an interview. Similarly, one study found that Asian Americans are less likely to be hired into positions that require social skills and are less likely to be promoted into such positions are than white candidates (Lai & Babcock 2013). In another study (Burdsey 2011), first-class Asian British cricket players indicated that, as ethnic minorities, they experienced many microaggressions (particularly ethnic jokes from opponents and teammates), felt pressured to adopt colorblind ideals, and felt forced to downplay the significance of the microaggressions they encountered.

Research indicates that members of the academe are not immune from perpetrating or receiving racial microaggressions. Constantine and colleagues (2008), for instance, reported that black faculty members in psychology departments struggled with issues of visibility and invisibility in the workplace, were provided inadequate mentorship, were expected to contribute extra service work beyond that of white colleagues, had difficulty distinguishing whether others' behaviors or remarks were attributable to race, and felt the need to be constantly aware of their appearance. Likewise, Cartwright, Washington, and McConnell's (2009) study of black faculty members in psychology programs confirmed that they were treated differently from and unequally to their white counterparts, suggesting that racial microaggressions toward people of color occur even in the institutions best equipped to identify and prevent them.

GENDER MICROAGGRESSIONS IN THE WORKPLACE

"Gender microaggressions" are "brief and commonplace daily verbal or behavioral indignities, whether intentional or unintentional, that communicate hostile, derogatory, or negative gender slights and insults that potentially have a harmful impact on women" (Sue 2010b, 164). A focus group study using female participants (Capodilupo, Nadal, Corman, Hamit, Lyons & Weinberg 2010) revealed eight recurring themes: (1) sexual objectification, or the viewing of women as sexual objects (e.g., catcalls); (2) assumptions of inferiority (e.g., assuming a woman cannot carry a large box); (3) assumptions of traditional gender roles (e.g., stating or enforcing that a woman should be responsible for duties such as cooking, cleaning, and nurturing); (4) use of sexist language (e.g., "bitch," "whore"); (5) denial of individual sexism (e.g., a man repudiating an accusation that he acted in a sexist manner); (6) invisibility (e.g., when women are overlooked when among men); (7) denial of the reality of sexism (e.g., declaring that sexism does not exist or that women are too sensitive); and (8) environmental gender microaggressions (e.g., media images that sexualize women). Gender microaggressions seem to pervade the workplace; women are less frequently offered positions (e.g., Gorman 2005), more frequently are paid less money than men for the same work, and have fewer opportunities for advancement.

Basford, Offerman, and Behrend (2013) used vignettes to investigate the extent to which employees could recognize gender microaggressions in fictional workplace scenarios. Women and men were both able to accurately identify gender microaggressions, but women perceived the discrimination to be more severe than men did, particularly when the discrimination was more subtle. In a study of medical school faculty members, Carr and colleagues (2000) found that women reported perceiving gender-based workplace discrimination more than twice as often as men did, and 72% of women (compared to 47% of men) reported a belief that gender bias negatively impacted their potential for career advancement. In a qualitative follow-up study, Carr, Szalacha, Barnett, Caswell, and Inui

(2003) interviewed 18 female medical school faculty members and found that 40% ranked gender discrimination as the top factor impeding their career advancement. The women described discriminatory experiences as negatively impacting their self-esteem, sense of collegiality, isolation, and career satisfaction, and noted that they do not feel prepared to effectively address or cope with discrimination in their professional settings.

Experimental studies also have revealed gender discrimination in academia. Moss-Racusin, Dovidio, Brescoll, Graham, and Handelsman (2012) found that reviewers for university laboratory jobs rated applicants with male names as being more competent and hirable than applications with female names, and offered the male applicants higher pay and more substantial mentoring than that offered to female applicants. This suggests that mentorship might be withheld from the most vulnerable employees—those who need it most. Interestingly, the gender of the faculty reviewing these applications did not significantly impact the manifestation of gender bias, demonstrating that both men and women hold the potential to perpetuate gender-based discrimination in employment.

SEXUAL ORIENTATION AND GENDER IDENTITY MICROAGGRESSIONS IN THE WORKPLACE

As public acceptance of LGBT individuals and support for their rights has increased over recent years, LGBT people increasingly are experiencing discrimination of a nature that is more subtle than overt (Nadal 2013; Sue 2010b). Thus, researchers recently have begun to focus on sexual orientation and gender-identity microaggressions. Nadal, Rivera, and Corpus (2010) delineated nine primary themes:

(1) Use of heterosexist/cissexist terminology (e.g., using derogatory terms such as "faggot," "dyke," or "tranny");
(2) Endorsement of heteronormative/cisnormative culture and behaviors (e.g., television shows predominantly featuring heterosexual and cisgender characters);
(3) Assumption of a universal LGBT experience (e.g., asking one individual to speak on behalf of all LGBT individuals);
(4) Exoticization (e.g., "I've always wanted a gay best friend!");
(5) Discomfort or disapproval of LGBT experiences (e.g., protesting an LGBT event as being immoral);
(6) Denying societal heterosexism or transphobia (e.g., the belief that LGBT discrimination is not real or that LGBT individuals are too sensitive);
(7) Assumption of pathology/abnormality (e.g., asking a lesbian woman what happened to her to make her gay);

(8) Denying one's own heterosexism (e.g., "I'm not homophobic/transphobic, I have a gay/trans friend!"); and

(9) Environmental microaggressions (e.g., institutional discrimination against LGBT people, such as restrictions on marriage rights).

Through a qualitative study, Nadal, Issa, and colleagues (2011) confirmed that these types of microaggressions were pervasive in the lives of lesbian, gay, and bisexual (LGB) people.

Research indicates that discrimination against LGBT individuals exists at many levels in the employment process, including interviews (Macan & Merritt 2011); hiring (Ahmed, Andersson & Hammarstedt 2013); callback decisions (Tilcsik 2011); and unequal pay, undue firing, denial of promotions, and negative performance evaluations (Badgett, Sears, Lau & Ho 2009). LGBT employees who reported experiencing discrimination most frequently experienced it directly following disclosure of their sexual orientation, suggesting that "coming out" could trigger an increase in workplace microaggressions (Ragins & Cornwell 2001). Further, the absence of gay men in local, state, and federal government (Lewis & Pitts 2011) sends a veiled message to LGB people conveying that they are not entitled to occupy these positions of political power.

To protect themselves from more direct forms of discrimination (e.g., slurs or obstacles to career advancement), many LGBT individuals choose to conceal their sexual orientation and gender identity in the workplace. Being "out" (i.e., being open about one's identifications) at work has been reported to engender negative career consequences (Mays & Cochran 2001). At the same time, although concealing one's sexual orientation might prevent some of the more direct forms of workplace microaggressions, LGBT individuals who do not disclose their sexual orientation still can experience an array of microaggressions, including a lack of visible LGBT employees in the upper ranks of a company; an organization offering benefits to heterosexual partners but not to same-sex partners; and interpersonal microaggressions from coworkers who do not realize that an individual identifies as LGBT.

In an Internet-based qualitative study of "outness" patterns in 88 lesbian, gay, bisexual, transgender, and questioning (LGBTQ) individuals (Davis 2014), respondents ranged from being completely "out" at work to being completely "closeted" at work, with the greatest number of respondents being out to just a portion of their colleagues. Several respondents explained that they avoid identification by dodging questions, failing to correct others' misconceptions about them, or altering their behavior in heteronormative ways (e.g., one gay man reported that he brought a woman with him to his office holiday party to maintain appearances). Davis (2014) also described how LGBTQ educators felt the need to "be very careful" about navigating sexual orientation in the workplace. One teacher noted that although her students would be unlikely to care about her sexual orientation, she worried about the parents' reactions. Stockdill and Danico (2012) provide another example as an anecdote in which one author's academic department posted a flyer equating homosexuality with incest and pedophilia. When the employee spoke up regarding the flyer's message of bigotry, he was reprimanded.

In a study of 514 kindergarten through 12 educators, 86% of LGBT educators reported hearing homophobic comments in school, and most of these educators find such remarks upsetting. Comments were heard not only from the mouths of students (reported by 96% of those who heard homophobic remarks), but also from the mouths of other educators (reported by 58% of those who heard homophobic remarks), and from school administrators (reported by 20% of those who heard homophobic remarks). The majority of LGBT educators reporting (73%) believed that rumors about them had been spread in their workplace. Very few educators reported seeing another educator or administrator intervene when such remarks were made in their presence, suggesting that LGBT educators might perceive a lack of support from faculty. Additionally, more than 75% of educators reported that LGBT individuals are absent from the school curriculum in their place of work; this conspicuous absence is potentially microaggressive toward LGBT employees and students alike.

Transgender Microaggressions

Although a great deal of research has emerged regarding microaggressions experienced by LGB individuals, research on transgender microaggressions is severely lacking. This population is frequently grouped with the larger "LGBT" community, but research supports independent consideration of unique transgender concerns, perceptions, and experiences (e.g., Meyer 2001). Despite the common conflation of sexual orientation and gender identity in extant research, a small body has emerged to specifically address the transgender population. Nadal, Skolnik, and Wong (2012) conducted a qualitative study of nine transgender (female and male) participants to explore themes of experiences of subtle discrimination such as microaggressions. The researchers discovered 12 themes of microaggressions experienced by transgender and gender nonconforming participants:

(1)   Use of transphobic or incorrect gender vocabulary (e.g., using the term "he-she" or "transvestite");
(2)   Assumption of a universal transgender experience (e.g., asking one transgender-identified individual to speak on behalf of all transgender people);
(3)   Exoticization (e.g., "I've always wanted a transgender friend!");

(4)   Discomfort with or disapproval of the transgender experience;
(5)   Enforcement of gender-conforming or binary gender behaviors (e.g., questioning the physical abilities of a male-to-female transgender individual working in construction);
(6)   Denying that transphobia exists;
(7)   Assumption of pathology/abnormality (e.g., assuming that a transgender individual is sexually deviant or mentally ill);
(8)   Physical threat or harassment;
(9)   Denial of individual transphobia (e.g., a cisgender individual saying he or she is not transphobic by virtue of having a friend who is transgender);
(10) Denial of personal bodily privacy (e.g., asking a transgender individual about their genitalia);
(11) Familial microaggressions (e.g., family members' continued use of a given name rather than a chosen name); and
(12) Systemic and environmental microaggressions (e.g., public restrooms labeled "men" and "women," which can be a source of stress for transgender individuals in transition, as well as nonbinary identified individuals).

Building upon the aforementioned taxonomy of transgender microaggressions, Nadal, Davidoff, Davis, and Wong (2014) conducted a qualitative investigation of emotional, cognitive, and behavioral reactions to microaggressive experiences among a sample of nine transgender participants. Participants reported responding emotionally to microaggressions with anger, feelings of betrayal, overall distress (e.g., describing the experience as "uncomfortable" or "traumatic"), hopelessness, and exasperation. Cognitive reactions included rationalization (e.g., justifying the microaggressor's behavior by blaming cultural influences) and feeling like they were in a "double-bind" (e.g., trying to navigate the different social privileges afforded to traditionally male or female behavior or weighing positive and negative aspects of gender-identity disclosure).

Behavioral reactions included direct confrontation (verbal responses directly to the microaggression, sometimes with elements of education regarding discrimination and its manifestations and impacts), indirect confrontation (such as contacting authorities or taking on a more aggressive demeanor as a preventative strategy for the future), and passive coping (such as trying to exit and minimize the situation by methods of avoidance or attempts to appease others). Given that previous research has found a high prevalence of depression and suicidal ideation among transgender individuals (Clements-Nolle, Marx & Katz, 2006; Nadal 2013), it is crucial to continue research on transgender experiences with microaggressions.

There is a dearth of research on the topic of transgender microaggressions in occupational settings (O'Neill, McWhirter & Cerezo 2008). In a series of interviews with nine female-to-male transgender individuals regarding career-related discrimination, Dispenza, Watson, Chung, and Brack (2012) found that participants experienced discrimination in the form of systemic microaggressions (e.g., discrimination embedded in health care, housing, and other government policies), as well as within-group oppression from other transgender coworkers. These experiences were associated with anxiety, depression, and interpersonal difficulties; however, they also positively impacted participants by inspiring them to seek out counseling and other resources, and to engage in active resistance against discriminatory policies.

Intersectional Microaggressions in the Workplace

When understanding how microaggressions manifest in the workplace, it is important to consider the notion of intersectional microaggressions. Intersectional microaggressions are "subtle forms of discrimination that are based on individuals' multiple social identities" (Nadal 2013, 36). In other words, because people hold an array of identities (e.g., race, gender, sexual orientation, ability status), they can experience microaggressions as a result of all of these identities. If a lesbian woman of color is discriminated against in the workplace, for example, is it because of her race, her gender, her sexual orientation, or some combination of all of these factors? The few studies that examine intersectional microaggressions provide some preliminary support that these types of microaggressions do affect the lives of people with multiple identities, particularly those with multiple marginalized identities. Balsam and colleagues (2011) created the LGBT People of Color Microaggressions Scale, addressing the racism in LGBT communities, heterosexism in racial/ethnic minority communities, and (c) racism in dating and close relationships. With their sample, they found that gay and bisexual men of color scored higher than did gay and bisexual women, lesbians and gay men scored higher than bisexual women and men, and Asian Americans scored higher than African Americans and Latina/Latinos, with higher scores indicating a greater prevalence of microaggressions. A quantitative study that examined Latinas'/Latinos' encounters with microaggressions found that intersectional identities affected the types of microaggressions that individuals experienced (Nadal, Mazzula et al. 2014). Their results revealed that Latinas experienced more microaggressions in the workplace or school settings and found that younger Latinos/Latinas, and those with less education, were more likely to experience microinvalidations. Another study that analyzed previous qualitative studies on microaggressions revealed that individuals are able to identify several types of intersectional microaggressions, even when they are not prompted to think about their multiple identities (Nadal, Davidoff, Davis, Wong, Marshall & McKenzie

2014). Examples of the many types of microaggressions that emerged in this study were: the exoticization of women of color; the disapproval of LGBT identity by racial, ethnic, and religious groups; and the invisibility and desexualization of Asian men. Finally, it is possible for individuals who encounter intersectional microaggressions to experience dual minority stress, or "the psychological distress that one experiences when she or he belongs to two marginalized groups" (Nadal 2003, 251).

There are a few ways that intersectional microaggressions can occur in the workplace. One is that an individual could feel excluded or isolated because people might not be fully comfortable with one or more of their identities. For instance, in one study examining experiences of lesbian women with disabilities, one participant stated:

> Gay professionals that I tried to go to cared about the disability and stuff and had never done their own work on that, so I couldn't go to them, and straight people couldn't deal with the lesbian thing. I've never found anybody who could get the lesbian and the disability pieces together. (Hunt, Matthews, Milsom & Lammel 2006, 169)

In this case, this woman feels that some heterosexual colleagues might not comfortable with her lesbian identity, and some gay colleagues might not be comfortable with her disability. As a result, she could feel isolated from others who do not share her multiple identities.

Sometimes, individuals with multiple marginalized identities may experience microaggressions perpetrated by individuals with whom they share a common identity. In one narrative, for instance, a gay African American man describes an instance in which he felt discriminated against by his heterosexual African American female coworker.

> My gay cultural identity was being deleted, denied, and dejected in my very presence . . . I feared that [she] represented one of those African Americans who gave lip service to being friends with an African American lesbian, gay, or bisexual (LGB) person but in reality was obviously not fully comfortable and accepting due to "the church." (Mobley & Pearson 2005, 89)

It seems that the speaker here is especially frustrated because he presumed (falsely) that his colleague would be more open-minded due to their shared racial identity. Perhaps microaggressions by individuals assumed to be empathetic might be more disappointing than those of others.

Furthermore, when exploring intersectional microaggressions, it is important to note that it might be easy for individuals with a marginalized identity to remain oblivious to instances in which they commit a microaggression against someone else because of a privileged identity (Nadal

2013). If a white woman experiences sexism in her everyday life, for example, then she might be able to identify and recognize instances when she is the target of sexism (e.g., sexual harassment in the workplace, being sexually objectified by a male stranger on the street). Because of this identity, however, it might be difficult for her to be aware of instances when her white identity could result in her committing microaggressions against people of color. In fact, when a Latino discusses encounters with racism, she might even say things like "As a woman, I know what it is like to experience discrimination." Although well-intended, this type of microaggression can be especially invalidating to a person of color, because, in essence, the white woman is stating that racism and sexism are the same and that, as a result, she knows what it feels like to be a person of color (Sue et al. 2007). Instead of making such statements, perhaps it would be more helpful for the woman in this case to instead validate the individual's experiences (e.g., "It's awful that you have to experience so much discrimination in your life."), and even being an ally (e.g., "If you ever want to talk about these things, I'd be happy to be a listening ear").

Lastly, it is important to note the literature involving mental health outcomes of individuals with multiple oppressed identities and how these studies could be related to intersectional microaggressions. For instance, it has been reported that LGBT people of color often feel excluded or mistreated by both their racial/ethnic communities and the white LGBT community, which in turn could have a negative impact on their mental health (Chung & Syzmanski 2006). Another study found that when black women and Latinas did not cope effectively with experiences of discrimination, they were more likely to be diagnosed with mood and anxiety disorders (McLaughlin, Hatzenbuehler & Keyes 2010). A different study (Cochran, Mays, Alegria, Ortega & Takeuchi 2007) found that gay Asian American men were more likely than heterosexual Asian American men to have reported a recent suicide attempt. Although there are likely numerous factors that contribute to mental health outcomes for individuals with multiple identities, it is important for practitioners and educators to recognize how encounters with microaggressions can influence these experiences.

Recommendations for Best Practices

Although the panacea for eliminating these pervasive experiences of microaggressions from the workplace remains elusive, several ideas hold promise. First, ambitious employers can target the source of discrimination—bias—by applying a variety of interventions supported by social psychological research. Employers also can address issues through assessment, education, policy change, and difficult dialogues.

Targeting the Source of the Problem: Interventions to Reduce Bias

Intergroup Contact

A number of factors—including in-group preference and inequalities in the workplace hierarchy—can lead employees to increase exposure to in-group members and reduce exposure to out-group members. This can be reflected in choices as small as whom to sit with at lunch. Pettigrew (1998) proposed that increased intergroup contact might reduce prejudice by increasing the availability of information about the out-group, changing behaviors, increasing affective bonding with out-group members, and reevaluating the in-group's superiority. Initial studies involved primarily interracial contact; however, a more recent meta-analysis by Pettigrew and Tropp (2006) indicated that similar effects were produced in studies of contact between other groups (e.g., differing sexual orientations, different religions). Employers might benefit from recognizing and utilizing many opportunities to increase intergroup contact among employees, including purposeful assignment of shared workspaces, shared eating spaces and times, and group outings and events. This also might promote opportunities for "individuation"—the process of obtaining specific, personal information about out-group members—which encourages evaluation of others as individuals rather than group members, thus reducing dependence on stereotypes for evaluation (Brewer 1988). Encouraging employees to get to know each other on a more personal level could reduce prejudice toward out-group coworkers.

Pursuit of a Common Goal

Promoting employees to work together toward a common goal is likely to reduce their prejudice toward out-group members and to improve intergroup relations. Sherif's (1966) research, for example, indicated that putting two mutually hostile groups together again to reach a superordinate goal gradually reduced hostility and promoted harmony between the groups. When individuals from different groups rely on each other to succeed, they begin to perceive out-group members as part of their in-groups (Gaertner, Dovidio, Anastasio, Bachman & Rust 1993) and begin to like them more, which might result in a decrease in microaggressions.

Addressing Existing Problems

Assessment. Employers should assess the experiences of employees on an ongoing basis to understand how microaggressions are operating in their workplace. Goals of assessment can include determining the pervasiveness of the problem, identifying routine offenders and victims, determining whether certain marginalized groups are more disadvantaged than others, and inquiring how microaggressions might affect employees' enjoyment of and commitment to their jobs. Assessments must be conducted in culturally competent ways, and protection from reprisals must be ensured to obtain the most honest data. This might be best achieved by collecting data anonymously; however, when workplaces are small or not representative of diverse populations, minority individuals will know that their data will be identifiable.

Policies and procedures. Once assessment has been conducted and the extent of the problem is revealed, formalized procedures for addressing microaggressions in the workplace could relieve some of the strain on individual employees. Organizations are likely to have policies and procedures in place to address severe incidents of discrimination, but rarely do policies address the less extreme manifestations of bias that take a daily toll on marginalized employees. When individuals are not intrinsically motivated to reduce their discriminatory behavior, perhaps company policies that uphold values of inclusivity and penalize acts of discrimination could assist in decreasing microaggressions. Following recommendations by Carr et al. (2013) and Lukes and Bangs (2014), a position could be designated to enforce the application of these procedures, by overseeing *difficult dialogues*—challenging and potentially stressful conversations about issues of diversity, inclusion, and equity—in the aftermath of microaggressive workplace behavior. Having such policies in place can assist in helping targeted individuals to not feel that they must address microaggressions alone.

Education. Employers who are committed to reducing discrimination in their workplaces could find that mandatory employee education has the potential to prevent or lessen the negative impact of discrimination and inequality in the workplace. Research (e.g., Becker & Swim 2011; Zawadski Danube & Shields 2012) has indicated that educating employees about gender discrimination yields positive outcomes, although such efforts might be met with resistance from both male and female employees. Programs that emphasize empathy for privileged group members and highlight self-efficacy for marginalized groups could serve to quell resistance. Education should not only cover organizational policies and procedures to ensure employees' understanding of their rights and responsibilities, but should also explore what constitutes prejudice/bias/discrimination and how discrimination affects those who experience it. External consultants can be utilized to dismantle the structural hierarchy, thus placing all organization members (regardless of position or rank) in the role of student.

CONCLUSION

Lastly, in addition to efforts to curtail discrimination in the workplace, employers can consider providing support for targets of discrimination.

Although it is clear that both overt and covert discrimination have detrimental effects on employees' mental health and job performance, some research indicates that discrimination also can hold the potential to promote resiliency. For example, Meyer, Ouellette, Haile, and McFarlane (2011) found that although experiences with LGB discrimination were related to decreased access to career opportunities, discrimination also appeared to increase participants' sense of identification with the LGB population. This increased sense of identification facilitated the development of a more positive LGB identity and more positive self-perceptions regarding that identity. Branscombe, Schmitt, and Harvey (1999) obtained similar results among a sample of African American participants, finding that although discriminatory experiences related negatively to well-being, such experiences also related to positive minority-group identification. Additionally, Cronin, Levin, Branscombe, Van Laar, and Tropp (2012) conducted a longitudinal investigation of discrimination and group identification with a sample of 252 Latino students across a period of four years. They found that discrimination was significantly correlated with group identification, and that group identification significantly correlated with higher levels of well-being. This small body of research suggests that positive interventions can take place following experiences of discrimination through the development of supportive group identifications.

Future research on microaggressions in the workplace should investigate means of building resiliency in marginalized employees to improve the well-being of targets of microaggressions. Additionally, as the concept of microaggressions has become solidified, a shift away from major discriminatory acts in the workplace toward more pervasive, small-scale forms of discrimination is necessary to keep the literature up to date with employees' experiences in the modern world. It will be particularly important to compare workplaces with various levels of microaggressions to determine what factors can promote or inhibit the incidence of microaggressions in the workplace. Finally, the areas of transgender and intersectional microaggressions in the workplace have been particularly neglected and are deserving of further study.

REFERENCES

Ahmed, A., Andersson, L., and Hammarstedt, M. (2013). Are gay men and lesbians discriminated against in the hiring process? *Southern Economic Journal* 79, 565–585. doi: 10.4284/0038-4038-2011.317

Alleyne, A. (2004). Black identity and workplace oppression. *Counseling and Psychotherapy Research* 4, 4–8.

Badgett, M. V. L., Sears, B., Lau, H., and Ho, D. (2009). Bias in the workplace: Consistent evidence of sexual orientation and gender identity discrimination. *Chicago-Kent Law Review*, 559–596.

Balsam, K. F., Molina, Y., Beadnell, B., Simoni, J., and Walters, K. (2011). Measuring multiple minority stress: The LGBT people of color microaggressions scale. *Cultural Diversity and Ethnic Minority Psychology* 17, 163–174. doi: 10.1037/a0023244

Basford, T., Offermann, L., and Behrend, T. (2013). Do you see what I see? Perceptions of gender microaggressions in the workplace. *Psychology of Women Quarterly.* Advance online publication. doi: 10.1177/0361684313 511420

Becker, J., and Swim, J. (2011). Seeing the unseen: Attention to daily encounters with sexism as way to reduce sexist beliefs. *Psychology of Women Quarterly* 35, 227–242. doi: 10.1177/0361684310397509

Bendick, M., Jackson, C. W., Reinoso, V. A., and Hodges, L. E. (1991). Discrimination against Latino job applicants: A controlled experiment. *Human Resource Management* 30, 469–484.

Blume, A. W., Lovato, L. V., Thyken, B. N., and Denny, N. (2012). The relationship of microaggressions with alcohol use and anxiety among ethnic minority college students in a historically white institution. *Cultural Diversity and Ethnic Minority Psychology* 18, 45–54. doi: 10.1037/a0025457

Branscombe, N. R., Schmitt, M. T., and Harvey, R. D. (1999). Perceiving pervasive discrimination among African Americans: Implications for group identification and well-being. *Journal of Personality and Social Psychology* 77, 135–149. doi: 10.1037/0022-3514.77.1.135

Brewer, M. B. (1988). A dual process model of impression formation. In *A dual process model of impression formation,* edited by T. K. Srull, R. Wyer, 1–36. Hillsdale, NJ England: Lawrence Erlbaum Associates, Inc.

Burdsey, D. (2011). That joke isn't funny anymore: Racial microaggressions, color-blind ideology and the mitigation of racism in English men's first-class cricket. *Sociology of Sport Journal* 28, 261–283.

Capodilupo, C. M., Nadal, K. L., Corman, L., Hamit, S., Lyons, O., and Weinberg, A. (2010). The Manifestation of gender microaggressions. In *Microaggressions and marginality: Manifestation, dynamics, and impact,* edited by D. W. Sue, 193–216. New York: Wiley.

Carr, P. L., Ash, A., Friedman, R. H., Szalacha, L., Barnett, R. C., Palepu, A., and Moskowitz, M. M. (2000). Faculty perceptions of gender discrimination and sexual harassment in academic medicine. *Annals of Internal Medicine* 132, 889–896.

Carr, P. L., Szalacha, L., Barnett, R., Caswell, C., and Inui, T. (2003). Faculty perceptions of gender discrimination and sexual harassment in academic medicine. *Journal of Women's Health* 12, 1009–1018. doi: 10.1089/154099903322643938

Cartwright, B. Y., Washington, R. D., and McConnell, L. R. (2009). Examining racial microaggressions in rehabilitation counselor education. *Rehabilitation Education* 23, 171–181.

Chung, Y., and Syzmanski, D. (2006). Racial and sexual identities of Asian American gay men. *Journal of LGBT Issues in Counseling* I, 67–93.

Clements-Nolle, K., Marx, R., and Katz, M. (2006). Attempted suicide among trans-gender persons. *Journal of Homosexuality* 51, 53–69. doi: 10.1300/J082v51n03_04

Cochran, S. D., Mays, V. M., Alegria, M., Ortega, A. N., and Takeuchi, D. (2007). Mental health and substance use disorders among Latino and Asian American lesbian, gay, and bisexual adults. *Journal of Consulting and Clinical Psychology* 75, 785–794. doi: 10.1037/0022-006X.75.5.785

Constantine, M. G., Smith, L., Redington, R. M., and Owens, D. (2008). Racial microaggressions against black counseling and counseling psychology faculty: A central challenge in the multicultural counseling movement. *Journal of Counseling & Development* 86, 348–355.

Cronin, T. J., Branscombe, N. R., Levin, S., Van Laar, C., and Tropp, L. R. (2012). Ethnic identification in response to perceived discrimination protects well-being and promotes activism: A longitudinal study of Latino college students. *Group Processes and Intergroup Relations* 15, 393–407.

Davis, L. S. (2014). *Outness in context: A quantitative and qualitative of LGBTQ experiences.* Manuscript in preparation.

Dispenza, F., Watson, L. B., Chung, Y. B., and Brack, G. (2012). Experience of career-related discrimination for female-to-male (FTM) transgender persons: A qualitative study. *Career Development Quarterly* 60, 65–81.

Gaertner, S. L., Dovidio, J. F., Anastasio, P. A., Bachman, B. A., and Rust, M. C. (1993). The common in-group identity model: Recategorization and the reduction of intergroup bias. *European Review of Social Psychology* 4, 1–26.

Gorman, E. (2005). Gender stereotypes, same-gender preferences, and organizational variation in the hiring of women: Evidence from law firms. *American Sociological Review* 70, 702–728.

Hunt, B., Matthews, C., Milsom, A., and Lammel, J. A. (2006). Lesbians with physical disabilities: A qualitative study of their experiences with counseling. *Journal of Counseling & Development* 84, 163–173.

Lai, L., and Babcock, L. C. (2013). Asian Americans and workplace discrimination: The interplay between sex of evaluators and the perception of social skills. *Journal of Organizational Behavior* 34, 310–326.

Lewis, G. B., and Pitts, D. W. (2011). Representation of lesbians and gay men in federal, state, and local bureaucracies. *Journal of Public Administration: Research and Theory* 21, 159–180. doi: 10.1093/jopart/mup030

Lukes, R., and Bangs, J. (2014). A critical analysis of anti-discrimination law and microaggressions in academia. *Research in Higher Education* 42, 1–15.

Macan, T., and Merritt, S. (2011). *Actions speak too: Uncovering possible implicit and explicit discrimination in the employment interview process (Vol. 26, 293–337).* St. Louis, MO: Wiley-Blackwell.

Mays, V. M., and Cochran, S. D. (2001). Mental health correlates of perceived discrimination among lesbian, gay, and bisexual adults in the United States. *American Journal of Public Health* 91, 1869–1876.

McLaughlin, K., Hatzenbuehler, M., and Keyes, K. (2010). Responses to discrimination and psychiatric disorders among Black, Hispanic, female, and lesbian, gay, and bisexual individuals. *American Journal of Public Health* 100, 1477–1484.

Meyer, I. H. (2001). Why lesbian, gay, bisexual, and transgender public health? *American Journal of Public Health* 91, 856–859. doi: 10.2105/AJPH.91.6.856

Meyer, I. H., Ouellette, S., Haile, R., and McFarlane, T. (2011). "We'd be free": Narratives of life without homophobia, racism, or sexism. *Sexuality Research and Social Policy* 8, 204–214. doi: 10.1007/s13178-011-0063-0

Mobley, M., and Pearson, S. M. (2005). Blessed be the ties that bind. In *Deconstructing heterosexism in the counseling professions: A narrative approach*, edited by J. M. Croteau, J. S. Lark, M. A. Liddendale, and Y. B. Chung, 89–96. Thousand Oaks, CA: Sage.

Moss-Racusin, C. A., Dovidio, J. F., Brescoll, V. L., Graham, M. J., and Handelsman, J. (2012). Science faculty's subtle gender biases favor male students. *Proceedings of the National Academy of Sciences of the United States of America* 109, 16474–16479. doi: 10.1073/pnas.1211286109

Nadal, K. L. (2013). *That's so gay! Microaggressions and the lesbian, gay, bisexual, and transgender community*. Washington, DC: American Psychological Association.

Nadal, K. L. (2011). The Racial and Ethnic Microaggressions Scale (REMS): Construction, reliability, and validity. *Journal of Counseling Psychology* 58, 470–480.

Nadal, K. L. (2010). Gender microaggressions and women: Implications for mental health. In *Feminism and women's rights worldwide: Vol. 2. Mental and physical health*, edited by M. A. Paludi, 155–175. Santa Barbara, CA: Praeger.

Nadal, K. L. (2008). Preventing racial, ethnic, gender, sexual minority, disability, and religious microaggressions: Recommendations for promoting positive mental health. *Prevention in Counseling Psychology: Theory, Research, Practice, and Training* 2, 22–27.

Nadal, K. L., Davidoff, K. C., Davis, L. S., and Wong, Y. (2014). Emotional, behavioral, and cognitive reactions to microaggressions: Transgender perspectives. *Psychology of Sexual Orientation and Gender Diversity* 1, 72–81. doi: 10.1037/sgd0000011

Nadal, K. L., Davidoff, K. C., Davis, L. S., Wong, Y., Marshall, D., and McKenzie, V. (2014). *Intersectional identities and microaggressions: Influences of race, ethnicity, gender, sexuality, and religion*. Manuscript under review.

Nadal, K. L., Griffin, K., and Wong, Y. (2011). Gender, racial, and sexual orientation microaggressions in the workplace: Impacts on women leaders. In *Women as transformational leaders: From grassroots to global interests, Volume 1: Cultural and Organizational Stereotypes, Prejudice, and Discrimination*, edited by M. A. Paludi, and B. Coates, 1–26. Santa Barbara, CA: Praeger.

Nadal, K. L., Griffin, K. E., Wong, Y., Hamit, S., and Rasmus, M. (2014). Racial microaggressions and mental health: Counseling clients of color. *Journal of Counseling and Development* 92, 57–66.

Nadal, K. L., Issa, M-A., Leon, J., Meterko, V., Wideman, M., and Wong, Y. (2011). Sexual orientation microaggressions: "Death by a thousand cuts" for lesbian, gay, and bisexual youth. *Journal of LGBT Youth* 8, 1–26. doi: 10.1080/19361653.2011.584204

Nadal, K. L., Mazzula, S. L., Rivera, D. P., and Fuji-Doe, W. (2014). Microaggressions and Latina/o Americans: An analysis of nativity, gender, and ethnicity. *Journal of Latina/o Psychology* 2, 67–78.

Nadal, K. L., Rivera, D. P., and Corpus, M. J. H. (2010). Sexual orientation and transgender microaggressions. In *Microaggressions and marginality: Manifestation, dynamics, and impact,* edited by D. Sue, 217–239. Hoboken, NJ: John Wiley & Sons.

Nadal, K. L., Skolnik, A., and Wong, Y. (2012). Interpersonal and systemic microaggressions toward transgender people: Implications for counseling. *Journal of LGBT Issues in Counseling* 6, 55–82. doi: 10.1080/15538605.2012.648583

Nadal, K. L., Wong, Y., Issa, M., Meterko, V., Leon, J., and Wideman, M. (2011). Sexual orientation microaggressions: Processes and coping mechanisms for lesbian, gay, and bisexual individuals. *Journal of LGBT Issues in Counseling* 5, 21–46.

O'Neil, M. E., McWhirter, E. H., and Cerezo, A. (2008). Transgender identities and gender variance in vocational psychology: Recommendations for practice, social advocacy, and research. *Journal of Career Development* 34, 286–308. doi: 10.1177/0894845307311251

Pettigrew, T. F. (1998). Intergroup contact theory. *Annual Review of Psychology* 49, 65–85.

Pettigrew, T. F., and Tropp, L. R. (2006). A meta-analytic test of intergroup contact theory. *Journal of Personality and Social Psychology* 90, 751–783.

Pierce, C., Carew, J., Pierce-Gonzalez, D., and Willis, D. (1978). An experiment in racism: TV commercials. In *Television and education,* edited by C. Pierce, 62–88. Beverly Hills, CA: Sage.

Ragins, B. R., and Cornwell, J. M. (2001). Pink triangles: Antecedents and consequences of perceived workplace discrimination against gay and lesbian employees. *Journal of Applied Psychology* 86, 1244–1261.

Sherif, M. (1966). *Group conflict and cooperation.* London: Routledge & Kegan Paul.

Stockdill, B. C., and Danico, M. Y. (2012). *Transforming the ivory tower: Challenging racism, sexism, and homophobia in the Academy.* Honolulu: University of Hawaii Press.

Sue, D. W. (2010a). *Microaggressions and marginality: Manifestation, dynamics, and impact.* New York: Wiley.

Sue, D. W. (2010b). *Microaggressions in everyday life: Race, gender, and sexual orientation.* Hoboken, NJ: Wiley.

Sue, D. W., Bucceri, J. M., Lin, A. I., Nadal, K. L., and Torino, G. C. (2010). Racial microaggressions and the Asian American experience. *Asian American Journal of Psychology* 88–101. doi: 10.1037/1948-1985.S.1.88

Sue, D. W., Capodilupo, C. M., Torino, G. C., Bucceri, J. M., Holder, A. M., Nadal, K. L., and Esquilin, M. E. (2007). Racial microaggressions in everyday life: Implications for counseling. *The American Psychologist* 62, 271–286.

Sue, D. W., Nadal, K. L., Capodilupo, C. M., Lin, A. I., Torino, G. C., and Rivera, D. P. (2008). Racial microaggressions against black Americans: Implications for counseling. *Journal of Counseling & Development* 86, 330–338.

Swim, J. K., and Cohen, L. L. (1997). Overt, covert, and subtle sexism: A comparison between the attitudes toward women and modern sexism scales. *Psychology of Women Quarterly* 21, 103–118.

Swim, J. K., Hyers, L. L., Cohen, L. L., and Ferguson, M. J. (2001). Everyday sexism: Evidence for its incidence, nature, and psychological impact from three daily diary studies. *Journal of Social Issues* 57, 31–53.

Swim, J. K., Mallett, R., and Stangor, C. (2004). Understanding subtle sexism: Detection and use of sexist language. *Sex Roles* 51, 117–128.

Tilcsik, A. (2011). Pride and prejudice: Employment discrimination against openly gay men in the United States. *American Journal of Sociology* 117, 586–626.

Wang, J., Leu, J., and Shoda, Y. (2011). When the seemingly innocuous "stings": Racial microaggressions and their emotional consequences. *Personality and Social Psychology Bulletin* 37, 1666–1678. doi: 10.1177/0146167211416130

Zawadski, M., Danube, C., and Shields, S. (2012). How to talk about gender inequity in the workplace: Using wages as an experiential learning tool to reduce reactance and promote self-efficacy. *Sex Roles* 67, 605–616. doi: 10.1007/s11199-012-0181-z

Chapter 8

Sexual Harassment of Low-Wage Immigrant Workers in the United States: Lessons from EEOC Lawsuits

Cynthia Deitch

These women often worked late nights in office buildings and churches, never seen by anyone, but silently suffering from terrible working conditions. These women were vulnerable and isolated, yet found the courage to come forward to tell what happened to them. . . . Some of the male supervisors and co-workers exposed themselves to the women, and groped them in their vaginal area. They also grabbed breasts, and forced the women to touch an erect penis. In one case, a woman was cleaning the bathroom, when a supervisor attempted to assault her by closing the door to the restroom, turning off the lights, and grabbing her legs and buttocks. One of the most unfortunate aspects of this case involved a woman who was raped. Other women were subjected to attempted assaults and sexual battery. Some of the claimants will tell you that when some of them were brave enough to complain, their hours were cut, and ultimately, they lost their jobs. In other instances, the complaints fell on deaf ears.

Equal Employment Opportunity Commission 2010

Anna Park, the regional attorney for U.S. Equal Employment Opportunity Commission (EEOC) delivered the above statement at a 2010 press conference announcing the $5.8 million settlement of a lawsuit filed by the EEOC against ABM Industries on behalf of 21 Latina immigrant janitorial workers (EEOC 2010). In recent years, the EEOC has brought and settled a growing number of sexual harassment lawsuits on behalf of immigrant workers, including many involving undocumented immigrants in agribusiness, food and cleaning service, and other low-wage sectors.

Although the allegations against ABM Industries were among the most egregious, this was not an isolated case. In the same press statement, Park (EEOC 2010) noted a marked increase in violent physical sexual harassment complaints made to the EEOC. Reports on immigrant women working in agriculture (Bauer & Ramirez 2010; Cediel & Bergman 2013; Meng 2012, Waugh 2010) document numerous examples of rape, sexual assault, and molestation. Whether the harassment is physical or verbal, workers who complain often are subject to severe retaliation—including termination and threats to notify immigration police. At Giumarra Vineyards, for example, when the parents and boyfriend of a teenage immigrant woman of indigenous Mexican Indian background tried to report sexual harassment of the woman by her foreman, all four were fired and as a result also lost their company housing (*EEOC v. Giumarra Vineyards* 2010).

On a more positive note, the EEOC lawsuits have resulted in significant monetary awards, along with court-overseen legal agreements for changes in workplace policies and practices that protect potentially hundreds of other workers under the same employer. Drawing on an examination of documents for 75 lawsuits, this chapter addresses the following questions: What can we learn from the lawsuits about the specific vulnerabilities to sexual harassment of low wage–earning, immigrant women of color in the United States? More specifically, how does the intersection of race, class, gender, and immigration status shape the organizational context of sexual harassment for immigrant workers? What types of interventions do the lawsuits provide, what are their limitations, what are the most promising practices promoted in the settlements?

Two overarching theoretical perspectives frame the chapter. One is intersectionality theory (e.g., Collins 1990; Crenshaw 1989; Ken 2010), which calls for an examination of the multiple ways that race, class, and gender combine to shape experiences of inequality. Following Welsh, Carr, MacQuarrie, and Huntley (2006), this chapter explores how immigration status complicates an intersectional approach to studying sexual harassment of workers who also are members of racial and ethnic minority groups as well as being low-wage employees. This chapter also considers both the narrow conception of intersectional discrimination in the law used by the EEOC where there are charges of both sex and race or national origin discrimination, and the broader understanding that gender, race, and class—as identities and as structures of inequality—shape the context of sexual harassment (Welsh, Carr, MacQuarrie & Huntley 2006).

The second framework is routine activities theory, which originated in criminology research on direct contact predatory crimes (Cohen & Felson 1979), but has been adapted to study sexual harassment and other bullying in the workplace (DeCoster, Estes & Mueller 1999; Lopez, Hodson & Roscigno 2009; Roscigno, Lopez & Hodson 2009; Stockdale & Nadler 2012). The routine activities model is used as a heuristic device to examine the workplace conditions that seem to make immigrant workers especially vulnerable to sexual harassment, and the interventions provided by the lawsuits. In the routine activities model, sexual harassment is most likely when three elements converge: "suitable targets" in the presence of "motivated perpetrators" with the absence of "capable guardians." During routine activities, some individuals and groups are exposed to this convergence more regularly than others. In studies of workplace sexual harassment, researchers have focused on characteristics of individuals as well as the organizational environment that define suitable targets. Perpetrator motivation usually is imputed rather than directly observed, invoking various theories of why men (most theories assume men) harass. Capable guardians, in the organizational context, include the presence of supportive coworkers and supervisors as well as institutional structures and processes such as sexual harassment policies and grievance procedures.

TITLE VII AND IMMIGRATION LAW

The 1986 Immigration and Control Act (IRCA) requires employers to verify employee immigration status or face penalties. The IRCA also states that undocumented workers cannot be denied Title VII and other employment law and civil rights. Immigrant rights advocates and other critics argue that immigrant workers and their rights bear the brunt of IRCA sanctions policy (Chen 2012; Meng 2012; Smith & Cho 2013). The EEOC interprets the law and the EEOC mission to mean that immigration status makes no difference in treating civil rights violations. *EEOC v. Tanimura & Antle* was a precedent-setting EEOC settlement secured in 1999 by the EEOC San Francisco office on behalf of an undocumented Mexican farmworker—a single mother who was forced to have sex as a condition of hiring and was fired when she protested. When the U.S. Supreme Court, in *Hoffman Plastic v. NLRB* (2002), however, interpreted the IRCA to limit remedies for undocumented workers who experience unlawful discharge for reporting workplace abuses, it cast a shadow over immigrant workers' prospects to challenge discrimination and other employment law violations (Chen 2012; Smith & Cho 2013). Despite this shadow and uneven lower-court responses to undocumented workers' rights, the EEOC has continued to bring lawsuits on behalf of immigrant workers, regardless of their immigration status.

OVERVIEW OF THE LAWSUIT DATA

The sample of 75 immigrant worker sexual harassment lawsuits was developed in several ways. Nine cases were drawn from an earlier project (Hegewisch, Deitch & Murphy 2011); additional cases were identified from EEOC press releases or other EEOC documents, and from law review articles discussing employment rights of immigrants.[1] Of the 75 lawsuits examined, 1 resulted in a favorable jury verdict, 1 was denied by a jury, 8 appear to be not yet resolved as of this writing, and the remaining 65 were resolved in settlements entered between 1999 and early 2014. Sources included the legal documents such as complaints (lawsuit charges filed by the EEOC), consent decrees (settlement agreements), EEOC press releases, and any media coverage.

Thirty of the cases were in agribusiness, and included food packing, processing, or distribution; at least 20 of the agribusiness cases primarily were farmworkers; 18 cases were restaurants or food service; six were janitorial; the rest were a mix of manufacturing, hotels, retail, laundry, and other businesses. Geographically, incidents for 34 cases had occurred in California, and another 16 occurred in states and territories (Washington, Oregon, Nevada, Hawaii, and Guam) that also were covered by the San Francisco or Los Angles EEOC regional offices, which have actively pursued many of the agribusiness and other cases. The national origins of the workers mentioned in the lawsuits included Mexican (most common, by far), several indigenous Mexican Indian groups, Guatemalan, Salvadoran, Filipino, Chinese, Haitian, and unspecified "African immigrants." Six lawsuits were for the sexual harassment of men. None of the lawsuits examined appeared simply about nuanced or possibly innocent or joking comments that might have been misinterpreted. Many of them charged both quid pro quo and hostile environment harassment. Many also charged retaliation for reporting a complaint.

The industries and geographic distribution of cases described here reflect EEOC priorities as well as demographic realities. Undocumented and other low-wage immigrant women are concentrated in agriculture, food service, and janitorial work (Passel & Cohn 2011). The San Francisco EEOC district office has been especially active in litigating farmworker cases, beginning in the 1990s. In recent years, the national EEOC strategic plan (EEOC 2012) has made the harassment of immigrant and migrant workers a priority. Although it certainly is likely that more middle-class immigrant workers also experience sexual harassment, the EEOC sexual harassment lawsuits examined here all concerned immigrant workers in very low-wage jobs.

It is important to remember that the lawsuits in sample represent only the very tip of the proverbial iceberg for sexual harassment of immigrant workers. Missing from the lawsuit sample are the many instances of sexual harassment that never were reported, of reported complaints that never got as far as the EEOC, and of harassment of workers in workplaces not covered by Title VII—such as employers with fewer than 15 employees and including many domestic workers (Vellos 1996), as well as the informal sector. Of all the complaints filed with the EEOC, most either are found not to have probable cause, or are resolved without filing a lawsuit (e.g., through the EEOC mediation or conciliation process). When Title VII lawsuits are filed, parties usually are represented by private attorneys; the EEOC selects only a small minority of cases to litigate.

EEOC lawsuits, however, are important for several reasons. Low-wage immigrants typically cannot afford private attorneys, and pro bono attorneys have limited resources. The EEOC is less constrained by class certification rules and better able to include unnamed "similarly situated" individuals. As with the EEOC cases, most employment discrimination lawsuits settle rather than go to trial. Unlike private-attorney litigated cases, EEOC lawsuit settlements are public, not confidential, and therefore are available for study. The settlements often are publicized widely, giving them a role in shaping the behavior of other employers in a given industry or locale. Most important for the present examination, EEOC settlements almost always include some kind of programmatic injunctive relief whereby the employer agrees to make specific changes in policy and practice that then apply not only to those workers who were part of the lawsuit, but also to the larger group of current and subsequent employees.

Although the offenses alleged in the lawsuits are not statistically representative of the frequency of sexual harassment of immigrant workers, they also are not necessarily outliers or extreme cases. Ethnographic and interview research on immigrant women shows that the range, context, and patterns of abuse alleged in the lawsuits are quite similar to what women not involved in any lawsuits have reported to researchers (Bauer & Ramirez 2010; Castañeda & Zavella 2003; Meng 2012; Waugh 2010).

FINDINGS

The findings given here identify several patterns of interest that illustrate common dynamics across industry sectors in the production of targets of sexual harassment. These include combined sexual and national origin harassment charges, abuse of power by supervisors, and physical context of the work. Following the routine activities model, the chapter then discusses targets, perpetrators (very briefly), and the absence of protectors. It then discusses how the lawsuit interventions remedy the problem by requiring protectors and protections in efforts reduce sexual harassment and promote better practices by employers.

COMBINED SEXUAL HARASSMENT AND NATIONAL ORIGIN DISCRIMINATION LAWSUITS

In line with routine activities theory, researchers have hypothesized that racial minority women might be in double jeopardy as targets of sexual harassment (Berdahl & Moore 2006); motivated perpetrators will select as suitable targets members of racial or ethnic groups, or people of national origin that the perpetrators view as inferior (Lopez, Hodson & Roscigno 2009; Roscigno, Lopez & Hodson 2009). Empirical evidence is mixed with some evidence that this is true for more severe forms of harassment (Berdahl & Moore 2006). Analyses focused on the content and context of sexual harassment of racial minority women have examined racialized sexual harassment that combines verbal expressions of racism or racial stereotypes with sexual harassment (Cho 1997; Cortina, Fitzgerald & Drasgow 2002; Texeira 2002; Welsh 1999). Welsh et al. (2006) found that women in different racial minority and immigrant groups perceived, evaluated, and responded to sexual harassment differently. For immigrants in Welsh's Canadian study, both cultural differences and legal considerations related to citizenship status were important. Legal scholars such as Ontiveros (2002; 2009) have argued that Title VII law treats sexual harassment of immigrant women as only a matter of sex discrimination, failing to address the intersectional reality of their experience.

The present study specifically analyzed indications of racialized sexual harassment as well as all instances where sexual harassment charges were combined with charges of race or national origin discrimination. Nineteen of the 75 cases included formal complaints of both sex and national origin discrimination, which were combined in several different ways. The six cases that involved the sexual harassment of immigrant men also charged national origin (and sometimes racial) harassment. Only a few lawsuits involved the racialized (or ethnicized) sexual harassment of women as in supervisors repeatedly telling women that "all Mexican women are whores," and "Mexican women are only good for sex." Others combined nonsexual ethnic slurs with sexual harassment as at Knouse Foods, a case in which the EEOC alleged that men made vulgar sexual gestures, exposed themselves, asked women for dates, and also called women "dumb Mexican" or "stupid Mexican." Several lawsuits combined complaints of sexual harassment of women with complaints of nonsexual, national origin harassment of men occurring in the same workplace.

EEOC Regional Attorney William Tamayo, reported to a 2007 meeting of the EEOC commissioners that, in cases handled by his office, Mexican women were targeted for harassment by non-Latino men. In one case against a restaurant chain, women were physically and verbally harassed (EEOC 2007); they were told, "Mexican bitches only are good for sex," and "go back to where you come from if you don't like it." Tamayo concluded, "In essence, the sexual violence against Latinas is rationalized by racism and xenophobia."

Some of the combined sexual and national origin cases involved harassment of one racial or ethnic minority by another, or harassment by immigrants from one country toward immigrants from another. As expected, all of the national origin cases involved sexual harassment by harassers of a different race, ethnicity, or national origin than the harassed workers. This is worth noting because many of the sexual harassment–only cases (no national origin discrimination complaint) included sexual harassment by members of the same national origin background as the victim, but with a somewhat more secure immigration and occupational status. Sometimes there was both same-ethnicity and cross-ethnicity harassment occurring in the same workplace.

SEXUAL HARASSMENT OF MEN

A small but interesting subcategory of the combined sexual and national origin cases involved the same-sex harassment of immigrant men by male supervisors. The U.S. Supreme Court recognized same-sex harassment as sex discrimination under Title VII in the landmark 1998 *Oncale v. Sundowner* case. Since then, the EEOC has filed a number of same-sex harassment of men lawsuits. It is interesting to note that all of the immigrant male sexual harassment lawsuits did include both charges as compared to relatively few of the women's cases. The harassment in the six male-immigrant cases included verbal sexual disparaging remarks, racialized sexual harassment, unwanted physical touching or groping, requests for sex, and a supervisor repeated exposing himself to subordinate men. In all six cases, the harassers were supervisors, managers, or owners; in one case it was a coworker promoted to supervisor despite complaints. The workplaces included a truck dealership, a fish market, a drywall company, an airline maintenance service, a janitorial service, and a tree farm. The immigrants' national origins were identified as Filipino, Salvadorian, Guatemalan; and ethnicities also included several indigenous Mexican groups and "African immigrants." In several of the cases, the harasser also was an immigrant or ethnic minority but had a different background. In at least two of the cases, nonimmigrant African Americans were subject to similar harassment in the same workplace.

Several of the male harassment cases were in traditionally or predominantly male workplaces such as a truck dealership and a drywall and plastering business. Men using a combination of racially and sexually demeaning language as well as sexually demeaning gestures toward other people are behaviors that are compatible with explanations of sexual harassment as a means for men to express their own masculinity and superior status to those they view as being subordinate. In these cases, it appears that sexual harassment was a means of demeaning an ethnic group that was viewed as inferior or disliked by the harasser.

POWER RELATIONS, ABUSIVE SUPERVISORS

Some researchers use routine activities theory to predict that workers in the most vulnerable positions in the workplace hierarchy are more likely to experience harassment (Lopez, Hodson & Roscigno 2009; Roscigno, Lopez & Hodson 2009). In this approach, employment insecurity, low-wage jobs, nonsupervisory positions, and jobs that allow little self-direction could be associated with increased incidence of harassment. Some studies have confirmed some of these patterns (Lopez, Hodson & Roscigno 2009; Roscigno, Lopez & Hodson 2009). Another line of analysis with considerable empirical support, however, finds that power-threat or "contra-power" positions often are stronger predictors of harassment (Chamberlain, Crowley, Tope & Hodson 2008; DeCoster, Estes & Mueller 1999; McLaughlin, Uggen & Blackstone 2012). Women in positions of authority can become targets of harassment by male subordinates (Chamberlain et al. 2008; DeCoster, Estes & Mueller 1999; McLaughlin, Uggen & Blackstone 2012). Women in predominantly male and normatively masculine work settings also could be perceived as challenging male privilege and masculinity (Gruber 1998). In both lines of analysis, power relations in the workplace are important for understanding sexual harassment. The present investigation examined how workplace power relations—especially between supervisors and subordinates—contributed to an organizational context conducive to sexual harassment of immigrant workers.

None of the 75 lawsuits for sexual harassment of immigrant workers that were examined fit the power-threat or contra-power explanation. None of the cases involved women in positions of power or authority over men. From the information available, none of the cases appeared to involve women in predominantly male jobs. It is true that agricultural labor, as a broad occupational category, statistically is a predominantly male occupation. In the settings in question, however, labor is segregated by gender within the workplace and women often are relegated to specific, predominantly female, lower-paying, less desirable jobs.

AN IOWA VIGNETTE

The case of *EEOC v. DeCoster Farms*, settled in 2002, involved the rape and abuse of undocumented immigrant women by supervisors at an Iowa egg-packing facility. As part of an earlier project (Hegewisch, Deitch & Murphy 2011), this chapter's author participated in conducting interviews with attorneys and others involved in this lawsuit.[2] The case was ground-breaking for its use of the U-visa[3] in a Title VII sexual harassment case to protect the immigrant victims of workplace sexual assault from deportation, but it also shares features with numbers of other cases, especially those in agribusiness. The women were recruited—basically trafficked—from villages in Mexico and Guatemala. Their abusers were supervisors who were Spanish-speaking legal residents with the power to terminate the women's employment, report them to immigration, humiliate them in their communities, and harm their families. The attorneys interviewed explained that the immigrant women had no reason to believe or understand that the white Iowan owners—with whom they had no direct contact—could possibly be legally liable for the sexual abuse perpetrated by the Latino supervisors (Hegewisch, Deitch & Murphy 2011).

A bilingual attorney who conducted legal outreach to the immigrant community for the Iowa Coalition Against Domestic Violence (ICADV) explained how the same few women kept showing up at every event at which she spoke—they were desperate to get help with their immigration status, which was something that the attorney was unable to help the women with. Finally, she asked them privately what was going on. When one woman said she wanted "to stop having sex at work," the attorney, who had worked on sexual trafficking cases, asked if the woman was a sex worker and learned that she worked at an egg-packing plant. The ICADV attorney contacted the EEOC and remained involved, as an advocate for the women, when the EEOC filed the lawsuit. The EEOC attorney for the lawsuit told us how he had to find new ways of working with complainants for this case, meeting with workers in a church basement, pursuing the case with full knowledge that the women were too afraid to testify if the case went to trial. The women were afraid their families might blame them if the sexual details were public. Even the U-visa could not protect families back home against retaliation by the abusers who had long since fled and were never punished or charged. According to the EEOC attorney, local law enforcement was not willing or interested in pursuing criminal charges for the rapes and sexual abuse (Hegewisch, Deitch & Murphy 2011).

A consistent pattern evident in almost all of the cases was the sexual harassment of subordinates by supervisors. The *DeCoster Farms* case described above illustrates the extensive power and its abuse by supervisors. As in *DeCoster Farms*, most of the harassers were first-line supervisors; only a few cases included any men who were considered managers or owners, and a few cases also included harassment by coworkers along with supervisors. As *DeCoster Farms* illustrates, in farm, food processing, food service, and janitorial cases (among others), men in relatively low-status, first-line supervisory positions had a considerable amount of unmonitored, discretionary power over the day-to-day working conditions of women in subordinate positions. This pattern also is documented in Meng's (2012) report for Human Rights Watch as being common for immigrant farm-workers. Supervisors could terminate workers, seemingly without any formal process. They could restrict allocation of work hours, shifts, and assignments. They exercised control over the physical movements and proximity of their targets in the sense that they could order a woman to go to an isolated room in the basement of a restaurant or assign "one woman to a barn" on a farm. With impunity, the harassing supervisors were able to retaliate—or threaten to retaliate—against women who resisted sexual contact or attempted to file complaints.

Although there is no evidence that the harassing supervisors in any of these cases felt threatened by the career success, or women's encroachment into men's domain, of their low-wage immigrant women subordinates, these often were men who might feel that they had relatively limited status, power, or money within their workplace and in the larger society. Perhaps sexually abusing subordinates was one way of asserting masculinity and power.

SPATIAL PROXIMITY AND PHYSICALITY OF WORK

Routine activities theory applied to sexual harassment in the workplace suggests that physical proximity is a factor that can determine whom perpetrators target (Lopez, Hodson & Roscigno 2009). Researchers have hypothesized that more populated workplaces offer more chances of harassment (DeCoster, Estes & Mueller 1999), or—to the contrary—that they offer more protection. Studies show that skewed gender ratios make a difference. Women in settings where men are numerically dominant tend to experience more harassment (Gruber 1998). Some research finds that predominantly female job settings are associated with lower incidence of severe forms of harassment (Chamberlain et al. 2008). Other studies show that it is not just the numbers but also the association of the job with traditional ideas of masculinity or femininity (Gruber 1998). Others call attention to the physicality of the work, suggesting that work or workplaces that emphasize normatively masculine physical strength or emphasize the body seem to be associated with increased incidence of sexual harassment (Chamberlain et al. 2008; Welsh 1999). This prompted examination of whether and how questions of physical proximity and the physicality of work relate to sexual harassment in the immigrant worker lawsuits.

Physical isolation emerged as a common theme across a number of cases. As demonstrated in the *ABM Industries* case discussed above, harassers often take advantage of routine activities that leave women (such as janitors cleaning empty buildings at night) physically isolated. At National Food's egg farm in Washington State, the EEOC alleged that a supervisor took advantage of the policy that each hen-barn was assigned one woman working in isolation. The supervisor would physically grab the barn worker and demand sex from her on a weekly basis. In the *EEOC v. Rivera Vineyards* settlement, to protect against sexual harassment, the consent decree specified that job-related training had to take place in designated places or in the presence of a female supervisor. This implicitly acknowledged the practices of some supervisors in farm settings of requiring women to follow them to an isolated location for supposedly job-related purposes, only to instead solicit or coerce sexual contact.

EEOC v. Kovacevich 5 Farms revealed how the systematic exclusion of women from the better-paying, predominantly male jobs on large corporate farms not only kept women at an economic disadvantage, but was perceived by the women as cutting off proximity to male family members who could potentially help them fend off harassers. Women perceived the gender segregation of work as contributing to sexual harassment. In the routine activities perspective, this can be interpreted as an element in the availability of targets and the absence of capable guardians. The EEOC alleged that Kovacevich 5 Farms had hired no women between 1998 and 2002, despite advertising more than 300 seasonal farmworker positions; the women applicants had been turned away. According to Tamayo (2009), the women who brought the lawsuit wanted to work in proximity to their male family members who would help protect them against the sexual harassment the women had experienced or knew was occurring elsewhere. Although this case might not appear to be about sexual harassment, it further illustrates how the organization of work along gender lines contributes to women's experience of vulnerability to sexual harassment. (Hegewisch, Deitch & Murphy 2011).

Several cases show how the physical demands of the job required body positions that left women vulnerable to attack. In the ABM case, a woman bent over cleaning a toilet in a small bathroom stall was grabbed from behind. In a number of the farmworker cases, and documented in studies of farmworkers, women report that when they are bending down to pick crops, men will grab or grope their buttocks (Castañeda & Zavella 2003).

The examples provided above suggest that it is also important to consider ways in which the physical organization of the work and the workplace and the routines of the job make workers in some occupations and settings especially vulnerable to harassment by predatory supervisors. Physical isolation removed women from possible intervention from supportive coworkers or managers. The examples further suggest that proximity is a factor that can be manipulated by a predatory supervisor and a correlate of hierarchical power relations. The discussion of proximity in the literature, however, usually is about the gender composition of the workplace (Chamberlain et al. 2008). The lawsuit examples expand the way of thinking about sexual harassment in relation to the gender segregation of work. The examples presented here suggest the need to think more broadly about the physicality of different types of labor and how that might relate to incidence of sexual harassment.

MOTIVATED PERPETRATORS

Presence of "motivated perpetrators" is one of the three elements in routine activities theory. In the literature on sexual harassment, some explanations for why men harass attribute sexual gratification as a motivation; others focus on demonstrating masculinity in the face of threat, and asserting male power or privilege (Welsh 1999). These are not mutually exclusive motivations. The present work does not include information on the harassers to analyze or impute motivations in the lawsuit cases other than to suggest that one or more of the above-listed motivations seem plausible in most if not all of the cases.

Roscigno, Lopez, and Hodson (2009) find that supervisors who bully and harass tend to have unfettered discretionary power over subordinates and little fear of sanctions or other disincentives not to harass. This view of perpetrator motivation fits well with the abuse of power by supervisors described above. It also connects to the third element, the absence of authorities or policies that provide negative sanctions for harassment.

ABSENCE OF VIABLE PROTECTORS

Studies that use routine activities theory for sexual harassment point to supportive supervisors and coworkers, and established formal policies and grievance procedures, as examples of "capable guardians" (Lopez, Hodson & Roscigno 2009; Roscigno, Lopez & Hodson 2009). In the lawsuits, many of the workplaces employing immigrant women did not have much in the way of sexual harassment or other grievance procedures; in other organizations, the policies existed but were not enforced. In many of the cases, complaints about sexual harassment were ignored. Supervisors often were the abusers instead of being the protectors. When supportive coworkers tried to help, they too were subject to retaliation such as firing and threats of deportation, as were family members who worked for the same employer and tried to intervene.

The police and criminal justice system often are absent from the "capable guardian" role for undocumented women who have been raped or have experienced other assault in the workplace. As in the *DeCoster* case, the police often are unwilling to intervene. An EEOC regional attorney, William Tamayo, stated in an interview (Cediel & Bergman 2013) that, to his knowledge, no accused rapist or abuser in any of the EEOC cases involving immigrant women ever has faced criminal charges. Additionally, immigrant workers might hesitate to go to the police due to fear of deportation.

In principle, the EEOC offers protection; but fear of deportation, language barriers, and other obstacles deter undocumented workers from reporting sexual harassment to a government agency (Cediel & Bergman 2013; Meng 2012). The U-visa protection only is possible in cases of rape, assault, or other violence and has other restrictions (Orloff, Isom & Saballos 2010). The EEOC, as well as private and nonprofit attorneys have developed strategies for trying to protect (keep confidential) immigration status of complainants as witnesses (Meng 2012; Cediel & Bergman 2013). In *EEOC v. Giumarra Vineyards*, as part of the discovery process, Giumarra sought information about the workers' immigration status. In this case, the parties and the court reached an agreement that the defense could ask about immigration status, but that the information would remain confidential, specifying exactly who could have access to the information and how confidentiality would be protected. Subsequently, the parties agreed to a far-reaching settlement praised by the EEOC. The EEOC and other plaintiff attorney efforts to prevent disclosure of immigration status, however, do not always work. In *EEOC v. Evans Fruit*, a lower court decided that claimants could not be required to disclose immigration status, but on appeal the decision was overturned by a higher court, resulting in the EEOC dropping roughly half of the complainants from the lawsuit. In the subsequent jury trial, 14 women testified about sexual abuse by one foreman at the prominent apple grower in Washington State, but a jury did not find the women's employer responsible and reportedly did not find the women's claims credible (Cediel & Bergman 2013).

It is amazing that despite all of the legal, logistical, language, and other obstacles, complaints do get to the EEOC. In many of the immigrant cases, workers first went to local legal assistance organizations that they knew and trusted, such as the domestic violence coalition that helped the DeCoster Farm workers. Other examples for the lawsuits examined for the present work include the Esperanza Project of the Southern Poverty Law Center, California Rural Legal Assistance (CRLA), Lideras Compesinas (a women farmworkers' organization), Oregon Law Center, Northwest Justice Project, Latino Justice PRLDF, and Coalition of Immolake Workers.

LAWSUIT INTERVENTIONS: WHAT DO THEY CHALLENGE?

The lawsuits, as interventions, have several types of potential impacts. One is publicity value. By routinely publicizing the initial lawsuits and the settlements with award amounts, the EEOC seeks to have other employers—especially those in the same industry or locale—pay attention and monitor their own practices, and to encourage other complainants to come forward. A search for media coverage of the lawsuits showed that employer-side law firms do tend to publicize EEOC lawsuits to their constituents, often with admonitions about the need to respond appropriately to sexual harassment. Publicity for the 1999 *EEOC v. Tanimura & Antle* settlement resulted in legal assistance organizations bringing a number of complaints of sexual harassment of immigrant farmworkers to the EEOC (Cediel & Bergman 2013). For some of the immigrant worker cases, the EEOC issued press releases in both Spanish and English, and sometimes emphasized the agency's commitment to protecting workers regardless of immigration status.

A second impact is that the individual relief provisions of settlements provide workers with monetary awards. Some add special protection against future retaliation, and they require purging of any negative evaluations and sanctions from employee records for those involved in the lawsuit. The focus herein is on the greater and longer-term potential impacts in stopping sexual harassment in the workplace found in the injunctive relief provisions of settlements.

A third impact is that injunctive relief provisions of the settlements mandate specific changes in employer policies and practices related to sexual harassment and, in some cases, other employment discrimination issues. The policy provisions apply to all workers, not just to those who participated in the lawsuit. As negotiated settlements, the employer voluntarily has agreed to the terms so as to avoid the cost and negative publicity of going to trial. The consent decrees then are approved by a judge and become legally mandated requirements, unless all parties and the court agree to make changes. The consent decrees typically cover a two- or three-year period (see Hegewisch, Deitch & Murphy 2011). Thus, the lawsuit resolution has potential impact on how sexual harassment complaints are handled.

The specific remedies most consistently found in the immigrant worker lawsuit settlements examined here, as well as in a larger sample of EEOC sexual harassment settlements not limited to immigrant workers which are analyzed elsewhere (Hegewisch, Deitch & Murphy 2011) include: posting of notices on Title VII law and company policy against sexual harassment; requiring training sessions to explain sexual harassment and sexual harassment policies to both managers and all other workers; and creating or revising written sexual harassment policies, including grievance procedures and procedures for investigating and reporting complaints.

Although the above provisions seem promising, several concerns exist. One is that it is not known how extensively or effectively these requirements are carried out. Another is that research on EEOC policy enforcement in organizations has concluded that posting notices and providing anti-harassment and antidiscrimination training either has no effect or the effect is not discernable (Dobbin & Kelly 2007). Nonetheless, these are typical forms of employer response to sexual harassment, consistent with what the courts have signaled are expected by employers to mount an affirmative defense in sexual harassment lawsuits.

Most of the immigrant lawsuit settlements go a step or two further by requiring that all of the remedies specified above be provided in the primary language of the workers. Many consent decrees specified Spanish and English, a few specified Creole or Chinese, some said the primary language(s) of the employees, and others mandated using the languages spoken by 30% or more of the workforce. In some of the West Coast farm-worker lawsuits, the languages specified were indigenous Mexican languages in addition to Spanish. Although obviously a helpful policy, at least two caveats on its potential impact exist. Research indicates that many of the most vulnerable undocumented workers might have little or no reading skills in any language (Passel & Cohn 2011). Gleeson (2010) shows that for other types of employment law violations, undocumented immigrants aware of the laws still refrain from making complaints, due to fear of termination and deportation, or because they don't believe the law will ever help them.

On a more optimistic note, nearly two-thirds (64%) of the consent decrees examined in full included at least one of several possible more substantively promising provisions. This means measures that previous research suggests are likely to make a difference in the workplace if implemented (see, e.g., Hegewisch, Deitch & Murphy 2011). Such measures include holding supervisors accountable for enforcement of sexual harassment and other EEO policy, and making EEO policy enforcement a factor in the evaluation of supervisors and managers; requiring the employer to hire an EEO consultant or EEO compliance officer to develop, supervise, and monitor new internal EEO policies; and appointing an external monitor to oversee the implementation of the consent decree and report to the EEOC and the court. Such provisions increase the presence of protectors in both number and authority. Nearly half (49%) required supervisor accountability, and almost one-third (31%) required hiring an EEO consultant, coordinator, or external monitor. These are somewhat greater percentages than found for nonimmigrant sexual harassment EEOC settlements in the data used by Hegewisch, Deitch & Murphy.[4]

Examples of other provisions of interest found in a few of the settlements include requirements for 24-hour external hotlines for reporting sexual harassment, and firing—and never rehiring—specific harassers. Conservatively, that author concludes that, at very least, the EEOC does not appear to be any less successful in negotiating substantive remedies in settlements covering immigrant workers than it is for others. At best, perhaps the immigrant worker settlements point to better practices for all workplaces seeking to reverse a history of sexual harassment problems.

DISCUSSION AND CONCLUSION

The study of sexual harassment lawsuits brought by the EEOC on behalf of immigrant workers contributes to an understanding of sexual harassment in two broad ways: It reveals some of the specific vulnerabilities to harassment experienced by immigrant women (and some men) of color in low-paying jobs, including how undocumented legal status exacerbates vulnerability to sexual harassment and retaliation. It also suggests how lawsuit settlements potentially serve as strategic interventions against sexual harassment in general, and for immigrant workers in particular.

Applying routine activities theory to a sample of 75 sexual harassment lawsuits filed by the EEOC on behalf of immigrant workers, the following results were found repeatedly and across many cases. The convergence of:

- Immigrant women as vulnerable targets,
- Men in positions of considerable discretionary power over subordinate women, and
- Absence of viable protectors or protections

produced environments in which sexual harassment flourished, often in violent and severe forms. Unchecked abuse of power by supervisors was a common theme. Harassed workers' fear of losing a job and—if undocumented—fear of being reported to immigration authorities, increased the harassing supervisors' leverage.

Using an intersectional analysis, the present work suggests that their status as economically disadvantaged, immigrant women of color was a major factor—*prior* to the harassment—in determining the types of jobs and workplaces in which they were employed. For most of the cases considered here, it is not possible to determine how much a person's national origin, versus immigrant status, versus subordinate occupational position contributed to being targeted for sexual harassment. It is not as if nonimmigrant white middle-class women were working alongside the other group to provide a basis of comparison. As Menjívar and Abrego observe, "immigrant workers are not undervalued (and underpaid) because of the work they do; rather, they are limited to labor sectors rampant with abuse precisely because they are undervalued" (Menjívar & Abrego 2012, 1404). Future research on sexual harassment in populations that include immigrants and nonimmigrants in comparable positions would be valuable.

Nineteen of the lawsuits involved EEOC charges of both national origin discrimination as well as sexual harassment. Just a few of these cases included racialized verbal sexual harassment whereby women clearly were targeted for both their gender and national origin, but in other cases it was not clear whether any individual woman was a target of both forms of Title VII violations. Interestingly, what the EEOC defines as intersectional discrimination was evident in all six cases involving sexual harassment of immigrant men by male supervisors, and sometimes also by coworkers. In the men's cases, it was more obvious that the harassed worker was targeted because of his national origin. Whereas Berdahl (2007) argues that "sexual harassers derogate others based on sex to protect or enhance their own sex-based social status." Thus a question that emerges for further research is how *sexual* harassment is also used to derogate others based on race, ethnicity, national origin, and anti-immigrant animus, both by itself and combined with racial-ethnic harassment.

The EEOC lawsuit settlements are a potentially effective intervention in workplaces with a history of sexual harassment problems because settlement agreements (consent decrees) routinely entail agreement by the employer to institute policies and practices aimed at stopping sexual harassment. In relation to the routine activities model, there no longer is an absence of viable protectors. Making policies and processes available in the primary languages of the workforce emerges as a "no-brainer" best practice.

Some studies show that incidence of sexual harassment is less frequent where any policies exist (Chamberlain et al. 2008). Other research, however, suggests that many of the standard practices such as posting notices of policy, (anti–)sexual harassment training, and grievance procedures are not necessarily effective in reducing harassment (Dobbin & Kelly 2007), thus the potential impact of the intervention could be muted. Among the most promising findings, almost half of the settlements examined for this study made supervisors accountable for implementing sexual harassment policies and procedures, and almost a third required the employer to hire an outside consultant, approved by the EEOC, to help design and implement new policy. These are promising practices for other settlements and for workplaces with a history of sexual harassment that have not (yet) been sued.

Unfortunately, even the best-crafted lawsuit settlements do not do much to address the conditions that make undocumented workers especially vulnerable to sexual harassment in the first place. It is feared that, as long as harassers and their employers have the threat of deportation as leverage, undocumented immigrant workers will remain targets of sexual harassment and face high risks for making complaints. Ultimately, current U.S. immigration policy serves to restrict the labor market for immigrants in ways that often put them in harm's way, feed immigrant vulnerability to sexual and other abuses on the job, and compromise access to legal recourse. The EEOC lawsuit settlements are an important tool for challenging abusive practices in the workplace, but are not a solution.

NOTES

1. Immigrant identity often is not specifically indicated in the source materials. I counted the lawsuit as involving immigrants if anything in the legal, EEOC, or other source material identified any of the workers as immigrants, foreign-born, or monolingual non-English speakers. The EEOC lawyers and other attorneys who

bring lawsuits on behalf of undocumented immigrants make a concerted effort to protect the confidentiality of the plaintiffs' immigration status. It therefore is not always evident whether the immigrants involved in the lawsuit are undocumented; often the undocumented worker can be among the unnamed "similarly situated" other parties cited in the lawsuit.

2. The research presented here began as an offshoot of an earlier project (Hegewisch, Deitch, and Murphy 2011), which analyzed more than 500 consent decrees for settlement of sex and race discrimination in employment lawsuits, including 171 sexual harassment settlements. The authors conducted interviews with attorneys and others involved with a handful of selected settlements. One of the selected cases was *EEOC v. DeCoster Farms*.

3. The U-visa allows undocumented immigrants who have been victims of certain violent acts such as sexual assault—and who assist law enforcement agencies in an investigation—to remain and work in the United States for a temporary period with a possibility of becoming a legal resident.

4. The comparable figures for nonimmigrant EEOC sexual harassment settlements are 27% for supervisor accountability and 14% for an outside consultant or monitor. These are unpublished calculations made by the author. The comparisons must be made with caution, given that the immigrant cases include a greater proportion of very severe cases (i.e., rape and assault), and are filed in the 9th Circuit, which is where Deitch & Hegewisch (2014) found stronger consent decree provisions for a broader sample of sex and race discrimination cases.

REFERENCES

Bauer, M., and Ramirez, M. (2010). *Injustice on our plates: Immigrant women in the US food industry.* Montgomery, AL: Southern Poverty Law Center.

Berdahl, J. L. (2007). Harassment based on sex: Protecting social status in the context of gender hierarchy. *Academy of Management Review* 32, 641–658.

Berdahl, J. L., and Moore, C. (2006). Workplace harassment: Double jeopardy for minority women. *Journal of Applied Psychology* 91, 426.

Castañeda, X., and Zavella, P. (2003). Changing constructions of sexuality and risk: Migrant Mexican women farmworkers in California. *Journal of Latin American Anthropology* 8, 126–150.

Cediel, A., and Bergman, L. (2013). Rape in the fields. *Frontline.* PBS.

Chamberlain, L. J., Crowley, M., Tope, D., and Hodson, R. (2008). Sexual harassment in organizational context. *Work and Occupations* 35, 262–295.

Chen, M. H. (2012). Where you stand depends on where you sit: Bureaucratic incorporation of immigrants in federal workplace agencies. *Berkeley Journal of Employment and Labor Law* 33.

Cho, S. K. (1997). Converging stereotypes in racialized sexual harassment: Where the model minority meets Suzie Wong. *The Journal of Gender, Race & Justice* 1, 177.

Cohen, L. E., and Felson, M. (1979). Social change and crime rate trends: A routine activity approach. *American Sociological Review,* 588–608.

Collins, P. H. (1990). *Black feminist thought: Knowledge, consciousness, and the politics of empowerment.* New York: Routledge.

Cortina, L. M., Fitzgerald, L. F., and Drasgow, F. (2002). Contextualizing Latina experiences of sexual harassment: Preliminary tests of a structural model. *Basic and Applied Social Psychology* 24, 295–311.

Crenshaw, K. (1989). Demarginalizing the intersection of race and sex: A black feminist critique of antidiscrimination doctrine, feminist theory and antiracist politics. *University of Chicago Legal Forum* 139.

DeCoster, S., Estes, S. B., and Mueller, C. W. (1999). Routine activities and sexual harassment in the workplace. *Work and Occupations* 26, 21–49.

Dobbin, F., and Kelly, E. L. (2007). How to stop harassment: Professional construction of legal compliance in organizations. *American Journal of Sociology* 112, 1203–1243.

Gleeson, S. (2010). Labor rights for all? The role of undocumented immigrant status for worker claims making. *Law & Social Inquiry* 35, 561–602.

Gruber, J. E. (1998). The impact of male work environments and organizational policies on women's experiences of sexual harassment. *Gender & Society* 12, 301–320.

Hegewisch, A., Deitch, C., and Murphy, E. (2011). *Ending sex and race discrimination in the workplace: Legal interventions that push the envelope.* Washington, DC: Institute for Women's Policy Research.

Ken, I. (2010). *Digesting race, class, and gender: Sugar as a metaphor.* Palgrave Macmillan.

Lopez, S. H., Hodson, R., and Roscigno, V. J. (2009). Power, status, and abuse at work: General and sexual harassment compared. *The Sociological Quarterly* 50, 3–27.

McLaughlin, H., Uggen, C., and Blackstone, A. (2012). Sexual harassment, workplace authority, and the paradox of power. *American Sociological Review* 77, 625–647.

Meng, G. (2012). *Cultivating fear: The vulnerability of immigrant farmworkers in the US to sexual violence and sexual harassment.* Washington, DC: Human Rights Watch.

Menjívar, C., and Abrego, L. (2012). Legal violence: Immigration law and the lives of Central American immigrants. *American Journal of Sociology* 117, 1380–1421.

Ontiveros, M. L. (2007). Female immigrant workers and the law: Limits and opportunities. In *The sex of class,* edited by D. S. Cobble, 235–252. Ithaca, NY: Cornell University Press.

Ontiveros, M. L. (2002). Lessons from the fields: Female farmworkers and the law. *Maine Law Review* 55, 157.

Orloff, L. E., Isom, K. C., and Saballos, E. (2010). Mandatory U-visa certification unnecessarily undermines the purpose of the Violence Against Women Act's immigration protections and its any credible evidence rules: A call for consistency. *Georgetown Journal of Gender and the Law* 11, 619.

Passel, J. S., and D'Vera Cohn, S. W. (2011). *Unauthorized immigrant population: National and state trends 2010.* Washington, DC: Pew Hispanic Center.

Roscigno, V. J., Lopez, S. H., and Hodson, R. (2009). Supervisory bullying, status inequalities and organizational context. *Social Forces* 87, 1561–1589.

Smith, R., and Cho, E. H. (2013). *Workers' rights on ICe*. National Employment Law Center.

Stockdale, M. S., and Nadler, J. T. (2012). Situating sexual harassment in the broader context of interpersonal violence: Research, theory, and policy implications. *Social Issues and Policy Review* 6, 148–176.

Tamayo, W. R. (2009). The EEOC and immigrant workers. *University of San Francisco Law Review* 44, 253.

Texeira, M. T. (2002). "Who protects and serves me?" A case study of sexual harassment of African American women in one US law enforcement agency. *Gender & Society* 16, 524–545.

U.S. Equal Opportunity Employment Commission (EEOC). (2012). Strategic enforcement plan for 2013–2016. http://www.eeoc.gov/eeoc/plan/sep.cfm. Accessed April 13, 2015.

U.S. Equal Opportunity Employment Commission (EEOC). (2010, September 2). Anna Park's remarks. http://www1.eeoc.gov//eeoc/litigation/settlements/abm_park.cfm?renderforprint=1. Accessed April 20, 2015.

U.S. Equal Opportunity Employment Commission (EEOC). (2007, February 28). Statement of William R. Tamayo. http://www.eeoc.gov/eeoc/meetings/archive/2-28-07/tamayo.html. Accessed April 20, 2015.

Vellos, D. (1996). Immigrant Latina domestic workers and sexual harassment. *American University Journal of Gender, Social Policy & the Law* 5, 407.

Waugh, I. M. (2010). Examining the sexual harassment experiences of Mexican immigrant farmworking women. *Violence Against Women* 16, 237–261.

Welsh, S. (1999). Gender and sexual harassment. *Annual Review of Sociology* 25, 169–190.

Welsh, S., Carr, J., MacQuarrie, B., and Huntley, A. (2006). "I'm not thinking of it as sexual harassment": Understanding harassment across race and citizenship. *Gender & Society* 20, 87–107.

LEGAL CASES CITED

EEOC v. Evans Fruit, No. CV-10-3033 (E.D. Wash.) (Jury verdict, April 2013)

EEOC v. Giumarra Vineyards Corporation, No. 1-09-CV-02255 (E.D. Cal. Feb. 9, 2010)

EEOC v. Iowa AG, LLC dba DeCoster Farms, No. 01-CV-3077 (N.D. Iowa Sept. 15, 2001)

EEOC v. Knouse Foods (M.D. Pa. July 22, 2010)

EEOC v. Kovacevich 5 Farms, No. CV-06-00165 (E.D. Cal. Feb. 6, 2006)

EEOC v. Rivera Vineyards, Inc., d/b/a Blas Rivera Vineyards et al., No. EDCV 03 01117 RT (C.D. Cal. Sept. 5, 2003)

EEOC v. Tanimura & Antle, C99-20088; Consent Decree (N.D. Cal. Feb. 9, 1999)

Hoffman Plastic v. National Labor Relations Board, 535 U.S. 137 (2002)

Oncale v. Sundowner Offshore Services Inc., 523 U.S. 75 (1998)

Chapter 9

Preventing and Responding to Sexual Harassment at the University of Zurich

Brigitte Tag and Pete Hirsch

In May 2007, the University of Zurich instituted specific regulations to ensure protection against sexual harassment. The campus serves as a role model for other universities and institutions within Switzerland. The University of Zurich (UZH) has seven faculties: Theology, Law, Economics, Medicine, Science, Veterinary Medicine, and Arts; and campus population includes approximately 26,000 students, 570 professors, 5,200 assistants and senior scientists, and 2,684 administrative and technical staff. The University board ranks above the executive board and the faculties, which are presided over by their Deans.

At UZH, protection against sexual harassment is integrated into ethical standards and is subject to a legal framework with a policy and code of conduct. In this spirit, the university conceived law as the so-called ethical minimum. As members of the UZH community, all staff and students are bound to act in an ethically responsible manner. Mutual respect and confidence, safeguarding of personal dignity, friendly and relaxed personal interaction, pleasant working atmosphere, and an agreeable study environment are cornerstones of these principles.

Important statutory sources within the legal and ethical framework of the protection against sexual harassment at the University of Zurich are the Swiss Criminal Code, the Swiss Criminal Procedure Code, and the Swiss Federal Act on Gender Equality. Of particular significance are the university regulations and general ethics.

The offences defined within the Swiss Criminal Code are felonies, misdemeanors, and contraventions. The new Swiss Criminal Procedure Code was not adopted until 2011. It reduced 29 Cantonal Criminal Procedure Codes to one single Federal Code. Some of its basic principles are

- Same procedural rules are used throughout the country,
- Extension of the rights of defense,
- Extension of the victim's rights, and
- General principle of equality of arms.

Under the direction of Professor Brigitte Tag, from 2003 to 2006 a working group of experts designed a draft of the specific regulations regarding protection against sexual harassment (RSH) at the University of Zurich. The regulations are based upon the following statutes: Swiss Federal Act on Gender Equality (Gleich-stellungsgesetz), Art. 5, Para. 3; University Decree on Human Resources (Personalverordnung) § 38; Cantonal University Act (Universitäts-gesetz) § 16; and the Code of Conduct on Gender Policy at the University of Zurich, Clause 5.

The Executive Board of the UZH enacted the RSH and later the University Council approved it. On March 1, 2007, the RSH came into effect. As a consequence, issues concerning RSH were resolved; actual assistance for the presumable victim and the suspected attacker was improved; and the liability of the university concerning the lack of regulations pertaining to sexual harassment was reduced. The spirit and purpose of the regulations are to provide prevention, to raise awareness, to resolve internal conflicts, and to avoid impending claims due to lack of appropriate measures.

The main purpose of the regulations according to § 1 is to protect against sexual harassment and thus safeguard the personal dignity of all university members and to prevent them from being hindered in performing their work, and to provide fair employment conditions, enable the completion of study course, and aid advancement in scientific or professional careers. Furthermore, the regulations define procedure in the event of alleged sexual harassment.

The Regulations on the Protection Against Sexual Harassment at the University of Zurich provide the following definitions of sexual harassment and sexist behavior:

- Sexual harassment is deemed to be any unwelcome or inappropriate behavior of a sexual nature that has the purpose or effect of violating an individual's dignity.
- Sexist behavior is deemed to be conduct that is not directly of a sexual nature but, based on the person's gender, is discriminatory or belittling.

The provisions apply to all members of the university community, including professors, private lecturers, associate lecturers, middle management, administrative and technical staff, as well as regular and auditor students (RSH § 3). According to sections 5 to 9, prevention and measures of the regulations are first and foremost, protection against sexual harassment in connection with all university-related activities, and provide general rules of conduct (§ 5), align the duties of senior staff and heads of institute (§ 6), arrange for information dissemination (§ 7), and facilitate awareness campaigns and training (§ 8).

Action for violation of the regulations ranges from supportive measures to dismissal or removal from the register of students (§ 9). Such action is taken independently of possible criminal proceedings initiated by victims. Victim's rights include the right to be advised and supported by specially designated and trained contact persons and to be advised by internal mediators or—in justified exceptional cases—by an external mediator and psychological or psychiatric counseling. Moreover, victims can request that an administrative investigation be conducted.

When sexual harassment occurs, individuals appeal to the designated contact persons for advice and support (§ 13): the head of the Office for Gender Equality or the general secretary of the university. For students, two collegiate contact persons of both sexes also are appointed. According to § 14, the tasks of the contact persons include providing support, advice, and information to clarify the proceedings and to also forward the relevant facts to the internal investigator.

The internal investigator at the University of Zurich presently is Dr. Brigitte Tag. Dr. Tag is assigned a deputy from the scientific staff and is supported by the university's legal service. According to § 18 of the regulations, the duties of the internal investigator are to establish the facts, to conduct the clarification proceedings, and to make a request to the Executive Board that the appropriate measures be taken (§ 9).

What is protection against sexual harassment and what it is not? Protection against sexual harassment first of all is a legal obligation. It is in the institution's own interest to protect and safeguard the staff and the scientists, the working atmosphere, the best interests of the institution, and its attractiveness and reputation as a place of research, education, and employment. Beyond that, is prevention of the abuse of power, and last but not least is one of a number of instruments to secure a favorable working atmosphere and an implementation of the right to be respected. Protection against sexual harassment is not an enforcement of certain moral beliefs; it is not a prohibition of friendly interpersonal relationships nor is it a "fun killer," an instrument of power against critics or unpopular persons, or a weapon for "gender struggles."

To publicize the regulations at the University of Zurich on campus, the Committee for Protection Against Sexual Harassment has designed an information sheet outlining the regulations' principles. This information sheet is available to all members of the university in both German and English; and it recently was translated into Portuguese and Spanish.

Chapter 10

Some Reflections on Gender Equality in Law Enforcement

Ian P. Lloyd, Jr.

My interest in gender equality and harassment led to my conducting interviews within one police department in upstate New York. This particular department consists of 127 sworn officers. Only 7 of the 127 sworn officers are female. A woman has never held the title of captain in this particular department. The highest ranking woman officer was employed a decade ago, and she attained the title of "sergeant."

Interviewing MK, a retired sergeant offered great insight to the experiences she had from her 20-plus years on the police force. MK was the highest ranking female officer. She began her work in 1987 as one of a handful of female police officers. In addition to MK, I interviewed P and B, female cohorts of MK, who each had retired after serving 20 years on the force.

When MK first started as a sworn officer she worked the midnight shift as all new officers do. The night captain who was her superior looked out for MK in the early part of her career. She identified him as the "Godfather" of the midnight shift. If any problems arose internally, she knew that he would handle it without any repercussions. When asked if she "ever felt she was treated any differently because of her gender, especially on

responding calls" she said "Never." MK said that she earned respect from
fellow officers for her work on responding calls. "When many new young
male officers would be starting off, my [male] partner and I would take
them out on responding calls, many would hesitate and kind of stand in
the back letting us take care of it." MK said that she "jumped right in" to
handle escalating situations on responding calls, especially early on in her
career; this was how she had earned the respect that she'd attained.

P and B were not as fortunate in their relationships with their colleagues. For example, B stated, "[I]t was hard, I mean it was male domi-
nated at the time and they just weren't used to us. It was hard, it was hard
at first." B further stated: "You know, I mean some guys wouldn't even
ride with me on patrols. When I was going through my training there was
some that just refused, they wanted nothing to do with us. . . . Even when
we retired, I felt that some people still didn't accept us."

MK had felt accepted all along and stated that nothing about that
changed from her first day until her last day. When P and B were asked
whether they felt female officers were treated fairly from the time they
started until the time they retired, both said:

> [D]efinitely not when we started. . . . There was a certain command
> officer who was kind of out there to get you. We would bid on a daily
> basis on where we were going to go and he would kind of think of
> the worst place he could possible place us.

P further stated, "I remember Thanksgiving night; I was put on the
downtown walking route in the middle of a blizzard . . . you know, once
the older school guys started to retire and leave, things became much easier." When asked what they believed was the reason for this treatment,
both stated firmly "it was definitely generational." P stated:

> [B]y the time that I left, people were more accepting, like I said the
> guys who thought of us as a lower standard were the biggest barrier,
> further identifying the atmosphere as "this was the old boys club."
> . . . It was more on an even plane; you didn't have to "prove your-
> self" as much. . . . [T]here were way more there female officers there
> when I left.

When asked what experiences JT has had in his tenure in regards to
gender inequality in policing, he stated,

> I think that question points out something that is little known, that
> male police officers—at least in my day when I was a young cop—
> approached females much differently; there was still that you know
> caution that the female was the weaker sex, until you get a punch in

the face from a female and realize that's not true. Today we have more women involved in violent crime; we suspect that right now there are three women who are shooters in the city. You know the tenure or connotation of them as criminals has changed. Internally, I had a female work for me when I was a sergeant that was the result of sexual harassment, and you know I took the steps that were available back then going back to the 80s and at least I was able to stop it, but certainly a lot of that has subsided, but there is no question that it was a prominent issue.

JT said that, in all of his years from a patrolman through the ranks to chief, he never experienced firsthand any mistreatment of women. He claimed he only recalled one time when a young female officer came to him as a result of what she felt was sexual harassment. Without delving too deeply into the details, JT said, "[U]nder my watch that wasn't going to happen." He took care of the matter and it never happened again. When asked if JT believed it was a prominent issue when this happened in the 1980s he responded "no question about it." When asked if JT believed the calls were filtered to men or women depending on the type of call, JT said,

[N]o; however, you bring up an interesting point. I'm considering starting a special victims unit that will handle all juvenile, domestic and sexual assault. I think the research shows that females are not any better equipped to handle those instances specifically, but what I do think is from the victim's side, they may be more likely to speak to a female. But it's unfortunate because due to our seniority provisions here I'm not allowed to assign a female to the unit. I think a lot of people are realizing that the only qualification to becoming an officer is what you set, gender doesn't matter, sexual orientation doesn't matter, you take the best candidate for the position.

When JT was asked why he believed it was so difficult for women to move through the ranks, and it seems as though women are hitting this ceiling, he commented,

I think that was just rank discrimination. You know bosses of the older days felt that it wasn't a women's place or something of that nature. Here our female officers are young, I do believe that some . . . are going to take the sergeants exam and I would really like to see them make it. And that's not because they're female, that's because they are good cops and work hard, I think they deserve it.

Another theme that was prevalent in the responses was awareness of policies in effect to ensure gender equality. The three female volunteers were unaware of any organizations or specific policies to ensure gender equality specifically on the police force. Due to his position in the department, however, JT was more aware of policies in effect. JT mentioned the civil rights act today, and federal and state legislations. He stated: "We have city and departmental harassment and discrimination policies." JT also mentioned his awareness of the National Association of Women Law Enforcement Executives (NAWLEE). JT encourages the current female officers to attend the group's workshops. NAWLEE provides female officers with the tools necessary to compete for promotions to higher positions. This theme in particular is intriguing because, although the three female respondents recognized NAWLEE, they did not necessarily know its function.

The final theme found in the present research was pregnancy discrimination. One woman stated,

> When I first started, there was another female officer who became pregnant and no one knew what to do. There was no policy or rules on the book pertaining to pregnancy because it had never happened before, at least not in our department. They gave her the decision that when she wanted to go on "light duty" as it's called now or "desk duty," to give them notice.

"The first thing they did was put her on desk duty and she didn't want to go on desk duty," P said, further stating there wasn't such a thing as "light duty." P also stated that

> there's nothing written, I don't want to say it was the city or even as much as a lack of policy even, but it was more of the guys and the union, because you're taking someone and putting them on the desk, then you have another individual on the road who says I want to bid the desk, I'm senior to her, I deserve it, but due to no light duty, there was nothing for that. Either you were on sick leave or you were working. There's no grey area in between, and she didn't want to go out, "I'm only 6 weeks pregnant," she wanted to be out there doing her job. My father, who was stout at the time actually had to give her some of his shirts because they didn't have big enough shirts for her. It was totally new ground. It threw everyone into a tizzy, because she was truly the first case, at least here.

JT affirmed these statements. He claimed,

> Right now I have a draft that I have been working on that is a pregnancy policy. I think it's only fair that females coming onto the job are aware of the benefits that would attach to that situation. We can't

identify them as sick, because it violates the national pregnancy antidiscrimination act that we have to follow. I personally believe that
a lot of departments are opening up the gates to litigation by labeling
pregnant officers as sick. "Oh you're pregnant we can't let you on the
road," and by law that's the officer's decision.

When JT was asked whether he experienced staffing issues and problems in regard to pregnancy, he stated: "It generates holes in the schedule,
but you know if you have a productive officer over the long term, the
short term leave doesn't matter to me. Does it affect some other chiefs? I
believe it may."

When asked whether JT thought the policy he was developing would
prohibit pregnancy discrimination, he responded,

I do because I modeled it after the federal legislation. And it's pretty
generic but it safeguards against a lot of provisions. Like we can't
reveal [that] an officer [i]s pregnant until she decides we can. She
could be in the ninth month of her pregnancy and if she wants to
work the road, that [is] her decision not ours. And many chiefs don't
know that; they say, "I don't want the liability," well, that's not your
liability, it's if she comes in here and we've had some officers come in
when they just found out and are nervous, so we give them light
duty assignment. You can't refer to her as being sick. We allow six
weeks after delivery, it can be amended if there . . . [are] medical
reasons, but I think it's fair that the officer knows what their right is.
What are the barriers you're facing with regards to lack of support?
It's this Byzantine thing called government. Something like that I
would pass through the city attorneys because of potential legality's
[sic] and it's something that moves pretty slow[ly].

P and B stated additionally, "I think it takes a certain woman to be a
police officer. I mean we had some who didn't make it, it just wasn't for
them." JT also had additional information he wanted to share.

I think the city is liable for a lawsuit on validity and I think either for
male or female, our physical testing for a candidate, you know you
do push-ups and sit-ups, I'm not sure they're job related. I'd much
rather us see go the way of the State police and test the job-related
skills rather than different standards for females and things like that.
And I think they are going to be challenged soon. I mean to say you
need to do 50 push-ups for this or that, you look at some of these officers and they couldn't do one. I won't see this in my tenure I don't
think though. I almost do hope we get a challenge so that would be
the impetus to change things. I'd also like to say I guess my view is a

little bit different you know—how many females, when are you going to promote a female. . . . I'm looking for the best person and I think the important thing is we aren't discriminating against the females so they don't get to those positions. We support them as much as anyone else, to me that's equality and that's treating people equally. And I think society as a whole has to move away from the preferential treatment, if you will, because that creates a stereotype on the other end. And nobody should be discriminated against for any reason; the best person should get the position.

Chapter 11

Sexual Harassment of Teenage Girls: Implications for Reporting Gendered Violence as Adults

Michele A. Paludi

INTRODUCTION

Violence against adolescent girls—including sexual harassment—has been recognized as a major public health (Fineran & Bolen 2006) and human rights issue (Paludi, Martin & Paludi 2007) that requires a coordinated response from parents, teachers, counselors, and providers in the teens' community. This violence has been explained by unequal power relations and patriarchal values. Additionally, factors embedded in the adolescent culture that influence and support violence include alcohol and drug use, religious influences, media portrayal of violence, devaluation of subordinated groups, and the sexualization of violence. Furthermore, research has identified that violence against adolescent girls exists along a continuum, from incivility and microaggressions to hate crimes, including assault and murder (Nadal 2010; Paludi 2010).

When schools fail to intervene in peer sexual harassment, students get the message that sexual harassment is accepted at the school. Strauss noted that this acceptance can be a "catalyst for increased sexual violence within the school and the community" (Strauss 2010, 189). Data support-ive of Strauss' contention were obtained by Pellegrini, who found that students who bullied their peers in sixth grade engaged in sexual harass-ment in seventh grade (Pellegrini 2002). Further, Klein (2006) noted that in the school shootings that occurred in the United States during a six-year period, 11 out of 13 of the victims were girls. Klein highlighted that sexual harassment was instrumental in instigating the shootings. According to Klein,

> Violence against girls is easy to render invisible because the behavior that precedes actual incidents is often perceived as normal; even af-ter fatalities have occurred, the gendered components of crimes do not seem to register . . . "normal" violence against girls—indeed, so-cial acceptance of male hostility towards girls tends to aid in conceal-ing even the most dramatic incidents. (Klein 2006, 148)

How teenage girls are assisted with sexual harassment has direct im-pact on whether they will report future experiences with gendered vio-lence at work and in school, whether they blame themselves for the victimization, and how they heal from the trauma. Consider the following statistics, for example:

- Thirty-five percent of high school girls know a peer who experienced relationship violence.
- Ten percent of teen girls report that they have experienced physical violence in their own relationships, including hitting, shoving, throwing of objects, grabbing, and other physical force used with the intention to injure, harm, or kill another individual.
- Approximately 71% of school-age females report being bullied. Between kindergarten and 12th grade, more than 4.5 million chil-dren and adolescents are targets of sexual harassment perpetrated by a school employee.
- Approximately 30% of adolescent girls are victims of childhood sex-ual abuse.

In 2002, the Girl Scouts of the United States of America released *The Net Effect: Girls and New Media* (Girl Scouts of the United States 2002). This study surveyed 1,000 adolescent girls aged 13 to 18 years to examine three major issues: (1) trends in adolescent girls' Internet habits; (2) adolescent girls' skills in dealing with difficult or emotional situations online; and (3) advice on how parents can empower adolescent girls so they can have safe online experiences. The Girl Scouts reported that 30% of the teens in the study indicated that they have been sexually harassed in an Internet chat room. Examples of harassment included demands for bra size, requests for cybersex, and receipt of unsolicited photos of naked men. Of these teens who reported that they had experienced sexual harassment,

- Seven percent indicated that they told their parents about the incidents;
- Thirty percent said they kept quiet about the harassment;
- Twenty-one percent indicated that they experience sexual harassment "all the time" and that it is "no big deal"; and
- Four percent said that "[n]othing is that bad online because it is not really real."

The American Association of University Women (AAUW 1992; 2001) conducted the first scientific national studies of academic sexual harassment of children and adolescents by their peers. The 1993 study included 1,632 girls and boys in grades 8 through 11 from 79 schools across the United States. The 2001 study was based on 2,064 students in grades 8 through 11. Both AAUW studies reported a high incidence of sexual harassment of girls in schools. The 2001 study, for example, found that 85% of girls reported experiencing some form of sexual harassment during their school lives. Girls experienced more sexual harassment than boys and also were more afraid of being sexually harassed. Furthermore, boys perpetrated more than twice as much sexual harassment than did girls. Sexual harassment reported by girls included name-calling, graffiti written about them in school bathrooms, dissemination of offensive drawings, unwanted touching, sexual rumors, and pressure for sex.

In the 2001 AAUW study, 38% of girls reported being harassed by a teacher or other school employee. Subsequent research conducted by the U.S. Department of Education (2004) found that approximately 10% of public school students were targeted with unwanted sexual attention by teachers and other school employees. Timmerman (2003) reported that 27% of sexual harassment of students was perpetrated by school employees, with teachers comprising 81% of the offenders.

Research also has been conducted on adolescents' experiences with sexual harassment in the workplace. Research by Strauss and Espeland (1992) reported that 30% of female vocational students had been sexually harassed at work. Most adolescents work in movie theatres, at fast-food chains, and for construction companies. Fineran (2002) found 35% of part-time employed adolescents experienced sexual harassment. Fineran and Gruber (2009) reported that more than half of the 260 adolescent employees surveyed experienced sexual harassment at their workplace. Compared to adult women employees, adolescents in Fineran and Gruber's study experienced more harassment and experienced it in a shorter time frame.

LEGAL DEFINITION OF SEXUAL HARASSMENT

Sexual harassment is legally defined as "unwelcome sexual advances, requests for sexual favors, and other verbal or physical conduct of a sexual nature" when any one of the criterion listed below is met (EEOC 1990).

- Submission to such conduct is made either explicitly or implicitly a term or condition of the individual's employment or academic standing.
- Submission to or rejection of such conduct by an individual is used as the basis for employment or academic decisions affecting the individual.
- Such conduct has the purpose or effect of unreasonably interfering with an individual's work or learning performance or creating an intimidating, hostile, or offensive work or learning environment.

The U.S. Department of Education, Office of Civil Rights (OCR) defined sexual harassment similarly.

Unwelcome sexual advances, request for sexual favors, and other verbal, nonverbal, or physical conduct of a sexual nature by an employee, by another student, or by a third party, which is sufficiently severe, persistent, or pervasive to limit a student's ability to participate in or benefit from an education program or activity, or to create a hostile or abusive educational environment. (U.S. Department of Education, Office of Civil Rights 1997)

These legal definitions describe two types of sexual harassment, quid pro quo sexual harassment and hostile environment sexual harassment. Quid pro quo sexual harassment refers to an individual with organizational power who either expressly or implicitly ties an academic or employment decision or action to the response of an individual to unwelcome sexual advances. A high school teacher, for example, might promise an adolescent student a reward for complying with a sexual request, such as an A for the course or letter of recommendation for college. Another example of quid pro quo sexual harassment would be a teacher who threatened a student who did not comply with the sexual requests; for example, threatening to fail the student.

Hostile environment sexual harassment involves a situation where an atmosphere or climate is set up by teachers, staff, or other students in the school or school-sponsored event, that makes it difficult or impossible for a student to study and learn because the student perceives the climate to be hostile, offensive, or intimidating.

Both quid pro quo and hostile environment sexual harassment of students is prohibited by Title IX of the 1972 Education Amendments, which states, "No person in the United States shall, on the basis of sex, be excluded from participation in, or denied the benefits of, or be subjected to discrimination under any educational program or activity receiving federal assistance."

Title IX is an antidiscrimination statute prohibiting discrimination on the basis of sex in any educational program or activity receiving financial assistance. Title IX extends to recruiting of students, admissions, educational activities and programs, course offerings, counseling, financial aid, health and insurance benefits, scholarships, and athletics.

Employed students (as are adults) are protected from quid pro quo and hostile environment sexual harassment by Title VII of the 1964 Civil Rights Act. According to the Equal Employment Opportunity Commission (EEOC 1999), sexual harassment of employees includes the following:

- The victim as well as the harasser could be a woman or a man. The victim does not have to be of the opposite sex.
- The harasser can be the victim's supervisor, an agent of the employer, a supervisor in another area, a coworker, or a nonemployee.
- The victim does not have to be the person directly harassed and could be anyone who is affected by the offensive conduct.
- Unlawful sexual harassment can occur without economic injury to or discharge of the victim.
- The harasser's conduct must be unwelcome.

Furthermore, sexual harassment can be physical, verbal, written, or visual. Sexual harassment can occur between individuals of the same sex or between opposite-sex individuals.

BEHAVIORAL EXAMPLES OF SEXUAL HARASSMENT

Sexual harassment includes:

- Unwelcome sexual advances;
- Sexual innuendos, comments, and sexual remarks;
- Suggestive, insulting, or obscene sounds;
- Implied or expressed threat of reprisal for refusal to comply with a sexual request;
- Pinching, patting, or brushing up against another person's body;
- Sexually suggestive books, magazines, objects, e-mail, photographs, or screen savers displayed in the school or work area; and
- Actual denial of an academic- or employment-related benefit for refusal to comply with sexual requests (Paludi, Martin & Paludi 2007).

SEXUAL HARASSMENT OF ADOLESCENT GIRLS BY PEERS AND TEACHERS

Peer Sexual Harassment

The AAUW reported results of the first national study of adolescents' experiences with peer sexual harassment. In this study, students were asked the following questions, based on the legal definition of sexual harassment presented above.

During your whole school life, how often, if at all, has anyone (this includes students, teachers, other school employees, or anyone else) done the following things to you when you did not want them to?

- Made sexual comments, jokes, gestures, or looks.
- Showed, gave, or left you sexual pictures, photographs, illustrations, messages, or notes.
- Wrote sexual messages/graffiti about you on bathroom walls, in locker rooms, etc.
- Spread sexual rumors about you.
- Said you were gay or lesbian.
- Spied on you as you dressed or showered at school.
- Flashed or "mooned" you.
- Touched, grabbed, or pinched you in a sexual way.
- Pulled at your clothing in a sexual way.
- Intentionally brushed against you in a sexual way.
- Pulled your clothing off or down.
- Blocked your way or cornered you in a sexual way.
- Forced you to kiss him or her.
- Forced you to do something sexual, other than kissing.

Eighty-one percent of students reported that they experienced one or more of these examples of sexual harassment during their school lives. Gender comparisons revealed that 85% of girls and 76% of boys reported experiencing sexual harassment. Additionally, African American boys (81%) were more likely to have experienced sexual harassment than white boys (75%) and Latinos (69%). For girls, 87% of white girls reported experiencing sexual harassment, compared with 84% of African American girls and 82% of Latinas. Thus, girls were thus more likely to report experiencing sexual harassment, regardless of race. The types of sexual harassment most reported by girls in this research are listed below.

- Sexual comments, jokes, gestures, or looks (76%)
- Touched, grabbed, or pinched in a sexual way (65%)

- Intentionally brushed against in a sexual way (57%)
- Flashed or "mooned" (49%)
- Had sexual rumors spread about them (43%)
- Had clothing pulled at in a sexual way (38%)
- Sexual pictures, photographs, illustrations, messages, or notes were shown, given, or left for them to find (31%)

Adolescents in this research reported experiencing behaviors that constitute hostile environment sexual harassment, especially in the hallways as they were going to and from class. The AAUW study also found that adolescents' experiences with sexual harassment were most likely to occur in the middle school or junior high school years of sixth to ninth grade.

Similar results were obtained by AAUW in its 2001 study. Furthermore, smaller, independent studies of peer sexual harassment of adolescents have confirmed the incidence rate initially reported by the AAUW. Roscoe (1994), for example, reported a significant percentage of early adolescents' experiences with peer sexual harassment. They reported that 50% of adolescent girls had been victimized, significantly more than the percentage of boys (37%). Fineran and Bennett (1999) reported that 87% of girls in their study were sexually harassed by their male peers. Research conducted by Murnen and Smolak (2000) found adolescent girls at school commonly experienced having an entrance blocked and being stared at. Other studies indicate between 50% and 90% of adolescent girls are victims of sexual harassment by peers (see, e.g., Brown & Leaper 2008; Fineran & Bennett 1999; Fineran & Bolen 2006; Roscoe, Strouse & Goodwin, 1994; Stratton & Backes 1997). Similar to the AAUW findings, all of these studies indicate that girls report experiencing sexual harassment more frequently than boys do, and boys perpetrate more sexual harassment than girls do.

When schools fail to intervene in peer sexual harassment, students get the message that sexual harassment is accepted at the school. Strauss noted that this acceptance can be a "catalyst for increased sexual violence within the school and the community" (Strauss 2010, 189). Data supportive of Strauss' contention were obtained by Pellegrini (2002), who found that students who bullied their peers in sixth grade engaged in sexual harassment in seventh grade.

PSYCHOLOGICAL DIMENSIONS OF PEER SEXUAL HARASSMENT

Hill and Silva offered some reasons boys identified for why they engage in sexual harassment of girls:

- I thought it was funny;

- I thought the person liked it;
- My friends encouraged or pushed me into doing it;
- I wanted something from that person; and
- I wanted that person to think I had some sort of power over them (Hill & Silva 2005, 22).

Paludi, Martin, and Paludi (2007) and Giladi (2005) noted that boys act out of extreme competitiveness or fear that they will lose their position of power. They don't want to appear less masculine or weak to their male peers, so they engage in sexual harassment of girls. Thus, girls are the objects of the game to impress other boys. De-individuation is common among adolescent boys; they discontinue self-evaluation and instead adopt group norms and attitudes. De-individuation causes group members to behave more aggressively than they would as individuals. Additionally, Doyle and Paludi (1995) and DeSouza (2004) noted that the male-as-aggressor theme is so central to many adolescent boys' self-concept that it spills over in to their relationships with girls.

Stein (1996) argued that peer sexual harassment is tolerated and characterized as "normal" by school administrators. Phinney (1994) also noted that sexual harassment is a "dynamic element" in the lives of adolescent girls because schools perpetuate this male dominance through pedagogical techniques and sports. (This issue is examined further elsewhere in this chapter.)

SEXUAL HARASSMENT OF ADOLESCENT GIRLS BY TEACHERS

Several studies have been conducted concerning the incidence of sexual harassment of adolescents by teachers. Strauss and Espeland (1992) found that 30% of high school students were sexually harassed by a teacher. Sexual harassment included sexually related remarks, staring, touching, gestures, and propositions. In its 2001 research, the AAUW reported that, of students who had been harassed, 38% identified teachers or other school employees as perpetrators. As another example, the U.S. Department of Education (2004) found that approximately 10% of high school students have been targeted with unwanted sexual attention by school employees, including teachers.

Although sexual harassment of adolescents by peers is more common than by teachers, incidence data could be difficult to obtain. Criminal rape laws and child abuse statutes may be filed against the teacher if the teen is less than 18 years old (Shakeshaft & Cohen 1995). Behavioral examples of sexual harassment by teachers include a variety of forms (Strauss 2010), including discussing girls' legs, commenting on their sex lives, touching a girl's breasts, fondling, and tickling.

SEXUAL HARASSMENT OF ADOLESCENT GIRLS ON THE INTERNET

There are a variety of behaviors that constitute online sexual harassment of adolescents, including unwelcome physical, verbal, and nonverbal behavior. Online sexual solicitation, for example, includes asking adolescents to discuss sex practices and requesting that the teen engage in a sexual act. Similar to child abductors who use a "confidence assault" (see Paludi & Kelly 2010), online harassers engage in an organized plot to lure teens into sexual solicitation. Online harassers initially try to gain the trust and confidence of the teen who is the targeted victim, for example. This trust then is used to manipulate the teen into physical and psychological vulnerability. By the time the teen realizes that the individual is violent, their ability to stop the behavior is limited. The harasser continues the confidence assault by convincing the teen that he or she is a participant in the crime or caused the crime.

Dewey (2002, cited in Fogarty 2009) and the Polly Klaas Foundation (2006; cited in Fogarty 2009) noted, with respect to online sexual solicitation of adolescent girls, that

- Thirty percent had been sexually harassed while they were in a chat room.
- Thirty-seven percent received links to sexually explicit content online.
- Thirty percent have discussed meeting someone they met online.
- Thirty-three percent had been asked about sexual topics online.

Research commissioned by Cox Communications and the National Center for Missing and Exploited Children (2005) reported that

- Fifty-one percent of parents do not have or are unaware of computer software that monitors their adolescents' online behavior.
- Forty-two percent of parents did not review the content of e-mail sent to their adolescent, or that of chat room discussions, or that of instant messages.

Online sexual harassment of adolescent girls indicates that the most vulnerable targets of the victimization are

- Girls between the ages of 14 and 17;
- Girls with major depressive symptoms;
- Girls who have experienced life transitions, including changing schools, not having many friends, and being worried about their parents divorcing;

- Girls who have close online relationships;
- Girls with high levels of Internet use;
- Girls with emotional problems are more likely to have formed online sexual relationships, have been asked for face-to-face encounters, and attend such encounters; and
- Girls whose Internet-safety awareness is low.

The Girl Scouts of America's study discussed previously in this chapter noted that "[I]nternet communication technology is a pervasive part of girls' lives. On average, girls report going online two to three times a week, with dedicated users going online several times a day. . . . Girls appear to spend the majority of their time online socializing" (Girl Scouts of the United States of America 2002, 9). According to the girls in their study (Girl Scouts of the United States of America 2002, 15, 16),

- "A guy threatened to come to my town if I didn't have cybersex with him" (13-year-old girl);
- "Some guy kept asking me if we could have cybersex and I kept saying 'no' but he kept asking. I got really scared and blocked him. He was so persistent and scary that he wouldn't go away. If it wasn't for the blocking feature, I probably wouldn't feel that safe" (15-year-old girl); and
- "I was chatting with two people who were friends [with each other] and after talking to them for like an hour, one of the guys [I didn't know them] told me that his friend had hacked into my computer and knew where I lived, and he told me that he was incredibly horny and was going to come find me" (16-year-old girl).

Berson, Berson, and Ferron (2002) reported that 74% of adolescent girls spend the majority of time online in chat rooms, sending e-mails, and sending instant messages.

Similar to research findings regarding school harassment of girls, girls who experience online sexual harassment are reluctant to tell their parents. This reluctance stems from fearing retaliation from their parents, including banning them from online socializing. Adolescent girls as well as boys want opportunities to vent about problems they experience, which is a normative part of this stage of life (Paludi 2002). Banning teenagers from using the Internet thus is perceived by adolescents as blocking them from having friends.

Online sexual harassment is not identical to cyberstalking (Chisholm 2006). Stalking involves being persistently watched or followed. Cyberstalkers bombard their targets with e-mails at work, on smartphones and similar devices, and at school. Because the online stalker remains anonymous, adolescents feel threatened, fearful, and filled with dread.

Online harassers and stalkers can engage in both forms of victimization against teen girls.

ADOLESCENT EMPLOYMENT AND SEXUAL HARASSMENT

Mortimer (2005) reported that approximately 80% to 90% of adolescents are employed during high school, especially in fast-food restaurants, retail sales, grocery stores, and health care fields. Strauss and Espeland (1992) found that 30% of 250 female vocational students surveyed from four Minnesota school districts had reported experiencing sexual harassment at their jobs. Fineran (2002) found that 35% of 332 part-time employed adolescents experienced sexual harassment, with girls being more likely to be victimized than boys (63% vs. 37%).

Fineran and Gruber (2009) indicated that out of 260 adolescents in a New England private high school, 52% of girls stated they experienced sexual harassment at work, with the majority of perpetrators being co-workers. The types of sexual harassment reported by these girls included unwanted sexual attention and sexual and sexist comments. Fineran and Gruber (2009) further noted that adolescent girls experience more sexual harassment than adult employed women and college women.

MENTAL HEALTH IMPACT OF SEXUAL HARASSMENT ON ADOLESCENTS

Research indicates a significant impact on adolescent girls' mental health following experiencing quid pro quo or hostile environment sexual harassment by peers, employers, teachers, or individuals in online chat rooms. Students in the AAUW study (AAUW 1992), for example, reported the following experiences:

- Embarrassment
- Self-consciousness
- Being less sure of themselves or less confident
- Feeling afraid or scared
- Doubting whether they could have a happy romantic relationship
- Feeling confused about who they are
- Feeling less popular

Larkin (1994) pointed out that adolescent girls' decline in self-esteem might be attributable to the sexual harassment they frequently experience. Additionally, Murnen and Smolak (2000) reported that adolescent girls were more likely than boys to perceive sexual harassment as being frightening. Timmerman (2002) and Duffy, Wareham, and Walsh (2004) also found that sexual harassment of adolescent girls contributed to their lower self-esteem and poorer psychological health. Girls in the research sample reported embarrassment, fear, and self-consciousness, all of which contributed to their participating fully in class.

Fineran and Gruber (2004) noted that adolescents who were sexually harassed experienced depression, sadness, anxiety, nightmares or disturbed sleep, isolation from family, and loss of friends; and that they also felt threatened, angry, and helpless. Fineran and Gruber (2004) further found that adolescents who experienced sexual harassment had increased post-traumatic stress as a result of their diminished emotional well-being. Sheffield (1993) argued that sexual harassment and other forms of gendered violence encourage adolescent girls to feel fearful and are part of what she described as "sexual terrorism."

Additionally, The Massachusetts Youth Risk Behavior Survey (Massachusetts Department of Elementary and Secondary Education 2007) reported that sexual minority adolescents who experienced sexual harassment had greater suicide rates than did heterosexual adolescents. Stein (1986, cited in Bogart, Simmons, Stein & Tomaszewski 1992) noted that sexual harassment victims often experience a second victimization when seeking resolution for the sexual harassment. Girls frequently are blamed for their own victimization as a consequence of individuals defining sexual harassment as seduction.

Another stereotype is that girls do not tell the truth. Additionally, Paludi and Barickman (1998) summarized research indicating that adolescents do not label their mental health–impact responses as being caused by, or contributed to, by sexual harassment. Their responses often are attributed by their family, friends, and school administrators to other events in the girls' lives, especially those related to hormonal changes and adolescent mood swings.

In addition to the mental-health impacts of sexual harassment on adolescent girls, research indicates that girls withdraw from school and from friends. Girls also experience lowered grades, lost educational opportunities, and more-limited career choices (Paludi, Martin & Paludi 2007). Further, as compared to adolescent girls who have not reported experiencing sexual harassment, adolescent victims of sexual harassment report nightmares, disturbed sleep, eating disorders, and reduced life satisfaction.

RESPONSIBILITIES OF SCHOOLS AND WORKPLACES IN PREVENTING AND DEALING WITH SEXUAL HARASSMENT OF ADOLESCENTS

Sexual harassment demands schools intervene since under Title IX, sexual harassment is an organizational responsibility with respect to prevention and reactive measures. Paludi and Paludi (2003) recommended that schools should exercise "reasonable care" to ensure a sexual harassment-free environment and retaliatory-free environment for students. This "reasonable care," adapted from the Supreme Court ruling in *Faragher v. Boca Raton* (1998) includes the following. School districts should

- Establish and disseminate an effective anti–sexual harassment policy;
- Establish and disseminate an effective investigatory procedure; and
- Offer training in sexual harassment in general and in the school's policy and procedures specifically.

Reasonable care is required of employers as well. With respect to sexual harassment, the EEOC (1990) has maintained that "It is unlawful to harass a person (an applicant or employee) because of that person's sex. Harassment can include 'sexual harassment' or unwelcome sexual advances, requests for sexual favors, and other verbal or physical harassment of a sexual nature."

Once a school district or employer is made aware of an alleged incident of sexual harassment, an investigation must be undertaken and completed as quickly as possible (Dowling 2011; Levy & Paludi, 2002; Paludi, Martin & Paludi 2007). In addition, a school or employer is required to investigate when a teacher or manager is told of sexual harassment, even if this individual is not the official designated complaint officer and even if the complaint is not made in an "official" manner. Thus, once the school or employer knows, the requirement of responsive action begins.

Schools also are legally required to facilitate training programs on sexual harassment awareness. Goals of effective training programs include

- Defining quid pro quo and hostile environment sexual harassment;
- Discussing the physical and emotional reactions to being sexually harassed;
- Discussing peer sexual harassment; and
- Discussing means of resolving complaints of sexual harassment (Paludi & Barickman 1998; Paludi, Martin & Paludi 2007; Paludi & Paludi 2003).

At the conclusion of training programs, students should be able to

- Assess their own perceptions of sexual harassment;
- Label adequately behaviors as illustrative of sexual harassment or not illustrative of sexual harassment;
- Identify peer sexual harassment;
- Describe the effects of sexual harassment on students;

- State components of the school's policy statement on sexual harassment; and
- State the proper procedure to follow if sexual harassment occurs.

Research has indicated the following with respect to training programs on sexual harassment awareness for adolescents:

- Training increases their tendency to perceive sexual harassment (Moyer & Nath 1998).
- Training increases students' knowledge acquisition and attitude change (Roscoe 1994).
- Training increases the reporting of sexual harassment (Roscoe 1994).

Paludi and Barickman (1998) noted that adolescents' level of cognitive development must be taken into account when schools are designing training programs (as well as policies and procedures). Thus, teens could need concrete examples rather than hypothetical, theoretical situations for them to understand the legal and psychological issues involved in sexual harassment.

ADDITIONAL EDUCATIONAL PROGRAMS

Additional educational programs for adolescents have been identified in the sexual harassment literature (e.g., AAUW 2001; Paludi & Paludi 2003).

- Include training on sexual harassment in new student and teacher orientation programs.
- Report annually on sexual harassment cases.
- Encourage teachers to incorporate discussions of sexual harassment in their classrooms.
- Encourage students to start an organization with the purpose of preventing sexual harassment.
- Facilitate a "sexual harassment awareness week" and schedule programs for students and teachers, including guided video discussions, guest lecturers, and plays.
- Provide educational sessions for parents about sexual harassment and the school district's policy and procedures.

CONCLUSION

Bullying versus Sexual Harassment in Schools

School districts increasingly have been focusing their attention on bullying (Stein 2005a). Bullying prevention is important, given findings by

Espelage and Holt (2001) and Lund, Ertesvag, and Roland (2010) among others that suggest at least 30% of adolescents are involved in bullying as bullies, victims, or both. Additionally, victims score within the clinical range on standard depression and anxiety measures (Sandler & Stonehill 2005). Focusing on bullying prevention also is important given findings by Lund, Ertesvag, and Roland (2010) that indicated adolescents identify nonsupportive school personnel to be the major explanation for why bullying occurs. A third reason to focus on bullying prevention concerns recent research that links workplace bullying to childhood and adolescent bullying that was never addressed properly (Daniel 2009).

Almost 30 years after the project on the Status of Education of Women used the term "hidden issue" to describe sexual harassment, we again have a backlash because schools are focusing on bullying instead. Despite the high incidence of various forms of sexual harassment and other forms of gendered violence against adolescent girls in schools, sexual harassment of girls is once again being "hidden" because it is being overshadowed by bullying (Paludi, Martin & Paludi 2007). In some school districts, sexual harassment is subsumed under bullying, which, according to Stein (2005a), further de-genders peer aggression. Sandler and Stonehill (2005) noted that, although sexual harassment might be seen as a form of sexual bullying, when schools focus on bullying prevention they are not likely to remember to deal with sexual harassment because they consider bullying and sexual harassment to be independent of each other. Stein noted that focusing on bullying ignores the fact that most victims of sexual harassment are girls to instead focus on boys' experiences with being bullied. According to Stein,

> [S]tate legislators have been passing laws on school bullying which may serve to placate the general public. Concurrently, however, there has been an increase of incidents of sexual harassment and sexual violence in schools, along with greater frequency of violence in teen dating relationships. Unfortunately, the bullying focus may serve to both degender the problem of sexual harassment and sexual violence and to take attention away from the increasing severity of these problems. (Stein 2005b, 7)

Attention to bullying rather than sexual harassment helps remove the school's responsibility in preventing and dealing with this form of violence against girls. Bullying is seen as an interpersonal problem that involves helping a pathological bully or group of bullies. Sexual harassment, however, is illegal and requires schools to both prevent and deal with sexual harassment when it occurs (Paludi, Martin & Paludi 2007). It is paramount to deal with sexual harassment from an institutional level of analysis, not an individual level (Paludi & Barickman 1998; Stein 1996).

Although the U.S. Department of Education has offered a definition of sexual harassment (discussed previously in this chapter), it has not defined bullying but it provides definitions of bullying from researchers. Sexual harassment is illegal but bullying is not. This fact has implications for adolescents seeking resolution to their complaints. If they define their experiences as sexual harassment, then they can use OCR's resolution procedures (described above). If adolescents define their experiences as bullying, however, then they do not have the same federal recourse. Stein (2003) has noted that state antibullying laws do not offer identical protection to adolescents as do federal laws.

COGNITIVE MATURITY OF ADOLESCENT GIRLS

Part of sexual harassment prevention for adolescents also includes school personnel recognizing and addressing Elkind's (1967) components of egocentrism characteristic of adolescence: imaginary audience and personal fable. The "imaginary audience" refers to adolescents feeling that they are the focus of attention; it is imaginary in that peers actually are not that concerned with the adolescent's thoughts, as they typically are focused on their own.

This concept has been used to explain why adolescent girls are self-conscious about their clothing and body image, spend many hours primping in front of mirrors, and feel that they are "on display"—and thus engage in eating disorders (Pipher 1994; Halpern, Udry, Campbell & Suchindran 1999). Ferron (1997) noted that approximately 75% of American adolescent girls in the study's sample believed they would be happier in their lives if they had a "flawless" body. Happiness was defined by these girls as having more friends, having an easier life, being accepted by a peer group, and finding love.

As a consequence of being absorbed with their own feelings, adolescents believe that their emotions are unique. Their belief in their uniqueness is expressed in a subjective story they tell themselves about their "special qualities." This subjective story is referred to as the "personal fable." Evidence of the personal fable is evident in diaries kept by adolescents; including stories about how they are immune from dangers suffered by others so they can dispense with using seat belts, contraceptives, and binge and purge. This is done because they are cognitively convinced that they are special and that nothing bad will happen to them.

Elkind (1967) noted that adolescent egocentrism disappears when girls have the role-taking opportunities that help to replace the imaginary audience with a real one and replace a subjective fable with an objective story. Egocentrism has been hypothesized to be declining by the time adolescents are 16 or 17 years old. Adolescent girls might not be given the role-taking opportunities at home or in school, however, or be encouraged to speak up about abuse—including their own and peers' victimization—because of stereotypic beliefs about them becoming argumentative and assertive, and therefore being unattractive as dates and potential mates (Leaper & Brown 2008; Paludi 2002). Thus, adolescent girls seriously harm themselves and others in their struggle to "fit in" with a peer group that demands silence about violence, including sexual harassment.

Sexual harassment prevention programs for adolescents must address these issues if the goal is to intervene before, during, and after incidents. The authors recommend a variation of the bystander education program developed for rape prevention by Banyard, Plante, and Moynihan (2005). Such programs can aid adolescents in understanding the importance of assisting themselves and others who are experiencing sexual harassment and other types of violence, including intimate partner violence.

The research on egalitarian and traditional gender-role orientations and intervening in sexual harassment is promising. In a study of 600 adolescent girls aged 12 years to 18 years, Leaper and Brown found that those who learned about feminism from their teachers, parents, or the media were more likely to recognize sexism—including sexual harassment—than those who were not educated about feminism. Further, according to Leaper and Brown,

> Exposure to feminism did not lead to increased reports of sexism for all girls equally. Feminist messages appeared to be most powerful for girls who either held moderately egalitarian attitudes or who were at least moderately discontent with gender norms. Thus, girls may need to be somewhat responsive to questioning the status quo for feminist messages to be most influential. (Leaper & Brown 2008, 699)

These results support in-class training programs for secondary students and utilizing sound pedagogy to provide the skills necessary for students to make connections among sexism, sexual harassment, illegal behavior, and reporting their experiences to school administrators. Such pedagogy includes case studies and scenarios that encourage adolescents to learn through guided discovery and teach them to think critically about discrimination (Carter 2002). The major objective of the training modules and pedagogical techniques is to facilitate transference to the classroom, other school-sponsored activities, and the workplace. Paludi, Martin, and Paludi (2007) note that part of this training must deal with confronting hidden biases and stereotypes about women, men, sex, and power. If these issues are not discussed, then adolescents will not challenge them.

REFERENCES

American Association of University Women (AAUW) Educational Foundation (1992). *The AAUW Report: How schools shortchange girls*. Washington, DC: Author.

American Association of University Women (AAUW) Educational Report (2001). *Hostile hallways: The annual survey on sexual harassment in America's schools.* Washington, DC: Author.

Banyard, V., Plante, E., and Moynihan, M. (2005). *Rape prevention through bystander education: Bringing a broader community perspective to sexual violence prevention.* Report to the U.S. Department of Justice. http://www.ncjrs.gov/pdffiles1/nij/grants/208701.pdf. Accessed October 7, 2010.

Berson, L., Berson, M., and Ferron, J. (2005). Emergency risks of violence in the digital age: Lessons for educators from an online study of adolescent girls in the United States. North Carolina. http://www.ncsu.edu/meridian/sum2002/cyberviolence/. Accessed April 14, 2015

Bogart, K., Simmons, S. Stein, S., and Tomaszewski, E. (1992). Breaking the silence: Sexual and gender-based harassment in elementary, secondary, and postsecondary education. In *Sex equity and sexuality in education,* edited by S. Klein, 191–221. Albany: State University of New York Press.

Brown, C., and Leaper, C. (2008, April). *Adolescent girls' reactions to academic sexism: Cognitive appraisals, coping strategies and academic outcomes.* Third Gender Development Research Conference, San Francisco, CA.

Carter, S. (2002). Matching training methods and factors of cognitive ability: A means to improve training outcomes. *Human Resource Development Quarterly* 13, 71–87.

Chisholm, J. (2006). Cyberspace violence against girls and adolescent females. *Annuals, New York Academy of Sciences* 1087, 74–89.

Cox Communications and the National Center for Missing and Exploited Children (2005). *Parents' Internet monitoring study.* http://www.cox.com/TakeCharge/includes/docs/results.pdf. Accessed October 10, 2010.

Daniel, T. (2009). *Stop bullying at work: Strategies and tools for HR and legal professionals.* Alexandria, VA: Society for Human Resource Management.

DeSouza, E. (2004, July). *Intercultural and intracultural comparisons of bullying and sexual harassment in secondary schools.* Paper presented at the Association for Gender Equity Leadership in Education, Washington, DC.

Dowling, J. (2011). Conducting workplace investigations. In *Praeger handbook on workplace discrimination,* edited by M. Paludi, C. Paludi, and E. DeSouza. Westport, CT: Praeger.

Doyle, J., and Paludi, M. (1995). *Sex and gender: The human experience.* New York: McGraw Hill.

Duffy, J., Wareham, S., and Walsh, M. (2004). Psychological consequences for high school students of having been sexually harassed. *Sex Roles* 50, 811–821.

Elkind, D. (1967). Egocentrism in adolescence. *Child Development* 38, 1025–1034.

Equal Employment Opportunity Commission (EEOC) (1999). *Enforcement guidance: Vicarious employer liability for unlawful harassment by supervisors.*

Equal Employment Opportunity Commission (EEOC) (1990). *Policy guidance on sexual harassment.*

Espelage, D., and Holt, M. (2001). Bullying and victimization during early adolescence. *Journal of Emotional Abuse* 2, 123–142.

Faragher v. City of Boca Raton, 524 U.S. 725 (1998).

Ferron, C. (1997). Body image in adolescence: Cross-cultural research results of the preliminary phase of a quantitative survey. *Adolescence 32*, 735–744.

Fineran, S. (2002). Adolescents at work: Gender issues and sexual harassment. *Violence Against Women* 8, 953–967.

Fineran, S., and Bennett, L. (1999). Gender and power issues of peer sexual harassment among teenagers. *Journal of Interpersonal Violence* 15, 626–641.

Fineran, S., and Bolen, R. (2006). Risk factors for peer sexual harassment in schools. *Journal of Interpersonal Violence* 21, 1169–1190.

Fineran, S., and Gruber, J. (2009). Youth at work: Adolescent employment and sexual harassment. *Child Abuse and Neglect* 33, 550–559.

Fineran, S., and Gruber, J. (2004, July). *Research on bullying and sexual harassment in secondary schools: Incidence, interrelationships and psychological implications.* Paper presented at the Association for Gender Equity Leadership in Education, Washington, DC.

Fogarty, K. (2009). *Teens and Internet safety.* http://edis.ifas.ufl.edu/fy848. Accessed October 9, 2010.

Giladi, A. (2005, August). *Sexual harassment or play? Perceptions and observations of young children's experiences in kindergarten and early schooling in Israel.* Paper presented at the Conference of the International Coalition Against Sexual Harassment, Philadelphia, PA.

Girl Scouts of the United States of America (2002). *The Net effect: Girls and new media.* http://www.girlscouts.org/research/pdf/net_effect.pdf. Accessed October 9, 2010.

Halpern, C., Udry, J., Campbell, B., and Suchindran, C. (1999). Effects of body fat on weight concerns, dating, and sexual activity: A longitudinal analysis of black and white adolescent girls. *Developmental Psychology* 35, 721–736.

Hill, C., and Silva, E. (2005). *Drawing the line: Sexual harassment on campus.* Washington, DC: American Association of University Women Educational Foundation.

Klein, J. (2006). An invisible problem: Daily violence against girls in school. *Theoretical Criminology* 10, 147–177.

Larkin, J. (1994). Walking through walls: The sexual harassment of high school girls. *Gender and Education* 6 (3), 263–280.

Leaper, C., and Brown, C. (2008). Perceived experiences with sexism among adolescent girls. *Child Development* 79, 685–704.

Levy, A., and Paludi, M. (2002). *Workplace sexual harassment, 2nd ed.* Englewood Cliffs, NJ: Prentice Hall.

Lund, I., Ertesvag, S., and Roland, E. (2010). Listening to shy voices: Shy adolescents' experiences with being bullied at school. *Journal of Child and Adolescent Trauma* 3, 205–223.

Massachusetts Department of Elementary and Secondary Education (2007). *Health and risk behaviors of Massachusetts youth, 2007: The report.* http://www.doe.mass.edu/cnp/hprograms/yrbs/. Accessed October 9, 2010.

Mortimer, J. (2005). *Working and growing up in America.* Cambridge, MA: Harvard University Press.

Moyer, R., and Nath, A. (1998). Some effects of brief training interventions on perceptions of sexual harassment. *Journal of Applied Social Psychology* 28, 333–356.

Murnen, S., and Smolak, L. (2000). The experience of sexual harassment among grade-school students: Early socialization of female subordination? *Sex Roles* 24, 319–327.

Nadal, K. L. (2010). Gender microaggressions: Implications for mental health. In *Feminism and women's rights worldwide; Vol. 2, Mental and physical health,* edited by M. Paludi, 155–175. Westport, CT: Praeger.

Paludi, C., and Paludi, M. (2003). Developing and enforcing effective policies, procedures, and training programs for educational institutions and businesses. In *Academic and workplace sexual harassment: A handbook of cultural, social science, management, and legal perspectives,* edited by M. Paludi and C. Paludi, 176–198. Westport, CT: Praeger.

Paludi, M. (2010, October). *The continuum of campus violence: Applying "broken windows theory" to prevent and deal with campus violence.* U.S. Department of Education National Meeting on Alcohol, Drug Abuse and Violence Prevention in Higher Education, National Harbor, MD.

Paludi, M. (2002). *The psychology of women.* Upper Saddle River, NJ: Prentice Hall.

Paludi, M., and Barickman, R. (1998). *Sexual harassment, work, and education: A resource manual for prevention.* Albany: State University of New York Press.

Paludi, M., and Kelly, K. (2010). Missing children and child abductions: An international human rights issue. In *Feminism and women's rights worldwide,* edited by M. Paludi, 47–80. Westport, CT: Praeger.

Paludi, M., Martin, J., and Paludi, C. (2007). Sexual harassment: The hidden gender equity problem. In *Handbook for achieving gender equity through education,* 2d ed., edited by S. Klein, 215–229. Mahwah, NJ: Erlbaum.

Pellegrini, A. (2002). Bullying, victimization, and sexual harassment during the transition to middle school. *Educational Psychologist* 37, 151–163.

Phinney, G. (1994). Sexual harassment: A dynamic element in the lives of middle school girls and teachers. *Equity and Excellence in Education* 27, 5–10.

Pipher, M. (1994). *Reviving Ophelia: Saving the selves of adolescent girls.* New York: Ballantine.

Roscoe, B. (1994). Sexual harassment: An educational program for middle school students. *Elementary School Guidance and Counseling* 29, 110–120.

Roscoe, B., Strouse, J., and Goodwin, M. (1994). Sexual harassment: Early adolescents' self-reports of experiences and acceptance. *Adolescence* 29, 515–523.

Sandler, B., and Stonehill, H. (2005). *Student to student sexual harassment in K–12: Strategies and solutions for educations to use in the classroom, school and community.* Lanham, MD: Rowman & Littlefield Education.

Shakeshaft, C., and Cohen, A. (1995). Sexual abuse of students by school person-
    nel. *Phi Delta Kappan* 76, 512–520.
Sheffield, C. (1993). The invisible intruder: Women's experiences of obscene phone
    calls. In *Violence against women: The bloody footprints*, edited by P. Bart and E.
    Moran, 73–78. Newbury Park, CA: Sage.
Stein, N. (2005a, August). *Gender safety in US schools*. Paper presented at the
    Conference of the International Coalition Against Sexual Harassment,
    Philadelphia, PA.
Stein, N. (2005b). A rising pandemic of sexual violence in elementary and second-
    ary schools: Locating a secret problem. *Duke Journal of Gender Law and Policy*
    12, 1–19.
Stein, N. (2003). Bullying or sexual harassment? The missing discourse of rights in
    an era of zero tolerance. *University of Arizona Law Review* 45, 783–799.
Stein, N. (1996). From the margins to the mainstream: Sexual harassment in K–12
    schools. *Initiatives* 57, 19–26.
Stein, N. (1993, August). *Secrets in full view: Sexual harassment in our K–12 schools*.
    Paper presented at the American Psychological Association, Toronto,
    Canada.
Stratton, S., and Backes, J. (1997, February/March). Sexual harassment in North
    Dakota public schools: A study of eight high schools. *High School Journal* 80,
    163–172.
Strauss, S. (2010). Sexual violence to girls and women in schools around the world.
    In *Feminism and women's rights worldwide. Vol. 1: Heritage, roles and issues*, ed-
    ited by M. Paludi, 187–231. Westport, CT: Praeger.
Strauss, S., and Espeland, P. (1992). *Sexual harassment and teens*. Minneapolis, MN:
    Free Spirit Publishing, Inc.
Timmerman, G. (2002). A comparison between unwanted sexual behavior by
    teachers and by peers in secondary schools. *Journal of Youth and Adolescence*
    31, 397–404.
United States Department of Education (2004). *Educator sexual misconduct: A syn-
    thesis of existing literature*. Doc. No. 2004-09. www2.ed.gov/rschstat
    /research/pubs/misconductreview/report. Accessed October 9, 2002.
United States Department of Education, Office of Civil Rights (1997). *Sexual harass-
    ment guidance: Harassment of students by school employees, other students, or
    third parties*. http://www2.ed.gov/about/offices/list/ocr/docs/sexhar00
    .html. Accessed October 9, 2010.

Part IV

Sexual Harassment of Students, Employees, and Faculty: Education and Training As Prevention

Chapter 12

Resistance to Sexual Harassment: Inspiring Girls Through Feminism

Jennifer L. Martin

INTRODUCTION

In August 2013, I attended the International Coalition Against Sexual Harassment (I-CASH) Conference in New York, NY. Scholars and activists from across the nation and spanning many countries attended and shared their research and outreach efforts to expand the knowledge base on sexual harassment and discuss strategies to prevent it in our schools, workplaces, streets, and larger society. At this conference I presented the findings of an empirical study of a sexual harassment intervention that I conducted with high school girls deemed "at-risk for school failure." (The study is summarized elsewhere in this chapter.) Later that year, in October 2013, I was invited to participate in an American Association of University Women (AAUW) Gender Studies Symposium in St. Louis, Missouri. Scholars, activists, and teachers from across the country were invited to share their experiences of teaching gender studies in K–12 schools and in bringing feminism to young people. These two transformational experiences have led me to share the strategies I implemented and the struggles I faced in engaging in this work. These experiences also inform the work that I share in this chapter and reinforce my commitment to advocating for the necessity of teaching gender studies and feminism, and for supporting feminist teachers in K–12 environments.

Whatever the label—gender studies; women's studies; women and gender studies; women's, gender, and sexuality studies—gender studies and feminism tend to be institutionalized within higher education (although not without controversy), but they have yet to be fully embraced within educational institutions that serve our young people. It is my hope that this chapter will communicate the absolute necessity of "doing gender" within K–12 schools. This chapter speaks to the need of feminism within high school environments. Had my students—whose stories are shared in this chapter—experienced such content at a younger age, they might not have faced gender-based offenses such as sexual harassment in their high school hallways. Some perpetrators, having experiencing the same content during their formative years, would have learned to respect the subjectivity—the very personhood—of others or, at least, would-be victims would have possessed the tools to grapple with such issues.

Teaching any content that threatens to dismantle the status quo always is controversial and dangerous work. To wit, the most challenging experience in my 20 years in public school and university teaching is without a doubt when I implemented a program to end the sexual harassment that was so prevalent in a high school where I was teaching. I often tell my students that nothing worthwhile is ever easy. That platitude epitomizes this experience. It was simultaneously the most important as well as the most difficult undertaking of my teaching life.

Before I share the findings of my empirical work with sexual harassment–reduction programming in high school, I first must set the stage. For 15 years I taught in an alternative high school for students labeled "at-risk for school failure." Most of my students had been adjudicated, had parole officers, faced various problems in schools throughout their educational histories, and experienced problems both at home and in the community. In other words, the school was not without conflict. Despite a variety of issues that we collectively handled, sexual harassment was at the forefront. My female students perplexed me, however, and perhaps it was because I was 10 years out from my own adolescent insecurity. Many girls would come to me upset, relaying the sexual- and gender-based victimization they faced at the hands of their male peers during school hours, yet at the same time they communicated that they did not want to proceed with reporting because they considered these same peers "friends." I immediately thought feminism was a crucial need for my students.

My passion for social justice collided with my female students' desires for answers paired with their existential paralysis at the thought of facing gender-based retaliation if they spoke out or stood up against their male peers, who, incidentally, were the dominant population of the school. I extensively researched the topic of sexual harassment prevention and found many parallels between college women identifying with feminism and an increased reporting of sexual harassment (Harris, Melaas & Rodacker 1999; Paludi 1997). Because at that time I did not find any comprehensive programs to reduce or prevent sexual harassment in high schools, I decided to create my own. The intervention I was inspired to create was a women's studies course focusing on sexual harassment reduction. This intervention was created solely for the female student population because they were the group with the most pressing need.

Through my work with critical pedagogy, I found that social engagement can reinvigorate the resistance to "talk back" to oppressive forces (Ginwright, Noguera & Cammarota 2006). Engaging in a resistant voice—which involves reading the world and questioning harmful societal or school practices—can facilitate gains in agency, belonging, and competence (Mitra 2004). Freire's concept of conscientization (Freire 1970), or the development of critical consciousness, strongly influenced me, and although my students had no qualms about verbally resisting adults—which, for some, was the only sense of power they possessed—I wanted to determine whether feminism and increased knowledge production/creation and communication would inspire my students to transcend the gender-based barriers they experienced through the examination of historical and current inequalities. The iteration of women's studies that I share in this chapter discusses the impact of feminism on high school–age girls labeled at-risk for school failure and provides empirical support for feminism in enriching these students' educational experiences. Overall, this course helped to facilitate heightened feminist identification, heightened internal motivation, and resistance to negative social forces—specifically sexual harassment—for my female students.

BACKGROUND

At the beginning of this chapter, I alluded to the fact that this course was the most difficult endeavor of my teaching career. Creating a space in which my students could share their experiences and learn together how to deal with their collective experiences as young women in the school was much more challenging than anticipated. In the first few days of the class, many students expressed the desire to drop the course. Common reasons included, "I cannot be in a room with all females. It is not safe"; "Girls talk too much stuff"; and "All my friends are guys." Initially, I was shocked at these responses. Although many of my female students had come to me in tears, relaying their experiences with sexual harassment, they also were fearful of being in a room with other females who experienced the exact same problems. Thus, I had to spend more time simply teaching my female students how to "get along." Many tears were shed throughout this process, but all of the students remained in the class.

Additionally, at the beginning of the course, many of the girls who experienced sexual harassment also communicated the general sentiment that sexual harassment was "normal"; something that girls and women have to face and nothing can be done about it. In other words, most of my students possessed an external locus of control; they expressed the fact that they had little control over what happened in their lives—their life experiences had taught them this. One's perception of the degree of control one has over situations (locus of control) has much to do with sexual harassment (Jordan, Price & Telljohann 1998; Schwartz 2000). Moreover, my students would take on a victim-blaming stance when learning of other students' experiences of sexual harassment; they did not have empathy for girls who experienced the same issues. This sentiment is not without precedent. According to De Judicibus and McCabe (2001) women who possess sexist beliefs ascribe more self-blame and other-woman blame for sexual harassment than do women who possess feminist beliefs. Many of my students would express satisfaction when other girls were harassed because that meant that they were momentarily safe. In sum, my students did not see their collective problems as women.

THE STUDENTS

My students attended an alternative high school in the Midwest. This school was labeled 100% at-risk and consisted of female and male students removed from traditional high schools because of behavior and attendance issues. The most common reason for female student attendance was conflict with other students (both physical and nonphysical). The women's studies course consisted of 20 female students. The ethnic composition of the sample was 40% African American (n=8), 5% Hispanic/Latina (n=1), 45% White/Euro-American (n=9), 10% Multiracial (n=2).

As stated, most of the students tended to exhibit an external locus of control in the school setting; in other words, they attributed life events to factors to chance or luck. My students traditionally had not experienced school success and most were externally motivated; to exacerbate this, they lived within a male-dominated school culture with high levels of sexual harassment, which further limited their sense of control.

THE CURRICULUM

According to Dewey (1902) one cannot move students forward without meeting them where they currently reside. Dewey's concept of experiential learning informs my pedagogical approach, whereby students lead and direct their engagement with the curriculum. The women's studies course that I created was based upon research of college women's studies courses, which have been found to increase empowerment, internal motivation, and reporting of sexual harassment (Harris, Melaas & Rodacker 1999; Jordan, Price & Telljohann 1998; Paludi 1997; Schwartz 2000), and encompassed the following areas of study: an examination of gender roles, gender history in the United States, global feminist activism, content on sex dynamics and aggression, an examination of gender roles in literature and the media, information on sexual harassment and strategies to deal with it, and assertiveness training. The course was 18 weeks in length and was divided into three six-week grading periods. The class met five days per week for approximately five hours.

I implemented the course curriculum via feminist pedagogy. The class was run as a student-centered environment where students felt safe to question, share information, and guide the learning through the selection of topics and areas of interest. Although this environment took time to create, the atmosphere was intended to empower students to feel safe and in control of their surroundings, the intention being to alter students' locus of control to become more internal. Feminist pedagogy presupposes an examination of all forms of oppression. My intention was that students would identify with others experiencing similar issues and devise strategies to either individually or collectively dismantle the oppressive forces in their lives, thereby also heightening students' internal motivation. An additional area of need, as mentioned, was to facilitate group cohesion through team-building exercises to promote peer-group responsibility and bonding among the students. I stressed the importance of female friendship to deepen the bonds between students and to further promote peer-group responsibility.

The semester's curriculum was what could be expected from a college introductory literature-based women's studies course, sans postmodern or highly philosophical texts. Students learned of the origins of women's secondary status, definitions of feminism, the effects of sexism and sexist language usage, and media literacy. Additional topics included gender equity, Title IX, sexual harassment (definitions and effects of), dating and domestic violence, relationships, boundary setting, body image, images of beauty in advertising/the media, female friendship, empowerment strategies, and intersectionality.

RATIONALE

The combination of conscientization with feminist sentiment can be truly powerful in inspiring students to examine the society in which they live (Ginwright, Noguera & Cammarota 2006). It is only through clear examination and reflection that they can then determine what societal changes are necessary to promote social justice and a more equitable world.

According to Lewis-Charp, Yu, and Soukamneuth,

> critical self-awareness not only helps an individual identify the seeds
> of her own problems, but also sheds light on dominant discourses
> that contribute to her marginalization and [the] oppression of others.
> Education about the "self" and identity is key to social transforma-
> tion because it helps individuals identify and articulate what it is
> that needs to be changed. (Lewis-Charp, Yu, and Soukamneuth 2006,
> 23)

Such critical reflection on society and one's place within it is powerful,
for it encourages students to look beyond themselves, to see themselves as
members of communities (Deeley 2010). When students feel that they can
make a difference in their own lives it can lead to a reduction in feelings of
alienation (Billig 2000). The next step is to promote the notion that students also can make a difference in transforming their schools, communities, and the world (Butin 2006). Through continued personal reflection,
students first transform themselves—which is an ongoing process—and
then, in turn, work to transform the world around them, whether it be
their school, their community, or to adopt a more global approach to social
service or social change. Ginwright, Noguera, and Cammarota advocate a
Freirian approach to social justice education, "one that posits [students']
capacity to produce knowledge to transform their world. In this regard,
youth should be recognized as *subjects* of a knowledge production that
underpins their agency for personal and social transformation" (Ginwright,
Noguera, and Cammarota 2006, xix). It is in this sense that education becomes transformative—to the individual and to the larger society.

THE PROCESS

This chapter represents a narrative retelling of an empirical study. In this
study, I first examined what ways and to what degree women's studies
could inspire my students to self-identify as feminists; then examined
how the choice to embrace the term "feminist" (and its corresponding philosophy) promoted the goals of female solidarity and increased internal
motivation within the school, and lastly, looked at how the aforementioned goals could serve to impact the sexual harassment that my students
faced within their school setting.

Feminist ethnography was the underlying framework through which
I examined changes in student ideas about feminism after participating
in the course. This lens provided a way to examine students' authentic
experiences and incorporate those experiences into the overall analysis.
Feminist ethnography uses the lens of gender to make the lives and experiences of women (and girls) visible (Reinharz 1992). Feminist

ethnography as defined by Reinharz (1992) encompasses three goals: To document women's lives, to understand women's experiences by utilizing their unique points of view, and to frame women's behavior as expressions of social contexts. I extended this definition to include the lives and experiences of girls: I centered on their voices by viewing them as key informants.

SOURCES OF DATA

As alluded to previously, this chapter represents the story of a classroom but it also is a retelling of an empirical study. Often, with time comes additional insight. Below I share the major findings detailing my students' transformation resulting from their participation in the course and, upon my reflection on this work, a delineation of progressive stages of sexual harassment awareness that most of my students experienced. To study changes in student perceptions, I gathered data from participant artifacts (reflections and assignments) and class discussions. I used journal entries, essays, and personal reflections as evidence of student growth.

I interviewed students on their individual impressions of the impact of the course one year after the course ended to determine what students remembered about the course and if they retained the objectives of the course over time. I conducted the interviews using open-ended questions; I audio-recorded them, transcribed them, and cross-checked transcripts with original recordings. Finally, I also used participant observer field notes as an additional source of data. Moch and Cameron (2000) discuss the importance of using journals to assist in processing the experience of conducting research. Wolf (1996) describes the importance of analyzing one's research experiences in terms that use "intuition, feelings, and viewpoint" (as cited in Angrosino & Mays de Perez 2000, 690). I kept a journal before, during, and after teaching the course to record my thoughts, observations, and impressions. To better understand elicited student responses and to assist in processing the experience of conducting research and teaching the course itself, for example, I recorded daily events. I discussed what we did in class that particular day, the challenges I faced in the course, and things that occurred outside of the classroom that were relevant to the goals of the study.

THE STORY OF THE COURSE

As noted, my students were resistant to this course at the beginning. Many expressed the desire to drop the course within the first few days. Upon examination, I learned that they feared the examination of issues such as sexual harassment and that they also were fearful of being in close proximity with so many other females who had experienced similar treatment. I did much work to simply teach my female students how to "get along." If a particular student was upset with another female student, instead of being direct and working out the problem, they instead would roll their eyes or talk behind the other student's back. As simplistic as it sounds, I cannot communicate enough how powerful the phrase "You hurt my feelings" was to this group. This phrase alone did much to reduce the conflict among my students. Additionally, I learned that these students did not know how to communicate their feelings of discomfort when faced with sexually harassing or otherwise degrading treatment. Having students practice naming the unacceptable behaviors as sexual harassment or as degrading—and the further indication that such behaviors not only made them feel uncomfortable but also were unacceptable—was a powerful exercise.

Additionally, much was done to help students to understand what their peers were experiencing; the sharing of individual stories helped them to gain empathy for their peers, who were experiencing the very same behaviors. The examination of affirmative texts written by scholars and practitioners who had experienced sexual harassment—as well as the sharing of strategies for what to do when faced with sexual harassment—assisted students in feeling as though they had recourse for the disparate treatment that they faced. Approximately halfway through the course, the girls had become a solid group. They began to stand together and "talk back" to males in the school who perpetrated sexually harassing behaviors as well as sexist comments about women. My students confronted these comments and behaviors and reported these behaviors to the counselor and to the administration with greater frequency.

Although I felt that this was a positive step in altering the school culture to be more egalitarian, I was surprised that a few of my colleagues were not equally supportive. When my students had progressed to the stage where they felt safe enough and brave enough to talk back to the male students perpetrating sexually harassing behaviors, for example, the school counselor came to me complaining that I was "making her job harder." I explained to her that this was a normal phase in cultural change, and that things eventually would get better. I asked her whether she preferred girls crying in her office or girls actually standing up for themselves. She indicated that a girl crying in her office was what she could handle, for this was on an individual basis and did not involve the counselor moving beyond her comfort zone to a chaos that intimidated her. Girls often stood collectively against sexual bullies, which was a new phenomenon and something the school community was not accustomed to. The school, however, was accustomed to dealing with male anger; in fact, this was a school norm. But female anger was something a bit too scary for many faculty and staff members to handle. These factors speak to the difficulty of this undertaking. Working with the girls on these issues was emotionally taxing for a variety of reasons, including working through their emotional pain in their sharing of what happened to them inside and outside of school pertaining to sexually harassing treatment, dealing with the resistance they faced in listening to and having empathy for stories just like their own, dealing with the sexually harassing behavior of my male students and, surprisingly, dealing with resistance from some of my colleagues, who I had assumed would be allies in this work.

I also experienced some pushback from the administration. The administration was not overtly supportive of this course and I had to do a lot of convincing to get it approved. Initially, my male administrator indicated to me that "this course will never work." Although he also communicated frustration to me at having to work harder to deal with problems that came to him with increased reporting of sexual harassment and additional paperwork, he eventually acknowledged that the harder work at the front end was worth it in the end. He realized that the end result—reduced sexual harassment and a healthier school culture in general—was worth the conflict in the midst of the learning. As stated, the work involved in and around this intervention was simultaneously the most difficult and the most rewarding work of my career.

FINDINGS

Feminist Identification

All of my students who participated in the women's studies course eventually indicated that feminism was a beneficial frame of reference to have, and all identified as feminists one year after the course ended. The following statement encapsulates how important feminism was to the lives of my students and how they used this philosophy to make connections with others.

> The word feminist means when you stand up for women and want to see women achieve, and give them encouraging advice. People who have not taken this class probably think it is all about downing men, saying negative things about them, and saying we are better than them. I feel the need to let people know what the word feminist really means. (Nairobe)

The importance of defining feminism and educating others about it was important to my students. They communicated concern that people have a false impression of the concept, which only serves to keep people from understanding one another and prevents women and their allies from joining forces for a common purpose—exactly what they had experienced in their own school with regard to sexual harassment. Nairobe expressed that feminism can be beneficial for all women. Without it, women can experience negative consequences, such as being labeled and degraded.

> I am a feminist because I feel that women should be treated equally; a lot people are not getting treated equally. . . . I used to say that songs don't matter, but they do, or women would not get treated the way they do. I learned stop degrading women just because of what they wear. (Cherise)

Cherise placed feminism in the context of equality. She expressed her feminism in terms of being treated as an equal. She expressed fear at the prospect of the course at the beginning, as did many of the girls, because it was an all-girl class; but over time she learned to identify with other girls. In the beginning she could not see a connection between how she spoke to other girls and how they spoke to her in reply.

April also spoke of her feminism in terms of equal rights.

> I believe that women and men should have equal rights. [This class] made me see that a woman should not be getting abused. Before I took this class, I thought that women deserved this. Or, I would say things like, "a woman gives a man a reason to hit her." But when I took the class it made me think differently—that women don't deserve this. Nobody does. (April)

April learned to stop engaging in victim-blaming behavior and learned that there was strength to be found in bonding with other girls and women. She expressed a desire to educate other girls and women on the ideas and strategies she learned in the course. Dominique also expressed a change in personal philosophy as a result of the course.

> After I took this course I would say I'm a feminist. It changed my whole outlook on the way I should be and how I should act because I am a woman and I need to have more respect for myself and not sit there and take being called a "ho." I think men show more respect for me now that I have more respect for myself. I think deep down a lot of people don't feel that they're feminists because they don't know the real term "feminist" because people use it the wrong way. (Dominique)

In the context of her own transformation, Dominique became concerned about terminology and language usage—her own, that of her classmates, and that of the members of her community.

At the end of the semester, 100% of students considered themselves feminists. They indicated that they had gained more respect for themselves and for others as a result of the course. They learned to stand up for themselves and others because of their realization of the common problems faced by girls and women; thus, they began identifying with other girls and women along these lines. They identified a causal relationship between media images of women and the treatment they received by their male counterparts. They saw certain media images of women as negative and damaging. In short, the students exhibited a change toward a feminist consciousness, which promoted many additional behavioral changes. Students altered their language usage, for example, to become less degrading to women in general and more egalitarian—they corrected the language usage of other students to be less degrading in general, and they stood up for themselves and for others when faced with degrading or harassing treatment.

SEXUAL HARASSMENT PREVENTION

As alluded to previously, the first time I analyzed my data I noticed that the majority of my students move through a series of progressive stages regarding sexual harassment awareness and prevention. After examining information on identity development (Downing & Roush 1985), I noticed a similarity between feminist identity development with the learning and progression through stages regarding sexual harassment awareness experienced by my students. In general, my students evolved through five stages of identity development regarding sexual harassment:

1. Passive acceptance,
2. Revelation,
3. "Emboldened-ness,"
4. Synthesis, and
5. Active commitment (adapted from Downing & Roush 1985).

Previous research on minority identity and feminist identity development is relevant to and provides a context for this discussion. Downing and Roush (1985) found that the women in their study of feminist identity development experienced several progressive stages including passive acceptance, revelation, embeddedness-emanation, synthesis, and active commitment. "Passive acceptance" involves unawareness or denial of the inequality experienced by women as women. As Downing and Roush state, "This woman carefully selects associates and experiences so as to avoid contact with ideas that may upset her sense of equilibrium" (Downing & Roush 1985, 698). Although I did not study this concept formally, my students exhibited this type of resistance when the class began. They passively accepted the idea that sexual harassment was just something that they, as females, had to face, as if it were a "normal" phenomenon. Likewise, my students exhibited a similar progression in their development of sexual harassment awareness. Prior to the start of the class the girls did not see their personal problem with sexual harassment as being a collective problem—one that they shared with other women.

According to Downing and Roush (1985), the second stage of feminist identity development is "revelation." At this stage, a crisis or series of events occurs that women cannot deny. Revelation involves an open questioning of the self and of socially prescribed sex roles. The results of this stage can cause both anger and dualistic thinking, in which women deem all men as being negative. I liken this second stage to my students realizing that they did indeed share a collective problem with their peers—the other females in the school—and with women in general. That collective problem was sexual harassment. Sexual harassment historically was a major problem within the alternative school. Students expressed that they were more aware of the problem, were more informed about potential strategies to deal with the problem, and thus ultimately dealt with it differently after participating in the course.

> At school, there are rumors going around about some people and guys will look at you if they hear these things—it's happened with me—guys are gonna look at you like, "Oh, I can touch you the way I wanna touch you, I can say whatever I wanna say to you because this has happened, or I have heard this has happened." They look at me like some type of toy that they can walk all over or talk to any way—no respect at all. I have been disrespected, and I have seen other people in school disrespected. (Dee)

Dee's statement (above) represented the second stage (revelation), which my students experienced after learning about sexual harassment as a collective problem affecting girls within this particular school context. Prior to the course they did not identify with one another in terms of shared experiences. As stated, they expressed relief if another girl was harassed because that meant they were momentarily safe from victimization; they expressed outrage at their own harassment but expressed no empathy for the experiences of other girls facing the same situation.

According to Downing and Roush (1985), the third stage is "embeddedness-emanation." This stage involves connecting with other women and affirming one's new identity. The thinking at this stage becomes more relativistic and less dualistic. The stage that my students experienced that similar to this I termed "emboldened-ness." My students did indeed connect with their peers over the issues that they shared; and in so doing they began to "talk back" when they heard sexist remarks and when they faced sexual harassment. Elizabeth expressed the third stage of development that took place as the course progressed, that of resistance.

> Now I speak my mind and I tell them. Before I didn't say anything; I just laughed about it too, knowing I was a girl I didn't even think about it. It was easier that way; if you say something back you feel like an idiot. But, now I don't care. Now, if they say something, I say something. (Elizabeth)

This is the stage that made some of my colleagues uncomfortable, for they were unaccustomed to girls as a group confronting a specific problem or issue within the school. There is power in the collective, and this caused fear and uncertainty for some of my colleagues.

The fourth stage is "synthesis." This stage involves the development of a positive feminist identity including, according to Downing and Roush (1985), a "flexible truce" with the world and the ability to evaluate men on an individual basis. I saw this level represented in my students in a variety of ways. They self-identified as feminists, they reported sexual harassment more frequently when they experienced it, and they thought about living differently in a world that does not value them equally with their male counterparts. This stage is expressed by Brittany:

> If I see something inappropriate, I'll say something, where before I would just keep to myself because sometimes that person would say something back to me and get smart with me and then it would just push my buttons and I would get angry. If you are sexually abused or molested tell somebody. Don't hide it because you're embarrassed. (Brittany)

The fifth stage is "active commitment." This stage involves commitment to meaningful action toward a more egalitarian world. This stage was represented by my students standing up for their peers when they witnessed sexual harassment. This progression in identity is relevant to both feminist identity development and a progression in thinking about sexual harassment awareness and prevention. At this stage, my students experienced the power of the peer group to stand up for one another when facing sexual harassment.

> In school, when people say disrespectful things to me or to other girls, I'll say, "That's not right." Now I actually speak up. I'll tell somebody about it. From this class I have gained a lot of strength. (Karissa)

Ultimately, my students not only took responsibility for their own treatment but also for the fair treatment of their classmates. This specific behavioral change—that students stood up for one another when faced with sexual harassment—was not found in the literature on adolescent females at the time of data collection for this study. This finding—that the peer group can directly impact the level of school-based sexual harassment—adds to the literature on adolescent girls and sexual harassment (Martin 2008).

All of the students gained the knowledge and confidence to develop at all five levels of sexual harassment awareness. The course acted as a consciousness-raising experience for them. After the course they regarded the phenomenon of sexual harassment in general very differently. They viewed it as something many people face, and could identify with other girls in the school who experienced it. Prior to the course they would overwhelmingly take on victim-blaming stances to experiences other than their own; they could not broaden their own experiences to identify a systemic problem. Thus, they were not identifying with one another, even though they all were facing the same school-based harassment. After time spent in the course and much examination of the phenomenon—including listening to guest speakers, researching national statistics, and sharing personal experiences—they changed their perspectives and began to relate to one another. This new identification and solidarity caused them to speak up and stand up for themselves and one another when experiencing and witnessing sexual harassment. They felt empowered to act.

INTERNAL MOTIVATION (LOCUS ON CONTROL)

In general, my students indicated that they felt more knowledgeable and therefore more informed and motivated to act against sexual harassment. This caused them to feel a heightened sense of internal motivation; no longer did they feel they had to accept certain actions and sentiments simply because they were female. They now felt more in control over what happened to them, and communicated a general sense of self-possession:

> I stand up for myself now. . . . Now, if somebody says something to me because of what I'm wearing or the way boys treat us, I report it, or try to help, stand up. (Damarti)

Prior to their work in the course, most students expressed the sentiment that there were certain aspects of life that were not open to them because of their gender. Additionally, they expressed that there were certain negative behaviors that they had to accept because of their sex. The students' transformation included a new world that defied the limitations that either they or society previously had placed upon them.

Previous studies have measured locus of control quantitatively and found that courses in feminism can result in increased internal motivation for girls (Martin 2008; Martin 2005). An earlier study of college women also found this to be the case (Harris, Melaas & Rodacker 1999). The present study examined locus of control qualitatively. I found a heightened sense of internal motivation in my students and a new sense of recourse they possessed when faced with degrading or harassing treatment. They no longer resigned themselves to feelings of powerlessness or victimization.

DISCUSSION

The key findings of the empirical study retold in this chapter include: group identification can be facilitated through curricular interventions, locus of control can be altered through curricular interventions, and students can learn to stand up for peers when facing school-based sexual harassment which in turn can impact school culture. These findings contribute to feminist theory, theory on sexual harassment, and theory on adolescent development. It was not clear at the conclusion of the study, however, what the long-term implications would be for my students.

The purpose for this telling is to communicate the impact of feminism on this group of high school–age girls who were labeled "at-risk" for school failure, and to advocate for teaching developmentally appropriate gender-studies content in grades K–12. The first issue examined was the ways that the course inspired students to self-identify as feminists. When students learned of various definitions of feminism (and eventually collectively created their own definition of feminism), the goals of feminism, and the need for feminist action, they embraced the term "feminist" as a self-identifier with greater frequency. Second, was observing how the choice to embrace the term "feminist" (and its corresponding philosophy) would promote the goals of female solidarity and increased internal motivation within the high school setting. Students exhibited increased solidarity by virtue of decreased victim blaming, refusal to tolerate or perpetuate sexist language, and increased internal motivation (standing up for themselves and fellow students when faced with sexual harassment and by virtue of their increased reports of incidents to school officials). Identifying with other girls and seeing themselves as members of a group that shares common problems enabled the students to gain a sense of empowerment and encouraged them to reexamine the problems found within their own school.

Students began to teach other students who were not involved in the course about the precepts of feminism, and began to correct sexist or demeaning behavior occurring within the school. Students desired to continue the spirit of feminism that began within the course. I can attest to the power of feminist and anti-oppressive education in the transformation of students and the culture of the school in general. These findings reveal that feminist thought and pedagogy still are relevant and beneficial for girls today. These findings also speak to the fact that social justice education possesses the capacity to produce transformative knowledge— knowledge that has the potential to change the lives of our students and, ultimately, the world—no matter how small a corner of the world it is (Ginwright, Noguera & Cammarota 2006).

This retelling is a testament to the power of bringing gender studies to the educational lives of our students prior to their entrance into higher education. In fact, many of my students have not yet made the decision to enter college, although they now are beyond the typical age of college entrance. This is not to say that these students will not one day choose to enter higher education; many may very well make this choice. Introducing gender studies into the high school curriculum where it was formerly absent, however, made a significant impact on the lives of these particular students.

Although important, this work is difficult; we must support those who are brave enough to engage in this work—often without the support of colleagues and administration. This work can be transformational, however, both for the practitioner and for the students. The end result—the "click" moment, the changes in our students—are more than worth the struggle and its corresponding challenges. I encourage readers to support such endeavors and to engage in them.

REFERENCES

Angrosino, M. V., and Mays de Perez, K. A. (2000). Rethinking observation: From method to context. In *Handbook of qualitative research*, edited by N. K. Denzin and Y. S. Lincoln, 673–702. Thousand Oaks, CA: Sage.

Billig, S. H. (2000). The effects of service-learning. *School Administrator* 57, 14–18.

Butin, D. W. (2006). The limits of service-learning in higher education. *The Review of Higher Education* 26, 473–498.

De Judicibus, M., and McCabe, M. P. (2001). Blaming the target of sexual harassment: Impact of gender role, sexist attitudes, and work role. *Sex Roles* 44, 401–417.

Deeley, S. J. (2010). Service-learning: Thinking outside the box. *Active Learning in Higher Education* 11, 43–53.

Dewey, J. (1902). *The child and the curriculum*. Chicago: University of Chicago Press.

Downing, N. E., and Roush, K. L. (1985). From passive acceptance to active commitment: A model of feminist identity development for women. *The Counseling Psychologist* 13, 695–709.

Freire, P. (1970) *Pedagogy of the oppressed*. New York: The Continuum Publishing Company.

Ginwright, S., Noguera, P., and Cammarota, J., eds. (2006). *Beyond resistance! Youth activism and community change: New democratic possibilities for practice and policy for America's youth*. New York: Routledge.

Harris, K. L., Melaas, K., and Rodacker, E. (1999). The impact of women's studies courses on college students of the 1990s. *A Journal of Research* 40, 969–977.

Jordan, T. R., Price, J. H., and Telljohann, S. K. (1998). Junior high school students' perceptions regarding nonconsensual sexual behavior. *The Journal of School Health* 68, 289–296.

Lewis-Charp, H., Cao Y, H., and Soukamneuth, S. (2006). Civic activist approaches for engaging youth in social justice. In *Beyond resistance! Youth activism and community change: New democratic possibilities for practice and policy for America's youth,* edited by S. Ginwright, P. Noguera, and J. Cammarota, 21–35. New York: Routledge.

Martin, J. L. (2008). Peer sexual harassment: Finding voice, changing culture, an intervention strategy for adolescent females. *Violence Against Women* 14, 100–124.

Martin, J. L. (2005, April). *Peer sexual harassment: Finding voice, changing culture.* Paper presented at the American Educational Research Association, Toronto, Canada.

Mitra, D. (2004). The significance of students: Can increasing "student voice" in schools lead to gains in youth development? *Teachers College Record* 106, 651–688.

Moch, S. D., and Cameron, M. E. (2000). Processing the researcher experience through discussion. In *The researcher experience in qualitative research,* edited by S. D. Moch and M. F. Gates, 77–82. Thousand Oaks, CA: Sage.

Paludi, M. A. (1997). Sexual harassment in schools. In *Sexual harassment: Theory, research, and treatment,* edited by W. O'Donohue, 225–249. Boston: Allyn and Bacon.

Reinharz, S. (1992). *Feminist methods in social research.* New York: Oxford University Press.

Schwartz, W. (2000). *Preventing student sexual harassment.* Report No. EDO-UD-00-9. Washington, DC: Office of Educational Research and Improvement (ERIC Document Reproduction Service No. ED448248).

Chapter 13

Teaching an Online Course on Sexual Harassment: A Course for Graduate and Undergraduate Students

Susan Fineran

This chapter describes an online course that introduces students of social work and women's studies to sexual harassment occurring in education and the workplace. Although sexual harassment evolved from a legal paradigm describing discrimination, this course examines sexual harassment from a criminal justice perspective. Using this perspective, many sexually harassing behaviors can be categorized as sexist violence against women, or heterosexist violence against individuals who are homosexual or perceived to be homosexual. The course also presents and discusses mental and physical health outcomes due to the experience of being sexually harassed at work or school.

RATIONALE FOR THE COURSE

Girls and women have long been negatively impacted by sexual harassment in primary and secondary education and in the workforce. For some it is an annoying background noise, interfering at a low level but invisibly restricting options on the path through school and into the workforce. For others, the experience is overwhelming and wrenching, forcing women to give up educational opportunities and derailing career goals. Regardless of women's personal experience, sexual harassment's effect is global. When women do not succeed their families suffer, fellow students and workplace colleagues suffer, and society suffers.

The unnamed should not be taken for the nonexistent. (MacKinnon 1979)

Even though Catherine MacKinnon coined the term "sexual harassment" in the late 1970s, many students recently taking the online class were unaware of the specific behaviors constituting sexual harassment. Even more importantly, most quickly realize that they have experienced a host of these behaviors during their school and work years. They just didn't have a name for what they experienced.

The first time I taught this sexual harassment course, this revelation caught me off guard. I had assumed that after the 1991 U.S. Supreme Court nomination hearing for Clarence Thomas' and Anita Hill's introduction to the public, people had become familiar with the term and what it entails. There have been quite a few hard-to-miss high–public profile cases since then, such as those involving President Bill Clinton and Monica Lewinsky; the Citadel; and Tailhook. It was striking that students of social work and women's studies—a group that usually is knowledgeable about and sympathetic to marginalized people—had not been aware of their own marginalization as females. What I have learned is that, for many of my students, this course not only informs them about sexual harassment in education and work, but also is the beginning of their personal understanding of how sexual harassment has affected their own lives and those of the people they care about. Unfortunately, a bystander can be affected just as much as a target is—and a discriminatory environment affects us all.

I would like to make several other observations about teaching this course. Although open to everyone, almost all of my students have been women. The two or three men who took the class came to conclusions similar to those of their female classmates regarding the outcome of sexual harassment. Those male students had heard their sisters, mothers, wives, and girlfriends complain about experiencing these negative behaviors at school or work. The course also makes clear that sexual harassment happens to both women and men. The material focuses on behaviors perpetrated by anyone upon anyone. For example, homophobic behavior is the primary form of sexual harassment experienced by men. In any negative environment, we all are potential targets. Bearing this in mind, I began offering the course online so that it might reach a broader audience, including those who might choose it as an elective.

WHAT IS COVERED?

The course is taught from a feminist perspective in which patriarchy, homophobia, sexism, heterosexism, and power are considered key elements in the social control of women. It is expected that students understand that discrimination does exist in society and that sexual harassment is a form of sex discrimination. Although I'm not one to shy away from a good debate, this course requires students to understand and apply these concepts as we cover the course material. There is too much information to convey in too little time to allow debate as to whether "women are equal to men" or "discrimination is dead." I have not had the experience of dealing with a misogynist in this class but know from my "Intro to Women's Studies" classes that this type of student (male or female) can be time-consuming. Most students of women's studies have a comprehensive grasp of women's history, and social work students usually have been steeped in social welfare history that includes discussion of the subjugation of women. The class, however, could include students studying nursing, English, business, or other less socially oriented disciplines; thus, all of the basic concepts (i.e., patriarchy, homophobia, sexism, heterosexism, power) are presented to provide a common platform upon which students can ground their opinions. The following section reviews basic information on Title VII and Title IX, patriarchy, and the types of sexual harassment presented in the course. A course guideline then is outlined.

BASIC INFORMATION GROUNDING THE COURSE

Title VII and Title IX

Sexual harassment is a specific type of sex discrimination that has been defined by the U.S. courts over the last 30 years. Ever since sex as a protected class was amended to the 1964 Civil Rights Act, there has been controversy surrounding the issue of providing equal employment and educational opportunities to women. In fact, equality for women in the United States has a relatively short history. A number of suits were filed between 1948 and 1971 to challenge state and federal statutes addressing sex. In all cases the Supreme Court found that women's rights under the federal constitution were not violated. The following examples reflect the scope of this discrimination.

- *Riley v. New York Trust Co.* (S. Ct. 1940)—Established as a matter of law that a wife's domicile is that of her husband.
- *Goesaert v. Cleary* (S. Ct. 1948)—Excluded women from specified employment.

- *Hogt v. Florida* (S. Ct. 1961)—States could systematically exclude women from serving on juries.
- *Yazell v. United States* (S. Ct. 1966)—States could deny married women the right to make contracts.
- *Williams v. McNair* (S. Ct. 1971)—Established separate single-sex schools.

This situation, however, has been ameliorated by legislative means. For instance, the Equal Pay Act of 1963, the Civil Rights Act of 1964, and a number of executive orders issued by President Johnson, President Nixon, and President Carter sought to correct racial and sex discrimination in the workplace. Specifically, Title VII of the Civil Rights Act of 1964 (42 U.S.C. § 2000e-2(a)) prohibits employment discrimination on the basis of race, color, religion, national origin, or sex.

In 1972, Title IX of the Education Amendments Act addressed the educational needs of minorities and women. It was thought that equal access to education was a necessary complement to Title VII of the Civil Rights Act and was imperative if women were to gain the necessary skills and training that would give them access to higher paying jobs, particularly in fields such as engineering and the sciences. It also prohibited sexual harassment in education and directed educational institutions to maintain a grievance procedure allowing for prompt and equitable resolution of all sex discrimination including sexual harassment. In general, the interpretation of what constitutes sexual harassment in an educational setting has followed the concepts developed under employment discrimination law. In 1980, the Equal Employment Opportunity Commission issued a definition of sexual harassment and included specific guidelines to prohibit it.

Equal Employment Opportunity Commission Sexual Harassment Definition

The EEOC guidelines define sexual harassment as unwelcome sexual advances, requests for sexual favors, and other verbal or physical conduct of a nature that constitute harassment when

1. Submission to the conduct is either explicitly or implicitly a term or condition of an individual's employment;
2. Submission to or rejection of such conduct by an individual is used as the basis for employment decisions affecting that individual; and
3. Such conduct has the purpose or effect of unreasonably interfering with an individual's work performance or creating an intimidating, hostile, or offensive working environment.

Equal Employment Opportunity Commission Guidelines

1. Title VII prohibits sexual harassment of employees;
2. Employers are responsible for the actions of their agents and supervisors; and
3. Employers are responsible for the actions of all other employees if the employer knew or should have known about the sexual harassment.

In 1986, the U.S. Supreme Court identified two forms of sexual harassment, "quid pro quo" and "hostile environment." "Quid pro quo" applies when a person with more power (a boss or supervisor) makes decisions that affect an employee's job based on whether the employee complies with the sexual demands of the person in power. "Hostile environment" applies when the harassing behavior of anyone in the workplace (not only a boss or supervisor) causes the workplace to become hostile, intimidating, or offensive, and unreasonably interferes with an employee's work (Langelan 1993). In education this definition has been expanded to include a school's responsibility for the actions of both its employees and students. Title IX of the 1972 Education Amendments requires that an institution receiving federal funds provide an environment free of discrimination:

> Title IX applies to any educational institution's programs or activities that receive federal funds and protects both employees and students. Sexual harassment of students is a violation of Title IX of the 1972 Education Amendments in that it constitutes differential treatment on the basis of sex.

Sandler and Hughes note that Title IX "clearly prohibits sexual harassment of students by faculty and staff. It can also prohibit harassment of students by students as well" (Sandler & Hughes 1988, xx).

The issues of sex discrimination and, in particular, sexual harassment were further addressed in the late 1980s by the passage of more empowering legislation. In 1988, the Civil Rights Restoration Act was passed, overturning the 1984 Supreme Court ruling *Grove City v. Bell*. The 1988 decision meant that schools no longer could legally fund programs such as sports that benefited mostly males without ensuring that equivalent opportunities were available to females. Until then, it had been common practice for schools facing major financial deficits to cut funding to girls' sports to help subsidize the boys' teams.

Sexual harassment is a problem for both girls and boys in schools, and its effects can be long term. Many students report that being the victim of sexual harassment leads to school performance difficulties including ab-senteeism, decreased quality of schoolwork, skipping or dropping classes, lower grades, loss of friends, tardiness, and truancy (AAUW 2011). These factors, in turn, can lead to ineligibility for specific colleges or merit schol-arships, and failure to get recommendations for awards, colleges, or jobs (Fineran 2002). All the difficulties listed above can lead to fewer career choices, decreased or lost economic opportunities, and possible job fail-ure—affecting a student for the rest of her or his life (Fineran & Bolen 2006; Gruber & Fineran 2008).

The Civil Rights Act of 1991, continuing support for the equal rights of women and minorities, expanded the scope of the original 1964 legislation. It allowed, for the first time, limited money damages for victims of sexual harassment and other intentional discrim-ination based on sex, religion, or disability. The act served to strengthen women's position in securing equal employment and educational opportunities.

POWER AND GENDER

Any consideration of sex discrimination and sexual harassment requires an examination of power and gender. Fitzgerald and colleagues (1988) discuss the concept of formal power versus informal power. The former comes from a position of authority. This concept usually comes into play with quid pro quo types of sexual harassment, in which a supervisor or teacher has power over a worker's job or a student's grades. This power can be wielded constructively or selfishly by women or by men. By con-trast, informal power inherently belongs to men in a patriarchal culture. This concept of power is more common in the hostile environment type of sexual harassment, where women are expected to defer to men's superior-ity (Fitzgerald, Shullman, Baily, Richards, Swecker, Gold, Oremerod & Weitzman 1988).

To clarify the differences between quid pro quo and hostile environ-ment sexual harassment, Langelan (1993) divides harassers into three dis-tinct types: (1) sexually predatory harassers, (2) dominance harassers, and (3) strategic or territorial harassers. Sexual predators, usually in authorita-tive power positions, prey on women (or men) for sex. Strategic harassers often are attempting to keep women out of predominantly male fields to maintain male privilege. Both the predator and strategic categories fit the more formal power structure in which the harasser is a supervisor or pro-fessor. Langelan (1993) points out that "male-dominance harassment is a social practice based on gender and power, not a demand for sexual ser-vice." Langelan identifies group harassment by males of females as a way of not only reaffirming male solidarity but also of upholding the status of the entire male group.

PATRIARCHY

When discussing power and gender it is important to examine the concept of patriarchy and its impact on the roles of women and men in our culture. Patriarchy generally is viewed as having two basic components: A structure in which men have more power and privilege than women, and an ideology that legitimizes this arrangement. Gerda Lerner (1986) wrote extensively on patriarchy and its effects on women and culture and history.

> Men and women live on a stage, on which they act out their assigned roles, equal in importance. The play cannot go on without both types of performers. Neither of them contributes more or less to the whole; neither is marginal or dispensable. But the stage set is conceived, painted, defined by men. Men have written the play, have directed the show, interpreted the meanings of the action. They have assigned themselves the most interesting, most heroic parts, giving women the supporting roles. (Lerner 1986, 12)

Lerner continues by describing how women who become aware of the difference in the way they fit into the play ask for more equality in the role assignments. They might upstage the men or substitute for a missing male performer. Eventually, they win the struggle for the right of access to equal role assignment. But now "qualifications" are set by the men to judge which women may have access to these parts. Women who are docile are favored over women who wish to assume the right to interpret their own role or who—even more outrageously—want to rewrite the script. Lerner continues,

> It takes considerable time for the women to understand that getting "equal" parts will not make them equal, as long as the script, the props, the stage setting, and the direction are firmly held by men. When the women begin to realize that and cluster together between the acts, or even during the performance, to discuss what to do about it, this play comes to an end. (Lerner 1986, 13)

This power inequality between the sexes forms the basis for discrimination against women in society, much of it in the form of sexual harassment. Another point is made regarding women's history and education. Because women have been denied significant participation in the public realm and are largely absent from history, Lerner asserts that women have been unable to learn and build from other women's experience due to this historical deprivation. This deprivation of knowledge has caused women to continually reinvent the wheel regarding their plight. Lerner points out that it has been men that have selected the events to be recorded and have interpreted them so as to give them meaning and significance. Thus, the recorded and interpreted record of the past of the human race is only a partial record, in that it omits the past of half of human-kind, and it is distorted, in that it tells the story from the viewpoint of the male half of humanity only. (Lerner 1986, 4)

Patriarchy has led to women's lack of history, and this in turn leads to another area of deficit, namely women's lack of educational opportunities. It is this concept of education deprivation that, although improved for them in modern times, still inhibits women from participating fully in the public domain. In the past, women have not had the access to the education enjoyed by their brothers, and they have not had access to information by women in the same way that men have been able to access information by men. These are the two main deficits that continue to hamper women today. By lacking a history that has developed over many centuries and subsequently lacking the same access to information available to men, women continue to experience discrimination in the educational system.

The above description, although broad, clearly outlines the obstacles that women continue to encounter in their quest for equality within the larger society and in educational institutions. Change comes slowly, and the factor of male power and its exertion over women (personally and politically) is an important variable to consider when examining sex discrimination and sexual harassment on any level and in any context.

COURSE ORGANIZATION

The seven-week course is organized on Blackboard, a common platform for teaching both online and face to face at universities around the world. (See www.blackboard.com for more information.) It begins with a three-week overview of sexual harassment in the workplace and of Title VII. For the next three weeks students switch to Title IX and sexual harassment occurring in school and college. The final week covers street harassment, which does not fall under Title VII or IX but which is loosely governed by free speech and public safety laws (Nielsen 2005).

Course Outline

- Class 1. Introduction and overview of current theory and research on sexual harassment
- Class 2. Legal implications under Title VII
- Class 3. The intersection of gender, sexual harassment, and mental health issues

- Class 4. Mental health and health and treatment interventions for adults
- Class 5. Diversity issues in the workplace
- Class 6. Title IX and sexual harassment: Current research and theory
- Class 7. Mental health and health implications for children and adolescents
- Class 8. Treatment interventions for children and adolescents
- Class 9. Prevention and intervention programs for individuals, groups, and schools
- Class 10. Mental health and health: Implications for young adults in college
- Class 11. Policy applications that support positive school and work environments
- Class 12. Sexual harassment and sexual assault: Criminal justice perspectives
- Class 13. Street harassment and the public response
- Class 14. Final Exam: View *Oleanna* video and answer Blackboard exam questions

Course Description

This online course examines sexual harassment occurring in the workplace and education from a mental health and sexual violence perspective. Students acquire skills for assessing individuals who have experienced sexual harassment, and utilize current practice interventions regarding post-traumatic stress disorder, depression, and other negative mental health outcomes. Students apply concepts drawn from the behavioral and social sciences and from clinical and community practice to contemporary educational and corporate environments. Intervention techniques are identified for individuals and groups experiencing oppressive systems based on racial, gender, ethnic, sexual orientation, and class characteristics. The interplay of interpersonal, environmental, and cultural forces that influence discriminatory behavior by individuals and companies also is explored based on current theory and research. In addition to evaluating treatment options for sexual harassment victimization, students also analyze and evaluate strategies for preventing sexual harassment in schools and in the workplace.

Class assignments are different for undergraduate and graduate students. All students are expected to have a working knowledge of Title VII and Title IX, and to become familiar with mental health outcomes common to people experiencing sexual harassment. Graduate social work students are assigned more complex papers involving diagnosis and mental health treatment interventions for sexually harassed employees or students. Grades for baccalaureate-level students of social work and women's studies typically are based on quizzes and tests, and on one paper that describes an aspect of sexual harassment in education or work that interests the student. All students complete an online final exam. Students are expected to respond to texts, readings, websites, videos, and assignments each week via the Blackboard Discussion Board.

Course Texts

The course is organized around four texts. The first, *The Women's Movement against Sexual Harassment*, by Carrie Baker, provides an excellent historical background on sexual harassment and covers information regarding both Title VII and Title IX. The second, *Sexual Harassment and Bullying: A Guide to Keeping Kids Safe and Holding Schools Accountable*, by Susan Strauss, is geared toward Title IX and children, adolescents, and schools. It includes information about sexual harassment and bullying plus prevention education for schools. For information regarding sexual harassment and college students, the 2005 American Association of University Women report *Drawing the Line: Sexual Harassment on Campus* provides outcome data on that population.

Two first-person stories illustrate different aspects of sexual harassment. Bingham and Gansler's book, *Class Action* (2002), describes Lois Jensen's personal experience with sexual harassment at the Eveleth Taconite Company. This story was made into the 2005 movie *North Country*, starring Charlize Theron, and portrays the experience of women miners trying to maintain their jobs amid harassment from their male co-workers. The second story is Dr. Frances Conley's personal account of sexual harassment experienced while she was a professor of neurosurgery at Stanford University (Conley 1998). Both books demonstrate that neither social status nor age prevent women from experiencing sexual harassment and sex discrimination on the job.

Course Readings

In addition to textbook chapters, readings are assigned each week. Many of the articles are classic studies written by leading researchers in the field, such as Louise Fitzgerald, Nan Stein, Jennifer Berdahl, Vicki Magley, Craig Waldo, Fritz Drasgow, and James Gruber. Articles are provided in the sample syllabus under the notes section. These studies examine many settings where sexual harassment occurs—in the military; between men; at a teenager's place of work; between peers at school; of persons with disabilities and—unusual and counterintuitive—worker-to-supervisor sexual harassment. Some articles provide information about mental and physical health outcomes from sexual harassment, and others provide information on training and prevention education in the workplace or schools. Students begin to understand the depth and breadth of this issue—it occurs in all walks of life and a significant number of people are affected by this behavior.

Websites

The first module encourages students to explore websites that provide information on the rights of both workers and students and also the laws that protect them. Websites for the Equal Employment Opportunity Commission, the U.S. Department of Education Office on Civil Rights, and the American Bar Association are featured. All three are critical resources for students examining sexual harassment and discrimination. Students learn about various forms of sex discrimination—such as the "glass ceiling"—from websites such as that for the *Fact-Finding Report of the Federal Glass Ceiling Commission,* and that of the *Ethnic Majority,* which describes the glass ceiling for African, Hispanic (Latino), and Asian American women. Teen work issues are addressed on the *ABA Journal* website and the Equal Employment Opportunity Commission's Youth at Work website. This latter cites recent cases of teenagers who filed sexual harassment claims. The American Bar Association's website featuring an article by labor law firm, Fox and Grove, Chartered, depicts how businesses can prevent sexual harassment. Another website allows students to read the comprehensive Tailhook report on sexual harassment in the U.S. Navy.

The U.S. Department of Education Office on Civil Rights, and the Gay, Lesbian, Straight Education Network (GLSEN) provide information on Title IX and the harassment of sexual minority students. Human Rights Watch's report "Hatred in the Hallways" addresses issues pertinent to gay and lesbian teenagers. Bernice Sandler—popularly considered the "godmother" of Title IX—has on her website a personal account, *Too Strong for a Woman,* about filing the first lawsuit that initiated Title IX. Students also are encouraged to explore other websites of interest regarding women's issues and discrimination in general. The National Organization for Women and the Feminist Majority Foundation have activist websites that provide information on how students can get involved in advocating for women's rights. The Institute for Women's Policy Research tracks and analyzes employment information that affects women's income and overall security.

Videos

The course is anchored by one video, *North Country,* which loosely depicts Lois Jensen's experience with the Eveleth Taconite Company. It is particularly compelling because it displays sexual harassment as behaviors very threatening and dangerous to women. Many of my students come away with a raw understanding of how dangerous job situations can be for women, particularly in a male-dominated workplace.

Thanks to YouTube, Hulu, and other public venues on the Internet, videos that explain or demonstrate sexual harassment are available to students. For those interested in exploring the experience of teen workers and sexual harassment, ABC-TV's "Good Morning America" program has a video about teen baristas at Starbucks who have experienced sexual harassment on the job. PBS also has a video, "Is your daughter safe at work?", which outlines scenarios in which teenage girls are exposed to sexual harassment while working. There also is a variety of interviews available regarding notable public cases, such as the Supreme Court hearing with Clarence Thomas and Anita Hill, and Laura Leedy Gansler speaking out about Lois Jensen and her experience at the Eveleth Taconite Company.

Students explore the various clips of the Hill-Thomas hearings available on You Tube, however, at the time of writing this chapter, a new video "Anita" by Freida Mock has been released. The raw footage of the hearings has been compelling viewing for students and I certainly will consider adding the new "Anita" video to the course.

There also are a few videos providing detailed Title IX concerns. "Title IX: Don't Let Our Daughters Grow Up Without It" explains how this law has improved girls' access to education, and "Let's Get Real" tells the story of middle-school students dealing with the bullying and sexual harassment occurring in their school. It addresses many types of differences and shows how students can change their behavior and their school environment so that all students feel welcome.

Because sexual harassment also can include sexual assault and other forms of violent behaviors against women, students also watch the video "Montreal Massacre." This video details the 1989 singling out and killing of female engineering students at the Ecole Polytechnique in Montréal, by a male gunman who hated feminists and believed they ruined his prospects in life.

The final two modules deal with street harassment of women, a behavior not covered under Title VII or Title IX. The video "Hollaback!" is a wonderful example of activist women who refused to take such abuse anymore and started a grassroots effort to deal with rude, threatening, and dangerous behavior exhibited in public areas. The subway systems in major metropolitan areas now have hotlines, websites, and posters addressing the issue of harassment. Women (or men) can take pictures or videos of perpetrators and upload them to secure sites so that people can be warned and then police can identify and fine or arrest violators.

Hollaback! now is an international organization with 79 member cities in 26 countries.

The final exam includes viewing the video *Oleanna*, a film version of the play by David Mamet which is not for the faint of heart. This video and the final exam are explained in more detail below.

COURSE ASSIGNMENTS

Course assignments are straightforward and offer choices so that students can follow their interests. Students are required to write a paper on either Title VII or Title IX and demonstrate their knowledge of a variety of manifestations of sexual harassment. Students interested in workplace issues often choose Title VII, and those interested in children's issues frequently pick Title IX. Social work graduate students are required to include a second part in their papers and address mental health or health issues and a treatment intervention component. All students must address prevention education for either schools or the workplace. Undergraduates also are required to take online quizzes.

In addition to writing a paper, students also have online discussion board assignments. Each module has a set of questions pertaining to its readings or video. Students must post their answers and engage in online dialog with their classmates. The discussion about each module depends on how fired up students are about the material. Students find the Hill-Thomas hearings very provocative based on the line of questioning demonstrated by the Senate Hearing Committee members. There usually is a lot of debate about how both Hill and Thomas were questioned.

Another assignment requires that students share their workplace or internship sexual harassment policies. Students form online "Wikis" to critique these policies. Some become activists, taking suggested changes back to the workplace to improve their work environment. If a student is not working or interning I have them critique our university policy with their classmates. This has provided some interesting responses as students think critically about how protected they are at school.

All students are required to take a final exam. As mentioned earlier, the film *Oleanna* is used and students answer a set of questions and substantiate their answers. Students must outline the Title VII and Title IX issues presented by both main characters, and then explain which they believe are more compelling and why. As the film is somewhat ambiguous, the issues and answers are not clear-cut. Students have to think hard about the initial behaviors presented by each character and then re-evaluate them at the end of the movie. As poor judgment is portrayed and some questionable mental health issues are present, students have a lot to consider when writing their responses.

SUMMARY

I have enjoyed teaching this course both in person and online. Even more meaningful to me than providing an intellectually challenging course is seeing a student realize how their own life has been affected by these behaviors. Additionally, many students are parents and they have remarked on how prepared they now feel they are to deal with their child and their child's school with regard to issues of sexual harassment and bullying. This is one of those courses where you see the application of theory and knowledge to course assignments transfer to real life. By the end of the course the following objectives have been covered, and students' final papers demonstrate their knowledge and application of the material.

- Assess individuals who have experienced sexual harassment based on the application of current theory using both a mental health and social justice empowerment perspective.
- Assess factors that contribute to environmental stress and discrimination in institutions utilizing general systems theory.
- Understand environmental and individual issues that impact mental health practitioners and social workers in providing services to clients who have experienced sexual harassment.
- Demonstrate competence in intervening with individuals and institutions based on knowledge of gender, race, social class, sexual orientation, and disability to effect positive outcomes.
- Identify and analyze the complex ethical and value issues faced by individuals who experience sexual harassment and the institutions that discriminate.
- Critically examine cultural assumptions about age, gender, race, social class, sexual orientation, and disability that contribute to sexual harassment in education and the workplace.
- Explore and analyze gender assumptions in traditional methodologies, theories and research of various disciplines that pertain to race, social class, sexual orientation, disability, and discriminatory behavior.
- Demonstrate knowledge of biological, psychological, and social aspects of discrimination and differences created by gender, race, social class, sexual orientation, and disability.
- Demonstrate knowledge of practice evaluation procedures and ethical research considerations based on gender, race, social class, sexual orientation, and disability when working with clients and institutions regarding issues of sexual harassment and discrimination.
- Develop and utilize a multidisciplinary approach in working collaboratively with other professionals that addresses sexism and sexist

attitudes and advocates for agency functioning which is nondiscriminating.

For those interested in organizing a course on sexual harassment, there is an abbreviated syllabus located at the end of this chapter that includes resources and articles. As educators, each of us brings an abundance of experience from our walk of life, so a course on sexual harassment can take many forms depending on the organizer. My particular lens embodies social justice, criminal justice, and mental health, but there is a variety of information to cover no matter what your focus.

Teaching practice courses to social work students always has been rewarding, mostly because the students are so eager to learn how to help people. Their enthusiasm for the course material is a joy for any professor who worries about being boring or irrelevant. Teaching a course on sexual harassment also has been personally satisfying to me, and the material dovetails beautifully with my passion for social work. Students find that sexual harassment, sex discrimination, and power inequality in society resonate with them; and their passion for the material is wonderful to observe. In an analogous fashion to social work, students apply their new knowledge both to their clients and to themselves. It is the observation of this self-growth and new understanding of themselves and their environment that is so satisfying. As a professor, I feel honored to see my students end the class feeling empowered and better positioned to not only help their clients but also to help themselves and everyone else in their challenging lives.

REFERENCES

American Association of University Women (AAUW) Educational Foundation. (2011). *Crossing the Line: Sexual harassment at school.* Washington, DC: Author.

Baker, C. N. (2008). *The women's movement against sexual harassment.* New York: Cambridge University Press.

Bingham, C., and Gansler, L. L. (2002). *Class action: The story of Lois Jenson and the landmark case that changed sexual harassment law.* New York: Doubleday.

Conley, F. K. (1998). *Walking out on the boys.* New York: Farrar, Straus and Giroux.

Fineran, S. (2002). Sexual harassment between same-sex peers: The intersection of mental health, homophobia, and sexual violence in schools. *Social Work* 47 (1), 65–74.

Fineran, S., and Bolen, R. M. (2006). Risk factors for peer sexual harassment in schools. *Journal of Interpersonal Violence* 21, 1169–1190.

Fitzgerald, L. F., Shullman, S., Baily, N., Richards, M., Swecker, J., Gold, Y., Oremerod, A. J., and Weitzman, L. (1988). The incidence and dimensions of sexual harassment in academia and the workplace. *Journal of Vocational Behavior* 32, 152–175.

Grove City College v. Bell, 465 U.S. 555 (1984).

Gruber, J. E., and Fineran, S. (2008). Comparing the impact of bullying and sexual harassment victimization on the mental and physical health of adolescents. *Sex Roles* 59 (1–2), 1–13.

Langelan, M. J. (1993). *Back off*. New York: Simon and Schuster.

Lerner, G. (1986). *The creation of patriarchy*. New York: The Oxford University Press.

MacKinnon, C. A. (1979). *Sexual harassment of working women*. New Haven, CT: Yale University Press.

Nielsen, L. B. (2005). *License to harass: Law, hierarchy, and offensive public speech (The cultural lives of law)*. Princeton, NJ: Princeton University Press.

Sandler, B. R., and Hughes, J. O. (1988). Project on the Status and Education of Women, Association of American Colleges. *Peer harassment: Hassles for women on campus*. Washington, DC.

Strauss, S. (2011). *Sexual harassment and bullying: A guide to keeping kids safe and holding schools accountable*. Lanham, Maryland: Rowman & Littlefield Publishers.

Title VII, Civil Rights Act of 1964, 42 U.S.C. § 2000e (1994).

Title IX, Education Amendments of 1972. Federal Register, Part II Department of Education. 45, 30955–30965.

VIDEOS

Chasnoff, D., Cohen, H. S., and Stilley, K. (Producers), and Chasnoff, D. (Director). (2005). *Let's Get Real* [DVD]. United States: Groundspark.

Hubert, N. (Producer), and Rogers, G. (Director). (1990). *After the Montreal Massacre* [DVD]. Canada: National Film Board of Canada.

Levine, H. (Producer), and Hadleigh-West, M. (Director). (1998). *War Zone* [DVD]. United States: A Film Fatale, Inc. / Hank Levine Film GmbH Production.

Mock, F. (Producer), and Mock, F. (Director). (2014). *Anita: Speaking Truth to Power* [Motion picture]. United States: Samuel Goldwyn Films.

Wechsler, N. (Producer), and Caro, N. (Director). (2005). *North Country* [Motion picture]. United States: Warner Brothers.

Wolff, P., and Green, S. (Producers), and Mamet, D. (Director). (1994). *Oleanna* [Motion picture]. United States: Metro Goldwyn Meyer Company.

WEBSITES

AAUW Report: Drawing the line: Sexual harassment on campus. http://history.aauw.org/files/2013/01/DTLFinal.pdf. Accessed April 20, 2015.

ABC Good Morning America. Trouble brewing at Starbucks. http://www.hulu.com/watch/122462. Accessed April 20, 2015.

ABC TV. Teen barista sues over "sex demands." http://abcnews.go.com/2020/video/teen-barista-sues-sex-demands-9640426. Accessed April 20, 2015.

After the Montreal Massacre. https://www.nfb.ca/film/after_the_montreal_massacre. Accessed April 20, 2015.

Equal Employment Opportunity Commission. http://www.eeoc.gov/laws /types/sexual_harassment.cfm. Accessed April 20, 2015.

Equal Employment Opportunity Commission. EEOC teen cases of sexual harassment. http://www.eeoc.gov/youth//cases.html. Accessed April 20, 2015.

Ethnic Majority Website. http://www.ethnicmajority.com/glass_ceiling .htm. Accessed April 20, 2015.

Feminist Majority Foundation. http://www.feminist.org/911/harass.html. Accessed April 20, 2015.

Gay, Lesbian & Straight Education Network. http://glsen.org/webinars. Accessed April 20, 2015.

Good for business: Making full use of the nation's human capital. http://md cbowen.org/p2/rm/aa/GlassCeiling.pdf. Accessed April 20, 2015.

Hollaback! http://hollabacknyc.blogspot.com/2007/06/war-zone.html. Accessed April 20, 2015.

Institute for Women's Policy Research. http://www.iwpr.org/. Accessed April 20, 2015.

Interview on NPR with Laura Leedy Gansler regarding Lois Jensen. http://www .npr.org/templates/story/story.php?storyId=1145275. Accessed April 20, 2015.

New troubles for teens at work. http://www.abajournal.com/magazine/new _troubles_for_teens_at_work/. Accessed April 20, 2015.

Oleanna. https://www.youtube.com/watch?v=P2KFG4ZibCQ. Accessed April 20, 2015.

PBS Program: Is your daughter safe at work? http://www.pbs.org/now /shows/508/. Accessed April 20, 2015.

Sexual Harassment: The employer's role in prevention. http://www.abanet.org /genpractice/magazine/1996/winter/w96shi.html. Accessed April 20, 2015.

Sexual harassment and Title IX. http://www2.edc.org/WomensEquity/pubs /digests/digest-title9-harass.html. Accessed April 20, 2015.

Sexual harassment in the workplace: A primer. http://www3.uakron.edu/lawrev /robert1.html. Accessed April 20, 2015.

"Too strong for a woman." The Five Words that Made Title IX a Reality. http:// bernicesandler.com/id44.htm. Accessed April 20, 2015.

U.S. Department of Education/Sex Discrimination. http://www.ed.gov/policy /rights/guid/ocr/sex.html. Accessed April 20, 2015.

Chapter 14

Sexual Harassment Training: Effective Strategies

William E. Schweinle and Christopher P. Roseman

Although attention to the problem of sexual harassment has increased in the last 30 years, its frequency appears to remain rather high. In the mid-1990s, for instance, approximately one-third of women employed in the health care sector claimed to be the victims of sexual harassment in the workplace (Burda 1996). A decade later, in 2004, the Equal Employment Opportunity Commission received 13,136 charges of sexual harassment; of the total, 15.1% were filed by men. In 2001, the American Association of University Women (AAUW 2001) reported that 81% of students are sexually harassed at some time during their education, with 59% reporting frequent sexual harassment. Given the attention sexual harassment has received, the more stringent criminal and civil laws against sexual harassment, and the training hours (and dollars) spent educating workers, such data are unexpected and thus are quite alarming.

Examples of sexual harassment even can be found within the perceived sanctity of the legal system itself. Widespread harassment and discrimination against female employees has occurred within the Los Angeles Police Department (LAPD). In one instance, the City of Los Angeles and LAPD officials agreed to pay $165,000 to a former female officer who was raped by a male colleague on Police Academy grounds in 1990. At the time, this particular case was the fifth case that dealt directly with sexual harassment within the LAPD (Williams & Kleiner 2001). An examination of these cases revealed a common theme of power and control in which the perpetrators acknowledged trying to protect themselves by covering up feelings or emotions tied to their victim. Outwardly the individuals appear strong; inside, however, they are not in control and are dealing with a multitude of mixed emotions, such as insecurity, anxiousness, or even anger. Oftentimes, to regain control, individuals attempt to compensate for this sense of losing control by becoming more rigid in not only their thinking but also in their behaviors, and do not choose appropriate responses.

Lenhart (2004) found that, when a sexual harassment case goes into litigation, there are no winners. Lenhart demonstrates this through case-based narratives and clearly shows that sexual harassment litigation probably is not a good place for sexual harassment victims to seek justice. Rather, it is more a gladiatorial arena that leaves everyone hurt. Prevention seems to be the best approach.

Further, sexual harassment results in lost productivity for an organization (see Paludi & Paludi 2003, for a review). Despite the painful consequences for sexual harassment plaintiffs, however, sexual harassment often is serious enough to warrant legal action. Thus, effective prevention is worth the expense and effort. Organizations are encouraged (if not outright ordered) by their attorneys to enact a structured, detailed, and comprehensive sexual harassment training and policy (Bisom-Rapp 2001; Martucci & Lu 2005; Perry, Kulik & Field 2009). Taken together, these findings suggest the need for thorough and ongoing assessment and development of more effective sexual harassment training methods.

SEXUAL HARASSMENT TRAINING

Most organizations, in fact, are committed to preventing sexual harassment by training their employees. In fact, as of 2005, 90% of U.S. businesses had employees participate in some form of sexual harassment training (Dolezalek 2005). Many businesses go so far as to have employees acknowledge by signature that they have received the training. Newman, Jackson, and Baker (2003) note that the sexual harassment training literature seems to share one conclusion: Sexual harassment training is vital to sexual harassment policy. Lastly, Reese and Lindenberg (2004) found that most people tend to view sexual harassment training as "very important." Given these findings, it would seem that sexual harassment training is widely provided and generally appreciated in organizations.

Despite these widespread practices, however, sexual harassment continues to be pervasive (Gruber 1997) and continues to create negative consequences for organizations and victims (Benson & Thomson 1982; Charney & Russell 1994; Collinsworth, Fitzgerald & Drasgow 2009; Fitzgerald, Drasgow, Hulin, Gelfand & Magey 1997; Gutek 1985; Rederstorff, Buchanan & Settles 2007; Richman, Flaherty & Rospenda 1996; Richman, Flaherty, Rospenda & Christensen 1992; Richman, Rospenda, Nawyn, Flaherty, Fendrich, Drum & Johnson 1999; Schneider, Swan & Fitzgerald 1997; Yagil 2008; Yoon, Funk & Kropf 2010).

Primarily for these reasons, this chapter reviews the literature relevant to the effectiveness of sexual harassment training and offers some suggestions based on recent scientific findings for possibly improving such training. It starts with an overview of organizational codes of ethics, their role in preventing sexual harassment, and their role as sources of learning objectives for sexual harassment training.

CODE OF ETHICS

An organizational code of ethics must promote and enforce the organization's commitment that each employee acts within the boundaries of professional comportment in successfully representing and working in their place of employment. One of the most simplistic strategies to educate employees on regarding sexual harassment is to teach how to "self-communicate." Employees must ask themselves, "Will this decision cost me or the company?" Lipman argues that a large number of sexual harassment cases could be avoided if employees simply paused for a moment to ask themselves this question before acting (Lipman 1997).

The Code of Ethics is a two-pronged tenet that requires organizations to protect the employee within the work environment and describes for all employees a comprehensive policy of a higher moral and professional code. The Code is expected to be understood by all internal staff members—including all new hires at orientation—and is critical to establishing the rights of individuals within an organization and within the framework of daily interaction. At all times, a compliant organization will provide the following to all/each staff/employee:

- A nonhostile work environment
- An anonymous and secure system for employees to report sexual harassment and ethical concerns
- Quick and responsive, unbiased, comprehensive, and objective investigation of all claims
- A safe and courteous atmosphere for the client population and employees
- An environment devoid of preferential treatment

- An environment devoid of preferential treatment or discrimination based on gender
- Interim and annual training sessions conducted by the ethics committee for each employee, to assess knowledge and judgment in possible sexual harassment situations.
- A human resources staff with specialists in sexual harassment emotional support
- Security personnel with investigative training in sexual harassment case procedure
- An in-house syndicate dedicated to preventing further cases of sexual harassment

A more thorough, well-written discussion of sexual harassment policy development can be found in Paludi and Paludi (2003). We suggest that the above Code of Ethics can serve along with the recommendations by Paludi and Paludi as "talking points," and add that they could serve as a template around which sexual harassment training can be designed.

SEXUAL HARASSMENT TRAINING

Sexual harassment training is designed to teach organization members to inculcate the Code of Ethics into their relationships with coworkers and into their relationship with the organization. There are several sexual harassment training programs available and some well-established guidelines (see Paludi & Paludi 2003). Some are internally developed and some are commercially available (Newman, Jackson & Baker 2003).

Kaufman (2011), for instance, reported on a training program that he developed and that was adopted for use by several United Nations subentities. This program is designed to help workers learn from sexual harassment incidents and to restore a workplace that has been damaged by sexual harassment. On one hand, Kaufman reported that all of the feedback he has received about his program from human relations personnel and other staff members has been positive. On the other hand, there has not been an independent evaluation of Kaufman's method; it therefore is difficult to draw any conclusions about its effectiveness.

There are some "best practices" that guide much of the sexual harassment training being conducted (Perry, Kulik, Bustamante & Golom 2010). These best practices include conducting a pre-training assessment of the trainees and the organization to optimize the training to the needs of the organization and the trainees, and delivering training that is based on learning objectives and is methodologically designed to best achieve the objectives. Methods to use can include role-playing, lecture, and video. Objectives can include interpersonal skill development, recognition and response to sexual harassment incidents, and knowledge of sexual harassment policies and laws. A third best practice involves post-training activities that reinforce the training within the organizational context, including refresher training and an atmosphere that allows trainees to utilize their newly taught skills.

Several authors have noted that, however, regardless of training method or philosophy or requirement, there is a paucity of systematic investigation into the actual effectiveness of sexual harassment training (Goldberg 2011; Newman, Jackson & Baker 2003; M. Paludi cited in Perry, Kulik & Field 2009). There is substantial empirical literature addressing whether sexual harassment training is popular or unpopular with participants (Newman, Jackson & Baker 2003). There also is scientific evidence that sexual harassment training can change people's attitudes and their ability to recognize sexual harassment when it occurs (Antecol & Cobb-Clark 2003; Kearney, Rochlen & King 2004; York, Barclay & Zajack 1997).

Still, there is not any direct evidence that the frequency of sexual harassment has decreased as a result of sexual harassment training (M. Paludi as cited in June 2009). This could be due to the psychometric and other problems that investigators face when trying to measure their ultimate outcome variable: the frequency of sexual harassment. (See DeSouza & Solberg 2003, and Paludi & Paludi 2003, for a discussion of some of the psychometric obstacles to measuring sexual harassment.)

INDIRECT EVIDENCE OF WHAT WORKS

There are training and policy factors that have been indirectly shown to help reduce sexual harassment. Again, however, this evidence comes from indirect measurement of sexual harassment training effectiveness, for example trainee, trainer, and manager opinions and attitudes; and trainees' ability to recognize sexual harassment when it occurs. It is important to note that although sexual harassment training does appear to change attitudes regarding sexual harassment, this effect seems to be a function of the attitude measures used (Lonsway, Cortina & Magley 2008).

Context

There is some evidence that the context of the training bears on its effectiveness (Kraiger, McLinden & Casper 2004; Perry, Kulik & Field 2009). For instance, an organizational climate that is not tolerant of sexual harassment—one that allows trainees to use the training and includes supportive supervisors—appears to improve training effectiveness. Having sufficient resources for sexual harassment training reinforces this idea. Similarly, helping trainees understand *why* sexual harassment training is helpful to the organization and to the employees seems to help. Lastly, having a balanced job gender ratio, positive perception of management's leadership style, and prior socialization appear to improve the likelihood that sexual harassment training will be effective (Cogin & Fish 2007).

Who Sexual Harassment Training Seems to Affect Most

There are some differences in how people perceive the effectiveness of sexual harassment training. Newman, Jackson, and Baker (2003) found that single workers, men, and older workers tend to see sexual harassment training as more effective than do younger workers. Conversely, people with more education, higher pay-grades, and divorcees tend to see sexual harassment training as less effective. Intuitively, recent victims of sexual harassment also tend to view sexual harassment training as less effective. Although these results could appear to suggest for whom sexual harassment training might be improved, they do not speak directly to the objectively measured effectiveness of that training on sexual harassment behaviors.

Several findings support the attitudinal and learning effect that sexual harassment training has on men (Beauvais 1986; Blakely, Blakely & Moorman 1998; Moyer & Nath 1998). More recent results reported by Robb and Doverspike (2001), however, suggest that men who are high in sexual harassment proclivity (Pryor 1987) are not as likely (if at all) to be affected by training. This suggests the need for developing training designed specifically for men who are high in sexual harassment proclivity.

Men who participated in sexual harassment training could correctly identify incidents of sexual harassment more frequently than they could prior to the training (Antecol & Cobb-Clark 2003; Kearney, Rochlen & King 2004; York, Barclay & Zajack 1997), which supports the effectiveness of training male workers. This is an especially promising finding, given that the majority of sexual harassment is perpetrated by men. Men, however, were not less likely to tolerate workplace sexual harassment after receiving training (Kearney, Rochlen & King 2004). Further, the relationship between attitude and behavior is a relatively imperfect one (c.f. Ajzen & Fishbein 1977). Thus, until more direct evidence is collected, these findings offer some support (although it is not strong) for the conclusion that focusing sexual harassment training on male audiences will result in reduced sexual harassment.

Perry, Kulik, and Field (2009) report that trainees who are more mastery-motivated (e.g., those who are motivated to learn for its own sake rather than just to perform well on a test) will learn more from training. Whether this learning results in changes in behavior has not been documented at the time of this writing.

Goldberg (2007) studied an interesting aspect of sexual harassment training: its effect on potential victims. Trainees were taught to use a confrontational ("voice") strategy when sexually harassed, as opposed to an "exit" strategy, for example leaving the room or changing the subject. A voice strategy involves stating in clear terms to the harasser that the behavior is sexual harassment, that it is not acceptable, and that it should not happen again. Note that this strategy has been very well described in very accessible prose by Howard (2007). Goldberg found that people who were trained in *voice* strategy reported being more likely to confront a sexual harasser than people who did not receive *voice* training. However, this effect appeared to be moderated by the trainees' tendency to avoid conflict.

Whether confrontation (that is, "voice") training actually results in more use of voice strategy and whether use of voice strategy actually results in less sexual harassment has not been empirically demonstrated. Still, as Plaut (2008) notes, perhaps training in clearly establishing interpersonal and psychological boundaries in the workplace is a step toward more effective sexual harassment training.

The Trainer

Perry and colleagues (Perry, Kulik & Field 2009) also argue that the characteristics of the trainer are important to changing trainee attitudes. More motivating and knowledgeable trainers, for instance, should better improve attitudes. Several authors (Carey 1998; Milite 1999; Reinhart 1999) have suggested that outside consultants offer more motivating and more specifically knowledgeable trainers, who seem better able to create attitude change. There does not appear to be any direct evidence, however, that this is the case.

Quinn (2002) conducted an in-depth qualitative study of 43 working men and women and concluded that sexual harassment, specifically "girl watching," by men could be more an "act of ignoring" than an "act of ignorance." If this is the case, then sexual harassment training that focuses more on the "ignoring" behavior instead of the potential "ignorance" might be more effective; however, there is no direct evidence to support this conclusion.

The Training Itself

Perry, Kulik, and Field (2009) reviewed the relevant literature and argued that some characteristics of the training are vital to its impact. Having clear and common objectives (Biviano 1997; Newman, Jackson & Baker 2003), for instance, which include training in how to most effectively communicate in the workplace would help. Perry and colleagues further argue that role-playing and behavioral modelling also could be effective learning strategies.

Sogunro (2004) found that more-passive training methods—such as using a video or lecture—are less likely to change trainee attitudes. Similarly, June (2009) suggested that online sexual harassment training methods tend to foster a "check the box" mentality and that "one size fits all" online training is not as likely to change attitudes as is face-to-face training that enables trainees to explore the more subtle gray areas of sexual harassment and allows a trainer to take advantage of potential "teachable moments." Thus, face-to-face sexual harassment training that can be optimized to the audience appears to offer more potential for change. As noted below, however, differential effects from different training methods to not appear to be significant (Perry, Kulik, Bustamante & Golom 2010).

Some authors have suggested that sexual harassment training be mandatory for all employees (c.f. Orlov & Roumell 1999). There is no direct evidence, however, to support requiring sexual harassment training. Additionally, in terms of organizational training in general (and not sexual harassment training specifically), making training voluntary (versus mandatory) appears to increase learning and compliance (Salas, Cannon-Bowers, Rhodenizer & Bowers 1999). It stands to reason, then, that making sexual harassment training optional—but somehow encouraging the attendance of everyone in an organization—would be an effective strategy.

Another possible direction—although only theoretical and not yet supported—for sexual harassment training could extend from Quinn's (2002) argument and arguments put forth by Schweinle, Cofer, and Schatz (2009) and by Schweinle and Roseman (2011). Schweinle and colleagues found that men who were deficient in their empathic accuracy and biased to over-attribute criticism and rejection to women were more likely to sexually harass women (Schweinle, Cofer & Schatz 2009). Schweinle and Ickes (2007) found that more-abusive husbands also had this interpersonal bias, and that the more-abusive men maintained this inaccurate biased perceptual style by ignoring ("tuning out") women's emotional expressions and substituting inferences of criticism and rejection. If "tuning women out" (an act of ignorance or perhaps "active ignorance") also is a characteristic of male sexual harassers, then this would further support Quinn's conclusion. Roseman, Ritchie, and Laux (2009) made a similar plausible argument regarding the treatment of sex offenders.

Further, empathic accuracy training (Barone, Hutchings, Kimmel, Traub, Cooper & Marshall 2005) could be included in sexual harassment training curricula and might help reduce the incidence of sexual harassment. At minimum, workers would better understand one another. Lastly, this suggestion is further supported by an argument put forth by Olowu and Ilesanmi (2008) for a more psychotherapeutic approach to sexual harassment. At present, however, this is only speculation.

DIRECT EVIDENCE OF WHAT WORKS

"Best Practices"

Perry, Kulik, Bustamante, and Golom (2010) surveyed 288 human resources and personnel directors across a variety of organizations that reported having sexual harassment training. As noted above, business training "best practices" include a pre-training assessment, optimized training design and delivery, and post-training activities. Respondents were asked to note the inclusion (or omission) of various sexual harassment training best practices and to report on the success of the sexual harassment training within their organization. These reports included whether the number of sexual harassment complaints increased, decreased, or remained the same as the levels before the training. This rich dataset allowed Perry and colleagues to statistically compare among each of the three best practices in terms of resultant sexual harassment training success; that is, any change in the frequency of sexual harassment complaints. It is important to note that although the frequency of sexual harassment complaints might reflect the actual frequency of sexual harassment and could serve as a legal measure, it is not, as such, a direct scientific measure of sexual harassment frequency.

Interestingly, Perry and colleagues (Perry et al. 2010) found that the *only* best practice that appears to have any effect on sexual harassment training success was to include post-training activities. Post-training activities do appear to lessen the frequency of sexual harassment complaints. This effect, however, is moderated by *why* the organization held the training. Some organizations justify, contextualize, and conduct sexual harassment training to avoid legal repercussions. Other organizations use a more strategic motivational approach in which sexual harassment training is presented in the context of how both attending the training and refraining from sexual harassment can further the organization's (and the individual's) goals. The latter approach—an organizationally strategic method—does work and fits well with the finding by Salas, Cannon-Bowers, Rhodenizer, and Bowers (1999) that when people understand and want the benefits of sexual harassment training, they will reap those benefits. This also speaks to the importance of effective organizational leadership.

CONCLUSION

There currently are several sexual harassment training programs, curricula, and methods available. Unfortunately, based on ongoing and longitudinal studies of sexual harassment prevalence, it is clear that sexual harassment persists. This suggests that sexual harassment training might not be entirely effective.

For this reason, this chapter reviewed some of the evidence supporting the efficacy of sexual harassment training. The review suggests that, despite a substantial body of evidence that indirectly supports the efficacy of sexual harassment training, there is no scientifically strong evidence that sexual harassment decreases as a result of sexual harassment training. Studies have shown that sexual harassment training results in attitude change among trainees and that trainees—particularly male trainees—are better able to identify sexual harassment after training and the frequency of sexual harassment reports increases.

As yet, however, there does not appear to be a study that directly measures actual sexual harassment incidence rates before and after training. Further still, there does not appear to be a study reported in which people or organizations were randomly assigned into either a "training" group or a "no training" control group and monitored over time for actual frequency of sexual harassment—not reports of sexual harassment, but the actual frequency of incidents. Such a randomized controlled study would very clearly indicate whether sexual harassment training indeed is effective.

As Michele Paludi (as cited in June 2009) and several other authors have argued, there is a significant need for more research into the effects of sexual harassment training on the actual frequency of sexual harassment. Such research also might inform the development of more effective sexual harassment training and, perhaps, the cessation of sexual harassment altogether.

Conversely, it stands to reason that sexual harassment training at minimum serves as a warning to potential sexual harassers—a warning that, once given, allows the organization to legally and morally terminate such an employee. As long as the organization is willing to sever its relationship with a sexual harasser, this sends the message throughout the organization that the sincerity of the organization's code of ethics and sexual harassment policies are not to be tested. This, by itself, is a good argument for the effectiveness of sexual harassment training.

REFERENCES

Ajzen, I., and Fishbein, M. (1977). Attitude-behavior relations: A theoretical analysis and review of empirical research. *Psychological Bulletin* 84, 888–918.

American Association of University Women (AAUW) (2001). *Hostile hallways: Bullying, teasing and sexual harassment*. Washington, DC: Harris Interactive Research.

Antecol, H., and Cobb-Clark, D. (2003). Does sexual harassment training change attitudes? A view from the federal level. *Social Science Quarterly* 84, 826–842.

Barone, D. F., Hutchings, P. S., Kimmel, H. J., Traub, H. L., Cooper, J. T., and Marshall, C. M. (2005). Increasing empathic accuracy through practice and feedback in a clinical interviewing course. *Journal of Social and Clinical Psychology* 24, 156–171.

Beauvais, K. (1986). Workshops to combat sexual harassment: A case study of changing attitudes. *Journal of Women in Culture and Society* 12, 130–145.

Benson, D., and Thomson, G. (1982). Sexual harassment on a university campus: The confluence of authority relations, sexual interest and gender stratification. *Social Problems* 29, 236–251.

Bisom-Rapp, S. (2001). An ounce of prevention is a poor substitute for a pound of cure: Confronting the developing jurisprudence of education and prevention in employment discrimination law. *Berkeley Journal of Employment and Labor Law* 22, 1–47.

Biviano, D. (1997).Training effectiveness of a sexual harassment training program. PhD Dissertation. Spokane, WA: Gonzaga University.

Blakely, G., Blakely, E., and Moorman, R. (1998). The effects of training on perceptions of sexual harassment allegations. *Journal of Applied Social Psychology* 28, 71–83.

Burda, D. (1996). ACHE survey response spurs expedited sexual harassment policy. *Modern Healthcare* 26, 2. http://search.proquest.com/docview/211917247?accountid=13044. Accessed March 21, 2011.

Carey, R. (1998). Hazardous material. *Successful Meetings* 47, 42–53.

Charney, D., and Russell, R. (1994). An overview of sexual harassment. *American Journal of Psychiatry* 151, 10–17.

Cogin, J., and Fish, A. (2007). Managing sexual harassment more strategically: An analysis of environmental causes. *Asia Pacific Journal of Human Resources* 45, 333–352.

Collinsworth, L., Fitzgerald, L., and Drasgow, F. (2009). In harm's way: Factors related to psychological distress following sexual harassment. *Psychology of Women Quarterly* 33, 475–490.

DeSouza, E., and Solberg, J. (2003). Incidence and dimensions of sexual harassment across cultures. In *Academic and workplace sexual harassment,* edited by M. Paludi and C. Paludi, 3–30. Westport, CT: Praeger.

Dolezalek, H. (2005). 2005 industry report. *Training* 41, 14–28.

Fitzgerald, L., Drasgow, F., Hulin, C., Gelfand, M., and Magey, V. (1997). Antecedents and consequences of sexual harassment in organizations: A test of an integrated model. *Journal of Applied Psychology* 82, 578–589.

Goldberg, C. (2011). What do we really know about sexual harassment training effectiveness? In *Praeger handbook on understanding and preventing workplace discrimination,* edited by M. Paludi, C. Paludi, and E. DeSouza, 45–48. Santa Barbara, CA: Praeger.

Goldberg, C. (2007). The impact of training and conflict avoidance on responses to sexual harassment. *Psychology of Women Quarterly* 31, 62–72.

Gruber, J. E. (1997). An epidemiology of sexual harassment: Evidence from North America and Europe. In *Sexual harassment: Theory, research, and treatment,* edited by W. O'Donohue, 84–98. Boston: Allyn & Bacon.

258 Sexual Harassment in Education and Work Settings

Gutek, B. (1985). *Sex and the workplace*. San Francisco, CA: Jossey-Bass.

Howard, L. G. (2007). *The sexual harassment handbook*. Pompton Plains, NJ: Career Press.

June, A. (2009, February 20). Online programs to stop sexual harassment: Easy to use but not always enough. *Chronicle of Higher Education* 55, A10–A13.

Kaufman, M. (2011). Red light, green light: A more effective approach to preventing and responding productively to workplace harassment. In *Praeger handbook on understanding and preventing workplace discrimination*, edited by M. Paludi, C. Paludi, and E. DeSouza, 39–44. Westport, CT: Praeger.

Kearney, L., Rochlen, A., and King, E. (2004). Male gender role conflict, sexual harassment tolerance, and the efficacy of a psychoeducative training program. *Psychology of Men and Masculinity* 5, 72–82.

Kraiger, K., McLinden, D., and Casper, W. (2004). Collaborative planning for training impact. *Human Resource Management* 43, 337–351.

Lenhart, S. (2004). *Clinical aspects of sexual harassment and gender discrimination: Psychological consequences and treatment interventions*. New York: Brunner-Routledge.

Lipman, P. (1997). Restructuring in context: A case study of teacher participation and the dynamics of ideology, race, and power. *American Educational Research Journal* 34, 3–37.

Lonsway, K., Cortina, L., and Magley, V. (2008). Sexual harassment mythology: Definition, conceptualization and measurement. *Sex Roles* 58, 599–615.

Martucci, W., and Lu, Z. (2005). Sexual-harassment training: The wave of the future in state legislative efforts. *Employment Relations Today* 32, 87–95.

Milite, G. (1999). What you know about harassment can hurt you. *Human Relations Focus* 76, 9–10.

Moyer, R., and Nath, A. (1998). Some effects of brief training interventions on perceptions of sexual harassment. *Journal of Applied Social Psychology* 28, 333–356.

Newman, M., Jackson, R., and Baker, D. (2003). Sexual harassment in the federal workplace. *Public Administration Review* 63, 472–483.

Olowu, A., and Ilesanmi, O. (2008). Psychotherapy for peace and conflict resolution. *Psychologia: An International Journal* 16, 153–172.

Orlov, D., and Roumell, M. (1999). *What every manager needs to know about sexual harassment*. New York: AMACOM.

Paludi, C., and Paludi, M. (2003). Developing and enforcing effective policies, procedures, and training programs for educational institutions and businesses. In *Academic and workplace sexual harassment: A handbook of cultural, social science, management, and legal perspectives*, edited by M. Paludi and C. Paludi, 175–198. Westport, CT: Praeger.

Perry, E., Kulik, C., Bustamante, J., and Golom, F. (2010). The impact of reason for training on the relationship between "best practices" and sexual harassment training effectiveness. *Human Resources Development Quarterly* 21, 187–208.

Perry, E., Kulik, C., and Field, M. (2009). Sexual harassment training: Recommendations to address gaps between practitioner and research literatures. *Human Resource Management* 48, 817–837.

Plaut, M. (2008). Sexual and nonsexual boundaries in professional relationships: Principles and teaching guidelines. *Sexual and Relationship Therapy* 23, 181.

Pryor, J. (1987). Sexual harassment proclivities in men. *Sex Roles* 17, 269–290.

Quinn, B. (2002). Sexual harassment and masculinity: The power and meaning of "girl watching." *Gender and Society* 16, 386–402.

Redersdorff, J., Buchanan, N., and Settles, I. (2007). The moderating roles of race and gender role attitudes in the relationship between sexual harassment and psychological well-being. *Psychology of Women Quarterly* 31, 50–61.

Reese, L., and Lindenberg, K. (2004). Employee satisfaction with sexual harassment policies: The training connection. *Public Personnel Management* 33, 99–119.

Reinhart, A. (1999). *Sexual harassment: Addressing sexual harassment in the workplace—A management information booklet*. Geneva, Switzerland: International Labour Office.

Richman, J., Flaherty, J., and Rospenda, K. (1996). Perceived workplace harassment experiences and problem drinking among physicians: Broadening the stress/alienation paradigm. *Addiction* 91, 391–403.

Richman, J., Flaherty, J., Rospenda, K., and Christensen, M. (1992). Mental health consequences and correlates of medical student abuse. *Journal of the American Medical Association* 267, 692–694.

Richman, J., Rospenda, K., Nawyn, S., Flaherty, J., Fendrich, M., Drum, M., and Johnson, T. (1999). Sexual harassment and generalized workplace abuse among university employees: Prevalence and mental health correlates. *American Journal of Public Health 89*, 358–363.

Robb, L., and Doverspike, D. (2001). Self-reported proclivity to harass as a moderator of the effectiveness of sexual harassment–prevention training. *Psychological Reports* 88, 85–88.

Roseman, C. P., Ritchie, M., and Laux, J. M. (2009). A restorative justice approach to empathy development in sex offenders: An exploratory study. *Journal of Addictions & Offender Counseling* 29, 96–109.

Salas, E., Cannon-Bowers, J., Rhodenizer, L., and Bowers, C. (1999). Training in organizations: Myths, misconceptions, and mistaken assumptions. *Research in Personnel and Human Resource Management* 17, 123–161.

Schneider, K., Swan, S., and Fitzgerald, L. (1997). Job-related and psychological effects of sexual harassment in the workplace: Empirical evidence from two organizations. *Journal of Applied Psychology* 82, 401–415.

Schweinle, W., Cofer, C., and Schatz, S. (2009). Men's sexual harassment of women and men's biased inferences of women's criticism and rejection. *Sex Roles* 60, 142–150.

Schweinle, W., and Ickes, W. (2007). The role of men's critical/rejecting overattribution bias, affect and attentional disengagement in marital aggression. *Journal of Social and Clinical Psychology* 26, 175–199.

Schweinle, W., and Roseman, C. (2011). Men's empathic accuracy in sexual harassment training. In *Praeger handbook on understanding and preventing workplace discrimination,* edited by Paludi, M., Paludi, C., and DeSouza, E., 33–38. Santa Barbara, CA: Praeger.

Sogunro, O. (2004). Efficacy of role-playing pedagogy in training leaders: Some reflections. *Journal of Management Development* 23, 355–371.

Williams, J., and Kleiner, B. H. (2001). Sexual harassment and discrimination in law enforcement. *Equality, Diversity and Inclusion: An International Journal* 20, 100.

Yagil, D. (2008). When the customer is wrong: A review of research on aggression and sexual harassment in service encounters. *Aggression and Violent Behavior* 13, 141–152.

Yoon, E., Funk, R., and Kropf, N. (2010). Sexual harassment experiences and their psychological correlates among a diverse sample of college women. *Journal of Women and Social Work* 25, 8–18.

York, K., Barclay, L., and Zajack, A. (1997). Preventing sexual harassment: The effect of multiple training methods. *Employee Responsibilities and Rights Journal* 10, 277–289.

Part V

Sexual Harassment: Complaint Resolution

Chapter 15

From Litigation to Mediation: Sexual Harassment Dispute Resolution in the 21st Century

Phoebe Morgan

In August 1974, Paulette Barnes filed a discrimination lawsuit against the director of U.S. Environmental Protection Agency, Douglas Costle. In the suit, Barnes claimed that her rejection of Costle's sexual advances had cost her promotions and eventually her job. The lawsuit initially was dismissed, with the judge claiming that her complaint was a "personal matter" and therefore not legally actionable. In 1975, that decision was appealed and a very public four-year battle for justice ended with Barnes being awarded $18,000 for back pay and the reimbursement of related medical expenses (*Barnes v. Costle* [1977]). Fortunately for Barnes, much of her legal aid was provided pro bono, as $18,000 barely scratched the surface of the expenses incurred, and the notoriety she incurred by the media's coverage of this benchmark case did little to advance her employment career. Despite her vilification by the press, in the pages of feminist law reform history Barnes is given credit as the first woman to file a sexual-harassment lawsuit.

In August 2013, Irene McCormack Jackson made similar accusations against her boss, San Diego's mayor Bob Filner. After only four days of mediation, Jackson and Filner struck a deal that included a public apology by Filner, his immediate resignation, and the imposition of a cap on the city's budget for Filner's legal defense. In a highly publicized meeting, the San Diego City Council called Jackson a "hero" and thanked her for her brave service to the city. Because all parties signed confidential agreements we will never know how many, if any, concessions Jackson had to make to settle her complaint. Similarly, exactly how much and in what ways Filner's misbehavior cost the City of San Diego also remains a secret. As Filner was checking into a clinic specializing in sexual disorders, however, he vowed to fight the sexual harassment claims of the other 20 women who came forward.

When read together, these two accounts dramatize the extent to which the legal terrain we now call "sexual harassment" has changed over the past 40 years. In the 20th century the only path to justice for the sexually harassed was through the courts. As in the cases of plaintiffs like Paulette Barnes, Lois Jenson, Michelle Vinson, and Teresa Harris, only those who felt they had no other choice were likely to embark on such a long, expensive, and emotionally arduous journey. For these pioneers the rewards were small compared with today's—typically little more than monetary compensation for lost wages. As a result of the precedents their cases set, however, today's jury awards can exceed more than 60 times the amount awarded in Paulette Barnes' case (Fuchs 2012).

To earn a multimillion-dollar award a case must go to trial, and in the 21st century those cases have become the exception; and informal and confidential alternative dispute resolution (ADR) such as negotiation, mediation, settlement conference, or conciliation are the norm (Calkins 2008). For those who take the alternative path, the journey to justice is measured in days rather than in years. The cost of dispute resolution is less than one day in court and often is paid for by the employer.

Lawsuits resolve sexual harassment complaints in monetary terms. Thus, in the previous century sexual harassment plaintiffs were "made whole" through financial compensation for lost pay, legal fees, pain, and suffering. Today, settlements arrived at through alternative dispute resolution are much more creative. Standard fare for out-of-court settlements are such things as reinstatements and resignations, mandatory trainings and policy reviews, continuation of medical benefits, and even public apologies.

Lastly, in the 20th century sexual harassment plaintiffs, defendants, and their witnesses ran a gauntlet of media scrutiny and workplace gossip. Regardless of the outcome, such publicity undermines the credibility and employability of the plaintiff and the defendant. Even when plaintiffs lose, employers lose valuable goodwill. For ADR participants, both the nature of their participation and the actual terms of agreement are confidential. Thus, all spared the indignity of public scrutiny.

In short, the path to justice traveled by sexual harassment complainants of the 21st century looks quite different from the path cut just 40 years ago. What happened? The following chapter provides a historical overview of the key events that shaped this transformation. The overview begins at the moment when sexual harassment was deemed legally actionable by U.S. Equal Employment Opportunity Commission (EEOC) and concludes with speculation about how landmark cases of the 20th century would have fared had they been filed today.

20th-CENTURY SEXUAL HARASSMENT DISPUTE RESOLUTION

Forty years ago, unwanted sexual behavior was a private trouble. Today, it is without doubt illegal. But sexual harassment is not a crime and there are no statutes prohibiting it. Sexual harassment law is case-made law. More than 40 years of litigation and appeals have defined what constitutes legal action, who is liable, and the acceptable remedies and appropriate sanctions.

The application of discrimination doctrine to the problem of sexual harassment might be one of the great legal innovations of the 20th century (MacKinnon 1979; Morgan 2003). Initially, whether the conceptualization of unwanted sexual behavior could be a form of legally actionable discrimination was an open question. Hundreds of thousands of lawsuits have since tested the discrimination theory, however, and 11 Supreme Court opinions have consistently (and often unanimously) upheld it. Thanks to the hard work and sacrifices of an untold number of litigants, the law's capacity to transform organizational culture and personal attitudes about sex and work is no longer debatable (MacKinnon 1995). Consequently, most of today's U.S. organizations have anti–sexual harassment policies informed by this case-made law. Additionally, governments around the world have adopted whole-cloth key elements of this U.S.-made law to institute a variety of anti–sexual harassment laws and criminal statutes. As a result, most transnational organizations today have policies designed to comply with the laws and statutes of the multiple jurisdictions in which they operate (Morgan & Gruber 2011).

Just 40 years ago the only path to remedy was through the courts. Often unemployed and frequently retaliated against for their efforts, the sexually harassed initially were dependent upon the expertise of trained legal activists or attorneys specializing in workplace discrimination to voice their concerns. Even with high-powered litigators by their sides, the pioneers that cut the first path through the court system paid exceptionally high prices. Most notably, even those who won often were shunned by their coworkers, blackballed within their professions, vilified in the media, and then countersued by their harassers (Stambaugh 1997; Morgan 2004).

Even in the 21st century, sexual harassment litigants still have a tough row to hoe. Making a sexual harassment case takes about two years and rarely do the awards exceed the cost of litigation. Only 20% of those who make it to trial actually win their cases. Although million-dollar awards can happen (CNN Money 1998), they are extremely rare. Lastly, winning any sexual harassment lawsuit comes with substantial losses. In addition to the cost of time and money, litigation and adjudication tend to ruin the relationships among all involved, thus foreclosing a plaintiff's future employment and career options (Morgan 1999; Whittenbury 1997).

In fact, in many instances the experience of litigation adds insult to harassment injury. Most find the reduction of their experience to dollar amounts insulting (Harkavy 2001). Often the things that the sexually harassed most want or need—such as apologies or character restitution—cannot be accomplished with a lawsuit. When asked what they would select if given a choice, for example, most prefer the cessation of the offending behavior and employment over monetary gain (Morris 1994).

THE DIVERSIFICATION OF EEOC RESOLUTION OPTIONS

In 1981, the Equal Employment Opportunity Commission published guidelines to encourage the establishment of internal procedures for investigating reports and remediating complaints. Before 1981 that manner in which allegations were handled varied greatly. In some cases, the sexually harassed turned to their personal attorneys who used the threat of litigation to leverage privately negotiated agreements. Others turned to their unions, and representatives would bargain on their behalf. Those without lawyers or unions depended upon their direct supervisors or human resource personnel to investigate and negotiate remediation. Unfortunately, retaliation is a common outcome of poorly handled reports. In fact, retaliation for reporting sexual harassment to authorities is the primary reason that the sexually harassed sue (Cooney 2003).

In addition to providing guidance to employers, in 1981 the EEOC established new protocols for the handling of sexual harassment complaints. In the early years, the EEOC primarily investigated claims, assessed the cause for legal action, and litigated select cases. Although the EEOC's goal is to investigate and resolve claims within 180 days, since 1991 the agency has struggled with a backlog that has delayed resolution by two to four months (Bond 1997; FDPK Law 2014). But a time frame of 180 to 300 days can be an unbearable amount of time to spend joblessness and blackballed (Billikopf 2004). Even when an ongoing EEOC investigation protects a complainant from more overt retaliations such as job loss or demotion, it often exacerbates hostilities and therefore can provoke more subtle forms of retaliation like shunning and isolation (Bond 1997). Thus, throughout much of the 20th century the EEOC's resolution efforts not only were inefficient, they also were risky.

Recognizing that fact, throughout the 1990s the EEOC piloted and then instituted a number of alternatives to formal investigation and litigation. As a result, those who contact the agency today are now offered an expanded menu of both formal and informal options that include such extra-legal processes such as mediation, settlement conference, and conciliation (EEOC 2014). A 2000 assessment of the meditation program reported that 91% of those who participated in mediation were satisfied with the outcome and 96% said they would use the program again (McDermott 2000). With mediation, the average time frame from report to resolution is only 84 days. Additionally, a bench or jury trial can take a month, and a typical EEOC mediation session takes about a day.

There is evidence that at the EEOC, mediation now is the norm and litigation is the exception. From 1999 to 2012, the number of EEOC mediation sessions increased by 65% and the number of successful resolutions nearly doubled. In 2012, the monetary benefits agreed upon in EEOC mediation ($158 million) exceeded those earned from the agency's litigation ($38.6 million) by 24% (EEOC litigation statistics; EEOC mediation statistics; http://www.eeoc.gov/eeoc/statistics/index.cfm. Accessed May 27, 2014).

Key elements of the EEOC's sexual harassment guidelines for employers and their own resolution processes have been widely adopted by other federal agencies (see, e.g., Office for Civil Rights; U.S. Department of Education). By the dawn of the 21st century, state-level agencies had followed suit (Kelly & Stambaugh 1992). Thus, regardless of the agency, those seeking governmental help now have some choice in how their sexual harassment concerns are addressed. The traditional methods of formal fact-finding and litigation still are in operation, but they are the alternative for a broad range of more expeditious and cost-effective alternatives to litigation.

The evolution of sexual harassment case law, government guidelines, and organizational practice has dramatically transformed the reporting and resolution landscape. As a result, 21st century sexual-harassment report investigation and complaint resolution is quite different from how they were handled 40 years ago. Today's complainant has access to a wide variety of venues and processes. An employee or student can report sexual harassment and seek resolution within multiple domains internal to their organization. At any point they can go outside of the organization and consider a plethora of alternatives available through federal and state government agencies. Regardless of whether a complainant chooses an internal or an external process, the options available vary by degree of formality. The vast majority of sexual harassment reports are now disposed "off the record," that is, through informal conversation, negotiation, or mediation.

"On the record" resolutions can include the published conclusions of a grievance hearing, the issuing of a government agency's investigative findings, or a court verdict. Today, formal grievances and court trials are the last resort rather than the only resort and nearly always are the result of botched or unsatisfactory informal resolutions. Thus, those who eventually opt for court typically have participated in one or more informal processes.

In sum, the plethora of dispute resolution alternatives available to today's sexual harassment complainant is the product of 20th century lawsuits. Ironically, sexual harassment complainants more often than not are *required* (e.g., by government agency regulation, court order, or by the terms of an employment contract) to attempt an alternative resolution method before they are permitted to file a lawsuit. The alternatives to litigation are so abundant and the pressures to use them so ubiquitous that, in the 21st century, litigation is the "new alternative" and the alternatives to litigation now are the standard fare (Barrett & Barrett 2010; Jarrett 2010). A key driver affecting this sea change has been the success of the alternative dispute resolution movement (Calkins 2008; Hensler 2003).

THE QUEST FOR ALTERNATIVES

From the historian's point of view, the 20th century was an era defined by excessive litigation (Friedman 2005). Optimists claim litigation has been the engine driving the cause of human and civil rights (Abel 1982). Others note that the prospect of punitive damages has held multinational corporations and governments accountable for their commitments to their workers and the communities in which they reside (Branson 2010). The more pessimistic observers characterize the late 20th century as a time of unbridled litigiousness (Will 2014). Some worry that law reforms of the 1970s and 1980s—like sexual harassment law—now fuel a litigation industry (Larson 1996). From this perspective, a workforce lacking fundamental conflict-management skills sustains the litigation industry (Gilbert 2011).

For still others, the rise in civil litigation is a harbinger of today's excessive divide between the "haves" and the "have-nots." As a consequence, the wealthy and corporate citizens outmatched ordinary litigants in every court of law (Galanter 1974). Regardless of point of view, toward the end of the 20th century there was increasing concern about the negative effects of this rising tide of litigation. In particular, judges and court administrators noted that the increased use of the courts to test innovative legal theories such as sexual harassment, to hold corporations accountable, and to sustain the historic expansion of rights had created a caseload problem of crisis proportion (Galanter 1986–1987). As the turn of the century approached, there emerged concerns that the 20th-century court system was out of step with the emerging needs and interests of the 21st century's public (Levin, Russell & Wheeler 1979). Justice Burger characterized court trials as uncivilized and Justice Scalia declared them unchristian (as cited in Calkins 2008). Court exit-survey data throughout the 1970s and 1980s documented a growing dissatisfaction extending beyond the bench to include all trial participants. As a result, a court reform movement coalesced around the need for alternatives to adversarial litigation and bench and jury trials (Feeley 2013).

A rising caseload and a corresponding spike in public dissatisfaction with traditional justice provoked a revolutionary proposition: that the courts should offer a menu of dispute resolution options tailored to the specific needs and particular tastes of the community. On this menu would be alternatives to formal adjudication and the traditional courtroom trial. For ease of conversation, the American Bar Association coined the phrase "multi-door courthouse" to reference this model of court justice. Throughout the 1980s and 1990s court systems across the country and at all levels experimented with numerous alternatives to traditional justice. By far the most commonly instituted alternatives have been mediation and arbitration programs (Harrington 1985). Initial results of pilot programs proved promising. Initial exit surveys suggested that the multidoor courthouse works. Judges and court administrators found that the ability to offer alternatives to litigation improved trial scheduling and administration. Even more importantly, however, satisfaction rates among those who participated in the piloting of informal alternatives such as mediation and conciliation were significantly greater than those of the participants who chose traditional court (Kolb 1994). As the news spread, courts across the country and around the world began "adding doors."

In 1990, the Civil Justice Reform Act required all federal district courts to implement at least one alternative to traditional trial. State legislatures followed suit and, consequently, most state district courts now offer at least one trial alternative. The trend has trickled down to the lower courts such that most courts today offer at least one alternative to trial. Alternatives to trial are particularly prevalent in those courts specializing in civil trials—which is where sexual harassment lawsuits are filed. Although mediation and arbitration are the most popular programs, today's court-annexed programs also include short trials, settlement conferences, private adjudication (commonly called "rent-a-judge"), or some combination of programs. In the 21st century, for example, courts routinely offer mediation with arbitration. Similarly, settlement conferences regularly run concurrent with trials, and conciliation can be tacked on after trial.

And so, 40 years ago, the phrase "alternative to trial" simply meant an out-of-court settlement arrived at by lawyers through traditional bargaining. Today, the term references an almost infinite range of processes and strategies; and the menu of options varies by region, jurisdiction, and constituent. In California's civil courts, for example, private adjudication (rent-a-judge) is exceptionally popular among the business class (Kasendorf 2003). In Hawaii, the alternative "door" outsources the Court's alternative dispute resolution work to private practitioners (Chiem 2010). Although short-trial programs are popular in metropolitan Nevada (http://www.clarkcountycourts.us/ejdc/courts-and-judges/adr/short_trial/short_trial.html), in rural New Mexico settlement conferences are the preferred alternative (https://firstdistrictcourt.nmcourts.gov/ADR1.htm). Depending upon the legal mandates, the court's legal culture, and amount of funding for alternatives, today's sexual harassment litigants could be offered the opportunity to choose between a short trial and a traditional trial. They might be given the choice of an arbitration panel or a bench trial. They also could be given permission to jump the trial queue entirely by renting a retired judge.

PROLIFERATION BY MANDATE

Key features distinguishing the 21st-century courthouse from that of the 1980s are the judicial and legal mandates that pressure litigants to at least consider—if not use—alternatives to litigation (Lee & Lakhani 2012). In the late 1990s, a raft of executive orders and statutes mandated the institutionalization of ADR programs throughout the federal government. Most notably, in 1995 the U.S. Attorney General ordered the appointment of a senior council for alternative dispute resolution. Just one year later, Congress passed the Administrative Dispute Resolution Act. This law required the formation of a task force charged with "encouraging the development and further expansion of ADR Programs." In combination with the previously mentioned Civil Justice Reform Act, these mandates have provided pressures and incentives for courts and federal agencies to institutionalize and promote ADR programs.

Judges increasingly have relied upon court orders to promote ADR. Although the initial vision of the multidoor courthouse consisted of a menu from which disputants could freely choose, today many judges now *require* litigants to consider or use an alternative to trial. In some cases, a judge might make the scheduling of a court date contingent upon the litigants' demonstration of a "good faith effort" at resolving their disagreements through an informal process such as mediation or conciliation. Consequently, sexual harassment complainants seeking redress through a state or federal court could be ordered to participate in a mediation, arbitration, or settlement conference.

The growing reliance on court orders to promote ADR has been controversial. Critiques of mandatory ADR are concerned that requiring documentation of participation in an ADR process makes accessing the adjudication door unduly onerous for those who could benefit the most from using it (Ward 2007). From this perspective, access to court justice is a sacred right, and the pathway to trial should be unencumbered by ADR detours. ADR practitioners have been equally critical but for different reasons. Most fundamentally, mandating participation in an ADR process undermines the key feature that most distinguishes ADR from traditional adjudication—self-determination (Hedeen 2005). Many meditators, for example, require their disputants to pledge voluntary participation and will not facilitate a session if there is evidence that a party feels coerced or pressured into participating. For the sexually harassed, coercion by a judge or an attorney to participate in any dispute resolution process—alternative or otherwise—that does not comport with one's justice orientation or conflict-management style can feel like it's adding insult to injury.

Although concerns abound, court-ordered ADR is not without benefits for the sexual harassment plaintiff. It is important to note that in most sexual harassment cases there is an inherent power differential such that an ordinary citizen is taking an entire organization to court. Employers typically have disproportionately more resources for winning a court trial than an under-resourced employee or former employee. When this is the situation, an employer might prefer to deplete the opponent's meager resources through a lengthy deposition phase before considering a settlement. A judge can level the field by forcing an employer to participate in a less costly mediation or a settlement conference before scheduling a trial date. Even if a mediation session or settlement conference fails to generate an agreement, the process can resolve extralegal issues and bring into sharper focus the most relevant legal ones. In fact, through dialogue and diplomacy, sexual harassment litigants can hone the case down to its most essential elements, paving the way for a more expeditious trial and therefore reducing the possibility of an appeal.

A third, less obvious mandate involves the now ubiquitous mandatory ADR contract clause. Today most contracts include a clause that stipulates the use of some form of ADR to resolve disputes. In some cases, the signatories waive their rights to trial entirely. In others, they agree to use mediation or arbitration before resorting to trial. Today, as a result, the vast majority of nonunion workers have signed employment contracts with mandatory ADR clauses.

THE UBIQUITY OF INTERNAL DISPUTE RESOLUTION

In 1994, the U.S. Postal Service settled a class action lawsuit in which postal workers claimed the EEO's resolution process was too slow, remote, and ineffective (USPS 2008). A key component of the lawsuit's settlement was an agreement to institute an on-site, on-demand workplace dispute resolution program. The first of its kind; the REDRESS Program provides resources to facilitate the resolution of disagreements between coworkers and between coworkers and direct supervisors. Today the program is staffed by 1,500 neutral (e.g., they are not employed by USPS) on-call volunteers who facilitate mediations at the participants' worksite. Postal workers offended by unwanted sexual attention can call upon a REDRESS mediator to facilitate meaningful dialogue with the offender and negotiate agreements with them and their supervisor to prevent future offensive behavior. Conversely, coworkers or supervisors who feel wrongly accused of sexual harassment can ask a REDRESS mediator to facilitate a dialogue to clarify misunderstandings.

Needless to say, the REDRESS Program has been extensively evaluated and researched. Consistently, a key finding is the high satisfaction rates among the workers who participate in these onsite informal processes (Bingham 1997). As a result, by 1998 more than half of all federal agencies had voluntarily instituted ADR programs similar to REDRESS. The 2000 Congress passed a law mandating that all federal agencies make alternative dispute resolution processes available at all phases of the EEO complaint process.

For private employers, programs like the REDRESS experiment suggest a possible link between workplace productivity, job turnover, and access to on-site informal dispute resolution. These programs provide a liability hedge should a complaint become a lawsuit and serve as a backstop for frivolous litigation. Consequently, organizations of any significant size now provide some form of on-site dispute resolution program. Although some programs are extensions of employee health and wellness programs, others emanate from human resources or personnel management offices. Credentialed ADR professionals staff some of them, but most are staffed by cross-trained personnel who have collateral duties. In academic settings, volunteer peer-mediation programs are becoming increasingly popular.

Of particular interest is the increased deployment of the ombudsmen model for handling workplace disputes in general and sexual harassment complaints in particular. As of 2013, 785 organizations had staffers who were members of the International Ombudsman Association, and the organization's membership has been growing steadily by as much as 15% per year (IOA 2013). Further, during the last economic downturn, the number of new ombudsman offices instituted well exceeded the offices that were shuttered. Interestingly, IOA members rank "conflict management and dispute resolution," as the most important services they provide (IOA 2008). About 40% of the concerns handled by IOA members are regarding discrimination and about another 30% involve inappropriate or unprofessional behavior. Because ombudsmen are prohibited from participating in formal processes, the majority of concerns are resolved informally through back-channel diplomacy or confidential mediation.

In addition to supporting workplace productivity, in-house ADR programs like these provide organizations with a low-cost hedge against liability and their workers with a low-risk mechanism for resolving problems before they become legally actionable. These programs also provide management with feedback that facilitates the fine-tuning of anti–sexual harassment initiatives (Gutek 1993). At the first sign of trouble, a worker can seek a confidential reality check from an EEO officer, ombudsman, or a peer mediator. If sufficiently trained, these types of on-site ADR workers can assess the legalities of the concerns and put complainants on the appropriate path to a just resolution. It also is at this early stage that disputes fueled by miscommunication or inadequate training can be resolved before they become grievances. In-house mediators can effectively resolve complaints about unwanted sexual attention by brokering agreements to stop offending sexual behaviors, to complete a sensitivity workshop, or even to enroll into a detoxification or therapy program. They can also work as a complaint sieve, helping to sort out personality conflicts for which there are no formal remedies from those that, if left unresolved, could become legally actionable.

But the sorting of issues embedded in a sexual harassment report requires skill, as sexual harassment complaints tend to be both multifaceted and dynamic (Marshall 2005). Most workplace ADR workers receive less than a day of dispute resolution training and less than half of that training regarding the EEOC guidelines for handling sexual harassment reports. Consequently, frontline personnel rely upon their limited experience and personal knowledge. Too often the result is a reframing of unwanted sexual attention as an inevitable personality conflict or a harmless personality peccadillo (Quinn 2000).

In the 20th century, sexual harassment reporting was simple. Employees complained to a direct supervisor or voiced their concerns in an EEO or human resource office. Today, the sexually harassed can raise concerns with a supervisor, an EEO officer, an ombudsman, or a peer mediator. Their complaints could be addressed through casual conversation, shuttle diplomacy, or a mediation session. Resolutions could be signified by a handshake, communicated in an e-mail, or codified by signed letters of understanding. Should informal efforts prove unsatisfactory or if the resolutions are not honored, then more formalized options in the form of written complaint or grievance are available. Because sexual harassment complaints often are related to, or emerge from, other complaints, it is not uncommon for claims to be acted on by multiple ADR personnel and be processed multiple times. Depending upon the amount of cooperation provided by the accused and the degree of diligence performed by those responsible for investigating and resolving reports, the sexually harassed likely will participate in more than one resolution process before the legality of their claims is clear.

THE CHALLENGE OF ABUNDANCE

When viewed together, these trends have contributed to both a proliferation and diversification of resolution options. Today, sexual harassment complaints can be handled informally or formally, internally or externally, and in a courtroom or in a conference room. Before becoming a lawsuit, a sexual harassment complaint has been attended to in multiple venues at multiple levels of formality. For the most part, for those whose job it is to resolve sexual harassment complaints, the growing abundance of options is welcomed as they provide more resources for tailoring the processes and remedies to the unique needs and interests of those they serve (Barendrecht & deVries 2006).

Such abundance, however, brings a new set of challenges to those seeking relief from unwanted sexual attention. The ability to make an informed choice requires some knowledge about the alternatives to litigation, their goals, weaknesses, and strengths. Just comprehending the legal parameters of sexual harassment reporting—that is, what behaviors are legally actionable; what are one's legal rights; what are the limits of an employer's liability; and determining deadlines for reporting, responding, and filing—takes some effort. Today, an informed choice demands additional learning about the finer distinctions between such things as formal and informal processes, mediation and conciliation, and binding and nonbinding agreements. Deciding whether to seek help internally or externally, whether to opt for a formal or informal process, and deciding when it is time to sue can be daunting tasks—especially if one already is stressed and depleted from coping with sexual harassment.

Without sufficient knowledge of the resolution options available to them, the sexually harassed might learn the finer distinctions of them through trial and error. Rather than make a proactive choice, only when a resolution process fails to satisfy will they choose a different tact and, when they do, they potentially bring with them unresolved disappointments regarding the previous effort, thus compounding their sexual harassment injuries with the insult of a negative dispute resolution experience.

In addition to knowledge about how various resolution processes work, a wise choice requires some reflection on one's own dispute resolution style, justice orientation, and needs. Even holding constant such things as the type of harassment, degree of formality, or the location of the process (internal verses external), the terms for a satisfying disposition of a sexual harassment complaint vary a great deal. Extralegal considerations such as household economics, familial support, as well as direct experiences of other forms of discrimination can strongly shape the justice consciousness of a sexually harassed person (Buchanan 2005; Morgan 2001). Personality, culture, economics, and previous victimization can produce a wide variety of expectations within a singular process or venue. For some, symbolic resolutions such as private apologies or public vindication are essential. For others, direct action in the form of policy revision or the writing of a check will suffice.

The severity of the harassment, however, as well as the onerousness of the reporting and complaint process can have an even greater bearing on satisfaction with a dispute resolution option. Depending upon the severity of the harassment and its effects, some are satisfied with nonmonetary remedies such as a pledge to transform organizational culture (Holcombe & Wellington 1992). For others nothing short of punitive damages will satisfy (Martin 2000).

Finally, the ability of those charged with the responsibility to address sexual harassment reports to navigate such diverse terrain can significantly affect how the sexually harassed move through the reporting and resolution system. Certainly, their knowledge of sexual harassment law and organizational rules for handling sexual harassment reports is essential. Their knowledge and experience with the various dispute resolution techniques, however, can make a big difference. Direct supervisors, for example, might try to minimize organizational liability by handling reports promptly. Without sufficient training in conflict management, however, in their haste they could inadvertently escalate the complaint rather than resolve it. In fact, mishandling of reports at the worksite is the primary reason complainants contact the EEOC Office. It is not uncommon for those dissatisfied with the handling of their concerns—either by their employer or a government agency—to complain about it to the media; and botched internal resolutions increase rather than minimize employer liability (Flahardy 2013).

In sum, the ADR Movement has proliferated the range of both the internal and external resolution options available to the sexually harassed. As internal dispute resolution programs have become the norm, a growing number of employees and students are turning to ombudsmen and mediators to help them solve their sexual harassment problems. Those who contact a federal agency now can expect an array of dispute resolution options tailored for every stage of the resolution process. Those who seek legal counsel are likely to find private mediation or settlement conference on their attorney's menu of services. Those who choose a trial might be required to demonstrate a good-faith effort to settle or participate in some form of mediation before the judge will schedule a trial. Despite these realities, there has not been much discussion of their impacts. In the 20th century there essentially only was one path to justice and it led to court. Today, the number of paths is only limited by the imaginations of those who seek resolution and those whose job it is to help find it.

CONCLUSION

As sexual harassment law was being written one lawsuit at a time, almost in tandem another legal innovation was emerging. As feminist law reformers were working hard to reform laws and create legal processes to protect the rights of women, court reformers and federal bureaucrats were seeking better ways to satisfy the growing diversity of needs and expectations brought to the courts and the government. The result has been a dramatic transformation in how individuals, organizations, and institutions understand workplace disputes.

In the 20th century, Michele Vinson was fired for not having sex with her supervisor. She took her employer to court, and after five years of trial and appeal she eventually won monetary compensation for her legal fees and lost wages (*Meritor Bank v. Vinson* [1985]). Had Michele Vinson lost her job today, however, her journey would be quite different. Odds are that her employment contract has a clause that limits the conditions under which she can take her employer to court. In signing it, she might have agreed to use mediation or arbitration to resolve her complaint. Long before losing her job, her employer might have provided her with dispute resolution training and she could have used those skills to negotiate a change of behavior with her sexual harasser. While still an employee, an organizational ombudsman or a coworker participating in a peer-mediation program could have attempted to resolve the problem with such extralegal remedies as shuttle diplomacy, therapy, and retraining. Vinson's management could have seized the opportunity to address systemic factors that had created such a hostile environment.

If, despite internal efforts, Vinson did lose her job, before issuing her a "right to sue" letter, the EEOC could offer her another menu of alternatives to trial. At this point, Vinson could engage the services of an EEOC mediator or schedule a settlement conference. Even if she rejected those options and filed suit, the judge likely would require evidence of a good-faith effort at settling her lawsuit outside of court before setting a trial date. The judge might point her to another menu of alternatives provided by the court.

Most practicing attorneys today have taken ADR training. Thus Vinson's attorney could either offer to mediate the complaint or help her shop for a mediator. Even if she were to get a trial date, she might be offered an alternative trial format—or even be pressured by her attorney or the judge to consider one. Thus, today, the case of *Vinson v. Meritor* most likely would have been decided in less than a day and perhaps without the option of appeal.

Forty years and thousands of lawsuits ago, feminists launched a campaign to raise the public's consciousness and politicize the highly personal and private indignation of unwanted sexual attention (Farley 1975;

MacKinnon 1979). The result is a formidable body of case law that clearly defines unwanted sexual attention as legally actionable discrimination. Although there is no doubt that sexual harassment is legally actionable, in the 21st century the vast majority of sexual harassment reports are resolved quickly, quietly, creatively, and off the record. This chapter has shown how this shift has occurred and highlighted some of the implications it has for the men and women who seek relief from unwanted sexual attention.

REFERENCES

Abel, R. (1982). *The politics of informal justice*. Waltham, MA: Academic Press.

Barendrecht, M., and deVries, B. (2006). Fitting the forum to the fuss with sticky defaults. *Unknown 13*, 83–118.

Barrett, J., and Barrett, J. B. (2004). *A history of alternative dispute resolution*. San Francisco, CA: Josey-Bass.

Billikopf, G. (2004). Sexual Harassment Complaints. Department of Agri-Labor Management, University of California-Berkeley. http://www.cnr.berkeley.edu/ucce50/ag-labor/7article/article03.htm. Accessed March 28, 2014.

Bingham, L. (1997). Alternative dispute resolution in public administration. In *The handbook of public law and public administration*, edited by C. Newland & F. Cooper, 546–566. San Francisco, CA: Jossey-Bass.

Bond, C.A. (1997). Shattering the myth: Sexual harassment disputes in the workplace. *Fordham Law Review* 65, 2489–2533.

Branson, D. (2010). Holding multinational corporations accountable: The Achilles heels in alien tort claims. *Santa Clara Journal of International Law*. University of Pittsburgh Legal Studies Research Paper No. 2010-30.

Buchanan, N. (2005). The nexus of race and gender domination: Racialized sexual harassment of African American women. In *In the company of men*, edited by J. Gruber and P. Morgan, 294–320. Boston: Northeastern University Press.

Calkins, R. (2008). The ADR revolution. *Rutgers Conflict Resolution Law Journal* 1, 1–68.

Chiem, L. (2010). Mediation gains popularity as the number of civil lawsuits rise. *Bizjournals* (November 19). http://www.bizjournals.com/pacific/print-edition/2010/11/19/mediation-gains-popularity-as-number.html?page=all. Accessed June 2, 2014.

CNN Money (1998). Mitsubishi settles for 34 M. http://money.cnn.com/1998/06/11/companies/mitsubishi/. Accessed May 20, 2014.

Cooney, L. (2003). Understanding and preventing workplace retaliation. *Massachusetts Law Review* 88, http://www.massbar.org/publications/massachusetts-law-review/2003/v88-n1/understanding-and-preventing-workplace-retaliation, last accessed: May 27, 2014.

Farley, L. (1975). *Sexual shakedown*. New York: McGraw Hill.

Feeley, M. (2013). *Court reform on trial*. New York: Quid Pro Quo Books.

Feinstein, D. & Payne & Kravic Law (FDPK Law) (2014). EEOC backlog. (January 15, 2014): http://www.fdpklaw.com/eeoc-backlog/ (last accessed: May 21, 2014).

Flahardy, C. (2013). Law firm files counterclaim in sexual harassment lawsuit. Inside Counsel Magazine (April 3). http://www.insidecounsel.com/2013/04/03/law-firm-files-counterclaim-in-sexual-harassment-s. Accessed May 22, 2014.

Friedman, L. (2005). *A history of American law*. New York: Touchstone Publishing.

Fuchs, E. (2012). The 9 most damning workplace sexual harassment lawsuits filed in America. *The Business Insider* (September 3). http://www.businessinsider.com/the-9-most-damning-workplace-sexual-harassment-lawsuits-filed-in-america-2012-8?op=1. Accessed: June 20, 2014.

Galanter, M. (1986–87). The day after the litigation explosion. *Maryland Law Review* 46, 3–26.

Galanter, M. (1974). Why the haves come out ahead: Speculations on the limits of legal change. *Law & Society Review* 9, 95–160.

Gilbert, L. (2011). Reducing the litigious climate in organizations. National Center for Preventative Law, California Western School of Law. http://www.preventivelawyer.org/main/default.asp?pid=essays/gilbert.htm. Accessed June 2, 2014.

Gutek, B. (1992). Disputes and dispute-processing in organizations. *Studies in Law, Politics and Society* 12, 31—52.

Harkavy, J. (2001). Privatizing workplace justice: The advent of mediation in resolving sexual harassment disputes. *Wake Forest Law Review* 34, 135.

Harrington, C. (1985). *Shadow justice: The ideology and institutionalization of alternatives to court*. Santa Barbara, CA: Praeger Press.

Hedeen, T. (2005). Coercion and self-determination in court-connected mediation. *The Justice System Journal* 26, 273–291.

Hensler, D. (2003). Our courts ourselves: How the ADR movement is reshaping our legal system. *Pennsylvania State Law Review* 108, 165–197.

Holcombe, B. J., and Wellington, C. (1992). *Search for justice*. Walpole, NH: Stillpoint Press.

International Ombudsman Association (IOA) (2013). *Annual Report*: http://www.ombudsassociation.org/sites/default/files/2013_IOA_AnnualReport.pdf. Accessed June 20, 2014.

International Ombudsman Association (IOA) (2008). Jobs analysis. http://www.ombudsassociation.org/sites/default/files/IOA-Final_Job%20Analysis%20Report-IOA_website_version.pdf. Accessed June 20, 2014.

Jarrett, B. (2010). Beauty and the beast: Mediating workplace sexual harassment claims. *Rutgers Conflict Resolution Law Journal* 7, 36.

Kasendorf, M. (2003). Rent-a-judges forced out of California courts. *USA Today* (April 24). http://usatoday30.usatoday.com/news/nation/2003-04-24-rentajudge-usat_x.htm. Accessed April 20, 2015.

Kelly, R., and Stambaugh, P. (1992). Sexual harassment in the states. In *Men and women of the states*, edited by M. Guy, 109–124. Armonk, NY: Sharpe.

Kolb, D. (1994). *When talk works: Profiles of mediators.* San Francisco, CA: Jossey-Bass.

Larson, E. (1996). The economic costs of sexual harassment. *The Freeman* (August 01). http://www.fee.org/the_freeman/detail/the-economic-costs-of-sexual-harassment. Accessed June 02, 2014.

Lee, Y. & Lakhani, A. (2012). The case for mandatory mediation to effectively address child custody issues. *International Journal of Law, Policy and the Family* 26, 327–350.

Levin, A, Russell, R., and Wheeler, R. (1979). *The pound conference: Proceedings of the National Conference on the Causes of Popular Dissatisfaction with the Administration of Justice.* Eagan, MN: West Publishing Company.

MacKinnon, C. (1995). Sexual harassment, its first decade in court. In *The criminal justice system and women*, edited by B. Price, and N. Sokoloff, 297–311. New York: McGraw Hill.

MacKinnon, C. (1979). *The sexual harassment of working women.* New Haven, CT: Yale University Press.

Marshall, A. (2005). Idle rights: Employee rights consciousness and the construction of sexual harassment policies. *Law and Society Review* 39, 83–124.

Martin, E. (2000). *Stopping the train.* Mt. Pleasant, SC: Corinthian Press.

McDermott, P. (2000). An evaluation of the EEEOC mediation program. EEOC Order No. 9/0900/7632/2: http://www.eeoc.gov/eeoc/mediation/report/index.html, last accessed May 27, 2014.

Morgan, P. (2004). Risking relationships. In *The social organization of law*, edited by A. Sarat, 191–200. Los Angeles, CA: Roxbury Press.

Morgan, P. (2001). Sexual harassment: Violence against women at work. In *The sourcebook on violence against women*, edited by C. Renzetti, J. Edleson, and R. Kennedy Bergen, 209–223. Los Angeles: Sage Publications.

Morgan, P. (1999). Risking relationships: Understanding the litigation choices of sexually harassed women. *Law & Society Review* 33, 67–92.

Morgan, P., and Gruber, J. (2011). Sexual harassment: Violence At work and in schools. In *The sourcebook on violence against women*, edited by C. Renzetti, J. Edleson & R. Kennedy Bergen, 75–94. Los Angeles, CA: Sage Publications.

Morris, C. (1994). *Bearing witness: Sexual harassment and beyond.* New York: Little & Brown.

Quinn, B. (2000). The paradox of complaining: Law, humor, and harassment in the everyday work world. *Law & Social Inquiry* 25, 1151–85.

Stambaugh, P. (1997). The power of law and the sexual harassment complaints of women. *National Women's Studies Association Journal* 9, 23–42.

U.S. Equal Employment Opportunity Commission (EEOC) (2014). History of the EEOC mediation program. http://www.eeoc.gov/eeoc/mediation/history.cfm. Accessed: May 21, 2014.

U.S. Postal Service (USPS) (2008). REDRESS: Conflict resolution that works. Publication 98 (September). http://about.usps.com/publications/pub94/pub94_002.htm. Accessed April 20, 2015.

Ward, E. (2007). Mandatory court annexed ADR. *St. John's Law Review* 81, 77–98.

Whittenbury, E. (1997). Sexual harassment claims: When can mediation work? *Business and Economic Review* 43.

Will, G. (2014). Thin skins, litigiousness and prayer. *The News & Advance* (May 10). http://www.newsadvance.com/opinion/columnists/will_george/thin -skins-litigiousness-and-prayer/article_4bb0f1b8-d7b5-11e3-a83e-0017a4 3b2370.html. Accessed April 20, 2015.

LEGISLATION, EXECUTIVE ACTION AND COURT CASES

Barnes v. Costle (1977). U.S. Court of Appeals, District of Columbia Circuit, 561, F2d 983. http://law.justia.com/cases/federal/appellate-courts/F2/561/983 /419011/#fn16. Accessed June 20, 2014.

U.S. Administrative Dispute Resolution Act (1996).

U.S. Alternative Dispute Resolution Act (1998). Public Law No. 105-315; 112 Stat. 2993.

U.S. Associate Attorney General (1995). "Promoting the Broader Appropriate Use of Alternative Dispute Resolution Techniques." General order: OBD/H-1' OBD/F-2; SPL-23.

U.S. Civil Rights Act (1991). Public Law No. 102-166, 118, 105 Stat. 1071, 1081.

Chapter 16

Protocol for the Standardization of Sexual Harassment Investigations: A Mediational Approach

William T. O'Donohue, Adrian H. Bowers, and Gwendolyn C. Carlson

INTRODUCTION

Wagner (1992) estimated that Fortune 500 companies incur an annual per-company cost of $ 6.7 million due to sexual harassment, not including litigation costs. The U.S. Merit Systems Protection Board (USMSPB 1981) attributed a 10% turnover rate of federal employees to sexual harassment. In a follow-up study (USMSPB 1988) it was estimated that the cost to the federal government of sexual harassment is more than $250 million over a two-year period. More recent data revealed that in 2006 there were 12,025 total sexual harassment claims made to the U.S. Equal Employment Opportunity Commission (EEOC), with the vast majority being made by women (84.6%) (Cunningham & Benavides-Espinoza 2008). Over a 12-year period, companies paid an average of $47.8 million in sexual harassment lawsuits (EEOC 2009). Mainiero and Jones (2013) noted that, due to the increased popularity of social media technologies in recent years, there is an increased risk for miscommunication regarding personal and professional interactions. Due to this risk, a clear understanding of the distinction between workplace romance and sexual harassment is increasingly critical. Even if this distinction is clear, however, sexual harassment investigations face the challenge of determining whether claims are creditable or spurious (Burns 1995; Feldman-Schorrig 1996).

This chapter provides a detailed protocol for sexual harassment investigation. The sexual harassment–investigation protocol is designed to improve the quality of these investigations and reduce the costs associated with sexual harassment by providing a thorough and systematic manual for investigation and mediation procedures. The goals of the protocol are to gain an accurate understanding of what has and has not happened in the past, to prevent further harm, to reduce any harm that already has occurred, and to attempt to resolve the dispute in a way that is fair and efficient.

WHAT IS SEXUAL HARASSMENT?

Although there is no agreement regarding the definition of sexual harassment, there is general consensus based on laws, legal precedents, psychological research, and general opinion that are quite consistent. Perhaps the best place to start is with the legal background of sexual harassment. Due to various court rulings, in 1980 the EEOC issued strict guidelines regarding sexual harassment under Title VII. Sexual harassment is composed of behaviors that include

> [making] unwelcome sexual advances, requests for sexual favors, and other verbal or physical conduct of a sexual nature when participation or submission is an explicit or implicit necessity for employment, used to decide employment decisions, or these acts have the purpose or effect of unreasonably interfering with a person's work performance or creating an intimidating, hostile, or offensive working environment. (EEOC 1980, 74676)

Sexual harassment basically is viewed as falling under two categories—quid pro quo and hostile environment harassment. "Quid pro quo" is Latin for "this for that." It refers to the explicit or implicit communication that the employee must endure various types of workplace sexualization to remain employed or to receive certain job perks. Examples include cases in which a supervisor uses his or her power and authority to coerce an employee into performing sexual acts or endure sexual behaviors (Burns 1995; Maypole & Skaine 1983). A hostile environment sexual harassment claim is established when an employee's workplace is sexualized in such a manner or for the "purpose or effect of unreasonably interfering with a person's work performance or creating an intimidating, hostile, or offensive working environment" (EEOC 1980, 74676).

Gruber (1992) developed a typology of sexual harassment. Gruber posits that there are three behaviorally referenced subcategories: (1) verbal requests (e.g., sexual bribery, sexual advances, relational advances, subtle pressure or advances); (2) verbal comments (e.g., personal remarks, subjective objectifications, sexual categorical remarks); and (3) nonverbal displays (e.g., sexual assault, sexual touching, sexual materials). Generally, all aspects of verbal comments and nonverbal displays are related to the determination of a hostile environment sexual harassment charge, and all the aspects of verbal requests are related to the determination of a quid pro quo sexual harassment charge. The following is a noninclusive list of some of the types of conduct that could constitute sexual harassment.

- Sexual bribery
- Sexual blackmail
- Sexual favors
- Unwanted touching
- Inquiry regarding personal life
- Discussion by the harasser of his or her own sex life or alleged sexual prowess
- Simulated sexual acts
- Viewing sexual materials
- Requests for dates
- Comments on body parts
- Repeated (albeit apparently innocent) remarks on appearance
- Gender-oriented remarks
- Rumor mongering
- Inappropriate visual display
- Threats or intimidating physical posturing
- Invasion of personal space
- Gender discrimination
- Staring
- Business trip to inappropriate establishment
- Inappropriate behavior at business gathering or party
- Apparently nonsexual hostile conduct that results from the rejection of a sexual advance

It is important to remember that victims of sexual harassment often hold back crucial information. The investigator might have to gently ask pointed and direct questions about different types of behaviors to discover the full extent of the problem.

GENERAL PRINCIPLES OF SEXUAL HARASSMENT INVESTIGATIONS

The U.S. justice system uses the premise that someone is innocent until proven guilty. The justice system works to minimize both "Type I" and "Type II" errors, but protects against Type I errors more thoroughly. Type I errors represent an outcome in which someone is judged as guilty of committing a crime that he or she did not do (a "false positive"). Type II errors refer to situations in which someone is not convicted of a crime that he or she did commit (a "false negative") (Kaiser 1960). By proving "beyond a reasonable doubt" that someone committed a crime, courts support this bias toward minimizing Type I errors. Although the bias toward minimizing Type I errors is crucial, sexual harassment investigations must grapple with how this decision rule materializes given the peculiar circumstances of a sexual harassment investigation. The basic question is, "What standard of proof ought to be applied to these investigations and who has the burden of meeting this standard?"

The predicament can be seen more clearly by comparing a typical sexual harassment investigation to a typical criminal investigation. In many cases, there is no physical evidence in a sexual harassment accusation and the accuser might have many significant reasons to fabricate the account of the sexual harassment. Conversely, the accused will have significant motivation to deny sexual harassment allegations even if the accusation is true (Burns 1995; Feldman-Schorrig 1996). Because of these problems in sexual harassment investigations, a new understanding of "burden of proof" must be developed. A sexual harassment investigation must view its responsibility as two separate subinvestigations: (1) Did the alleged harasser sexually harass? (2) Is the accuser giving an accurate account of the alleged harassment? The credibility of the accounts of both the accused and the accuser is under investigation, and both the accused and the accuser should be considered innocent until the final conclusion of the investigation is determined.

PROBLEMS WITH CURRENT SEXUAL HARASSMENT INVESTIGATIONS

Evidence of the need for a systematic and comprehensive protocol is found in the numerous efforts of companies to standardize their sexual harassment investigations (Spann 1990). Many companies have developed—and others are developing—company sexual harassment–investigation guidelines to augment sexual harassment policies. Very little research has examined the accuracy or effectiveness of sexual harassment investigations, however. To date, there are no empirically validated sexual harassment–investigation protocols. The guidelines underlying sexual harassment investigations largely are based on a legal perspective (i.e., company liability, risk management) rather than a scientific perspective. Because lawyers and human resource staff often draw from these guidelines, they tend to be rather insensitive to the behavioral implications that the guidelines entail. From a psychological perspective, many components that would improve outcomes for all parties can be added to sexual harassment investigations, particularly regarding how information is gathered from witnesses during the investigation (Collins, Lincoln & Frank 2002; Dodd & Bradshaw 1980; Loftus 1975; Oxburgh & Dando 2011; Sharman & Powell 2012).

In an attempt to create a standardized measure of sexual harassment Fitzgerald, Gelfand, and Drasgow (1995) modified the Sexual Experiences Questionnaire (SEQ) to assess an individual's self-reported experiences of the following dimensions: gender harassment, unwanted sexual attention, and sexual coercion (for a review, see Gelfand, Fitzgerald & Drasgow 1995; Stark, Chernyshenko, Lancaster, Drasgow & Fitzgerald 2002). Although it is standardized, the measure does not consider the possibility of spurious claims and, due to the nature of such claims, a self-report measure of sexual harassment would be insufficient and inappropriate. This illustrates the second limitation with previous sexual harassment investigation guidelines. That is, sexual harassment investigations guidelines fail to consider all possible hypotheses that could account for a sexual harassment claim, particularly in the context of missing relevant information and spurious claims (Burns 1995; Feldman-Schorrig 1996).

Further, previous guidelines fail to consider how companies should proceed if investigators conclude that the claim is false or if there is not enough information to draw a definitive conclusion. For instance, Galdin and Pino (1997) list concerns that a third-party mediator should consider regarding the perspective of the accuser during sexual harassment claim mediation including: "They want things to go back to normal" (Galdin & Pino 1997, 143) and "They do not want to get the person who harassed them in trouble" (Galdin & Pino 1997, 144). Sexual harassment guidelines and recommendations such as these make assumptions about the occurrence of the alleged harassment as well as what outcome(s) the accuser(s) or victim(s) want as a result of the sexual harassment investigation and mediation procedures. Unlike previous sexual harassment investigation guidelines, the current protocol attempts to consider all plausible scenarios—that is, legitimate, spurious, and inconclusive claims—recognizing the variability of the investigative processes and how compensation for all principal parties is dependent on the conclusion of the investigation.

A third critique of previous sexual harassment investigation guidelines is their vagueness and the lack of instruction for investigators. Recommendations are given but no concrete instructions for investigators to carry out those recommendations are presented. Galdin and Pino (1997), for example, recommended that investigation and mediation procedures be conducted in a rapid and confidential manner, but provided no concrete instructions to help investigators implement these guidelines. Maypole and Skaine (1983) gave vague recommendations for changing the atmosphere of the workplace to mitigate the prevalence of sexual harassment claims and to reduce distress associated with sexual harassment claims. Additionally, Wright and Fitzgerald (2009) reported that an organization's climate is associated with sexual harassment class action, but gave no recommendations as to how an organization can positively modify its climate to reduce class action sexual harassment lawsuits. The current protocol attempts to overcome the limitations of previously recommended guidelines for sexual harassment investigation and mediation in the following ways:

- The protocol should be based on psychological theory and research rather than a legal framework;
- The protocol should consider all possible hypotheses (i.e., legitimate, spurious, inconclusive claims); and
- The protocol should describe how investigators and mediators respond to all hypothetical outcomes in a sexual harassment investigation.

PLANNING THE INVESTIGATION

The present chapter describes a comprehensive protocol for investigators to use when a sexual harassment claim has been made (see Table 1). Given the financial burden that sexual harassment claims place upon organizations, however, preventing sexual harassment in the workplace and eliminating the need for an investigation altogether is an obvious strategy for organizations to consider. A detailed description of how to prevent sexual harassment in the workplace is beyond the scope of this chapter (see Coleman 1993). The authors, however, recommend that investigators take the following steps prior to beginning a sexual harassment investigation:

- Investigators should be familiar with evolving state and federal laws concerning sexual harassment and other forms of discrimination.
- Investigations should conform to the sexual harassment policy of the individual institution.
- Investigators should pay special attention to promises that are made in the sexual harassment policy.

Inconsistencies between the sexual harassment policy and the sexual harassment investigation could yield fertile ground for litigation (Koen & Morgan 1997).

Before the investigation begins, the organization immediately should speak to the accuser about changing his or her work environment to possibly minimize additional harassment. Of course, this assumes that the claim is prima facie legitimate. Contact between the accused and the accuser should be as minimal as possible. Under typical circumstances, an investigation should be started within one working day of the first complaint and should be concluded within 30 days (Kobata 1995; Segal 1993). The EEOC *Guidelines on Discrimination Because of Sex* (1980) states that an employer is liable if "immediate and appropriate corrective action" is not taken (see, e.g., *Carr v. Allison Gas Turbine Div., Gen. Motors Corp,* 32 F.3d 1007 (7th Cir. 1994)). There are court precedents that reflect favorably on companies that quickly respond with an adequate investigation that results in appropriate remedial actions (see, e.g., *Saxton v. AT&T,* 10 F.3d 526 (7th Cir. 1993); *Wathen v. General Electric Co.,* 115 F.3d 400 (6th Cir. 1997)).

Additionally, when embarking upon an investigation, investigators should chart the investigative process as soon as possible and provide a detailed outline of the procedure. The investigator can review this outline with interested parties; it could help them understand how the investigator is trying to embody the principles of conducting a complete and fair inquiry (Segal 1993). Investigators determine the jurisdiction of the investigation as early in the process as possible. One problem with determining jurisdiction is that—by its nature—an investigation deals with unfolding evidence. What begins as a civil problem in fact could turn out to be a criminal matter. Another jurisdictional issue is the need for mutual investigations among companies. At times, harassment charges can bridge a number of companies. In this type of scenario, the investigator should attempt to coordinate investigative efforts among all the sites. It is beneficial to have any companies that the investigator is dealing with provide a clear and comprehensive document describing the boundaries of the investigative authority (Mainiero & Jones 2013). The investigator also should have a document including this information provided by the investigator's own company if it is not included in the investigator's job description.

After planning is complete, the proposed protocol for sexual harassment investigations should be conducted. When applicable, behavioral principles and theory guide the creation of the protocol at the three levels: (1) the overall structure surrounding the investigation procedure, (2) the investigation procedure, and (3) behaviors that occur during the actual investigative interviews. This protocol is designed to reduce harm to everyone involved in sexual harassment cases. It is roughly divided into two integrated functions. It first provides instructions on the intricacies of fact-finding and synthesis and then gives instructions for instantiating mediational concepts.

Table 16.1. Proposed Sexual Harassment Investigation Structure

1. Coordinating interviews and other data-gathering efforts
2. Gathering appropriate information (i.e., know what is not relevant information)
3. Determining welcomeness
4. Exploring and managing ancillary risk
5. Preventing retaliation
6. Dealing with danger from employees
7. Identifying problematic interviewer behaviors and replacing them with beneficial interviewer behaviors
8. Using the right style to maximize the collection of information
9. Alleviating victimization

THE INVESTIGATION PROCEDURE

Coordinating Interviews and Other Data-Gathering Efforts

Interview order should be based on logical and practical consider-ations. This helps maximize the effectiveness of the investigation, and minimize time and costs. Logically, investigators will want to conduct in-terviews in a sequence that provides the most amount of relevant informa-tion in the smallest amount of time (Oxburgh & Dando 2013). In most cases, interviews should start with the accuser. If other witnesses were privy to the instance of harassment (and if they are available for inter-views) they should be interviewed next. The accused then should be inter-viewed last. If a satisfactory conclusion cannot be made then more witnesses can be interviewed. This can be an iterative process in which previously interviewed individuals are re-interviewed as new informa-tion becomes available. Also, the investigator should conduct interviews in an order that precludes any groups or individuals from discussing ei-ther what the interview consisted of or what the next witness should say in the interview; it is important to prevent the temptation or opportunity for alliances to form that could upset the interview processes' validity (Kalmbach & Lyons 2006).

The limits of confidentiality should be discussed during the first con-tact with witnesses. Witnesses should be told that:

- Investigators take witnesses' privacy seriously and that confidential-ity will be maintained as much as possible;
- Strict confidentiality cannot be maintained because an investigation of sexual harassment necessarily deals with conflicting accounts of events given by two identifiable people; and

- Any type of retaliation will be dealt with swiftly and severely; proven retaliation is grounds for dismissal.

The default should be to maximize confidentiality unless otherwise indicated by the investigative needs. The rule to follow is to maintain confidentiality as much as possible, until breaking confidentiality becomes necessary to continue moving the investigation in a meaningful direction.

Exploring and Managing Ancillary Risk

Ancillary risks are risks that are incurred due to the investigative process; they include risks such as racial discrimination, slander, defamation, and various other countersuits. The investigator first must explore the possible ancillary risks. Are there any possible legal avenues that the accused could pursue to deter the investigation or seek revenge against the accuser or the company? Next, the investigator should manage potential risk by asking appropriate questions in the interview in terms of the type of questionnaire (open rather than closed or accusatory; Snook, Luther, Quinlan & Milne 2012) and the information about which the interviewer is inquiring (see Gathering Appropriate Information section). Risk closing questions would include: Has the company mistreated the individual in any way in the past? Has anyone at work been discriminatory toward the individual because of his or her race, creed, gender, or a similar reason? Ancillary risk also can be reduced by communicating the importance of confidentiality. Rumors spread while the investigation is being conducted can have a detrimental impact by tainting the reputation of the organization or employees, sapping of morale organizational productivity, and dissemination of false information (Michelson & Mouly 2004). Witnesses should be instructed to not spread rumors or hearsay about the investigation and be informed that doing so could directly affect their employment status at the company.

Gathering Appropriate Information

A common misperception in our society is that women who have had some number of sexual relationships are therefore legitimately open to men directing sexualized behaviors toward them. Related to this point are the important Rape Shield laws that have been adopted by many states. These laws protect the accuser in rape trials by preventing her (or his) past sexual history from being entered as evidence. A fine example is found in the case of *Burns v. McGregor Electrical Indus.*, 989 F.2d 959 (8th Cir. 1993). As such, investigators should not inquire about sexual history that is not relevant to that person's allegation or work life. Doing so could harm the individual and actually increase ancillary risk for the company.

A closely related topic is the accuser's history of sexual harassment accusations. If there is a pattern of "unfounded" or "spurious" sexual harassment claims, then the investigator must resolve three problems.

- The investigator must be sure that the prior investigations were of sufficient quality to have arrived at reasonable conclusions. Many sexual harassment investigations are inadequate and often come to erroneous decisions (Burns 1995).
- "Unfounded" does not mean that the allegation was false; it only means that there was insufficient evidence to decide that the sexual harassment actually occurred.
- Some individuals receive a greater rate of harassment than do others.

For both the accuser and the accused, if there is insufficient evidence to reveal a history of harassment or of making false accusations, then any past information along these lines should not be used to determine culpability in the present investigation.

Another line of evidence that could be important is the witness's history of credibility at work. Character credibility refers to the believability of the accuser's claim of sexual harassment (Burns 1995). This is not an easily rectified dimension. Some factors to consider are what the accuser possibly could gain by entering a damaging false charge of sexual harassment. Would the accuser obtain a job promotion that he or she is competing for with the accused? The accuser might have a history or a pattern of deceitfulness and falsification at work; this could be a sign that he or she is falsifying the current harassment charge. Again, however, only work character credibility should factor into the equation.

Determining "Welcomeness"

The question of "welcomeness" looms above both quid pro quo and hostile environment claims. In other words, if the accuser welcomed the sexualized environment or behaviors then sexual harassment did not take place. Welcomeness, however, is difficult to assess. In fact, in *Vinson v. Taylor,* Taylor—the alleged harasser in *Meritor Savings Bank v. Vinson*—claimed that all the sexual behaviors were voluntary (i.e., implicitly claiming welcomeness) and the behaviors therefore were not harassment. Taylor lost the case, however, which is not surprising given the fact that the Supreme Court described what Vinson endured as having to run a gauntlet of sexual abuse (as reported in Fitzgerald, Swan & Magley 1997). Clearly, one difficulty with establishing welcomeness is accurately reading the recipient's reactions. McFall (1997) has shown that individuals high in sexual assault potential often misread women's reactions in a positive direction.

The EEOC realizes the pivotal role that welcomeness plays in determining whether sexual harassment has occurred. The EEOC states that "sexual attraction may often play a role in the day-to-day social exchange between employees [thus], the distinction between invited, uninvited-but-welcome, offensive-but-tolerated, and flatly rejected sexual advances may well be difficult to discern" 29 C.F.R. 1604.11 (b). The EEOC's 1990 *Policy Guidance on Sexual Harassment* somewhat clarifies this murky area by specifying some considerations to determining welcomeness (EEOC 1990).

- Was a timely complaint made?
- What behaviors did the accuser engage in?
- Was the relationship consensual?
- Can a determination of welcomeness clearly be made?

Determining welcomeness also might play a pivotal role in determining the entire outcome of the investigation and any subsequent litigation.

Preventing Retaliation

Some form of retaliation—albeit subtle—is likely to occur in cases of sexual harassment. The accused or the accuser might retaliate (Cortina & Magley 2003). Investigators should educate both the alleged perpetrator and those people who tacitly permitted the sexual harassment about the company's policy and on the need to prevent retaliation. Investigators also should describe what actions will be taken in response to retaliation. They should give concrete examples of what is proscribed. Importantly, investigators periodically and discreetly should follow up for a substantial period after the investigation concludes to verify that any offending conduct has stopped and that retaliation isn't occurring.

One way to attempt to defuse low-level retaliation is with widespread sexual harassment training or retraining. Using data drawn from the U.S. Merit Systems Protection Board of the U.S. federal government, Antecol and Cobb-Clark (2003) found that after sexual harassment training, men were more likely to consider behaviors such as pressure for dates, sexual gestures, sexual remarks, and touching to be forms of sexual harassment. Kearney, Rochlen, and King (2004) also found that providing a psychoeducational workshop regarding what constitutes sexual harassment in the workplace was effective in changing the accuracy of male employees' perception of sexual harassment in the workplace. Based on these findings, investigators and companies should try to prevent retaliation by using sexual harassment training and education, admonitions, and warnings. If the situation warrants, then the alleged perpetrator should be transferred to a different location away from the accuser. A full description of sexual harassment training is beyond the scope of this chapter, however (for a review see Antecol and Cobb-Clark 2003; and Kearney, Rochlen, and King 2004).

DEALING WITH DANGER FROM EMPLOYEES

Danger is most likely to come from either disgruntled employees that feel wrongfully accused or from employees who feel that their charges were not taken seriously (Cortina & Magley 2003). Revenge is a common motive for violence; individuals can hurt themselves and other people (Bies & Tripp 2005; Neuman & Baron 1998). Given the spate of recent workplace shootings it is even more crucial to take these issues seriously. In the United States in 2005, half of all medium-sized companies (those having at least 1,000 employees) reported an incident of workplace violence (U.S. Department of Labor 2005). It is important to note, however, that violent behavior (to self and others) is notoriously unpredictable. Although workplace violence might seem more frequent given the availability heuristics from reports in the media, its frequency is quite low and even actuarial models cannot reliably predict its occurrence in the workplace (Dawes, Faust & Meehl 1989).

Fortunately, according to Baron and Neuman (1996) most aggression in the workplace is verbal, indirect, and passive rather than physical and active. Organizations, however, would likely prefer to err on the side of caution than to end up with a violent tragedy occurring. Investigators should be wary of warning signals such as erratic behavior; subtle threats; direct threats; talk about death, dying, or impermanence; and selling or giving away items (which could be a sign that an individual might be preparing to end his or her life) (Rudd et al. 2006). The investigator should ask the main participants if they are having difficulty dealing with their thoughts and feelings surrounding the alleged incident. If individuals make threats toward themselves or others, then the police should be contacted. If individuals are having difficulties such as those described here, then appropriate referrals to mental health care workers should be made.

IDENTIFYING BENEFICIAL AND PROBLEMATIC INTERVIEWER BEHAVIORS

Behaviors that occur during interviews can be beneficial (e.g., rapport building) or detrimental (e.g., leading questions) to the evidence-collection process either as displayed by the interviewer or the witness (O'Donohue & Fanetti 1996). There are, however, some crucial interview guidelines that investigators should follow.

- Investigators should describe the rationale of the interview to the witness. That is, the investigator should state that he or she is conducting a sexual harassment investigation and is gathering evidence to make a final determination concerning whether the sexual harassment took place or whether this judgment can be determined. The investigator should articulate to the witness that he or she is not being accused of anything, and emphasize that the interview is for information-gathering purposes only.

- Investigators should never say things that he or she is unsure of or that could be proven wrong.

- Investigators should not provide any conclusions during evidence collection. The investigator doesn't know what evidence found subsequently might reveal; therefore, any conclusions must be withheld until the final synthesis and conclusion of the investigation.

In addition to these basic guidelines, there are several information-gathering tactics that have been found to be effective in both forensic and clinical settings (Oxburgh & Dando 2011).

Beneficial Interview Behaviors

"Rapport" refers to the creation of a harmonious relationship between the witness and the investigator (Abbe & Brandon 2014). Due to the pleasant (or at least nonaversive) atmosphere that the investigator creates, the witness will feel more at ease and be more likely to divulge sensitive information. Poor rapport is characterized by a witness that is uncooperative, hostile, or deceitful (Collins, Lincoln & Frank 2011; Duchan & Kovarsky 2011). Revealing empathic understanding of the witness's difficult situation in clear, straightforward communication can help to build rapport. Empathetic listening techniques include validating the interview's experience (e.g., "It sounds like your situation is difficult"), reflecting or paraphrasing what the interviewee recently stated, and summarizing multiple statements made by the interviewee (Norfolk, Birdi & Walsh 2007; Passmore 2011).

Another beneficial interview behavior and empathetic listening technique is asking open-ended questions. Open-ended questions are questions that suggest as little information as possible to the witness, and allow the witness the greatest latitude of possible responses (Hassan 2012). This means that questions are constructed in such a way that they do not aid the witness in guessing the response that he or she thinks that the investigator wants. For all questions, however, some context must be provided. For example, the investigator could say the following, "Mr. X states that you sexually harassed him on the morning of the seventh in the copying room, can you tell us what happened from your point of view?"

The previous question gives enough detail to the witness to determine the circumstance of the alleged incident but does not give specifics that could become useful in determining guilt or innocence.

Asking about specific domains of sexual harassment might only be necessary if the witness is excessively vague or is not able to articulate what events occurred and how or why they were offensive; events occurred that were sexual harassment but the witness does not report them because he or she believes that the events were outside the realm of what sexual harassment encompasses; or the witness is too embarrassed to discuss what occurred (e.g., a witness might feel uncomfortable stating that the alleged harasser constantly stared at a body part).

A third beneficial interview behavior is emphasizing the importance of truthful information. It is recommended that investigators do not pressure witnesses to answer a question if the witnesses do not understand the question or claim to not know or possess information relevant to the question. Emphasizing the importance of the truth and transparency interviews can reduce social desirability (i.e., tendency of interviewees to respond in manner that they believe will be viewed favorably by others) as well as mitigate the impact of authority figures on behavior (Milgram 1963). Witnesses might attempt to please investigators they perceive as authority figures; that is, witnesses could report false information to please investigators, particularly if the witnesses are pressured to disclose information they do not possess. Similar patterns have been observed when interviewers are perceived as experts or perceived as attractive to interviewees (Kerr & Dell 1976).

Although under the circumstances described above witnesses might be deliberately deceptive, in other instances outside contamination can be insidious and witnesses might be unaware of how their memories have been corrupted. Therefore, another reason for investigators to emphasize the importance of truth during interviews is avoiding outside contamination. Outside contamination refers to information (or to physical evidence, traditionally) that is changed or distorted by some other source (Loftus 1975; Sharps, Herrera, Dunn & Alcala 2012; Thorley 2013). For example, an employee might have overheard other employees talking about something that they had seen. When the employee is asked a question he or she responds by saying that he or she saw the event (instead of reporting that he or she only heard people talking about it). For this reason, investigators should always ask follow-up questions about the circumstances surrounding the witnesses' information. By attempting to establish a context, memory retrieval and accuracy of reporting are enhanced (Smith & Vela 2001).

Problematic Interview Behaviors

In addition to beneficial interview behaviors, there are problematic interview behaviors to avoid. One tactic interviewers should avoid is asking leading questions. Leading questions are questions directed at witnesses that hint at or include the correct response within the question (Sharman & Powell 2012); for example, at the very start of the interview, asking, "For how long did X grab you?" This is a leading question unless the witness already had said that X did, indeed, grab him or her. Leading questions are problematic for a number of reasons, including that they could reveal what the interviewer thinks actually happened; they can suggest that the interviewer doesn't believe X's or Y's account of what happened; they can change what the witnesses say in response to the question. This last possibility perhaps is the most problematic, because leading questions can cause the witnesses to lie, distort the truth, or omit details—either deliberately or unintentionally (Dodd & Bradshaw 1980; Sharman & Powell 2012).

A second interview behavior to avoid is "disconfirmation." Disconfirmation refers to the investigator behavior of expressing disbelief in certain witness responses. An example would be the witness saying "and then he took his hand and slid it up my leg," then the investigator says, "Now come on, I don't think that happened." Disconfirmation is problematic because it could reveal what the investigator thinks actually happened, it can imply that the investigator doesn't believe X's or Y's account of what happened, it can change what witnesses say in response to the question, and it can invalidate the witnesses' emotional experience and increase psychological problems (Norfolk, Birdi & Walsh 2007). Investigators should try to prevent disconfirmation by responding as if they believe the witnesses regardless of the content of their statements.

A third interview behavior to avoid is repetitive questioning. Repetitive questioning refers to the practice of the investigator asking numerous questions about a certain topic when an answer already has been given (Shaw & McClure 1996). An example would be an investigator asking "Did X say anything when he was touching you?" The witness then says, "No, X didn't say anything to me while he was touching me." Then the investigator asks, "When X was touching you did he say anything to you?" The minor rewording does not negate the fact that the second question is repetitive; the witness clearly answered this question after it was posed the first time. Repetitive questioning is a problematic investigative practice because it could reveal what the investigator thinks actually happened, it can hint that the investigator doesn't believe X's or Y's account of what happened, it can change what witnesses say in response to the question, it can frustrate witnesses and decrease their confidence in the investigative procedure because they think that they are not being heard, and it can invalidate witnesses' experience and increase psychological suffering (Poole & White 1991; Thorley 2013).

ALLEVIATING VICTIMIZATION

Overall, the proposed investigation is designed to minimize unwarranted negative consequences for all parties. In particular, if harassment did take place then the accuser can be retraumatized by the investigative procedure. In rape investigations, for example, poor investigatory technique has been called the "second victimization" (Patterson 2011). This is especially problematic when an investigation ends in a conclusion of "unfounded" but the harassment did in fact take place. A number of negative psychological consequences can result from any traumatic experience, including sexual harassment. Further, the psychological risk increases with the severity of the harassment. A person's response to sexual harassment, however, can be very idiographic (Galatzer-Levy & Bryant 2013). One person can endure much harassment without symptoms and another person might not be able to endure even slight harassment without dire consequences.

The absence, presence, or severity of PTSD symptoms should not be used as evidence that the alleged sexual harassment did or did not occur. That being said, it is important for investigators to understand the range of sexual harassment response sequelae and to avoid belittling anyone for their response to harassment. As described, confidentiality and empathetic listening techniques can be implemented to avoid further harm from either the primary distress from the alleged harassment or a secondary victimization due to the investigative procedures. Although the harassment might seem slight to the investigator, it is the accuser's perception of the harassment that determines his or her response to the harassment. If witnesses indicate that they are not handling the situation in productive ways or that their emotional lives are out of control, then they should be referred to an appropriate mental health resource. As described, if someone indicates that they are a danger to themselves or to someone else, then investigators should contact the police and a mental health care worker immediately.

CONCLUDING THE INVESTIGATION AND BEGINNING MEDIATION

Hypothesis Testing and Synthesis of Information

After the relevant information has been collected, the investigator can start the process of synthesizing the information and testing the hypothesis. It is best to wait until all relevant information is collected before starting the information synthesis (Ross & Nisbett 1991). Synthesis of information deals with the grouping of evidence into a coherent whole, into an account of what the evidence indicates has occurred. There always exist multiple ways of constructing the past and the investigator should construct a number of possible scenarios before beginning hypothesis testing. Hypothesis testing is the process that determines which account seems most likely to have occurred. It is important to remember that even though many scenarios can be created, the true state of affairs might not be represented in any of the scenarios. Just because the investigator has many scenarios does not mean that one of these is accurate, or—even if one is accurate—that the investigator will be able to discern this from the evidence. Nevertheless, the more scenarios created, the greater the probability of one of them being accurate or close to accurate.

After all possible scenarios have been developed, the next step is to evaluate these scenarios. This process is accomplished by generating hypotheses and then testing these hypotheses against the different scenarios. By doing this, the investigator gains a better perspective on which scenarios are more likely to have occurred, and which are highly unlikely to have occurred. Hypotheses should be generated based on the information that these possibly could yield. Investigators should focus on high-yield hypotheses. For example, hypotheses that reveal the scenarios to be highly likely or unlikely based on logical inconsistencies, problems with timelines, motives, consistencies in behavior, corroboration of evidence, relevancy of evidence, type of evidence, quality of evidence, and the total body of evidence will be very important to the investigation's conclusion.

Fatal Incongruence

The first type of important incongruence is one that refutes one or more possibilities. This is known as a "fatal incongruence." A fatal incongruence is a piece of information that is so dysynchronous within the context that it is purported to be placed that it disconfirms the entire context. For example, say a very severe case of sexual harassment takes place—a sexual assault. DNA evidence was collected. The main person who is accused does not have an ironclad alibi. A fatal incongruence occurs when it is determined that the main accused does not have the same DNA match as the DNA that was collected as evidence. The information about the incongruity between the evidence DNA and the main accused's DNA is sufficient to totally disconfirm the scenario that the accused was the rapist—someone else must have committed the assault.

Collective Incongruence

Collective incongruence occurs when a sufficient number of weaker incongruencies call into question the validity of the context in which they are placed—"the facts don't add up." Usually when this type of incongruence is encountered the investigator will not be able to draw a definitive conclusion about the occurrence or nonoccurrence of a scenario. Rather, it significantly decreases the probability that the investigator can be sure about an outcome (i.e., start to seriously consider mediation as crucial to the resolution). A collective incongruence could occur, for example, where the following are all found: a problem with a timeline, a major discrepancy in the account of incidents by eye witnesses, and significantly different accounts of the incident are provided by accuser and accused when questioned the first time and a second time. Clearly, there are so many problems with any one scenario that a definitive decision of culpability cannot be made.

Nine Conclusions and Their Validities

Given that a sexual harassment investigation actually focuses on the investigation of both the accuser and the accused, the investigative conclusion is significantly more complex than in a typical criminal investigation. In a typical criminal investigation the accused is found to be guilty or not guilty. Because a sexual harassment investigation investigates both the accuser and the accused, however, the possible investigative conclusions are expanded. Furthermore, for both the accuser and the accused, their respective accounts can be judged to be false or true or to have insufficient evidence available to judge the account's veracity. In other words, either the harassment occurred, it did not occur, or it might have occurred. Therefore, nine (realistically eight) potential investigative outcomes can be created by combining each of three investigative findings about the accuser with the three investigative findings about the accused (see Table 16.2).

Hypothesis 1. Harassment—Yes; Spurious—Yes.

This conclusion concerns an interesting finding where there is reasonable and sufficient evidence to conclude that both harassment occurred and a spurious charge was made. Although unlikely, these conditions can be met if (a) harassment must have occurred, (b) the charge must contain allegations that are unequivocally false (and not just unfounded), and (c) the allegations that are unequivocally false must not be fabricated due to ignorance (i.e., there is indication of malice). Further, because both parties clearly are at fault they have very few options during mediation; the company, not its faulty employee, has the advantage in the mediation process. Because harassment took place, however, the company might have certain liabilities as well, depending on the circumstances of the case. (Should the company have known about this harassment? Should it have been able to prevent it?) If the company is found to be indirectly responsible for

Table 16.2. All Possible Hypotheses in a Sexual Harassment Investigation

	Spurious: Yes	Spurious: No	Spurious: Possible
Harassment: Yes	Hypothesis 1	Hypothesis 2	Hypothesis 3
Harassment: No	Hypothesis 4	Hypothesis 5	Hypothesis 6
Harassment: Possible	Hypothesis 7	Not Applicable*	Hypothesis 9

* Hypothesis 8 is impossible. In square 8 it makes no sense to say the harassment could have taken place—either the charge is not spurious and harassment is substantiated, or the charge is not spurious (because of the accuser's confusion about harassment) and harassment did not take place.

the harassment as well, then the company also has limited mediation options.

Hypothesis 2. Harassment—Yes; Spurious—No.

This conclusion refers to a finding where it is clear that the harassment occurred and the harassment charge was not spurious (i.e., it was not malicious, was made in good faith, and was a good approximation of the harassment). He or she harassed someone and this will result in fewer choices of mediation options. Contrarily, the accuser is in a position where he or she will have many mediational options. Again, if the company should have known about the harassment or prevented it, then the company might have fewer mediation options.

Hypothesis 3. Harassment—Yes; Spurious—Possible.

This conclusion refers to a finding where there is sufficient evidence to clearly indicate harassment occurred and there also are some indications that the charge might be spurious. However, there is insufficient information to say for certain that the harassment is spurious. As such, the accuser's mediation options are not reduced and he or she has a greater advantage in the mediation process. Because the charge of spuriousness only is possible, it does not reduce the mediation options. Of course, the same criterion applies to a charge of "possible harassment"— this finding does not reduce the accused's mediation options. This conclusion means that the accused is culpable. He or she harassed someone and this will result in fewer choices of mediation options. Contrarily, the accuser is in a position where he or she will have many mediation options. If the company should have known about the harassment or prevented it, then the company might be in a position of having few mediation options.

Hypothesis 4. Harassment–No; Spurious—Yes.

This conclusion refers to a finding that there is sufficient evidence to conclude that harassment did not occur and that the charge of harassment was spurious (i.e., malicious and not just misguided as to what is truly harassment). This conclusion means that the accuser is culpable. He or she entered a false charge and this will result in fewer choices of mediation options. Contrarily, the accused is in a position where he or she will have many mediation options. There currently are no legal provisions regarding a company's liability related to spurious charges of sexual harassment. The prudent company, however, still is well advised to examine its role in the perpetuation of a false charge. A company could be found guilty of slander, libel, defamation, and other such legal penalties relating to how it handles a sexual harassment charge. If the company should have handled the case more professionally, known about the spurious charge, or prevented its promulgation, then the company might be in a position of having fewer mediation options.

Hypothesis 5. Harassment—No; Spurious—No.

This scenario occurs where there is sufficient information to conclude that harassment did not occur and that the original charge was not spurious. Basically, this refers to a misunderstanding by the accuser of what sexual harassment entails. The sexual harassment charge was not malicious and harassment did not occur. This finding means that both the accuser and the accused parties have a number of mediation options. The company has slightly more mediation options in this situation, however, because it is clear that no wrongdoing took place. As such, the company has more leeway in deciding upon an acceptable resolution.

Hypothesis 6. Harassment—No; Spurious—Possible.

This finding refers to a case in which there is sufficient information to conclude that harassment did not occur but that the initial charge might be spurious. This is likely to be a rare finding. The question of whether the charge is spurious depends on whether harassment occurred, whether the harassment that occurred was the harassment recounted in the charge, whether the charge was entered with malice, and whether the charge was entered with ignorance about definitional harassment. In this particular case, because harassment did not occur the relevant issue is whether the charge was based on malice, ignorance, or both. If this issue is unclear then the decision of a possibly spurious charge should be accepted. A finding of "possibly" spurious must be treated the same as a definite non-spurious charge in the mediational process. As such, the accuser's mediation options are not reduced. Of course, the same criterion applies to a charge of "possible harassment"—this finding does not reduce that accused's mediation options. Because the charge was "possibly spurious," however, the company does not have more mediation options than the other two parties.

Hypothesis 7. Harassment—Possible; Spurious—Yes.

This finding refers to a scenario in which there is evidence to suggest that harassment might have occurred but the initial charge was spurious. This is likely to be a rare finding. Because the charge is spurious (i.e., maliciously fabricated) then, by definition, the events that the charge refers to did not occur. However, there still exists the possibility that other sexual harassment could have taken place and that if this evidence is present but is insufficient to unequivocally point to harassment, then a conclusion of "possible" harassment should be accepted. As discussed, in the mediational process prior findings of "possible" harassment or "possibly" spurious charges are to be treated as if there is no reduction in bargaining options for those parties. Because the conclusion is only "possible" (inconclusive) then the mediator should not see the party as being culpable. Culpability, conversely, usually does entail a reduction in bargaining options and reduced mediational power. This conclusion means that the accuser is culpable. He or she entered a false charge that resulted in less choice of mediational options for him or her. Contrarily, the accused is in a position where he or she will have many mediational options. Currently there are no legal provisions regarding a company's liability related to spurious charges of sexual harassment. A prudent company, however, still is well advised to examine its role in the perpetuation of a false charge. A company could be found guilty of slander, libel, defamation, and other such legal penalties relating to how it handles a sexual harassment charge. If the company should have handled the case more professionally, known about the spurious charge, or prevented its promulgation, then the company might have fewer mediation options.

Hypothesis 9. Harassment—Possible; Spurious—Possible.

This is a common finding in which it is unclear as to whether harassment occurred and unclear as to whether the charge is spurious. This situation occurs when there is insufficient evidence to confirm or refute the occurrence of harassment and insufficient evidence to confirm or refute that the harassment charge was spurious. Unfortunately, this is a common occurrence in sexual harassment investigations even when they are carefully conducted and all the relevant avenues of evidence are explored. This conclusion means that there is no clear picture of culpability. As such, all parties retain the same number of mediation options. One possible exception could occur if a company has badly handled the events leading up to the investigation. In this case, the company could be partially liable and this in turn might result in a reduction of bargaining options and reduced mediational power for the company.

COMMUNICATING THE FINDINGS TO THE RESPECTIVE PARTIES

Although mediation for the purposes of simplification can be viewed as a separate activity from the fact-finding aspects of the investigation, the investigator must be looking for ways of solving the dilemma throughout the investigation, considering retaliation, dangerous employees, and alleviating victimization as described. After all evidence is gathered, the investigator (i.e., mediator) is now in harm-reduction mode (Marlatt 1996). Harm should be reduced as much as possible to the accuser, the accused, and the company or society. Communicating the findings to the participants must be handled very carefully, as it is one of the occurrences most likely to evoke participants' strong emotions. The investigative findings will not be conveyed to the participants in the manner that they are presented in this protocol. This is because of the complexity of the investigatory conclusion process and the subsequent likelihood of it being misinterpreted by participants who are not familiar with the entire investigational-mediational activity. In other words, the eight investigative findings are kept solely for the mediation process and participants are not directly informed of which cell contains the final conclusion. The nine conclusions then have clear and direct implications for the mediation approaches and options that are described below.

MEDIATIONAL APPROACHES

Integrative mediation is the first goal in mediation. Basically this refers to the process of expanding the possibilities of acceptable solutions (see Emery 1994; Fisher & Ury 1981). This process enables the mediator to expand the "pie" for everyone; all participants stand to gain from this process. The mediator's role is to maximize gains and minimize losses for everyone. This approach to mediation is particularly relevant to sexual harassment hypotheses in which two or more of the parties (the accused, the accuser, or the company) have a relatively equal number of mediation options (e.g., hypotheses 1, 5, 6, and 9). It is better for parties to generate options first and then, if they are stymied, the mediator can offer some suggestions about potential solutions, given the knowledge they have regarding each parties respective mediation power.

Mediation Options

One striking difference between sexual harassment mediation and typical mediation (including divorce mediation) is the lack of face-to-face dialogue between parties. In most mediation scenarios, parties discuss and brainstorm potential solutions together. Because of the sensitive issues in sexual harassment mediation, however, face-to-face contact is prohibitive. The accuser and the accused could have a volatile in-session encounter that would end mediation and start litigation. Perhaps the most compelling reason not to have face-to-face sessions among participants is that sexual harassment often is predicated on power differentials and fear. The ability of the accused to potentially continue subtle threats and exercise power in-session counter-indicates party-to-party interactions. Revictimization and further psychological harm are real possibilities.

As stated, parties should be given the opportunity to offer options first. This is because, psychologically, most individuals have better long-term satisfaction with decisions if they have actively chosen a course of action (Festinger & Carlsmith 1959; Martinie, Milland & Olive 2013); parties most likely will be able to describe their wants and wishes better than the investigator could; and if the mediator offers a suggestion first it can be insulting, too generous, or be "cognitively sensitizing." Cognitive sensitizing refers to the occurrence of someone thinking a certain thought because another thought was recently activated. For example, if a mediator says, "We will offer you $2,000 to resolve this problem," then the party might be sensitized to money as a sole solution. The participant's ability to create new and different solutions could be seriously hampered. Instead, all of the participant's new solutions involve differing amounts of money. Conversely, if the mediator says, "We will offer you an apology from the accused and companywide training concerning sexual harassment," then the participant's new solutions likely will include some form of these offerings and might not include money. Mediation can be worked into numerous potential solutions, such as the following domains:

- Apologies,
- Letter of reprimand,
- Psychotherapy/treatment,
- Demotion,
- Transfer,
- Forgo raise or bonus,
- Severance package,
- Monetary settlement, or
- Vacation time.

Remember that these are just some of the potential solutions that can be used singly or in combination within the mediational framework to benefit the participants involved with the sexual harassment charge. The mediator must decide which of these options seems most likely to be accepted by all participants. After ranking the solutions on desirability, the mediator then must present the most desirable solution to the participants. If that solution is not desirable to some of the participants then the mediator can try to make that solution look more desirable or move on to the next potential solution on the list.

Best Alternative to a Negotiated Agreement

In some cases and for multiple reasons mediation sometimes breaks down. "Best alternative to a negotiated agreement" or "BATNA" (Fisher & Ury 1981) refers to what a mediator will do if the mediation breaks down. Interestingly, the mediator will want to know the BATNA for the company but should not discuss this with the parties. Furthermore, participants should not be told about the concept of BATNA, because it refers to the next best realistic option for a party. What will realistically happen if the mediation breaks down? What will the company do next? If mediation dissolves, what is the most likely scenario to occur next? Sometimes BATNA is confused with a bottom line. A "bottom line" refers to the lowest threshold that is acceptable to a party as an acceptable solution during mediation. For example, a company's bottom line could be $300,000 for a settlement; anything more than this amount could cause severe financial difficulties for the company. A BATNA, however, is what the company's next best option is, excluding mediation. In other words, the second best solution if mediation is not used or if mediation breaks down. Understanding the BATNA is very important to mediation and bargaining. Basically, it enables investigators to gauge more effectively loss-gain endpoints. In turn, loss-gain endpoints determine how much effort and to what lengths investigators will have to go to either reach a mediated solution or explore other options.

ENDING MEDIATION

Throughout the investigation and mediation process investigators will want to look for opportunities to shut down liability. In the larger scheme of things, closing liability is not confined to asking specific liability-closing questions. Closing liability is a more diffuse topic that involves making parties satisfied with the outcome of the mediated solution and the investigation. One important way to close liability is to have signed documents by participants saying that they are satisfied with the investigation and mediation's conclusion and recommendations. These documents should be signed with—at minimum—a court recorder present (for sworn statements), and consultation with a lawyer is strongly recommended. A sworn and signed document is not the final goal, however. Even after this step, mediators always should treat parties with respect and must remember that anything less could result in future dissatisfaction and eventual litigation.

Mediation should be ended when an acceptable solution has been found; a solution that maximizes the greatest satisfaction for the greatest number of the participants. After all of the participants have agreed to the solution, a lawyer should be contracted to write it up as a legally binding contract. Of course, the participants must sign this contract. Again, just because it is legally binding does not mean that once the participants sign they have no future legal recourse. It is possible that some of the participants will not accept the mediated solution. This can sometimes be expected. Even with the most creative gerrymandering of a group of peoples' wishes, some will not be satisfied. This is acceptable as long as their BATNA is not likely to cause significant problems for the company or other parties. For example, the accuser's BATNA might be to seek external litigation, which likely will result in the loss of millions of dollars by the company. Mediators always should examine and anticipate all parties' BATNAs; this procedure determines what sort of leverage the parties have as compared to the mediators and what sort of concessions mediators should or should not make during mediation. Further, even if an investigation or mediation ends in a lawsuit, the fact that a thorough and competent investigation or mediation process took place will greatly increase the likelihood of a good outcome for the organization. Recent court findings (e.g., *Saxton v. AT&T*, 10 F.3d 526 (7th Cir. 1993); *Wathen v. General Electric Co.*, 115 F.3d 400 (6th Cir. 1997)) have sided with the company when a comprehensive and fair investigation took place. Thus, this investigative protocol reduces liability in two important ways, by helping to prevent lawsuits, and by increasing the likelihood of the court siding with the company if a lawsuit does occur.

CONCLUSIONS

Sexual harassment claims are a burden for both the individual employees and the larger organization involved. Despite an overwhelming need, there currently is no empirical research regarding the effectiveness of sexual harassment claim investigation protocols. The current protocol attempted to improve upon previous sexual harassment investigation guidelines by including procedures that are consistent with psychological theory and research, considering all possible investigation outcomes, and describing investigation and mediation procedures in a clear and detailed manner. Essential components of the proposed sexual harassment investigation protocol included coordinating interviews and other data-gathering efforts, gathering appropriate information, determining welcomeness, exploring and managing ancillary risk, preventing retaliation, dealing with danger from employees, identifying problematic and beneficial interviewer behaviors, using the right style to maximize the collection of information, and alleviating victimization.

Following the completion of evidence collection, the investigators are advised to examine the evidence and come to one of eight possible conclusions derived from both occurrence of the harassment and the validity of the claim. The mediation options are described for each potential outcome, which then guides whether an integrative approach or a distributive approach to mediation is implemented. The goals of the protocol are to gather accurate information, prevent and reduce any harm, and resolve the dispute in a way that is fair and efficient. This investigative protocol is designed based on the assumption that, at times, people can be unpredictable. The protocol is designed to maximize gains and minimize risks on average. Harm reduction, however, is predicated on a calculation of probability; that is, correct courses of action only are probabilistically correct. The unexpected can occur; people can feel hurt and the organization could end up in a lawsuit. This outcome, however, is much more likely to occur if an investigative protocol is poorly conceived or not used at all.

REFERENCES

Abbe, A., and Brandon, S. E. (2014). Building and maintaining rapport in investigative interviews. *Police Practice & Research: An International Journal* 15, 207–220. doi: 10.1080/15614263.2013.827835

Antecol, H., and Cobb-Clark, D. (2003). Does sexual harassment training change attitudes? A view from the federal level. *Social Science Quarterly* 84, 826–842.

Baron, R. A., and Neuman, J. H. (1996). Workplace violence and workplace aggression: Evidence on their relative frequency and potential causes. *Aggressive Behavior* 22, 161–173.

Bies, R. J., and Tripp, T. M. (2005). The study of revenge in the workplace: Conceptual, ideological, and empirical issues. In *Counterproductive work behavior: Investigations of actors and targets,* edited by S. Fox, and P. E. Spector, 65–81. Washington, DC: American Psychological Association. doi: 10.1037/10893-003

Burns, S. E. (1995). Issues in workplace sexual harassment law and related social science research. *Journal of Social Issues* 51, 193–207.

Coleman, F. T. (1993). Creating a workplace free of sexual harassment. *Association-Management* 45, 69–75.

Collins, R., Lincoln, R., and Frank, M. G. (2002). The effect of rapport in forensic interviewing. *Psychiatry, Psychology and Law* 9, 69–78.

Cortina, L., and Magley, V. (2003). Raising voice, risking retaliation: Events following interpersonal mistreatment in the workplace. *Journal of Occupational Health Psychology* 8, 247.

Cunningham, G. B., and Benavides-Espinoza, C. (2008). A trend analysis of sexual harassment claims: 1992–2006 1. *Psychological Reports* 103, 779–782.

Dawes, R. M., Faust, D., and Meehl, P. E. (1989). Clinical versus actuarial judgment. *Science* 243, 1668–1674.

Dodd, D. H., and Bradshaw, J. M. (1980). Leading questions and memory: Pragmatic constraints. *Journal of Verbal Learning and Verbal Behavior* 19, 695–704.

Duchan, J., and Kovarsky, D. (2011). Rapport and relationships in clinical interactions. *Topics In Language Disorders* 31, 297–299. doi:10.1097/TLD.0b013e31823baf91

Emery, R. E. (1994). Renegotiating family relationships: Divorce, child custody, and mediation. New York: Guilford press.

Feldman-Schorrig, S. (1996). Factitious sexual harassment. *Journal of the American Academy of Psychiatry and the Law Online* 24, 387–392.

Festinger, L., and Carlsmith, J. M. (1959). Cognitive consequences of forced compliance. *Journal of Abnormal and Social Psychology* 58, 203–210.

Fisher, R., and Ury, W. (1981). *Getting to yes: Negotiating agreement without giving in.* 1st ed. New York: Penguin.

Fitzgerald, L. E, Swan, S., and Magley, V. J. (1997). But was it really sexual harassment? Legal, behavioral, and psychological definitions of the workplace victimization of women. In *Sexual harassment: Theory, research and treatment,* edited by W. O'Donohue, 5–28. Boston: Allyn & Bacon.

Fitzgerald, L. F., Gelfand, M. J., and Drasgow, F. (1995). Measuring sexual harassment: Theoretical and psychometric advances. *Basic and Applied Social Psychology* 17, 425–445.

Galatzer-Levy, I. R., and Bryant, R. A. (2013). 636,120 ways to have posttraumatic stress disorder. *Perspectives on Psychological Science* 8, 651–662. doi: 10.1177/1745691613504115

Galdin, M., and Pino, E. W. (1997). *Neutrality: What an organizational ombudsman might want to know.* Dallas: Ombudsman Association.

Gelfand, M. J., Fitzgerald, L. F., and Drasgow, F. (1995). The structure of sexual harassment: A confirmatory analysis across cultures and settings. *Journal of Vocational Behavior* 47, 164–177.

Gruber, J. (1992). A typology of personal and environmental sexual harassment: Research and policy implications for the 1990s. *Sex Roles* 26 (11–12): 447–464.

Hassan, I. (2012). Skill development in the use of open- and closed-ended questions. *Australasian Psychiatry* 20, 534–535. doi: 10.1177/1039856212458165

Kaiser, H. F. (1960). Directional statistical decisions. *Psychological Review* 67, 160.

Kalmbach, K. C., and Lyons, P. M. (2006). Ethical issues in conducting forensic evaluations. *Applied Psychology in Criminal Justice* 2, 261–290.

Kearney, L. K., Rochlen, A. B., and King, E. B. (2004). Male gender role conflict, sexual harassment tolerance, and the efficacy of a psychoeducative training program. *Psychology of Men & Masculinity* 5 (1), 72.

Kerr, B. A., and Dell, D. M. (1976). Perceived interviewer expertness and attractiveness: Effects of interviewer behavior and attire and interview setting. *Journal of Counseling Psychology* 23 (6), 553.

Kobata, M. T. (1995). Minimize risk by investigating complaints promptly. *Personnel Journal* 74, 38–39.

Koen, C. M., and Morgan, J. D. (1997). Guidelines for conducting effective sexual harassment investigations. *Supervision* 58, 6–10.

Loftus, E. F. (1975). Leading questions and the eyewitness report. *Cognitive Psychology* 7, 560–572.

Mainiero, L. A., and Jones, K. J. (2013). Sexual Harassment versus workplace romance: Social media spillover and textual harassment in the workplace. *The Academy of Management Perspectives* 27, 187–203.

Marlatt, G. A. (1996). Harm reduction: Come as you are. *Addictive Behaviors* 21 (6), 779–788.

Martinie, M., Milland, L., and Olive, T. (2013). Some theoretical considerations on attitude, arousal and affect during cognitive dissonance. *Social and Personality Psychology Compass* 7 (9), 680–688. doi:10.1111/spc3.12051

Maypole, D. E., and Skaine, R. (1983). Sexual harassment in the workplace. *Social Work* 28, 385–390.

Michelson, G., and Mouly, V. S. (2004). Do loose lips sink ships? The meaning, antecedents and consequences of rumour and gossip in organisations. *Corporate Communications: An International Journal* 9, 189–201.

Milgram, S. (1963). Behavioral study of obedience. *The Journal of Abnormal and Social Psychology* 67, 371.

Neuman, J. H., and Baron, R. A. (1998). Workplace violence and workplace aggression: Evidence concerning specific forms, potential causes, and preferred targets. *Journal of Management* 24, 391–419.

Norfolk, T., Birdi, K., and Walsh, D. (2007). The role of empathy in establishing rapport in the consultation: A new model. *Medical Education* 41, 690–697. doi: 10.1111/j.1365-2923.2007.02789.x

O'Donohue, W. T., and Fanetti, M. (1996). Assessing the occurrence of child sexual abuse: An information processing, hypothesis testing approach. *Aggression and Violent Behavior* 1, 269–281.

Oxburgh, G. E., and Dando, C. J. (2011). Psychology and interviewing: What direction now in our quest for reliable information? *British Journal of Forensic Practice* 13, 135–144.

Passmore, J. (2011). Motivational interviewing techniques reflective listening. *The Coaching Psychologist* 7, 50–53.

Patterson, D. (2011). The linkage between secondary victimization by law enforcement and rape case outcomes. *Journal of Interpersonal Violence* 26, 328–347.

Poole, D. A., and White, L. T. (1991). Effects of question repetition on the eyewitness testimony of children and adults. *Developmental Psychology* 27, 975.

Ross, L., and Nisbett, R. E. (1991). *The person and the situation: Perspectives of social psychology.* New York; England: McGraw-Hill.

Rudd, M. D., Berman, A. L., Joiner, T. E., Nock, M. K., Silverman, M. M., Mandrusiak, M., . . . and Witte, T. (2006). Warning signs for suicide: Theory, research, and clinical applications. *Suicide and Life-Threatening Behavior* 36, 255–262.

Segal, J. A. (1993). Proceed carefully, objectively to investigate sexual harassment claims. *HR Magazine* 38, 91–95.

Sharman, S. J., and Powell, M. B. (2012). A comparison of adult witnesses' suggestibility across various types of leading questions. *Applied Cognitive Psychology* 26, 48–53.

Sharps, M. J., Herrera, M., Dunn, L., and Alcala, E. (2012). Repetition and reconfiguration: Demand-based confabulation in initial eyewitness memory. *Journal of Investigative Psychology and Offender Profiling* 9, 149–160.

Shaw, J. S., III, and McClure, K. A. (1996). Repeated postevent questioning can lead to elevated levels of eyewitness confidence. *Law and Human Behavior* 20, 629–654.

Smith, S. M., and Vela, E. (2001). Environmental context-dependent memory: A review and meta-analysis. *Psychonomic Bulletin & Review* 8, 203–220.

Snook, B., Luther, K., Quinlan, H., and Milne, R. (2012). Let 'em talk! A field study of police questioning practices of suspects and accused persons. *Criminal Justice and Behavior* 39, 1328–1339.

Spann, J. (1990). Dealing effectively with sexual harassment: Some practical lessons from one city's experience. *Public Personnel Management* 19, 53–69.

Stark, S., Chernyshenko, O. S., Lancaster, A. R., Drasgow, F., and Fitzgerald, L. F. (2002). Toward standardized measurement of sexual harassment: Shortening the SEQ-DoD using item response theory. *Military Psychology* 14, 49–72. doi: 10.1207/S15327876MP1401_03

Thorley, C. (2013). Memory conformity and suggestibility. *Psychology, Crime & Law* 19, 565–575.

U.S. Department of Labor, Bureau of Labor Statistics. (2005). *News: Survey of workplace violence prevention, 2005.* http://www.bls.gov/iif/oshwc/osnr0026.pdf. Accessed April 16, 2015.

U.S. Equal Employment Opportunity Commission (EEOC). (2009). Fiscal year 2009 annual report. http://www.eeoc.gov/eeoc/litigation/reports/09annrpt.cfm. Accessed April 16, 2015.

U.S. Equal Employment Opportunity Commission (EEOC). (1990). Policy guidance on current issues of sexual harassment. http://www.eeoc.gov/eeoc/publications/index.cfm. Accessed June 28, 2010.

U.S. Equal Employment Opportunity Commission (EEOC). (1980). Guidelines on discrimination because of sex. *Federal Register* 45, 74676–74677.

U.S. Merit Systems Protection Board (USMSPB) (1988). *Sexual harassment in the federal government: An update.* Washington, DC: U.S. GPO.

U.S. Merit Systems Protection Board (USMSPB) (1981). *Sexual harassment in the federal government: Is it a problem?* Washington, DC: U.S. GPO.

Wagner, E. (1992). *Sexual harassment in the workplace: How to prevent, investigate, and resolve problems in your organization.* New York: American Management Association.

Wright, C. V., and Fitzgerald, L. F. (2009). Correlates of joining a sexual harassment class action. *Law and Human Behavior* 33, 265–282. doi: 10.1007/s10979 -008-9156-6

Chapter 17

Understanding Sexual Harassment Dilemmas: Complaint Management, Investigation Processes, and Workplace Impact

Katie L. Pustolka

Each day in the media, stories of harassment and inappropriate conduct abound—in schools, the workplace, and public venues alike. Teasing and bullying can lead to harassment, conduct that is proven to have damaging, lasting effects on those subjected to it. Sexual harassment—harassment that is sexual in nature or gender based—often is the action that gets the most press and has the most potential for serious consequences for businesses, victims, and the accused.

THE TRUE MEANINGS OF BULLYING AND HARASSMENT

Over the past several years, "bullying" has been a hot-button word in academia, pop culture, and in workplaces. Conduct from managers such as insults, humiliation, and mocking unfortunately are not uncommon in the United States, but are not exactly illegal either. This conduct—"bullying"—certainly is not professional and can border on harassment if the conduct is severe.

In general, harassment is a form of employment discrimination that violates Title VII of the Civil Rights Act of 1964, the Age Discrimination in Employment Act of 1967 (ADEA), and the Americans with Disabilities Act of 1990 (ADA). For the purposes of this discussion, it is assumed that employers would meet the coverage requirements of the legislation—employers with 15 or more employees must abide by Title VII and the ADA, and those with 20 or more employees must abide by the ADEA. Harassment is considered any unwelcome conduct that is based on race, color, religion, sex (including pregnancy), national origin, age (40 years old or older), disability, or genetic information. Harassment becomes unlawful when enduring the offensive conduct becomes a condition of continued employment, or if the conduct is severe and pervasive enough to create a work environment that a reasonable person would consider intimidating, hostile, or abusive. Petty annoyances and isolated incidents (unless very serious) generally do not rise to the level of harassment, although it could be argued that the effects of such conduct have many of the same effects as harassment (discussed elsewhere in this chapter).

To understand the impact that sexual harassment can have on the alleged victims, the alleged harasser, and the company, one must fully understand the definition of sexual harassment. Sexual harassment is a form of sex discrimination that violates Title VII of the Civil Rights Act of 1964. Companies, organizations, and government agencies with 15 or more employees must abide by Title VII. According to the U.S. Equal Employment Opportunity Commission (EEOC), sexual harassment includes unwanted sexual advances, requests for sexual favors, and other verbal or physical harassment of a sexual nature when this conduct explicitly or implicitly affects an individual's employment; unreasonably interferes with an individual's work performance; or creates an intimidating, hostile, or offensive work environment. Title VII also prohibits an employer from discriminating or retaliating against anyone who has made a claim of harassment or anyone who has testified, assisted, or participated in an investigation or hearing related to the claim.

The EEOC also considers offensive remarks about an individual's sex to be harassment. Importantly, the complainant and the harasser can be either male or female, and the complainant and harasser can be of the same or opposite sex. The circumstances in which sexual harassment can occur are wide ranging. What makes prevention and management of harassment difficult is that essentially anyone can be accused of harassment—supervisors, coworkers, vendors, suppliers, customers. Equally difficult, is that victims certainly are the individuals to whom the unwelcome conduct was directed, but they also can be any bystanders who found the conduct offensive.

With so many variables in sexual harassment situations, the potential for litigation is serious. Unfortunately, many instances of sexual harassment are not reported, but those that are and that reach litigation can have detrimental effects on an organization. In addition to long-standing psychological effects, poor publicity, and low morale and productivity, the financial costs are steep. In the past few decades, millions of dollars have been paid in restitution to employees who suffered from sexual harassment. In 1990, for example, in the case of *Bihun v. AT&T Information Systems*, a personnel manager was awarded $2 million for suffering mental distress after receiving unwelcome advances from her supervisor (Larson 1996). In 1998, a UPS employee who said she was punished after accusing a coworker of poking her in the breast was awarded $80.7 million (Ahmad 1998). Also in 1998, Mitsubishi agreed to pay $34 million to female workers at the Normal, Illinois, plant after it allowed a hostile setting to exist since 1990 (Fabio 1996). With just a few examples, it's clear that sexual harassment cases are taken seriously in court and must be taken seriously by company management as well.

The financial risks of sexual harassment suits are climbing, because in 1991, the Civil Rights Act allowed juries to award both compensatory *and* punitive damages to plaintiffs. For example, settlement awards from 1991 to 1997 rose from $7.1 million to $49.4 million (Ahmad 1998). After Supreme Court Justice Clarence Thomas was accused of sexual harassment in 1991, offerings of Employment Practices Liability (EPL) insurance began. Employment Practices Liability insurance is a type of coverage that protects employers against lawsuits relate to Title VII violations, among other laws, such as the ADEA, ADA, and FMLA. Although some organizations might think that EPL is an added protection, the morality of taking out such insurance coverage has been debated by legal experts and civil rights groups—for example, are companies insuring themselves against intentional acts of discrimination and harassment (Ahmad 1998)? Rather than take out insurance to save face (and finances), employers should foster a work environment free from harassment, prevent harassment from occurring in the first place, and have clear procedures for issues as they arise.

BEST PRACTICES FOR COMPLAINT MANAGEMENT AND INVESTIGATIONS

A sexual harassment claim in and of itself indicates that something has gone awry in policy, prevention, or in an individual's judgement. It is imperative that all employers (especially those with 15 or more employees covered by Title VII) have a sexual harassment policy in place as well as a complaint and investigation procedure. As Trotter and Zacur (2012) outline, it is the responsibility of the employer to have an understanding of relevant law, to develop a thorough and publicized sexual harassment policy (that can be easily understood by all staff), to train employees and managers to help them understand (and carry out) the policy, and a have procedure for complaints and investigations. Having a sexual harassment policy in and of itself is not enough to avoid an EEOC charge—the crux of sexual harassment complaints often lies in the investigation and subsequent action taken by the employer.

From the moment a manager, supervisor, or company official is made aware of a sexual harassment complaint, prompt action must be taken. Trotter and Zacur (2012) consider the first manager to learn of the complaint as the "intake manager." This first point of contact for the complainant should display sensitivity for the matter at hand, and still keep in mind the best interests of the company. It is recommended that this initial manager should have a private meeting with the employee (complainant) and record in writing everything said at this meeting, including the date and time. It is also recommended that the employee review the notes to ensure their accuracy and then sign them. These notes then should be forwarded to the human resources department so that a prompt investigation can begin.

The human resources department, or a designated investigator, must be prompt in the assessment of the complaint, first deciding whether the complaint merits a sexual harassment investigation. Some questions to consider include

- Does the company policy mandate an investigation?
- How serious is the complaint?
- What are the implications of the complaint?
- Is the party complaining a member of a protected class?
- Is there, or has there been, more than one related concern?
- Is litigation looming? (Hastings 2010)

Even if the complaint is from the "rumor mill," it must be followed up on, and managers always should assume that the rumor is true. If the complaint does not merit an investigation, it certainly still warrants follow-up. Addressing issues efficiently—even those not considered immediate harassment—can protect an employer from a hostile work environment charge in the future.

Once a complaint is deemed to warrant an investigation, there are specific steps that must be taken for an investigation to be considered legally valid. At a minimum, an investigation must include interviewing the complainant, the alleged harasser, and any witnesses that are able to corroborate either story. Trotter and Zacur (2012) note that prior to beginning an investigation interview the investigator also should verify whether the complainant is part of a union. From the first day a complaint is made everything must be documented, and the information be housed in a separate file.

Upon beginning the process, the investigator should review the company's sexual harassment policy and confidentiality statement, and should reinforce protection against retaliation prior to asking any investigation questions. When questions are presented to any involved parties, they should be open ended yet allow the investigator to obtain specific information such as who was involved; who might have seen the incident; who might've been told about the incident; exactly what happened and when; and the places, dates, and times. Finding out whether there is a pattern to a specific behavior also is imperative. Investigators should request any evidence that the complainant, harasser, or witnesses might have. In today's technological age, this could include e-mails, screenshots or printouts of social media posts, text messages, and voice mail. After determining whether sexual harassment occurred, the investigator must determine what appropriate corrective or disciplinary action to take against the harasser. Finally, the investigator should update all parties involved—the complainant, the accused, and witnesses (on a "need-to-know" basis). Periodic follow-up meetings with the complainant and the harasser should occur to ascertain whether the situation has been resolved to the complainant's satisfaction and to ensure that retaliation has not occurred. Hastings (2011), states it well—the investigator should "tie the investigation up in a bow by getting back to the complainant to ensure he [or] she is satisfied with what was done."

INVESTIGATION DON'TS—DILEMMAS TO AVOID

There are numerous EEOC and Supreme Court rulings that demonstrate the responsibility employers have when it comes to proper complaint and investigation procedures. Employers may be held liable for not establishing, disseminating, or consistently enforcing a sexual harassment policy (Trotter & Zacur 2012). Of equal importance to creating and upholding a proper policy, it is crucial company officials and human resources professionals be aware of what *not* to do with a sexual harassment complaint or investigation.

Consider the following example. Hastings (2011) describes how the *Pittsburgh Tribune-Review* published a news article describing how a Pittsburgh bar owner was alleged to have posted threatening messages on an employee's Facebook page after the employee had filed a complaint. At the time of the article, the complaint still was under investigation, but actions such as this are far too common in the business world. Employers and staff alike must be aware that posting harassing messages on social media sites (such as Facebook, Twitter, LinkedIn, and Instagram) can be just as damaging as verbal or physical conduct, if not more so.

Although it is important for business leaders to carefully consider complaints from employees, there might be a few individuals who seem to complain about everything—from their workload, to their coworkers, to the types of food served in the company cafeteria. Although these employees can be trying, if any employee alerts a company official of a sexual harassment complaint, the complaint must be investigated—even if the complainant complains about everything. Equally difficult is if a sexual harassment complaint comes from an executive who just wants to make a company official (human resources department, company attorney, or other company officer) aware, but does not wish for any action to be taken. It is the responsibility of the investigator to take every complaint seriously—verbally or written—even if the individual requests that no action be taken. Executives and high-ranking officials can prove problematic in the complaint procedure in other ways—they might think that an investigation is not necessary, that an employee is being dramatic, or that there are more important tasks to focus on. Hastings (2011) suggests building a file of news reports and case settlements to provide to the executive or CEO—a person might quickly change his or her tune after seeing the implications in black and white.

The investigator himself or herself also can prove to be a liability. A company must have a procedure for choosing an individual to investigate complaints of sexual harassment. Investigators most often are members of the human resources department, but not always. When choosing an investigator it's important to evaluate that individual's familiarity with policies, procedures, the law itself, and his or her ability to maintain confidentiality. The company also must consider whether the investigator would make a good witness if he or she was put on the stand in a trial. Note that caution should be taken when choosing a company attorney to investigate complaints of sexual harassment—it should be fully considered whether attorney-client privilege would impact the investigation or—down the line—a trial. A neutral, outside investigator might be a preferable option, especially if the complaining party is "known to be litigious, if the allegations are against someone with significant authority, or if for other reasons the employer believes litigation is likely" (Trotter & Zacur 2012).

After choosing an individual to investigate and then beginning the investigation process, there are several actions that must be avoided. These might seem obvious but must be stated; the investigator must never joke about the incident with others; must not rush judgement or take sides; and, unlike the Pittsburgh bar owner, must never use text messaging, e-mail, or social media to discuss the complaint. Throughout the investigation, the investigator must be aware of comments and behaviors that could be considered retaliatory, such as threatening the employee or criticizing the employee for filing a charge; discussing the charge with the employee (outside of investigation fact-finding); discussing the charge with anyone outside of the company or anyone who does not "need to know"; ignoring the complainer in meetings, e-mails, or during office activities; or treating the worker differently by disciplining, demoting, or firing the worker (Hastings 2011).

Another dilemma for an organization and for a sexual harassment investigation is if the complainant has not been managed appropriately, or has had performance issues prior to the complaint. Consider the following example.

Jane Smith works in the Engineering Department of XYZ Company. She has been underperforming for months but her manager, Noreen Jones, feels uncomfortable having conversations regarding Jane's performance. Although Noreen is frustrated, she has not been properly documenting Jane's performance deficiencies. A few months down the line Jane attends a meeting. At the meeting one of the attendees makes a "joke" that Jane finds unsavory. The next day, Jane files a sexual harassment complaint with the human resources department. Throughout the investigation, Jane's performance continued to be sub-par, as it was prior to the incident. Throughout Jane's employment, Noreen did not keep Human Resources in the loop about performance issues prior to or during the complaint of sexual harassment. Noreen finally decided that she wanted to take disciplinary action.

At this point, the manager in the above example, Noreen, has put the investigation and the company at risk for multiple reasons. The first reason is that Noreen mismanaged Jane's performance. The second misstep was that Noreen poorly documented performance issues, and only after a complaint was submitted was she finally so dissatisfied that she wanted to take disciplinary action. Although performance must be managed appropriately, Noreen and the human resources staff must tread lightly in this situation. Jane likely would be able to go to trial and claim that disciplinary action was based on her complaint of sexual harassment and not on her performance issues (as there was no documentation of any performance problems). The lesson to learn from this example is that managers must consistently and accurately document performance issues and follow up as soon as action is necessary. Waiting until it is too late proves problematic and can open up the company to even more risk, especially when paired with a harassment claim. It should also be mentioned that perhaps even worse than conducting an inappropriate, incomplete, or biased investigation, is not conducting one at all.

IMPACT OF SEXUAL HARASSMENT AND CROSS-CULTURAL CONSIDERATIONS

It is well known that time and effort allocated to sexual harassment investigations, EEOC claims, legal fees, and potential court settlements are costly. But what are the true costs of harassment claims—to the victim, the harasser, the work group, and the overall company climate?

Harassment claims—especially sexual harassment—are not measured merely in dollars—although, for a Fortune 500 company, sexual harassment can cost about $6.7 million dollars per year (Crawford 1995). Other indirect costs of harassment are difficult to measure, such as a negative public image for a company as the result of a publicized sexual harassment suit. It is well documented that only a fraction of sexual harassment incidents actually are formally reported (Goldberg 2007; Kath, Swody, Magley, Bunk & Gallus 2009; Ulusoy, Swigart & Erdemir 2011). Incidents that are not reported and remedied appropriately can result in turnover, low morale, resentment and distrust, and decreases in productivity (Crawford 1995; Kath et al. 2009).

It is not surprising that men and women experience harassment differently. According to Crawford (1996), women who have experienced harassment are nine times more likely to quit, five times more likely to transfer, and three times more likely to be dismissed. Employees subject to sexual harassment also experience low morale at work—as could their colleagues and workgroup. Employees could start to resent or mistrust their employer (Crawford 1995) based on how complaints are handled. They also could view their employer's response—or lack thereof—as a lack of support (Kath et al. 2009).

In addition to gender impacting the way an individual is affected by harassment, culture plays an integral role as well. Several studies have demonstrated the way in which sexual harassment is viewed and dealt with cross-culturally (Crocker & Kalemba 1999; Goldberg 2007; Ulusoy et al. 2011). From denying that a harassment incident ever occurred, to blaming oneself, to confrontation, employees have various reactions to having endured sexual harassment—many of which are deep-rooted based on cultural background. Human resources and management personnel who are aware of cultural differences might be better prepared to respond to harassment claims (whether complainant, perpetrator, or investigation team member).

In a recent study conducted in Turkey, researchers found that in the medical profession almost 68% of female doctors surveyed had experienced sexual harassment by a patient or a patient's family member (Ulusoy et al. 2011). Some of the most common harassing behaviors included staring at the doctor in a lewd manner, asking for dates or asking questions about private sexual matters, making threats, and inappropriate touching. The harassment these doctors-in-training experienced directly impacted their work performance—for example, Ulusoy and colleagues (2011) found that to cope with the harassment, the doctors most commonly discharged, or asked to discharge, the harasser or stopped all contact with the individual. This brings up an interesting dilemma—in the medical profession, doctors have a responsibility (and have taken an oath) to care for their patients. When the patient or family member is also a perpetrator of harassment, that behavior impacts not only the work performance of the physician, but affects the potential care the patient might receive as well. Similar outcomes would be expected in other work environments—deadlines might not be met, customers might not be served, and businesses might not run efficiently. In response to the harassment, only 4% of the women surveyed in the Ulusoy (2011) study sought help from a supervisor or manager. Had a supervisor been aware of the conduct, perhaps the doctors could have been assigned to other patients without having to endure the harassment.

Rather than seek out assistance, it has been demonstrated that Turkish women are more likely to use avoidance and denial as coping mechanisms when subjected to sexual harassment. These coping mechanisms could be rooted in Turkish culture—Turkish men are more likely to believe that sexual harassment is provoked by the way women dress, behave, or talk, and feel that any woman who is harassed has brought it on herself (cited in Ulusoy et al. 2011). With this understanding of the cultural opinions on harassment, it is not surprising that the doctors-in-training most often paid attention to their own verbal and nonverbal communication and manner of dress when dealing with harassers. It is very common in any workplace for the victim of harassment to internalize and blame herself or himself rather than blame the harasser. The doctors also expressed an interest in security and protection, but were not comfortable with requesting such help outright. As such, management and supervisors must provide an effective method for bringing complaints and concerns to the forefront. This also illustrates how imperative it is that organizations (for-profit or not-for-profit) have clear harassment and complaint procedures.

Similar to the experience of female Turkish doctors, a survey of 1,990 working women in Canada found that 56% of the respondents experienced harassment the year prior to the survey, with 77% having experienced harassment in the workplace at some point during their work lives (Crocker & Kalemba 1999). The most common issues the women in Canada faced were staring and inappropriate jokes (likely contributing to a hostile working environment). In contrast to the study conducted in Turkey, 30% of women surveyed who had been subject to sexual harassment reported that their job was affected—by increased stress (reported by 45% of the women) and feeling hindered and unable to do their jobs (48%) (Crocker & Kalemba 1999). Additionally, the Canadian women admitted to personal issues as a result of the sexual harassment, including preoccupation (41%), stress in the home (29%), and distrust of men (19%) (Crocker & Kalemba 1999).

Interestingly, Canadian women were just as likely to respond to sexual harassment directly, such as reporting or confrontation, as they were to respond indirectly, by way of ignoring the harasser, not responding, or changing one's behavior. Although clearly people's personalities influence the way in which they respond to sexual harassment, Crocker and Kalemba (1999) found that women harassed by coworkers were more likely to confront the situation than to ignore it; harassment from supervisors was often dealt with by not responding or by quitting; and harassment by clients or customers often was ignored. Harassment from clients or customers presents a difficult situation. Often, employees in customer service or sales roles are dependent on their customers for their livelihood. Additionally, high-wealth or high-value clientele might create a sense of fear in employees. If these individuals are responsible for harassment, then employees might not report such incidents for fear of upsetting management, losing business, or—ultimately—losing their jobs.

In addition to culture, the climate of an organization—the attitudes and standards of a company—has been shown to impact the psychological outcomes for men and women who have experienced harassment (Kath et al. 2009). A company climate is created by the messages sent by upper management through to the comments and opinions expressed by staff members. Kath and colleagues (2009) describes two types of climates in an organization—a "beneficial climate" and a "detrimental climate." According to Kath et al. (2009), a beneficial climate is one where harassing behaviors are discouraged or not tolerated, and there is strong procedural justice for correcting harassment. For example, complaints that are filed in an organization with a beneficial climate are taken seriously and acted upon. Those employees found to have violated a harassment policy are subject to punishment. Kath and colleagues (2009) describe a detrimental climate as one where harassing behaviors are perceived to be tolerated or even encouraged.

Climate can be an important influence on those affected by sexual harassment—employees can feel empowered by their environment to report an incident and have faith it will be handled appropriately (beneficial climate), or employees can work in a climate that makes them feel as though a claim would not be taken seriously or kept confidential (detrimental climate). Kath and colleagues (2009) found that men who worked in a beneficial climate did not experience issues with job satisfaction after experiencing sexual harassment. Conversely, women who experienced sexual harassment in a beneficial climate had the opposite experience— working in a beneficial climate and experiencing moderate to frequent sexual harassment was "particularly devastating" to the women's job satisfaction. Women can feel especially impacted by experiencing sexual harassment in a beneficial climate because they feel they are to blame for the conduct that was forced upon them. Additionally, males and females can define and view sexual harassment differently.

An individual's perceptions of harassment, prior experience, sexist attitudes, and gender roles all impact the way in which he or she views harassment. Although the only people to blame for harassment are those perpetrating it, it has been shown that males attribute more blame to females who have been subject to harassment, rather than to the actual harasser (De Judicibus & McCabe 2001). This can have a direct impact on the way an employee interacts with supervisors, subordinates, and coworkers, especially if these individuals have any involvement in a harassment claim or the investigation process. Opinions from supervisors also can trickle down to subordinates and to workgroups, thus fostering an environment that can prove hostile and harassing in and of itself.

SUGGESTIONS FOR TRAINING

The only way to create a welcoming and productive work environment free from harassment is to change perceptions and attitudes. After a harassment policy has been developed, a company-wide training program should be instituted with support from top management. The training should include information on the sexual harassment policy, clear explanations on the complaint procedure, and examples of conduct that is not appropriate. Management and those involved in investigations should attend a separate, thorough training on their specific roles. All new staff should be trained upon hire, and all existing staff should be trained annually.

If a company is concerned about perceptions or biases of the staff, then a separate training should enable individuals to learn about their own biases and how to prevent these biases from impacting their management of staff, or how they would handle a complaint or investigation. After the training the organization should begin to foster a more welcoming environment by encouraging open discussion by employees to earn their trust and loyalty, and checking in periodically with staff to gauge their opinions on the changing culture of the organization. Training does not create instantaneous change, but with perseverance and follow-up it ultimately can change a work environment for the better.

Sexual harassment and inappropriate workplace conduct are unfortunately commonplace situations not only laden with legal concerns but with long-term implications for those affected by it, as well. Human resources personnel and management must be aware of the legislation pertaining to sexual harassment, create a transparent policy and compliant procedure against harassment, and spend time training all staff on harassment "do's and don'ts." It also is crucial that management become aware of the cultural differences that can impact the way in which staff members respond to harassing situations, as these differences can directly impact how individuals react to such situations. Awareness of the long-term effects of harassment also can assist companies in mediating consequences such as low morale, turnover, and litigation.

REFERENCES

Ahmad, S. (1998, March 2). Get your sex insurance now. *U.S. News & World Report* 124, 8, 61.

Crawford, S. (1995). Economic impact of sexual harassment in the workplace. *USA Today Magazine* 123, 25, 35–36.

Crocker, D., and Kalemba, V. (1999). The incidence and impact of women's experiences of sexual harassment in Canadian workplaces. *CRSA/RCSA* 36, 4, 541–558.

De Judicibus, M., and McCabe, M. (2001). Blaming the target of sexual harassment: Impact of gender role, sexist attitudes, and work role. *Sex Roles* 44, 7/8, 401–417.

Fabio, M. (2006, June). Five biggest sexual harassment cases. *Legalzoom.* http://www.legalzoom.com/legal-headlines/corporate-lawsuits/five-biggest-sexual-harassment-cases. Accessed May 13, 2015.

Goldberg, C. (2007). The impact of training and conflict avoidance on responses to sexual harassment. *Psychology of Women Quarterly* 31, 62–72.

Hastings, R. (2011, January 26). What not to do with employee complaints. *SHRM.* http://www.shrm.org/hrdisciplines/employeerelations/articles/Pages/WhatNottoDo.aspx. Accessed May 13, 2015.

Hastings, R. (2010, March 22). Expert provides guidance on investigation dilemmas. *SHRM, N/A.* http://www.shrm.org/hrdisciplines/employeerelations/articles/Pages/InvestigationDilemmas.aspx. Accessed April 20, 2015.

Kath, L. M., Swody, C. A., Magley, V. J., Bunk, J. A., and Gallus, J. A. (2009). Cross-level, three-way interactions among work-group climate, gender, and frequency of harassment on morale and withdrawal outcomes of sexual harassment. *Journal of Occupational and Organization Psychology* 82, 159–182.

Larson, E. (1996, August 1). The economic costs of sexual harassment: Expansion of a crime's definition obscures genuine instances of it. *The Freeman: Foundation for Economic Education.* http://www.fee.org/the_freeman/detail/the-economic-costs-of-sexual-harassment#axzz2YPaiN5ac. Accessed July 2, 2013.

Trotter, R., and Zacur, S. (2012). Investigating sexual harassment complaints: An update for managers and employers. *SAM Advanced Management Journal* (Winter 2012), 28–37.

Ulusoy, H., Swigart, V., and Erdemir, F. (2011). Think globally, act locally: Understanding sexual harassment from a cross-cultural perspective. *Medical Education* 45, 603–612.

Appendix A: Street Harassment and Students

Delaney Rives, Olivia Emigh, Anna Youngmann, and David Morales

As seniors at the Sister Thea Bowman Center for Women on the Siena College campus, many of us have been reflecting on the types of programming we want to implement during our last year of our undergraduate studies. Members of the Peace and Non-Violence committee chose to focus specifically on "anti-slut shaming" and "anti-street harassment"; two controversial issues that have only briefly been touched on in campus programming. Our devotion to ending street harassment, and more specifically to ending sexual harassment on college campuses, is due to the fact that every single female member of our staff easily could recall an instance when she had been publicly harassed on campus.

One student recalled being called a "slut" while merely walking across campus in sweatpants; another remembers hearing "Where's that ass going tonight?" shouted at her as she left her townhouse. One student told the story of how a friend was followed by a man who tried to take "upskirt" pictures of her to post on Instagram. Derogatory epithets and disgusting phrases such as, "I want your pussy, shaved or not!" are shouted out of dormitory windows every weekend, because perpetrators are able to hide behind a screen of anonymity. Most often, women are told that it's their fault for provoking these unwanted remarks due to their appearance, dress, or even the time of day or their location when the harassment occurred. Based on the experiences of these women, however, it is obvious that there is a more subtle and subversive force that allows men the license and feelings of entitlement to women's bodies.

We think that some men are socially conditioned to believe that they have the right to comment on women's bodies. Conversely, women are conditioned to believe that these comments are not an issue. Street harassment and catcalls are experienced so often—especially on college campuses—that women do not realize that they have a legal right to a safe educational environment free from such hostile encounters and that the day-to-day harassment they experience violates this right.

Our committee decided to focus on this issue during our programming throughout the year and has developed several different programs to combat street harassment and sexual harassment in the form of slut-shaming. Our first initiative was to create an educational poster titled "Campus Catcalls: Breaking Down Street Harassment" to be installed in every single classroom on campus. This is a huge success in terms of access to campus facilities because there are so many policies that restrict student promotion of events. With the help of our campus Title IX Coordinator, Michele Paludi, however, we were able to use Title IX regulations to reinforce the importance of this issue and that students have the right to know their options when it comes to encountering and reporting these forms of harassment.

Additionally, we currently are developing a public program about violent language, to address some of the common phrases or remarks that presently are used in our society. Our hope is that by raising awareness of the subconscious influence of these terms we can effectively change our campus culture to be more peaceful, just, and welcoming to a diverse range of students. Some phrases we're deconstructing include "Man, I just raped that exam," "What a retard," and "That's so gay." This program is a great way to address slut-shaming as well, because referring to women as "sluts," "whores," and other terms referring to actual or rumored sexual behavior is a gendered form of bullying that ultimately is dehumanizing. These terms and phrases are dangerous because they desensitize issues of rape and sexual assault and allow for victim-blaming to run rampant in our everyday conversations around these unfortunately common crimes.

Appendix B: Organizations

Amanda Knipple, Susan Strauss, and Michele A. Paludi

9 to 5: Winning Justice for Working Women. http://9to5.org/

American Association of University Women (AAUW): Know Your Rights at Work. http://www.aauw.org/what-we-do/legal-resources/know-your-rights-at-work/workplace-sexual-harassment/

American Civil Liberties Union: Women's Rights. https://www.aclu.org/womens-rights

Department of Defense Sexual Assault Prevention and Response. http://www.defense.gov/home/features/2012/0912_sexual-assault/

Department of Justice Office on Violence Against Women. http://www.ovw.usdoj.gov/overview.htm

Department of Labor Women's Bureau. http://www.dol.gov/wb/

Equal Employment Opportunity Commission: Sexual Harassment. http://www.eeoc.gov/laws/types/sexual_harassment.cfm

Equal Rights Advocates. http://www.equalrights.org/legal-help/know-your-rights/sexual-harassment-at-work/

Feminist Majority Foundation. http://www.feminist.org/default.asp

Hollaback. http://www.ihollaback.org/

INCITE. http://www.incite-national.org/

Institute for Women's Policy Research (IWPR). http://www.iwpr.org/

International Coalition Against Sexual Harassment (ICASH). http://jan.ucc.nau.edu/~pms/icash.html

Legal Momentum—Women's Legal Defense and Education Fund. https://www.legalmomentum.org/

Mexican American Legal Defense and Education Fund. https://www
    .facebook.com/MALDEF
National Asian Pacific American Women's Forum. http://napawf.org
    /about/staff/
National Bar Association, Women Lawyers Division. http://www.national-
    bar.org/women_lawyers
National Center for Victims of Crime. http://www.ncvc.org/
National Council of Black Women. http://nationalcongressbw.org/
National Council of Negro Women, Inc. http://www.ncnw.org/
National Domestic Violence Hotline. http://www.thehotline.org/
National Organization of Women (NOW). http://now.org/
National Sexual Assault Hotline. https://www.safehelpline.org
    /?gclid=CjkKEQjw5qmdBRCn--70gPSo074BEiQAJCe7zUVJlsmn
    UYHrQ92dqnqykN235_pmwJ-S9ESH6_7dS8Tw_wcB
National Sexual Violence Resource Center. http://www.nsvrc.org
    /organizations
National Women's Law Center. http://www.nwlc.org/about-national
    -womens-law-center
Rainbo. http://www.rainbo.org/organizations-fight-for-womens-rights/
RAINN—Rape, Abuse & Incest National Network. http://www.rainn
    .org/get-information/types-of-sexual-assault/sexual-harassment
Sexual Assault Resource Agency (SARA). http://saracville.org/
Society for Human Resource Management (SHRM). https://www.shrm
    .org/Pages/default.aspx
Stop Street Harassment. http://www.stopstreetharassment.org/wp-
    content/uploads/2012/08/2014-National-SSH-Street-Harassment-
    Report.pdf
UC Berkeley Gender Equity Resource Center. http://geneq.berkeley.edu
    / sexual_and_dating_violence_additional_resources
U.S. Department of Education Office for Civil Rights and Title IX. http://
    www.ed.gov/category/keyword/titleix
U.S. Department of Labor, Women's Bureau. http://www.dol.gov/wb
    /stats/stats_data.htm
Victim Rights Law Center. https://www.victimrights.org/
Women Employed. http://womenemployed.org/
YWCA USA. http://www.ywca.org/site/c.cuIRJ7NTKrLaG/b.7515807
    /k.2737/YWCA__Eliminating_Racism_Empowering_Women.htm

Appendix C: Sample Training Program Outlines

Michele A. Paludi

AN ETHIC OF CARE AND RESPECT: TRAINING FOR EMPLOYEES

Diversity versus Inclusivity

The New Workforce: Increased Participation of

- Individuals of Color
- Women
- Older Individuals
- LGBT Individuals
- Mentally and Physically Challenged Individuals
- "In-Between Generation"

Stereotypes, Prejudice, and Discrimination

- Federally Protected Categories
- State-Protected Categories
- Discrimination Defined Legally
- Harassment Defined Legally

Sexual Harassment

- Quid Pro Quo
- Hostile Environment
- Behavioral Examples of Sexual Harassment
- Behavioral Examples of Discrimination
- Hostile Work Environments
- Third-Party Harassment
- Contrapower Harassment
- Domestic Violence
- Dating Violence
- Stalking
- Rape
- Consent
- Incapacitation

IMPACT OF DISCRIMINATION, HARASSMENT, AND SEXUAL MISCONDUCT ON INDIVIDUALS AND ORGANIZATION

Legal Responsibilities

- Effective and Enforced Policy
- Effective and Enforced Procedures
- Training Programs
- Retaliation

FACULTY DEVELOPMENT WORKSHOPS FOR TEACHING ABOUT SEXUAL HARASSMENT IN UNDERGRADUATE AND GRADUATE TRAINING PROGRAMS

- Introduction
- Sexual Harassment as a Threat to Educational Equity and Career Development
- Academe as Transformational
- Courses: Catalysts for Change

Common Approaches to Discussing Sexual Harassment in the Curriculum

- Add On

- Curriculum Infusion
- Transformation

Culturally Responsive Teaching Obstacles to Transforming the Curriculum Faculty Development

- Process of Training
- Needs Assessment Phase
- Training Phase
- Evaluation Phase
- Training Content
- Training Pedagogy
- Exit Competencies Desired
- Conclusion

PSYCHOLOGY OF THE VICTIMIZATION PROCESS OF SEXUAL MISCONDUCT

- Introduction
- Emotional Responses of Sexual Misconduct
- Physical Responses to Sexual Misconduct
- Social-Interpersonal Responses to Sexual Misconduct
- Career Impact
- Self-Concept Impact
- Unhealthy Coping
- Healthy Coping

Trauma and Recovery Stages

- Pre-Impact Terror
- Acute Stage of Trauma
- Denial
- Reactivation
- Anger

Integration

- Internal Coping Strategies
- External Coping Strategies

- Long-Term Effects of Sexual Misconduct
- Assisting Survivors
- Assisting Bystanders
- Conclusion

TITLE IX TRAINING FOR ATHLETIC STAFF

- Introduction
- Responsibilities of "Responsible Employees"

Heritage of Title IX

- Legal Definition
- Reasons for Needing Legislation
- Programs to Which Title IX Is Applied

Gender Equity in Athletics

- NCAA Gender Equity Task Force
- Compliance Areas for Athletics
  - Sexual Harassment
  - Participation
  - Financial Aid
  - Treatment of Student Athletes
  - Equity in Treatment

Title IX and Definitions and National Incidence Data of Campus Violence

- Rape
- Stalking
- Domestic Violence
- Dating Violence

Requirements of Title IX

- "Not Alone" Campus Policy
- Harassment and Discrimination
- Federally Protected Categories

- State-Protected Categories
- Behavioral Examples

Sexual Harassment

- Quid Pro Quo
- Hostile Environment

Behavioral Examples

- Third-Party Harassment
- Contrapower Harassment
- Psychology of the Victimization Process
- Retaliation
- Consent
- Incapacitation
- Resolution Options on Campus

Concluding Comments

TRAINING FOR CAMPUS SAFETY OFFICERS

- Introduction
- Respect, Dignity of Individuals in Complaint Proceeding
- Title IX
- Legal Overview
- Pre-Passage of Title IX

APPLICATION OF TITLE IX TO CAMPUS PROGRAMS

- Clery Act
- Violence Against Women Act
- National Incidence Data of Campus Violence
- Requirements of Title IX
- Requirements of the Clery Act
- "Not Alone" Programs
- Federally Protected Categories
- State-Protected Categories

PSYCHOLOGY OF THE VICTIMIZATION PROCESS

- Emotional Responses
- Physical Responses
- Career Effects
- Interpersonal Effects
- Self-Concept Impact

QUESTIONS FROM SURVIVORS OF SEXUAL MISCONDUCT

- Unhealthy Coping
- Healthy Coping

STAGES OF TRAUMA AND RECOVERY

- Pre-Impact Terror
- Acute Stage of Trauma
- Denial
- Reactivation
- Integration

RESPONDING TO SURVIVORS: AVOIDING VICTIM BLAMING

- Avoiding Judgmental Questions
- Sensitive Statements
- Sensitive Verbal and Nonverbal Communications
- Recommendations for Active Listening
- Resolution Options on Campus
- Retaliation Is Prohibited

Concluding Comments

Index

About the Editors and Contributors

EDITORS

Michele A. Paludi, PhD, is the series editor for Praeger's "Women's Psychology," and "Women and Careers in Management" series. Dr. Paludi is the author or editor of 52 college textbooks and more than 200 scholarly articles and conference presentations on sexual harassment, campus violence, psychology of women, gender, and discrimination. Her book, *Ivory Power: Sexual Harassment on Campus* (1990, SUNY Press), received the 1992 Myers Center Award for Outstanding Book on Human Rights in the United States.

Dr. Paludi served as chair of the U.S. Department of Education's Subpanel on the Prevention of Violence, Sexual Harassment, and Alcohol and Other Drug Problems in Higher Education. She was one of six scholars in the United States to be selected for this subpanel. She also was a consultant to and a member of former New York State governor Mario Cuomo's Task Force on Sexual Harassment. Dr. Paludi serves as an expert witness for court proceedings and administrative hearings on sexual harassment. She has extensive experience in conducting training programs and investigations of sexual harassment and other Equal Employment Opportunity (EEO) issues for businesses and educational institutions. Additionally, Dr. Paludi has held faculty positions at Franklin & Marshall College, Kent State University, Hunter College, Union College, Hamilton College, and Union Graduate College, where she directs the human resource management certificate program. She is on the faculty in the School of Management. Her four-volume edited set, *Managing Diversity in Today's Workplace*, received the 2014 RUSA Outstanding Business Reference Source and the 2014 RUSA/ BRASS Notable Business Reference Source awards.

Jennifer L. Martin, PhD, is an assistant professor of education at the University of Mount Union. Prior to working in higher education, Dr. Martin worked in public education for 17 years, 15 of those as the department chair of English at an urban alternative high school for students labeled at-risk for school failure in metropolitan Detroit. Additionally, she taught graduate and undergraduate courses in research methods, multicultural education, educational leadership, and women and gender studies. Currently, she teaches graduate courses in curriculum and undergraduate courses in multicultural education, gender studies, and content area literacy. Dr. Martin is committed to incorporating diverse texts in all her courses and inspiring culturally responsive pedagogical practices in current and future educators. She is the editor of the two-volume series *Women as Leaders in Education: Succeeding Despite Inequity, Discrimination, and Other Challenges* (Praeger, 2011), which examines the intersections of class, race, gender, and sexuality for current and aspiring leaders from a variety of perspectives. Dr. Martin's current book project is *Racial Battle Fatigue: Insights from the Front Lines of Social Justice Advocacy*, which contains personal stories of the repercussions of doing social justice work in the field and in the university. Activists and scholars share experiences of microaggressions, racial battle fatigue, and retaliation because of who they are, for whom they advocate, and what they study. Dr. Martin has numerous publications on bullying and harassment, educational equity, and issues of social justice. She is currently studying the development of culturally responsive leadership practices.

James E. Gruber, PhD, is a professor of sociology at the University of Michigan–Dearborn. He has published extensively on workplace sexual harassment and has presented workshops and expert witness testimony on the topic since the early 1980s. He co-edited a book in 2005 with Dr. Phoebe Morgan, *In the Company of Men: Male Dominance and Sexual Harassment*, which offers new "directions in theory and research on the topic." Currently, Dr. Gruber is conducting research with Dr. Susan Fineran on bullying and sexual harassment in middle schools and high schools.

Susan Fineran, PhD, MSW, is professor of social work and women and gender studies at the University of Southern Maine. During the past 20 years, Fineran has conducted research examining mental health and school performance outcomes experienced by junior high and high school students who were sexually harassed and bullied by peers. Dr. Fineran is one of the first researchers to examine sexual harassment that teenagers experience while working their first jobs and while attending school. Fineran has received two campus grant awards from the Department of Justice Office on Violence Against Women, to reduce sexual assault, dating violence, domestic violence, and stalking on college campuses.

CONTRIBUTORS

Adrian H. Bowers, PhD, is a licensed clinical psychologist and currently works as a quality manager senior psychologist specialist for the California Correctional Healthcare Services. His current work focuses on rehabilitation efforts via quality management improvements in large health care systems. Dr. Bowers' research interests include personality disorders, false allegations of sexual harassment, and quality management.

Gwendolyn C. Carlson is a graduate student in the Clinical Psychology Doctoral Program at University of Nevada, Reno. She received her undergraduate training at Drake University (Des Moines, IA). Her research interests include retraumatization, risk factors of potentially traumatic events, and health risk behaviors.

F. Edward Coughlin, OFM, currently is serving as the interim president at Siena College (Albany, NY). He served as the VP for the Franciscan Mission (2005–2014) and as director of the Franciscan Institute (1991–1996). He served in the Provincial Office of the Province of Friars Minor (1996–2005) and previously held various positions in the Province's formation program (1977–1987).

Brother Edward holds a PhD in counseling from Catholic University (1975) and an MA in pastoral ministry (Boston College 1981). He contributed an article to *Blessed Ambiguity: Brothers in the Church* and has written articles for *Human Development*, *Review for Religious*, *The Cord*, and *New Theology Review*. Brother Ed wrote the introduction for, edited, and annotated volume X of the *Works of St. Bonaventure: Writings on the Spiritual Life* (Franciscan Institute 2006) and served for a number of years on the editorial board for the Bonaventure Texts in Translation Series. More recent publications include "Can Ethics Be Taught? Harvard's Question, SCOTUS' Ethics and Twenty-First Century College Students," *The ACFU Journal* 6.1 (January 2009), and "Serving Generously and Loving Rightly: Insights for a Value Centered Life from the Franciscan Tradition," *The ACFU Journal* 7.1 (January 2010).

Brother Edward lectures widely and has led a variety of programs in the areas of human-spiritual formation, spiritual direction, organizational development, and Franciscan spirituality. He has also served as a process and organizational consultant to a variety of religious communities.

Lindsey Sank Davis, MA, is a doctoral student in clinical forensic psychology and an adjunct professor of Psychology at John Jay College of Criminal Justice, CUNY. She received her BA in psychological and brain sciences from Dartmouth College and her MA in forensic psychology from John Jay College. Davis conducts research on microaggressions and LGBTQ issues under the advisement of Dr. Kevin Nadal and is completing her dissertation on hate crime under the advisement of Dr. Louis Schlesinger.

Cynthia Deitch is an associate professor of women's studies, sociology, and public policy at The George Washington University, and the associate director of the Women's Studies Program. She received her PhD from the University of Massachusetts at Amherst. Her research and publications often focus on the intersection of gender, race, and class in the labor market, including studies of economic restructuring and displaced workers, work-family conflicts and employment benefits, the evolution of Title VII, sex and race discrimination lawsuits, and occupation-segregation among physicians. Dr. Deitch also has published research on public opinion on abortion and on social-welfare policies. She is an affiliated researcher with the Institute for Women's Policy Research.

Sandra Ellenbolt received her JD from the University of South Dakota in 2003. She currently is the institutional review board manager for Avera Health in Sioux Falls, South Dakota. Sandra's prior background includes working as a rural grant attorney for an area domestic violence shelter and as an advocate for families of children with special needs.

Olivia Emigh was a mathematics major at Siena College, and graduated in May 2015. She is the president of the Peer Education and Empowerment Program at Siena, which empowers students to take an active role in violence prevention. She also works for the Sr. Thea Bowman Center for Women as a member of the Peace and Non-Violence Committee.

Joy Galarneau holds a BA in religious studies from the College of St. Rose, an MTS in systematic theology from the University of Notre Dame, and a PhD in contemporary systematic theology from Fordham University. Dr. Galarneau currently serves as associate dean of students at Siena College, where she also teaches in the Department of Religious Studies.

Mo Therese Hannah, PhD, is professor of psychology at Siena College. A clinical psychologist who specializes in couples' therapy, she is as an academic faculty member of Imago Relationships International, the professional training organization for Imago Therapy. Dr. Hannah has published seven books and produced numerous articles and presentations on topics related to relational psychology. She is the author of The EQ (Social-Emotional Intelligence) Program, which teaches elementary-school children the principles and practices of good character and of equitable and respectful relationships. Dr. Hannah's interest in abusive dynamics and their impact on interpersonal relationships led her to become the co-founder and chair of the annual Battered Mothers Custody Conference, now in planning for its 11th year.

Pete Hirsch, PhD, is managing director of the Committee "Protection Against Sexual Harassment" at the University of Zurich and member of the Chair for Criminal Law, Criminal Proceedings and Medical Law. Dr. Hirsch has been head of Traffic Department, Zurich Metropolitan Police, chief of staff of a foreign private bank in Zurich, and the commanding officer of Swiss Mountain Infantry troops.

Amanda Knipple attends Siena College in Loudonville, New York. She is a political science major with minors in French and business. She hopes to work in a nonprofit organization in the future.

Ian P. Lloyd, Jr., is a graduate of Siena College, and majored in political science. He currently is seeking avenues to expand upon studies regarding gender inequality. In January 2015 Mr. Lloyd began attending SUNY Albany, pursuing an MA and a PhD in public policy.

David Morales is a biology major with a minor in sociology at Siena College. He will graduate in December 2015. Mr. Morales works as a member of the Sr. Thea Bowman Center for Women and sits as a member of the Peace and Non-Violence Committee.

Phoebe Morgan holds a BA in education (UNC-CH), and masters and PhD in justice studies (ASU-Tempe). She is a professor of criminology, a board certified ombudsman, and a credentialed mediator. Internationally renowned for her research on sexual harassment and compliance, her research has been published in the *Law and Society Review*, *The Journal for the National Association for Women Studies*, *The Study of Law and The Humanities*, *Affilia*, *Violence Against Women*, and *The Journal for the International Association of Ombudsmen*. Dr. Morgan's currently is researching the privatization of alternative dispute resolution. She is a lifetime member of the Society for the Study of Social Problems and presently serves on the SSSP executive board. At Northern Arizona University, Dr. Morgan teaches undergraduate and graduate classes on law and alternative dispute resolution. For the past seven years, she also has conducted leadership workshops on conflict management, and she regularly provides employers with professional consultation and sensitivity training.

Wendy Murphy, JD, is adjunct professor of sexual violence law at New England Law–Boston, where she also co-directs the Women's and Children's Advocacy Project under the Center for Law and Social Responsibility. A former visiting scholar at Harvard Law School, Ms. Murphy prosecuted child abuse and sex crimes cases for many years. In 1992, she founded the first U.S. organization for providing pro bono legal services to crime victims. She is an impact litigator whose work in state and federal courts has changed the law to better protect the constitutional rights of victimized women and children. Ms. Murphy writes and lectures widely on the rights of women and children, and on criminal justice policy. She is a contributing editor for *Women's eNews* and writes a regular column for *The Patriot Ledger*. Ms. Murphy has published numerous scholarly articles on novel legal issues, including using third-party attorneys in criminal cases to enforce women's rights and prevent gender bias; the relationship between sexual assault and Title IX; rape victims' constitutional privacy rights in therapeutic counseling files; and testimonial accommodations for disabled crime victims in criminal cases. Dubbed the "Goddaughter of Title IX" by the "Godmother of Title IX," Dr. Bernice Sandler, Ms. Murphy's work in the area of campus sexual assault—beginning in the late 1990s and including her 2002 first-of-its-kind complaint with the Office for Civil Rights at the Department of Education against Harvard—led to widespread awareness and reforms in the redress and prevention of campus sexual assault. A popular and bold speaker on the lecture circuit, Ms. Murphy also is a well-known television legal analyst who has been described by Emmy Award–winning journalist Emily Rooney as the "best talker" on television with a "finger on the pulse of victims' and women's rights." Ms. Murphy has worked for NBC, CBS, CNN, and Fox News. She regularly provides legal analysis for network and cable news programs. Her first book, *And Justice for Some*, was published by Penguin/Sentinel in 2007.

Kevin L. Nadal, PhD, is an associate professor of psychology at John Jay College of Criminal Justice–City University of New York (CUNY), as well as the executive director of CLAGS: The Center for Lesbian, Gay, Bisexual, Transgender, and Queer Studies at the CUNY Graduate Center. The author of 5 books and more than 60 other publications, Dr. Nadal's research focuses on multicultural issues in psychology and education.

Jeffrey J. Nolan, JD, is an attorney with the firm of Dinse, Knapp & McAndrew (www.dinse.com). He consults with clients and provides training throughout the United States on campus threat assessment, Title IX/Clery Act compliance, and sexual violence response–related issues. Mr. Nolan and also speaks frequently at client sites and public conferences on issues relating to workplace violence prevention, crisis management planning, at-risk individuals assessment, and related privacy and disability law issues. He participated in the development and piloting of the DOJ National Center for Campus Public Safety trauma-informed sexual assault response training that is mentioned in "Not Alone: The First Report of the White House Task Force to Protect Students from Sexual Assault." Mr. Nolan often collaborates with colleagues at Margolis, Healy & Associates (www.margolis-healy.com) and Sigma Threat Management Associates (www.SigmaTMA.com). He co-authored a chapter on threat assessment in higher education (with Gene Deisinger, PhD, and Marisa Randazzo, PhD) in the *International Handbook of Threat Assessment*, published recently by the Oxford University Press. Mr. Nolan is listed in Chambers & Partners America's Leading Lawyers for Business in the area of labor and employment law, and in The Best Lawyers in America in the area of labor and employment law.

William T. O'Donahue, PhD, is a licensed clinical psychologist and a professor of psychology at the University of Nevada–Reno. He has published more than 70 books and 250 journal articles and book chapters. For the past 20 years, Dr. Donahue has directed a clinic supported by the National Institute of Justice providing free assessment and therapy to children who have been sexually abused and adults who have been sexually assaulted.

Shannon O'Neill holds a BA in psychology and women's studies from St. Catherine's University and a PhD in social psychology from the State University of New York at Albany. Dr. O'Neill currently serves as director of the Sr. Thea Bowman Center for Women at Siena College, where she also teaches in the Women's Studies Program.

Katie L. Pustolka, PHR, is a human resources professional living and working in upstate New York. She specializes in staffing and recruitment initiatives, benefits administration, and employee health and wellness initiatives. Ms. Pustolka is a certified professional in human resources and holds a BS in psychology with a minor in classics from Union College, as well as a certificate in human resources management from Union Graduate College. She is a member of the Society of Human Resource Management's national and local chapter. Ms. Pustolka has published several book chapters and other writings, most recently publishing in the area of women's cancers. In 2013, Ms. Pustolka was a panel moderator at the conference of the International Coalition Against Sexual Harassment.

Delaney Rives is a sociology major at Siena College with a minor in women's studies, and is graduating in May 2015. Ms. Rives is the prevention educator at the Sr. Thea Bowman Center for Women, vice president of the

Peer Empowerment and Education Program, and sits on the Title IX Committee at Siena. As a member of these organizations Ms. Rives is dedicated to working to prevent and end violence against women.

Christopher P. Roseman holds a PhD from the University of Toledo in counselor education and supervision. His research interests have focused on an offender's lack of shame and guilt, and the impact that has on empathy development, as well as working with victims and survivors in innovative offender treatment programming to enhance empathy development. Dr. Roseman is currently an assistant professor in the University of South Dakota Counselor Education Program and director of the Counseling and School Psychological Services Center.

William E. Schweinle received his PhD in experimental psychology (social and quantitative) from the University of Texas at Arlington. He is currently an associate professor of biostatistics at the University of South Dakota. Dr. Schweinle's research interest is primarily in empathic accuracy, which involves the accuracy with which people "read" one others' minds, that is, understand what another person is thinking and feeling. He applies empathic accuracy methods to the study of social cognition in close relationships and to abusive male-female dyadic interaction, among a number of health care–related projects.

Susan Strauss, RN, EdD, is a national and international speaker, trainer, and consultant. Her specialty areas include harassment and workplace bullying, organization development, and management/leadership development. Her clients are from business, education, health care, law, and government organizations from both the public and private sectors. Dr. Strauss has authored book chapters, articles in professional journals, curriculum and training manuals, as well as the book *Sexual Harassment and Teens: A Program for Positive Change*. She has been featured on *The Donahue Show*, *CBS Evening News*, and other television and radio programs, and has been interviewed for newspaper and journal articles for publications such as the *Times of London*, *Lawyers Weekly*, and the *Harvard Education Newsletter*. Dr. Strauss has presented at international conferences in Botswana, Egypt, Thailand, Israel, and the United States, and has conducted sex discrimination research in Poland. She has consulted with professionals from other countries including England, Australia, Canada, and St. Martin.

Brigitte Tag, PhD, earned her master's degree in public administration in Germany. She earned her PhD in criminal law and economic offenses from the University of Heidelberg. Since 2002, Dr. Tag has been a full professor at the University of Zurich and chair of Criminal Law, Criminal Proceedings and Medical Law. She earned her attorney's license in 2004. Presently Dr. Tag is president of the Gender Equality Commission.

Chassitty Whitman is a doctoral student studying clinical psychology at the City University of New York (CUNY) Graduate Center–John Jay College of Criminal Justice. Her past research focused on Facebook use and personality, aggression and coping styles, and LGB identity and psychological well-being. Current research interests center on gender identity development and factors of risk and resiliency among transgender-identified populations.

Anna Youngmann graduated in 2015 with a religious studies major at Siena College. Her passion for anti-human-trafficking work drew her to the Peace and Non-Violence Committee at the Sr. Thea Bowman Center for Women, where she has worked during all four years of college. Ms. Youngmann also is a member of the Anti-Violence Task Force and was a resident assistant for two years.